Stephen Birnbaum Travel Guides

Acapulco
Bahamas, Turks & Caicos
Barcelona
Bermuda
Boston
Canada
Cancun, Cozumel, and Isla Mujeres
Caribbean
Chicago
Disneyland
Eastern Europe
Europe
Europe for Business Travelers
Florence
France
Great Britain
Hawaii
Ireland
Italy
Ixtapa & Zihuatanejo
London
Los Angeles
Mexico
Miami & Ft. Lauderdale
New York
Paris
Portugal
Rome
San Francisco
South America
Spain
United States
USA for Business Travelers
Venice
Walt Disney World
Western Europe

CONTRIBUTING EDITORS

Jane Warslaw
Mary Dempsey
Connie Goddard
Nellie Goddard
Lee Hill
William Hurlbut

Adam Lisberg
Beth Lisberg
Mike Michaelson
Stuart Silverman
Michael Shymanski
Melinda Tang

MAPS Mark Carlson
      Susan Carlson

SYMBOLS Gloria McKeown

A Stephen Birnbaum Travel Guide

Birnbaum's
CHICAGO
1992

Stephen Birnbaum
Alexandra Mayes Birnbaum
EDITORS

Lois Spritzer
EXECUTIVE EDITOR

Laura L. Brengelman
Managing Editor

Mary Callahan
Ann-Rebecca Laschever
Beth Schlau
Dana Margaret Schwartz
Associate Editors

Gene Gold
Assistant Editor

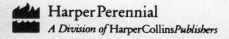 HarperPerennial
A Division of HarperCollins*Publishers*

FIRST EDITION

ISSN: 0749-2561 (Stephen Birnbaum Travel Guides)
ISSN: 1056-4365 (Chicago)
ISBN: 0-06-278024-7 (pbk.)

92 93 94 95 96 CC/OPM 10 9 8 7 6 5 4 3 2 1

Contents

GETTING READY TO GO

All the practical travel data you need to plan your vacation down to the final detail.

When and How to Go

Preparing

On the Road

THE CITY

Thorough, qualitative guide to Chicago. Each section offers a comprehensive report on the city's most compelling attractions and amenities, designed to be used on the spot.

DIVERSIONS

A selective guide to more than a dozen active and/or cerebral theme vacations, including the best places in Chicago to pursue them.

DIRECTIONS

Sixteen of the most delightful walks through Chicago.

A Word from the Editor

I suppose I could regale you with encomiums to the architecture and ambience of Chicago, all in an effort to convince you that it is the aesthetic aspects of the so-called Second City (now actually the third) that draw me back again and again. But that would be misleading — and also untrue.

I go to Chicago to eat. That's it, plain and simple, and it is not in the least hyperbolic to report that as I leave O'Hare Airport I mentally tuck a napkin under my chin. Oh, I like Chicago's citizenry a lot, the skyline is at least as impressive as advertised, and the lakeshore setting is spectacular, but it is Chicago's extraordinary spectrum of menus that really gets my attention.

And it is more than mere food that draws me to Chicago's dining tables. In a restaurant world that has gone more than a little bonkers in offering nouvelle nonsense as a substitute for real food, Chicago has kept its head on straight. For folks who prefer straightforward meals to small portions of radicchio slathered in raspberry sauce, Chicago is a gastronomic shrine.

Chicago helped me remember what real food is. Like so many others, I was initially taken in by the foodies who insisted that the self-consciously precious new style of cooking was really what was happening. I found myself paying much more attention to the artistic arrangement of comestibles on my plate than to how those edible still lifes tasted.

Then I came back to Chicago. Specifically, an old friend took my confused palate out to dinner at *Carson's* on Wells Street. There, amid the perfectly grilled baby back ribs and the salad with the thick, creamy, anchovy dressing, I regained my gastronomic balance. Chicago has a way of showing visitors just what truly is important in life.

My own evolution as a traveler (which happily continues) is mirrored by the evolution of our guidebook series. When we began our series of modern travel guides, we logically began with "area" books, attempting to publish guides that would include the widest possible number of attractive destinations. When the public seemed to accept our new way of delivering travel data, we added titles covering only a single country, and when these became popular we began our newest expansion phase, which centers on a group of books that deal with only a single city. Now, we can not only highlight our favorite urban destinations, we can describe how to get the very most out of a visit.

Such treatment of travel information only mirrors an increasingly pervasive trend among travelers — the frequent return to a treasured travel spot. Once upon a time, even the most dedicated travelers would visit distant parts of the country no more than once in a lifetime — usually as part of a larger tour. But greater numbers of would-be sojourners are now availing themselves of the opportunity to visit a favored part of the planet over and over again.

So where once it was routine to say you'd "seen" a particular city or country after a very superficial, once-over-lightly encounter, the more perceptive travelers of today recognize that it's entirely possible to have only skimmed the surface of a specific travel destination even after having visited that place more than a dozen times. Similarly, repeated visits to a single site permit true exploration of special interests, whether they be sporting, artistic, or intellectual.

For those of us who now have spent the last several years working out the special system under which we present information in this series, the luxury of being able to devote nearly as much space as we'd like to just a single city is as close to paradise for guide writers and editors as any of us expects to come. But clearly this is not the first guide to the glories of Chicago — one suspects that guides of one sort or another have existed at least since the days when trappers first paddled their pelts up the Chicago River — so a traveler might logically ask why a new one is suddenly necessary.

Our answer is that the nature of travel to Chicago — and even of the travelers who now routinely make the trip — has changed dramatically of late. For the past 200 years or so, travel to even a town within our own country was considered an elaborate undertaking, one that required extensive advance planning. But with the advent of jet air travel in the late 1950s and of increased-capacity, wide-body aircraft during the late 1960s, travel to and around once distant destinations became extremely common. Attitudes as well as costs have changed significantly in the last couple of decades.

Obviously, any new guidebook to Chicago must keep pace with and answer the real needs of today's travelers. That's why we've tried to create a guide that's specifically organized, written, and edited for this more demanding modern audience, travelers for whom qualitative information is infinitely more desirable than mere quantities of unappraised data. We think that this book — and all the other guides in our series — represent a new generation of travel guides, one that is especially responsive to modern needs and interests.

For years, dating back as far as Herr Baedeker, travel guides have tended to be encyclopedic, seemingly much more concerned with demonstrating expertise in geography and history than with a real analysis of the sorts of things that actually concern a typical modern tourist. But today, when it is hardly necessary to tell a traveler where Chicago is (in many cases, the traveler has been there nearly as often as the guidebook editors), it becomes the responsibility of those editors to provide new perspectives and to suggest new directions in order to make the guide genuinely valuable.

That's exactly what we've tried to do in this series. I think you'll notice a different, more contemporary tone to the text, as well as an organization and focus that are distinctive and more functional. And even a random reading of what follows will demonstrate a substantial departure from the standard guidebook orientation, for we've not only attempted to provide information of a more compelling sort, but we also have tried to present the data in a format that makes it particularly accessible.

Needless to say, it's difficult to decide precisely what to include in a guidebook of this size — and what to omit. Early on, we realized that giving up the encyclopedic approach precluded our listing every single route and restaurant, a realization that helped define our overall editorial focus. Similarly, when we discussed the possibility of presenting certain information in other than strict geographic order, we found that the new format enabled us to arrange data in a way we feel best answers the questions travelers typically ask.

Large numbers of specific questions have provided the real editorial skeleton for this book. The volume of mail I regularly receive emphasizes that modern travelers want very precise information, so we've tried to organize our material in the most responsive way possible. Readers who want to know the best restaurants or the most apectacular architectural sites in Chicago will have no trouble extracting that data from this guide.

Travel guides are, understandably, reflections of personal taste, and putting one's name on a title page obviously puts one's preferences on the line. But I think I ought to amplify just what "personal" means. I don't believe in the sort of personal guidebook that's a palpable misrepresentation on its face. It is, for example, hardly possible for any single travel writer to visit thousands of restaurants (and nearly as many hotels) in any given year and provide accurate appraisals of each. And even if it were physically possible for one human being to survive such an itinerary, it would of necessity have to be done at a dead sprint and the perceptions derived therefrom would probably be less valid than those of any other intelligent individual visiting the same establishments. It is, therefore, impossible (especially in a large, annually revised guidebook *series* such as we offer) to have only one person provide all the data on the entire world.

I also happen to think that such individual orientation is of substantially less value to readers. Visiting a single hotel for just one night or eating one hasty meal in a random restaurant hardly equips anyone to provide appraisals that are of more than passing interest. No amount of doggedly alliterative or oppressively onomatopoeic text can camouflage a technique that is essentially specious. We have, therefore, chosen what I like to describe as the "thee and me" approach to restaurant and hotel evaluation and, to a somewhat more limited degree, to the sites and sights we have included in the other sections of our text. What this really reflects is a personal sampling tempered by intelligent counsel from informed local sources, and these additional friends-of-the-editor are almost always residents of the city and/or area about which they are consulted.

Despite the presence of several editors, writers, researchers, and local correspondents, very precise editing and tailoring keep our text fiercely subjective. So what follows is the gospel according to the Birnbaums, and represents as much of our own taste and instincts as we can manage. It is probable, therefore, that if you like your cities stylish and prefer small hotels with personality to huge high-rise anonymities, we're likely to have a long and meaningful relationship. Readers with dissimilar tastes may be less enraptured.

I also should point out something about the person to whom this guidebook is directed. Above all, he or she is a "visitor." This means that such elements as restaurants have been specifically picked to provide the visitor with a representative, enlightening, stimulating, and above all, pleasant experience.

Since so many extraneous considerations can affect the reception and service accorded a regular restaurant patron, our choices can in no way be construed as an exhaustive guide to resident dining. We think we've listed all the best places, in various price ranges, but they were chosen with a visitor's enjoyment in mind.

Other evidence of how we've tried to tailor our text to reflect modern travel habits is most apparent in the section we call DIVERSIONS. Where once it was common for travelers to spend an urban visit in a determinedly passive state, the emphasis is far more active today. So we've organized every activity we could reasonably evaluate and arranged the material in a way that is especially accessible to activists of either athletic or cerebral bent. It is no longer necessary, therefore, to wade through a pound or two of superfluous prose just to find the very best steak to nibble or the hottest jazz licks within the city limits.

If there is a single thing that best characterizes the revolution in and evolution of current holiday habits, it is that most travelers now consider travel a right rather than a privilege. No longer is a family trip necessarily a once-in-a-lifetime thing; nor is the idea of visiting faraway places in the least worrisome. Travel today translates as the enthusiastic desire to sample all of the country's and the world's opportunities, to find that elusive quality of experience that is not only enriching but comfortable. For that reason, we've tried to make what follows not only helpful and enlightening but the sort of welcome companion of which every traveler dreams.

Finally, I also should point out that every good travel guide is a living enterprise; that is, no part of this text is carved in stone. In our annual revisions, we refine, expand, and further hone all our material to serve your travel needs better. To this end, no contribution is of greater value to us than your personal reaction to what we have written, as well as information reflecting your own experiences while using our book. We earnestly and enthusiastically solicit your comments about this guide *and* your opinions and perceptions about places you have recently visited. In this way, we will be able to provide the most current information — including the actual experiences of recent travelers — and to make those experiences more readily available to others. Please write to us at 60 E. 42nd St., New York, NY 10165.

We sincerely hope to hear from you.

STEPHEN BIRNBAUM

How to Use This Guide

A great deal of care has gone into the organization of this guidebook, and we believe it represents a real breakthrough in the presentation of travel material. Our aim is to create a new, more modern generation of travel books and to make this guide the most useful and practical travel tool available today.

Our text is divided into four basic sections in order to present information in the best way on every possible aspect of a Chicago visit. This organization itself should alert you to the vast and varied opportunities available, as well as indicate all the specific data necessary to plan a successful trip. You won't find much of the conventional "swaying palms and shimmering sand" text here; we've chosen instead to deliver more useful and practical information. Prospective itineraries tend to speak for themselves, and with so many diverse travel opportunities, we feel our main job is to highlight what's where and to provide basic information — how, when, where, how much, and what's best — to assist you in making the most intelligent choices possible.

Here is a brief summary of the four basic sections and what you can expect to find in each. We believe that you will find both your travel planning and en-route enjoyment enhanced by having this book at your side.

GETTING READY TO GO

This mini-encyclopedia of practical travel facts is a sort of know-it-all companion with all the precise information necessary to create a successful trip to Chicago. There are entries on about 2 dozen separate topics, including how to get where you're going, what preparations to make before leaving, what your trip is likely to cost, and how to avoid prospective problems. The individual entries are specific, realistic, and where appropriate, cost-oriented.

We expect you to use this section most in the course of planning your trip, for its ideas and suggestions are intended to simplify this often confusing period. Entries are intentionally concise, in an effort to get to the meat of the matter with the least extraneous prose. These entries are augmented by extensive lists of specific sources from which to obtain even more specialized data, plus some suggestions for obtaining travel information on your own.

THE CITY

The individual report on Chicago has been created with the assistance of researchers, contributors, professional journalists, and experts who live in the city. Although useful at the planning stage, THE CITY is really designed to be taken along and used on the spot. The reports offer a short-stay guide, including an essay introducing the city as a historic entity and as a contemporary place to visit. *At-a-Glance* material is actually a site-by-site survey of the most important, interesting (and sometimes most eclectic) sights to see, and things to do. *Sources and Resources* is a concise listing of pertinent tourist information meant to answer a range of potentially pressing questions as they arise — simple things such as the address of the local tourist office, how to get around, which sightseeing tours to take, when special events occur, where to find the best nightspot or hail a taxi, which are the chic places to shop, and where the best museums and theaters are to be found. *Best in Town* is our collection of cost-and-quality choices of the best places to eat and sleep on a variety of budgets.

DIVERSIONS

This section is designed to help travelers find the best places in which to pursue a wide range of physical and cerebral activities, without having to wade through endless pages of unrelated text. This very selective guide lists the broadest possible range of activities, including all the best places to pursue them.

We start with a list of possibilities that offer various places to stay and eat, and move to those that require some perspiration — sports preferences and other rigorous pursuits — and go on to report on a number of more cerebral and spiritual vacation opportunities. In every case, our suggestion of a particular location — and often our recommendation of a specific hotel — is intended to guide you to that special place where the quality of experience is likely to be the highest. Whether you seek a historic hotel, a compelling museum, or the best place to shop or sail, each category is the equivalent of a comprehensive checklist of the absolute best in Chicago.

DIRECTIONS

Here are 16 walks that cover the city, along its main thoroughfares and side streets, past its most spectacular landmarks and magnificent parks. This is the only section of the book that is organized geographically; itineraries can be "connected" for longer sojourns or used individually for short, intensive explorations.

Although each of the book's sections has a distinct format and a special function, they have all been designed to be used together to provide a complete inventory of travel information. To use this book to full advantage, take a few minutes to read the table of contents and random entries in each section to get a firsthand feel for how it all fits together.

Pick and choose needed information. Assume, for example, that you have always wanted to visit Chicago and sample one of its spectacular steaks — but you never really knew where to go. Choose specific restaurants from the selections offered in "Eating Out" in THE CITY, add some of those noted in each walking tour in DIRECTIONS, and cross-reference this list with those eateries in the roundup of the best in the city in the "Chicago's Best Restaurants" section in DIVERSIONS.

In other words, the sections of this book are building blocks designed to help you put together the best possible trip. Use them selectively as a tool, a source of ideas, a reference work for accurate facts, and a guide to the best buys, the most exciting sights, the most pleasant accommodations, the tastiest food — *the best travel experience* that you can possibly have in Chicago.

CENTRAL
CHICAGO

OAK ST
Tower
WALTON ST
AWARE PL
John Hancock
Blg.
CHESTNUT ST
Water Tower
Place
SON ST Armory
er Tower
CHICAGO AV
RTH SIDE
SUPERIOR ST
HURON ST
ERIE ST
ERIE ST
ONTARIO ST
ARIO ST
Museum
of Contemp Art
OHIO ST
GRAND AV
GRAND AV
GRAND AV
GRAND AV
Navy Pier
NOIS ST
ILLINOIS ST
BARD ST
WATER ST
River
WACKER DR
WATER ST
tial
Blg
Stand.
Oil Blg
RANDOLPH ST
Naval Armory

LAKE

MICHIGAN

MONROE DR
Institute
Petrillo Musicshell
JACKSON DR

Buckingham
Fountain

GRANT
BALBO DR
PARK

COLUMBUS DR
LAKE SHORE DR

Shedd
Aquarium
SOLIDARITY DR
Adler Planetarium
Illinois
Central
& Gulf
Station
Field Museum
McFETRIDGE DR
INDIANA AV
Soldier
Field

GETTING READY TO GO

When and How to Go

When to Go

The most popular time to visit Chicago traditionally is June to September, but autumn may be the best season for a sojourn here. It is at that time of year that the days are most pleasant in Chicago — generally clear and brisk, with temperatures in the 50s and 60s. On autumn nights, temperatures can drop into the 40s or even 30s, and occasional chilly winds may make it feel even a bit cooler. The city's brisk and cool spring season, with an average daytime temperature in the 50s and nighttime temperatures dropping into the 30s, may be the second-best time to visit. Winter can be formidable, with fierce winter winds and wind-chill factors that occasionally measure 60F below zero! Summer has the highest precipitation (about 4 inches in an average June) and feels muggy even though temperatures rarely climb higher than the 80s.

There are good reasons for visiting Chicago any time of the year, possibly excepting winter. There are no real off-season periods in this city. That means visitors are unlikely to arrive at an attraction and find the gates locked. It also means that prices stay pretty much within the same range year-round. If anything, hotel room bargains are available on weekends, when business travel is slow, rather than during any particular season of the year.

WEATHER: Travelers who want to find out about the weather in Chicago can get current temperature readings and 3-day Accu-Weather forecasts through *American Express Travel Related Services'* Worldwide Weather Report number. Simply dial 900-WEATHER and punch in the area code for Chicago (312), and an up-to-date recording will provide the current temperature, sky conditions, wind speed and direction, heat index, relative humidity, local time, beach and boating reports in warm weather, and highway reports. This 24-hour service can be accessed from any touchtone phone in the US and costs 95¢ per minute. The charge will show up on your phone bill.

CULTURAL EVENTS: Autumn signals the beginning of the year's cultural calendar. The famed *Chicago Symphony Orchestra* starts its season in September, and the *Lyric Opera* runs a busy schedule from September through February each year. Check with the tourist board for an update. Baroque chamber music, jazz concerts, and folk, country, and rock groups can be heard at a variety of clubs around the city. Drum and bugle corps, swing bands, and choral groups of all persuasions add to the musical mix.

Chicago also is rich in theater. Since the city is a favorite place for Broadway tryouts, playgoers can often catch a future Broadway hit (or flop) here. The *Steppenwolf Theater Company* and other, smaller companies are among the institutions that contribute to the cultural scene.

More than 22 museums, including the *Art Institute of Chicago, Museum of Contemporary Art,* and the *Museum of Science and Industry* draw visitors from all over the world.

FESTIVALS: Three music festivals are held annually: the *Chicago Blues Festival* in

June, the *Chicago Country Music Festival* in July, and the *Chicago Jazz Festival* in August. All are highly celebrated events that draw thousands upon thousands of participants from all over the world. The *Ravinia Festival,* held in Highland Park from early June until *Labor Day,* is a series of outdoor concerts by the *Chicago Symphony Orchestra* and other headliners.

More than a thousand international artists are invited to the *Chicago International Art Expo* in May. Exhibitions are held in *Donnelly Hall.*

Among the most savory ways to experience the city of Chicago is to attend the *Taste of Chicago,* held each year in Grant Park from the last weekend in June until *July Fourth.* The week-long gastronomical extravaganza features more than 70 of the city's restaurants and their chefs. Two and a half million participants lick their way through the event every year.

The 85th Annual *Chicago to Mackinac Island Yacht Race* will be held this year in July. More than 200 contestants participate in the race, which attracts thousands of spectators.

Traveling by Plane

Flying is the quickest, most convenient means of travel between different parts of the country. It *sounds* expensive to travel across the US by air, but when all costs are taken into account for traveling any substantial distance, plane travel usually is less expensive per mile than traveling by car. It also is the most economical way to go in terms of time. Although touring by car, bus, or train certainly is the a more scenic way to travel, air travel is far faster and more direct — and the less time spent in transit, the more time spent in Chicago.

SCHEDULED FLIGHTS: Numerous airlines offer regularly scheduled flights to Chicago's O'Hare International Airport, which is located 25 miles from the city center and handles international and domestic traffic.

Listed below are the major national air carriers serving Chicago and their toll-free telephone numbers:

American and American Eagle: 800-433-7300.
America West: 800-247-5692.
Continental and Continental Express: 800-525-0280.
Delta and Delta Connection: 800-221-1212.
Midway: 800-866-9000.
Northwest, NW Airlink, and Northeast Express: 800-225-2525.
TWA: 800-221-2000.
United: 800-241-6522.
USAir and USAir Express: 800-428-4322.

Among the international carriers that serve Chicago are *Aer Lingus, Air Canada, Air France, Alitalia, British Airways, El Al, Lufthansa, Sabena,* and *Swissair.*

Tickets – When traveling on regularly scheduled flights, a full-fare ticket provides maximum travel flexibility, because there are no advance booking or other ticketing requirements — except seat availability. It is advisable, however, to reserve well in advance during popular vacation periods and around holiday times.

Fares – Full-fare tickets are followed by a wide variety of discount fares, which even experts find hard to keep current. With these fares, the less you pay for your ticket, the more restrictions and qualifications are likely to be attached to the ticket purchase, including the months (and the days of the week) during which you must travel, how far in advance you must purchase your ticket, the minimum and maximum amount of time you may or must remain away, and your willingness to decide and stick with a return date at the time of booking. It is not uncommon for passengers sitting side by side on the same plane to have paid fares varying by hundreds of dollars.

In general, domestic airfares break down to four basic categories — first class, business class, coach (also called economy or tourist class), and excursion or discount fares. In addition, Advance Purchase Excursion (APEX) fares offer savings under certain conditions.

A **first class** ticket admits you to the special section of the aircraft with larger seats, more legroom, better (or more elaborately served) food, free drinks, free headsets for movies and music channels, and above all, personal attention. First class fares cost about twice those of full-fare (often called "regular") economy.

Behind first class often lies **business class**, usually a separate cabin or cabins. While standards of comfort and service are not as high as in first class, they represent a considerable improvement over conditions in the rear of the plane, with roomier seats, more leg and shoulder space between passengers, and fewer seats abreast. Free liquor and headsets, a choice of meal entrées, and a separate counter for speedier check-in are other inducements. Note that airlines often have their own names for their business class service — such as Ambassador Class on *TWA* and Medallion Class on *Delta*.

The terms of the **coach** or **economy** fare may vary slightly from airline to airline, and in fact from time to time airlines may be selling more than one type of economy fare. Coach or economy passengers sit more snugly, as many as 10 in a single row on a wide-body jet, behind the first class and business class sections. Normally, alcoholic drinks are not free, nor are the headsets.

In first, business, and regular economy classes, passengers are entitled to reserve seats and are sold tickets on an open reservation system. They may travel on any scheduled flight they wish, buy a one-way or round-trip ticket, and have the ticket remain valid for a year. There are no requirements for a minimum or maximum stay or for advance booking and no cancellation penalties. The fare also allows free stopover privileges, although these can be limited in economy.

Excursion and other **discount** fares are the airlines' equivalent of a special sale and usually apply to round-trip bookings only. These fares generally differ according to the season and the number of travel days permitted. They are only a bit less flexible than full-fare economy tickets, and are, therefore, often useful for both business and holiday travelers. Most round-trip excursion tickets include strict minimum and maximum stay requirements and can be changed only within prescribed time limits. So don't count on extending a ticket beyond the specified time of return or staying less time than required. Different airlines may have different regulations concerning the number of stopovers permitted, and sometimes excursion fares are less expensive during midweek. The availability of these reduced-rate seats is most limited at busy times such as holidays. Discount or excursion fare ticket holders sit with the coach passengers and, for all intents and purposes, are indistinguishable from them. They receive all the same basic services, even though they may have paid anywhere between 30% and 55% less for the trip. Obviously, it's wise to make plans early enough to qualify for this less expensive transportation if possible.

These discount or excursion fares may masquerade under a variety of names and invariably have strings attached. A common requirement is that the ticket be purchased a certain number of days — usually no fewer than 7 or 14 days — in advance of departure, though it may be booked weeks or months in advance (it has to be "ticketed," or paid for, shortly after booking, however). The return reservation usually has to be made at the time of the original ticketing and cannot be changed later than a certain number of days (again, usually 7 or 14) before the return flight. If events force a passenger to change the return reservation after the date allowed, the difference between the round-trip excursion rate and the round-trip coach rate probably will have to be paid, though most airlines allow passengers to use their discounted fares by standing by for an empty seat, even if the carrier doesn't otherwise have standby fares. Another common condition is the minimum and maximum stay requirement; for example, 1 to 6 or 6 to 14 days (but including a Saturday night). Last, cancellation penalties of up to 50% of the full price of the ticket have been assessed — check the specific penalty in effect when you purchase your discount/excursion ticket — so careful planning is imperative.

Of even greater risk — and bearing the lowest price of all the current discount fares — is the ticket where no change at all in departure and/or return flights is permitted, and where the ticket price is totally nonrefundable. If you do buy a nonrefundable ticket, you should be aware of a new policy followed by many airlines that may make it easier to change your plans if necessary. For a fee — set by each airline and payable at the airport when checking in — you *may* be able to change the time or date of a return flight on a nonrefundable ticket. However, if the nonrefundable ticket price for the replacement flight is higher than that of the original (as often is the case when trading in a weekday for a weekend flight), you also will have to pay the difference. Any such change must be made a certain number of days in advance — in some cases as little as 2 days — of either the original or the replacement flight, whichever is earlier; restrictions are set by the individual carrier. (Travelers holding a nonrefundable or other restricted ticket who must change their plans due to a family emergency should know that some carriers may make special allowances in such situations.)

There also is a newer, often less expensive, type of excursion fare, the **APEX**, or **Advanced Purchase Excursion**, fare. As with traditional excursion fares, passengers paying an APEX fare sit with and receive the same basic services as any other coach or economy passengers, even though they may have paid 50% less for their seats. In return, they are subject to certain restrictions. In the case of domestic flights, the ticket usually is good for a minimum of 1 to 3 days (including a Saturday) away and a maximum, currently, of 1 to 6 months (depending on the airline and the destination); and as its name implies, it must be "ticketed," or paid for in its entirety, a certain period of time before departure — usually somewhere between 7 and 21 days.

The drawback to an APEX fare is that it penalizes travelers who change their minds — and travel plans. The return reservation must be made at the time of the original ticketing, and if for some reason you change your schedule, you will have to pay a penalty of $100 or 10% of the ticket value, whichever is greater, as long as you travel within the valid period of your ticket. But if you change your return to a date less than the minimum stay or more than the maximum stay, the difference between the round-trip APEX fare and the full round-trip coach rate will have to be paid. There also is a penalty of anywhere from $75 to $125 or more for canceling or changing a reservation *before* travel begins — check the specific penalty in effect when you purchase your ticket.

In addition, most airlines also offer package deals that may include a car rental, accommodations, and dining and/or sightseeing features along with the basic airfare, and the combined cost of packaged elements usually is considerably less than the cost of the exact same elements when purchased separately.

Reservations – When you're satisfied that you've found the lowest price for which you can conveniently qualify, make your booking. You may have to call the airline more than once, because different airline reservations clerks have been known to quote different prices, and different fares will be available at different times for the same flight because of a relatively new computerized airline practice called yield management, which adds or subtracts low-fare seats to a given flight depending on how well it is selling.

To protect yourself against fare increases, purchase and pay for your ticket as soon as possible after you've received a confirmed reservation. Airlines generally will honor their tickets, even if the price at the time of your flight is higher than the price you paid. If fares go up between the time you *reserve* a flight and the time you *pay* for it, however, you likely will be out of luck. Finally, with excursion or discount fares, it is important to remember that when a reservation clerk says that you must purchase a ticket by a specific date, this is an absolute deadline. Miss it and the airline usually will automatically cancel your reservation without telling you.

Frequent Flyers – Most of the leading US carriers offer a bonus system to frequent travelers. After the first 10,000 miles, for example, a passenger might be eligible for a first class seat for the coach fare; after another 10,000 miles, he or she might receive a discount on his or her next ticket purchase. The value of the bonuses continues to increase as more miles are logged.

Bonus miles also may be earned by patronizing affiliated car rental companies or hotel chains, or by using one of the credit cards that now offers this reward. In deciding whether to accept such a credit card from one of the issuing organizations that tempt you with frequent flyer mileage bonuses on a specific airline, first determine whether the interest rate charged on the unpaid balance is the same as (or less than) possible alternate credit cards, and whether the annual "membership" fee also is equal or lower. If these charges are slightly higher than those of competing cards, weigh the difference against the potential value in airfare savings. Also ask about any bonus miles awarded just for signing up — 1,000 is common, 5,000 generally the maximum.

For the most up-to-date information on frequent flyer bonus options, you may want to send for the monthly *Frequent* newsletter. Issued by Frequent Publications, it provides current information about frequent flyer plans in general, as well as specific data about promotions, awards, and combination deals to help you keep track of the profusion — and confusion — of current and upcoming availabilities. For a year's subscription, send $33 to Frequent Publications, 4715-C Town Center Dr., Colorado Springs, CO 80916 (phone: 800-333-5937).

There also is a monthly magazine called *Frequent Flyer,* but unlike the newsletter mentioned above, its focus is primarily on newsy articles of interest to business travelers and other frequent flyers. Published by Official Airline Guides (PO Box 58543, Boulder, CO 80322-8543; phone: 800-323-3537), *Frequent Flyer* is available for $24 for a 1-year subscription.

Low-Fare Airlines – Increasingly, the stimulus for special fares is the appearance of airlines associated with bargain rates. On these airlines, all seats on any given flight generally sell for the same price, which is somewhat below the lowest discount fare offered by the larger, more established airlines. It is important to note that tickets offered by the smaller airlines specializing in low-cost travel frequently are not subject to the same restrictions as the lowest-priced ticket offered by the more established carriers. They may not require advance purchase or minimum and maximum stays, may involve no cancellation penalties, and may be available one way or round trip. A disadvantage to low-fare airlines, however, is that when something goes wrong, such as delayed baggage or a flight cancellation due to equipment breakdown, their smaller fleets and fewer flights mean that passengers may have to wait longer for a solution than they would on one of the equipment-rich major carriers.

If making plane reservations through a travel agent, ask the agent to give the airline your home phone number, as well as your daytime business phone number. All too often the agent uses his or her agency's number as the official contact for changes in flight plans. Especially during the winter, weather conditions hundreds or even thousands of miles away can wreak havoc with flight schedules. The airlines are fairly reliable about getting this sort of information to passengers if they can reach them; diligence does little good at 10 PM if the airline has only the agency's or an office number.

Reconfirmation is not generally required on domestic flights. However, it always is a good idea to call ahead to make sure that the airline did not slip up in entering your original reservation, or in registering any changes you may have made since, and that it has your seat reservation and/or special meal request in the computer.

If you plan not to take a flight on which you hold a confirmed reservation, by all means inform the airline. Because the problem of "no-shows" is a constant expense for airlines, they are allowed to overbook flights, a practice that often contributes to the threat of denied boarding for a certain number of passengers (see "Getting Bumped," below).

Seating – For most types of tickets, airline seats usually are assigned on a first-come, first-served basis at check-in, although some airlines make it possible to reserve a seat at the time of ticket purchase. Always check in early for your flight, even with advance seat assignments. A good rule of thumb for domestic flights is to arrive at the airport *at least* 1 hour before the scheduled departure to give yourself plenty of time in case there are long lines.

Most airlines furnish seating charts, which make choosing a seat much easier, but there are a few basics to consider. You must decide whether you prefer a window, aisle, or middle seat. On those few domestic flights where smoking is permitted (see "Smoking," below), you also should indicate if you prefer the smoking or nonsmoking section.

The amount of legroom provided (as well as chest room, especially when the seat in front of you is in a reclining position) is determined by pitch, a measure of the distance between the back of the seat in front of you and the front of the back of your seat. The amount of pitch is a matter of airline policy, not the type of plane you fly. First class and business class seats have the greatest pitch, a fact that figures prominently in airline advertising. In economy class or coach, the standard pitch ranges from 33 to as little as 31 inches — downright cramped.

The number of seats abreast, another factor determining comfort, depends on a combination of airline policy and airplane dimensions. First and business classes have the fewest seats per row. Economy generally has 9 seats per row on a DC-10 or an L-1011, making either one slightly more comfortable than a 747, on which there normally are 10 seats per row. A 727 has 6 seats per row.

Airline representatives claim that most planes are more stable toward the front and midsections, while the seats farthest from the engines are quietest. Passengers who have long legs and are traveling on a wide-body aircraft might request a seat directly behind a door or emergency exit, since these seats often have greater than average pitch, or a seat in the first row of a given section, which offer extra legroom — although these seats are increasingly being reserved for passengers who are willing (and able) to perform certain tasks in the event of emergency evacuation. It often is impossible, however, to see the movie from seats that are directly behind the plane's exits. Be aware that the first row of the economy section (called a "bulkhead" seat) on a conventional aircraft (not a wide-body) does *not* offer extra legroom, since the fixed partition will not permit passengers to slide their feet under it, and that watching a movie from this first-row seat also can be difficult and uncomfortable. These bulkhead seats do, however, provide ample room for a bassinet or safety seat and often are reserved for families traveling with small children.

A window seat protects you from aisle traffic and clumsy serving carts, and also provides a view, while an aisle seat enables you to get up and stretch your legs without disturbing your fellow travelers. Middle seats are the least desirable, and seats in the last row are the worst of all, since they seldom recline fully. If you wish to avoid children on your flight or if you find that you are sitting in an especially noisy section, you usually are free to move to any unoccupied seat — if there is one.

If you are large, you may face the prospect of a long flight with special trepidation. Center seats in the alignments of wide-body 747s, L-1011s, and DC-10s are about 1½ inches wider than those on either side, so larger travelers tend to be more comfortable there.

Despite all these rules of thumb, finding out which specific rows are near emergency exits or at the front of a wide-body cabin can be difficult because seating arrangements on any two same-model planes usually vary from airline to airline. There is, however, a quarterly publication called the *Airline Seating Guide* that publishes seating charts for most major US airlines and many foreign carriers as well. Your travel agent should have copies, or you can buy the US edition for $39.95 per year. Order from Carlson Publishing Co., Box 888, Los Alamitos, CA 90720 (phone: 800-728-4877 or 213-493-4877).

Simply reserving an airline seat in advance, however, actually may guarantee very little. Most airlines require that passengers arrive at the departure gate at least 45 minutes (sometimes more) ahead of time to hold a seat reservation. It pays to read the fine print on your ticket carefully and follow its requirements.

A far better strategy is to visit an airline ticket office (or one of a select group of travel agents) to secure an actual boarding pass for your specific flight. Once this has been issued, airline computers show you as checked in, and you effectively own the seat you have selected (although some carriers may not honor boarding passes of passengers arriving at the gate less than 10 minutes before departure). This also is good — but not foolproof — insurance against getting bumped from an overbooked flight and is, therefore, an especially valuable tactic at peak travel times.

Smoking – One decision regarding choosing a seat has been taken out of the hands of most domestic travelers who smoke. Effective February 25, 1990, the US government imposed a ban that prohibits smoking on all flights scheduled for 6 hours or less within the US and its territories. The new regulation applies to both domestic and international carriers serving these routes.

Only flights with a *continuous* flying time of more than 6 hours between stops in the US or its territories are exempt. Even if the total flying time is longer, smoking is not permitted on segments of domestic flights where the time between US landings is under 6 hours — for instance, flights that include a stopover (even with no change of plane), or connecting flights. To further complicate the situation, several individual carriers ban smoking altogether on certain routes.

On those flights that do permit smoking, the US Department of Transportation has determined that nonsmoking sections must be enlarged to accommodate all passengers who wish to sit in one. The airline does not, however, have to shift seating to accommodate nonsmokers who arrive late for a flight or travelers flying standby. Cigar and pipe smoking are prohibited on all flights, even in the smoking sections.

For a wallet-size guide, which notes in detail the rights of nonsmokers according to these regulations, send a self-addressed, stamped envelope to *ASH (Action on Smoking and Health),* Airline Card, 2013 H St. NW, Washington, DC 20006 (phone: 202-659-4310).

Meals – If you have specific diet requirements, be sure to let the airlines know well before departure time. The available meals include vegetarian, seafood, kosher, Muslim, Hindu, high-protein, low-calorie, low-cholesterol, low-fat, low-sodium, diabetic, bland, and children's menus. There is no extra charge for this option. It usually is necessary to request special meals when you make your reservations — check-in time is too late. It's also wise to reconfirm that your request for a special meal has made its way into the airline's computer — the time to do this is 24 hours before departure.

(Note that special meals generally are not available on shorter domestic flights, particularly on small local carriers. If this poses a problem, eat before you board, or bring a snack with you.)

Baggage – Though airline baggage allowances vary slightly, in general all passengers are allowed to carry on board, without charge, one piece of luggage that will fit easily under a seat of the plane or in an overhead bin, and whose combined dimensions (length, width, and depth) do not exceed 45 inches. A reasonable amount of reading material, camera equipment, and a handbag also are allowed. In addition, all passengers are allowed to check two bags in the cargo hold: one usually not to exceed 62 inches when length, width, and depth are combined, the other not to exceed 55 inches in combined dimensions. Generally, no single bag may weigh more than 70 pounds.

Charges for additional, oversize, or overweight bags usually are made at a flat rate; the actual dollar amount varies from carrier to carrier. If you plan to travel with any special equipment or sporting gear, be sure to check with the airline beforehand. Most have specific procedures for handling such baggage, and you may have to pay for transport regardless of how much other baggage you have checked. Golf clubs may be checked through as luggage (most airlines are accustomed to handling them), but tennis rackets should be carried onto the plane.

To reduce the chances of your luggage going astray, remove all airline tags from previous trips, label each bag inside and out — with your business address, rather than your home address on the outside, to prevent thieves from knowing whose house might be unguarded. Lock everything and double-check the tag that the airline attaches to make sure that it is correctly coded — ORD — for Chicago's O'Hare Airport.

If your bags are not in the baggage claim area after your flight or if they're damaged, report the problem to airline personnel immediately. Keep in mind that policies regarding the specific time limit within which you have to make your claim vary from carrier to carrier. Fill out a report form on your lost or damaged luggage and keep a copy of it and your original baggage claim check. If you must surrender the check to claim a damaged bag, get a receipt for it to prove that you did, indeed, check your baggage on the flight. If luggage is missing, be sure to give the airline your destination and/or the telephone number where you can be reached. Also take the name and number of the person in charge of recovering lost luggage.

Most airlines have emergency funds for passengers stranded away from home without their luggage, but if it turns out that your bags are truly lost and not simply delayed, do not then and there sign any paper indicating you'll accept an offered settlement. Since the airline is responsible for the value of your bags within certain statutory limits ($1,250 per passenger for lost baggage on a US domestic flight) you should take the time to assess the extent of your loss (see *Insurance,* in this section). It's a good idea to keep records indicating the value of the contents of your luggage. A wise alternative is to take a Polaroid picture of the most valuable of your packed items just after putting them in your suitcase.

Considering the increased incidence of damage to baggage, now more than ever it's advisable to keep the sales slips that confirm how much you paid for your bags. These are invaluable in establishing the value of damaged luggage and eliminate any arguments. A better way to protect your gear from the luggage-eating conveyers is to try to carry it on board whenever possible.

Getting Bumped – A special air travel problem is the possibility that an airline will accept more reservations (and sell more tickets) than there are seats on a given flight. This is entirely legal and is done to make up for "no-shows," passengers who don't show up for a flight for which they have made reservations and bought tickets. If the airline has oversold the flight and everyone does show up, there simply aren't enough seats. When this happens, the airline is subject to stringent rules designed to protect travelers.

In such cases, the airline first seeks ticket holders willing to give up their seats voluntarily in return for a negotiable sum of money or some other inducement, such as an offer of upgraded seating on the next flight or a voucher for a free trip at some other time. If there are not enough volunteers, the airline may bump passengers against their wishes.

Anyone inconvenienced in this way, however, is entitled to an explanation of the criteria used to determine who does and does not get on the flight, as well as compensation if the resulting delay exceeds certain limits. If the airline can put the bumped passengers on an alternate flight that is *scheduled to arrive* at their original destination within 1 hour of their originally scheduled arrival time, no compensation is owed. If the delay is more than an hour but less than 2 hours on a domestic US flight, they must be paid denied-boarding compensation equivalent to the one-way fare to their destination (but not more than $200). If the delay is more than 2 hours after the original arrival time on a domestic flight, the compensation must be doubled (but not more than $400). The airline also may offer bumped travelers a voucher for a free flight instead of the denied-boarding compensation. The passenger may be given the choice of either money or the voucher, the dollar value of which may be no less than the monetary compensation to which the passenger would be entitled. The voucher is not a substitute for the bumped passenger's original ticket; the airline continues to honor that as well. Keep in mind that the above regulations and policies are for US flights only.

To protect yourself as best you can against getting bumped, arrive at the airport early, allowing plenty of time to check in and get to the gate. If the flight is oversold, ask immediately for the written statement explaining the airline's policy on denied-boarding compensation and its boarding priorities. If the airline refuses to give you this information, or if you feel it has not handled the situation properly, file a complaint with both the airline and the appropriate government agency (see "Consumer Protection," below).

Delays and Cancellations – The above compensation rules also do not apply if the flight is canceled or delayed, or if a smaller aircraft is substituted because of mechanical problems. Each airline has its own policy for assisting passengers whose flights are delayed or canceled or who must wait for another flight because their original one was overbooked. Most airline personnel will make new travel arrangements if necessary. If the delay is longer than 4 hours, the airline may pay for a phone call or telegram, a meal, and in some cases, a hotel room and transportation to it.

■ **Caution:** If you are bumped or miss a flight, be sure to ask the airline to notify other airlines on which you have reservations or connecting flights. When your name is taken off the passenger list of your initial flight, the computer usually cancels all of your reservations automatically, unless *you* take steps to preserve them.

CHARTER FLIGHTS: By booking a block of seats on a specially arranged flight, charter tour operators offer travelers air transportation for a substantial reduction over the full coach or economy fare. These operators may offer air-only charters (selling transportation alone) or charter packages (the flight plus a combination of land arrangements such as accommodations, meals, tours, or car rentals). Charters are especially attractive to people living in smaller cities or out-of-the-way places, because they frequently take off from nearby airports, saving travelers the inconvenience and expense of getting to a major gateway.

From the consumer's standpoint, charters differ from scheduled airlines in two main respects: You generally need to book and pay in advance, and you can't change the itinerary or the departure and return dates once you've booked the flight. In practice, however, these restrictions don't always apply. Today, although most domestic charter flights still require advance reservations, some permit last-minute bookings (when there are unsold seats available), and some even offer seats on a standby basis. Though charters almost always are round trip, and it is unlikely that you would be sold a one-way seat on a round-trip flight, on rare occasions one-way tickets on charters are offered.

Here are things to keep in mind about the charter game:

1. It cannot be repeated often enough that if you are forced to cancel your trip, you can lose much (and possibly all) of your money unless you have cancellation insurance, which is a *must* (see *Insurance,* in this section). Frequently, if the cancellation occurs far enough in advance (often 6 weeks or more), you may forfeit only a $25 or $50 penalty. If you cancel only 2 or 3 weeks before the flight, there may be no refund at all unless you or the operator can provide a substitute passenger.

2. Charter flights may be canceled by the operator up to 10 days before departure for any reason, usually underbooking. Your money is returned in this event, but there may be too little time for you to make new arrangements.

3. Most charters have little of the flexibility of regularly scheduled flights regarding refunds and the changing of flight dates; if you book a return flight, you must be on it or lose your money.

4. Charter operators are permitted to assess a surcharge, if fuel or other costs warrant it, of up to 10% of the airfare up to 10 days before departure.

5. Because of the economics of charter flights, your plane almost always will be full, so you will be crowded, though not necessarily uncomfortable. (There is, however, a new movement among charter airlines to provide flight accommodations that are more comfort-oriented, so this situation may change in the near future.)

To avoid problems, *always* choose charter flights with care. When you consider a charter, ask your travel agent who runs it and carefully check the company. The Better Business Bureau in the company's home city can report on how many complaints, if any, have been lodged against it in the past. Protect yourself with trip cancellation and interruption insurance, which can help safeguard your investment if you or a traveling companion is unable to make the trip and must cancel too late to receive a full refund from the company providing your travel services. (This is advisable whether you're buying a charter flight alone or a tour package for which the airfare is provided by charter or scheduled flight.)

Bookings – If you do fly on a charter, read the contract's fine print carefully and pay particular attention to the following:

Instructions concerning the payment of the deposit and its balance and to whom the check is to be made payable. Ordinarily, checks are made out to an escrow account, which means the charter company can't spend your money until your flight has safely returned. This provides some protection for you. To ensure the safe handling of your money, make out your check to the escrow account, the number of which must appear by law on the brochure, though all too often it is on the back in fine print. Write the details of the charter, including the destination and dates, on the face of the check; on the back, print "For Deposit Only." Your travel agent may prefer that you make out your check to the agency, saying that it will then pay the tour operator the fee minus commission. It is perfectly legal to write the check as we suggest, however, and if your agent objects too vociferously (he or she should trust the tour operator to send the proper commission), consider taking your business elsewhere. If you don't make your check out to the escrow account, you lose the protection of that escrow should the trip be canceled. Furthermore, recent bankruptcies in the travel industry have served to point out that even the protection of escrow may not be enough to safeguard a traveler's investment. More and more, insurance is becoming a necessity. The charter company should be bonded (usually by an insurance company), and if you want to file a claim against it, the claim should be sent to the bonding agent. The contract will set a time limit within which a claim must be filed.

Specific stipulations and penalties for cancellations. Most charters allow you to cancel up to 45 days in advance without major penalty, but some cancellation dates are 50 to 60 days before departure.

Stipulations regarding cancellation and major changes made by the charterer. US rules say that charter flights may not be canceled within 10 days of departure except when circumstances — such as natural disasters or political upheavals — make it physically impossible to fly. Charterers may make "major changes," however, such as in the date or place of departure or return, but you are entitled to cancel and receive a full refund if you don't wish to accept these changes. A price increase of more than 10% at any time up to 10 days before departure is considered a major change; no price increase at all is allowed during the last 10 days immediately before departure.

At the time of this writing, the following companies regularly offered charter flights to Chicago. As indicated, some of these companies sell charter flights directly to clients, while others are wholesalers and must be contacted through a travel agent.

Apple Vacations West (25 Northwest Point Blvd., Elk Grove Village, IL 60007; phone: 800-365-2775). This agency is a wholesaler, so use a travel agent.

Funway Holidays (PO Box 1460, Milwaukee, WI 53201-1460; phone: 800-558-3050). This agency is a wholesaler, so use a travel agent.

MLT Vacations (5130 Hwy. 101, Minnetonka, MN 55345; phone: 800-328-0025). This agency is a wholesaler, so use a travel agent.

MTI Vacations (1220 Kensington, Oak Brook, IL 60521; phone: 800-323-7285). Retails to the general public.

You also may want to subscribe to the travel newsletter *Jax Fax,* which regularly features a list of charter companies and packagers offering seats on US charter flights. For a year's subscription send a check or money order for $12 to *Jax Fax,* 397 Post Rd., Darien, CT 06820 (phone: 203-655-8746).

DISCOUNTS ON SCHEDULED FLIGHTS: Promotional fares often are called discount fares because they cost less than what used to be the standard airline fare — full-fare economy. Nevertheless, they cost the traveler the same whether they are bought through a travel agent or directly from the airline. Tickets that cost less if bought from some outlet other than the airline do exist, however. While it is likely that the vast majority of travelers flying within the US in the near future will be doing so on a promotional fare or charter rather than on a "discount" air ticket of this sort, it still is a good idea for cost-conscious consumers to be aware of the latest developments in the budget airfare scene. Note that the following discussion makes clear-cut distinctions among the types of discounts available based on how they reach the consumer; in actual practice, the distinctions are not nearly so precise.

Net Fare Sources – The newest notion for reducing the costs of travel services comes from travel agents who offer individual travelers "net" fares. Defined simply, a net fare is the bare minimum amount at which an airline or tour operator will carry a prospective traveler. It doesn't include the amount that normally would be paid to the travel agent as a commission. Traditionally, such commissions amount to about 10% on domestic fares — not counting significant additions to these commission levels that are paid retroactively when agents sell more than a specific volume of tickets or trips for a single supplier. At press time, at least one travel agency in the US was offering travelers the opportunity to purchase tickets and/or tours for a net price. Instead of making its income from individual commissions, this agency assesses a fixed fee that may or may not provide a bargain for travelers; it requires a little arithmetic to determine whether to use the services of a net travel agent or those of one who accepts conventional commissions. One of the potential drawbacks of buying from agencies selling travel services at net fares is that some airlines refuse to do business with them, thus possibly limiting your flight options.

Travel Avenue is a fee-based agency that rebates its ordinary agency commission to the customer. They will find the lowest retail fare, then rebate 7% to 10% (depending on the airline) of that price, minus a ticket-writing charge of $10 for domestic flights. The ticket-writing charge is imposed per ticket; if the ticket includes more than eight separate flights, an additional $10 fee is charged. Customers using free flight coupons pay the ticket-writing charge, plus an additional $5 coupon-processing fee.

Travel Avenue will rebate its commissions on all tickets, including heavily discounted fares and senior citizen passes. Available 7 days a week, reservations should be made far enough in advance to allow the tickets to be sent by first class mail, since extra charges accrue for special handling. It's possible to economize further by making your own airline reservation, then asking *Travel Avenue* only to write/issue your ticket. For travelers outside the Chicago area, business may be transacted by phone and purchases charged to a credit card. For information, contact *Travel Avenue* at 641 W. Lake, Suite 201, Chicago, IL 60606-1012 (phone: 312-876-1116 in Illinois; 800-333-3335 elsewhere in the US).

Consolidators and Bucket Shops – Other vendors of travel services can afford to sell tickets to their customers at an even greater discount because the airline has sold the tickets to them at a substantial discount (usually accomplished by sharply increasing commissions to that vendor), a practice in which many airlines indulge, albeit discreetly, preferring that the general public not know they are undercutting their own "list" prices. Airlines anticipating a slow period on a particular route sometimes sell off a certain portion of their capacity to a wholesaler or consolidator. The wholesaler sometimes is a charter operator who resells the seats to the public as though they were charter seats, which is why prospective travelers perusing the brochures of charter operators with large programs frequently see a number of flights designated as "scheduled service." As often as not, however, the consolidator, in turn, sells the seats to a travel agency specializing in discounting. Airlines also can sell seats directly to such an agency, which thus acts as its own consolidator. The airline offers the seats either at a net wholesale price, but without the volume-purchase requirement that would be difficult for a modest retail travel agency to fulfill, or at the standard price, but with a commission override large enough (as high as 50%) to allow both a profit and a price reduction to the public.

Travel agencies specializing in discounting sometimes are called "bucket shops," a term fraught with connotations of unreliability in this country. But in today's highly competitive travel marketplace, more and more conventional travel agencies are selling consolidator-supplied tickets, and the old bucket shops' image is becoming respectable. Agencies that specialize in discounted tickets exist in most large cities, and usually can be found by studying the smaller ads in the travel sections of Sunday newspapers.

Before buying a discounted ticket, whether from a bucket shop or a conventional, full-service travel agency, keep the following considerations in mind: To be in a position to judge how much you'll be saving, first find out the "list" prices of tickets to your destination. Then do some comparison shopping among agencies. Also bear in mind that a ticket that may not differ much in price from one available directly from the airline may, however, allow the circumvention of such things as the advance purchase requirement. If your plans are less than final, be sure to find out about any other restrictions, such as penalties for canceling a flight or changing a reservation. Most discount tickets are non-endorsable, meaning that they can be used only on the airline that issued them, and they usually are marked "nonrefundable" to prevent their being cashed for a list-price refund.

A great many bucket shops are small businesses operating on a thin margin, so it's a good idea to check the local Better Business Bureau for any complaints registered against the one with which you're dealing — before parting with any money. If you still do not feel reassured, consider buying discounted tickets only through a conventional travel agency, which can be expected to have found its own reliable source of consolidator tickets — some of the largest consolidators, in fact, sell only to travel agencies.

A few bucket shops require payment in cash or by certified check or money order, but if credit cards are accepted, use that option. Note, however, if buying from a charter operator selling seats for both scheduled and charter flights, that the scheduled seats are not protected by the regulations — including use of escrow accounts — governing the charter seats. Well-established charter operators, nevertheless, may extend the same protections to their scheduled flights, and, when this is the case, consumers should be sure that the payment option selected directs their money into the escrow account.

Listed below are some of the consolidators frequently offering discounted domestic fares:

>*Bargain Air* (655 Deep Valley Dr., Suite 355, Rolling Hills, CA 90274; phone: 800-347-2345 or 213-377-2919).
>
>*Maharaja Consumer Wholesale* (393 5th Ave., New York, NY 10016; phone: 212-213-2020 in New York; 800-223-6862 elsewhere in the US).
>
>*TFI Tours International* (34 W. 37th St., 12th Floor, New York, NY 10001; phone: 212-736-1140).
>
>*25 West Tours* (2490 Coral Way, Miami, FL 33145; phone: 305-856-0810; 800-423-6954 in Florida; 800-252-5052 elsewhere in the US).
>
>*Unitravel* (1177 N. Warson Rd., St. Louis, MO 63132; phone: 314-569-2501 in Missouri; 800-325-2222 elsewhere in the US).

Check with your travel agent for other sources of consolidator-supplied tickets.

■**Note:** Although rebating and discounting are becoming increasingly common, there is some legal ambiguity concerning them. Strictly speaking, it is legal to discount domestic tickets but not international tickets. On the other hand, the law that prohibits discounting, the Federal Aviation Act of 1958, is consistently ignored these days, in part because consumers benefit from the practice and in part because many illegal arrangements are indistinguishable from legal ones. Since the line separating the two is so fine that even the authorities can't always tell the difference, it is unlikely that most consumers would be able to do so, and in fact it is not illegal to *buy* a discounted ticket. If the issue of legality bothers you, ask the agency whether any ticket you're about to buy would be permissible under the above-mentioned act.

Last-Minute Travel Clubs – Still another way to take advantage of bargain airfares is open to those who have a flexible schedule. A number of organizations, usually set up as last-minute travel clubs and functioning on a membership basis, routinely keep in touch with travel suppliers to help them dispose of unsold inventory at discounts of between 15% and 60%. A great deal of the inventory consists of complete tour packages and cruises, but some clubs offer air-only charter seats and, occasionally, seats on scheduled flights.

Members generally pay an annual fee and receive a toll-free hotline number to call for information on imminent trips. In some cases, they also receive periodic mailings with information on bargain travel opportunities for which there is more advance notice. Despite the suggestive names of the clubs providing these services, last-minute travel does not necessarily mean that you cannot make plans until literally the last minute. Trips can be announced as little as a few days or as much as 2 months before departure, but the average is from 1 to 4 weeks' notice.

Among the organizations regularly offering such discounted travel opportunities in the US are the following:

Discount Club of America (61-33 Woodhaven Blvd., Rego Park, NY 11374; phone: 800-321-9587 or 718-335-9612). Annual fee: $39 per family.

Discount Travel International (Ives Building, 114 Forrest Ave., Suite 205, Narberth, PA 19072; phone: 800-334-9294 or 215-668-7184). Annual fee: $45 per household.

Encore Short Notice (4501 Forbes Blvd., Lanham, MD 20706; phone: 301-459-8020; 800-638-0930 for customer service). Annual fee: $48 per family.

Last Minute Travel (1249 Boylston St., Boston MA 02215; phone: 800-LAST-MIN or 617-267-9800). No fee.

Moment's Notice (425 Madison Ave., New York, NY 10017; phone: 212-486-0503). Annual fee: $19.95 per family.

Spur-of-the-Moment Tours and Cruises (10780 Jefferson Blvd., Culver City, CA 90230; phone: 213-839-2418 in California; 800-343-1991 elsewhere in the US). No fee.

Traveler's Advantage (3033 S. Parker Rd., Suite 1000, Aurora, CO 80014; phone: 800-548-1116). Annual fee: $49 per family.

Vacations to Go (2411 Fountain View, Suite 201, Houston, TX 77057; phone: 800-338-4962). Annual fee: $19.95 per family.

Worldwide Discount Travel Club (1674 Meridian Ave., Miami Beach, FL 33139; phone: 305-534-2082). Annual fee: $40 per person; $50 per family.

Generic Air Travel – Organizations that apply the same flexible-schedule idea to air travel only and sell tickets at literally the last minute also exist. Their service sometimes is known as "generic" air travel, and it operates somewhat like an ordinary airline standby service except that the organizations running it offer seats on not one but several scheduled and charter airlines.

One pioneer of generic flights is *Airhitch* (2790 Broadway, Suite 100, New York, NY 10025; phone: 212-864-2000). Prospective travelers register by paying a fee (applicable toward the fare) and stipulate a range of acceptable departure dates and their desired destination, along with alternate choices. The week before the date range begins, they are notified of at least two flights that will be available during the time period, agree on one, and remit the balance of the fare to the company. If they do not accept any of the suggested flights, they lose their deposit; if, through no fault of their own, they do not ultimately get on any agreed-on flight, all of their money is refunded. Return flights are arranged the same way. At the time of this writing, *Airhitch* did not offer domestic flights, but do check at the time you plan to travel.

Bartered Travel Sources – Suppose a hotel buys advertising space in a newspaper. As payment, the hotel gives the publishing company the use of a number of hotel rooms in lieu of cash. This is barter, a common means of exchange among hotels, airlines, car rental companies, cruise lines, tour operators, restaurants, and other travel service companies. When a bartering company finds itself with empty airline seats (or excess hotel rooms, or cruise ship cabin space, and so on) and offers them to the public, considerable savings can be enjoyed.

Bartered travel clubs often can give discounts of up to 50% to members, who pay an annual fee (approximately $50 at press time), which entitles them to select from the flights, cruises, hotel rooms, or other travel services that the club obtained by barter. Members usually present a voucher, club credit card, or scrip (a dollar-denomination voucher negotiable only for the bartered product) to the hotel, which in turn subtracts the dollar amount from the bartering company's account.

Selling bartered travel is a perfectly legitimate means of retailing. One advantage to club members is that they don't have to wait until the last minute to obtain flight or room reservations.

Among the companies specializing in bartered travel, several that frequently offer members travel services throughout the US include the following:

IGT (In Good Taste) Services (1111 Lincoln Rd., 4th Floor, Miami Beach, FL 33139; phone: 800-444-8872 or 305-534-7900). Annual fee: $48 per family.

Travel Guide (18210 Redmond Way, Redmond, WA 98052; phone: 206-885-1213). Annual fee: $48 per family.

Travel World Leisure Club (225 W. 34th St., Suite 2203, New York, NY 10122; phone: 800-444-TWLC or 212-239-4855). Annual fee: $50 per family.

OTHER DISCOUNT TRAVEL SOURCES: An excellent source of information on economical travel opportunities is the *Consumer Reports Travel Letter,* published monthly by Consumers Union. It keeps abreast of the scene on a wide variety of fronts, including consolidators, package tours, rental cars, insurance, and more, but it is especially helpful for its comprehensive coverage of airfares, offering guidance on all the options, from scheduled flights on major or low-fare airlines to charters and discount sources. For a year's subscription, send $37 ($57 for 2 years) to *Consumer Reports Travel Letter* (PO Box 53629, Boulder, CO 80322-3629; phone: 800-999-7959). For information on other travel newsletters, see *Sources and Resources,* in this section.

CONSUMER PROTECTION: Consumers who feel that they have not been dealt with fairly by an airline should make their complaints known. Begin with the customer service representative at the airport where the problem occurred. If your complaint cannot be resolved there to your satisfaction, write to the airline's consumer office. In a businesslike, typed letter, explain what reservations you held, what happened, the names of the employees involved, and what you expect the airline to do to remedy the situation. Send copies (never the originals) of the tickets, receipts, and other documents that back your claims. Ideally, all correspondence should be sent via certified mail, return receipt requested. This provides proof that your complaint was received.

Passengers with consumer complaints — lost baggage, compensation for getting bumped, smoking and nonsmoking rules, deceptive practices by an airline — who are not satisfied with the airline's response should contact the Department of Transportation (DOT), Consumer Affairs Division (400 Seventh St. SW, Room 10405, Washington, DC 20590; phone: 202-366-2220). DOT personnel stress, however, that consumers initially should direct their complaints to the airline that provoked them.

Remember, too, that the federal Fair Credit Billing Act permits purchasers to refuse to pay charges if they do not receive the services for which they've been billed, so the onus of dealing with the receiver for a bankrupt airline, for example, falls on the credit card company. Do not rely on another airline to honor any ticket you're holding from a failed airline, since the days when virtually all major carriers subscribed to a default protection program that bound them to do so are long gone. Some airlines may voluntarily step forward to accommodate the stranded passengers of a fellow carrier, but this is now an entirely altruistic act.

The deregulation of US airlines has meant that travelers must find out for themselves what they are entitled to receive. The Department of Transportation's informative consumer booklet, *Fly Rights,* is a good place to start. To receive a copy, send $1 to the Superintendent of Documents (US Government Printing Office, Washington, DC 20402-9325; phone: 202-783-3238). Specify its stock number, 050-000-00513-5, and allow 3 to 4 weeks for delivery.

On Arrival

 FROM THE AIRPORT TO THE CITY: O'Hare International Airport is about 25 miles west of the Loop and, depending on traffic, a 30- to 60-minute ride by cab; the fare should run about $25. *Continental Air Transport* (phone: 454-7800) charges $12.50 for van service to the airport from 24 city locations (including all the major hotels). The trip takes almost an hour, and vans run approximately every 30 minutes. Ask your hotel concierge for *Continental*'s return schedule. *Chicago Transit Authority* (phone: 836-7000 or 800-972-7000) *O'Hare Line* trains run from several downtown and North Side spots to O'Hare's main terminal in approximately 35 minutes; the fare is $1.25.

Midway Airport, which handles an increasing volume of domestic traffic, is 8 miles south of the Loop. A taxi ride to Midway from the Loop will take from 10 to 20 minutes and cost about $10. The No. 62 *Archer Express* bus (heading south) can be picked up from any stop along State St. in the Loop; transfer at Cicero Avenue to any southbound bus — they stop inside the airport. This ride takes about 30 minutes and costs $1.25. *Continental Air Transport* (phone: 454-7800) also provides van service to the airport from the *Palmer House, Hyatt Regency,* and *Marriott* hotels; schedules vary according to flights. The run to the airport takes about 40 minutes, and it costs $9.50.

CAR RENTAL: Unless planning to drive round trip from home, most travelers who want to drive while on vacation simply rent a car. They can rent a car through a travel agent or national rental firm before leaving home, or from a local company once they arrive in Chicago. Another possibility, also arranged before departure, is to rent the car as part of a larger package of travel services.

It's tempting to wait until arrival to scout out the lowest-priced rental from the company located the farthest from the airport high-rent district and offering no pick-up services. But if your arrival coincides with a holiday or peak travel period, you may be disappointed to find that even the most expensive car in the city was reserved months ago. Whenever possible, it is best to reserve in advance, anywhere from a few days in slack periods to a month or more during the busier seasons.

Often, the easiest place to rent (or at least pick up) the car is at the airport on arrival. The majority of the national car rental companies have locations at O'Hare Airport, where shuttle buses from each company pick up clients from the terminals and take them to the car rental locations. Travel agents can arrange rentals for clients, but it is just as easy to call and rent a car yourself. Listed below are the nationwide, toll-free telephone numbers of the major national rental companies that have locations in Chicago.

Alamo: 800-327-9633
Avis: 800-331-1212
Budget Rent-A-Car: 800-527-0700
Dollar Rent-A-Car: 800-800-4000
Hertz: 800-654-3131
National Car Rental: 800-CAR-RENT
Sears Rent-A-Car: 800-527-0770
Thrifty Rent-A-Car: 800-367-2277

If you decide to wait until after you arrive, you'll often find a surprising number of small companies listed in the local yellow pages. One such company is *Airways Rent-a-Car* (phone: 708-678-2300 in Illinois, or 800-952-9200 elsewhere in the US). Downtown locations include 410 E. Erie, 519 W. Jackson Blvd., and 70 E. Lake St. *Econo-Car* (phone: 312-951-6262) also has several downtown locations, including 850 N. State Ave., 320 S. Wells St., and 101 W. Lake St. Other local rental companies with airport locations include *Ace Rent-a-Car* (phone: 800-323-3221), with locations near the O'-Hare and Midway airports, and *Payless Rent-a-Car* (1450 E. Touhy, Des Plaines; phone: 708-635-6140), a 7-minute drive from O'Hare.

To economize on a car rental, also consider one of the firms that rents 3- to 5-year-old cars that are well worn but (presumably) mechanically sound; one such company is *Rent-a-Wreck* (4935 W. 63rd St., Chicago; phone: 800-421-7253), whose local office is located just across the street from Midway Airport.

At the other extreme, for those who feel like splurging, *Rent-A-Rollz* (1304 Algonquin, Schaumburg, IL 60173; phone: 800-273-0634 or 708-887-0634), which rents Rolls-Royces by the hour, can deliver one to your hotel.

Requirements – Whether you decide to rent a car in advance from a large national rental company or wait to rent from a local company, you should know that renting a car is rarely as simple as signing on the dotted line and roaring off into the night. If you are renting for personal use, you must have a valid driver's license and will have to convince the renting agency that (1) you are personally creditworthy, and (2) you will bring the car back at the stated time. This will be easy if you have a major credit card; most rental companies accept credit cards in lieu of a cash deposit, as well as for payment of your final bill. If you prefer to pay in cash, leave your credit card imprint as a "deposit," then pay your bill in cash when you return the car.

Note that *Avis, Budget, Hertz,* and other national companies usually *will* rent to travelers paying in cash and leaving either a credit card imprint or a substantial amount of cash as a deposit. This is not necessarily standard policy, however, as other national chains and a number of local companies will *not* rent to an individual who doesn't have a valid credit card. In this case, you will have to call around to find a company that accepts cash.

Also, keep in mind that although the minimum age to drive in most states is 16, the minimum age to rent a car is set by the rental company. (Restrictions vary from company to company, as well as at different locations.) Many firms have a minimum age requirement of 21 years, some raise that to 23 or 25 years, and for some models of cars it rises to 30 years. The upper age limit at many companies is between 69 and 75; others have no upper age limit or may make drivers above a certain age subject to special conditions.

Costs – Finding the most economical car rental will require some telephone shopping on your part. As a *general* rule, expect to hear lower prices quoted by the smaller, strictly local companies than by the well-known international names.

Comparison shopping always is advisable, however. Even the international giants offer discount plans whose conditions are easy for most travelers to fulfill. For instance, *Budget* and *National* offer discounts of anywhere from 10% to 30% off their usual rates (according to the size of the car and the duration of the rental), provided that the car is reserved a certain number of days before departure (usually 7 to 14 days, but it can be less), is rented for a minimum period (5 days or, more often, a week), is paid for at the time of booking, and, in most cases, is returned to the same location that supplied it or to another in the same area. Similar discount plans include *Hertz*'s Leisure Rates and *Avis*'s Supervalue Rates.

If driving short distances for only a day or two, the best deal may be a per-day, per-mile rate: You pay a flat fee for each day you keep the car, plus a per-mile charge. An increasingly common alternative is to be granted a certain number of free miles each day and then be charged on a per-mile basis over that number.

Most companies also offer a flat per-day rate with unlimited free mileage; this certainly is the most economical rate if you plan to drive over 100 miles. Make sure that the low, flat daily rate that catches your eye, however, is indeed a per-day rate:

Often the lowest price advertised by a company turns out to be available only with a minimum 3-day rental — fine if you want the car that long, but it's not the bargain it appears if you really intend to use it no more than 24 hours. Flat weekly rates also are available, as are some flat monthly rates that represent a further savings over the daily rate.

Another factor influencing the cost is the type of car you rent. Rentals generally are based on a tiered price system, with different sizes of cars — variations of budget, economy, regular, and luxury — often listed as A (the smallest and least expensive) through F, G, or H, and sometimes even higher. Charges may increase by only a few dollars a day through several classes of subcompact and compact cars — where most of the competition is — then increase by great leaps through the remaining classes of full-size and luxury cars and passenger vans. The larger the car, the more it costs to rent and the more gas it consumes, but for some people the greater comfort and extra luggage space of a larger car (in which bags and sporting gear can be safely locked out of sight) may make it worth the additional expense. Also more expensive are sleek sports cars, but again, for some people the thrill of driving such a car — for a week or a day — may be worth it.

Electing to pay for collision damage waiver (CDW) protection will add considerably to the cost of renting a car. You may be responsible for the *full value* of the vehicle being rented if it is damaged or stolen, but you can dispense with all of the possible liability by buying the offered waiver at a cost of around $11 to $13 a day. Before making any decisions about optional collision damage waivers, however, check with your own insurance agent and determine whether your personal automobile insurance policy covers rented vehicles; if it does, you probably won't need to pay for the waiver. Be aware, too, that increasing numbers of credit cards automatically provide CDW coverage if the car rental is charged to the appropriate credit card. However, the specific terms of such credit card coverage differ sharply among individual card companies, so check with the credit card company for information on the nature and amount of coverage provided. Business travelers also should be aware that, at the time of this writing, *American Express* had withdrawn its automatic CDW coverage from some corporate *Green* card accounts and limited the length of coverage — watch for similar cutbacks by other credit card companies.

When inquiring about CDW coverage and costs, be aware that a number of car rental companies now automatically are including the cost of this waiver in their quoted prices. This does not mean that they are absorbing this cost and you are receiving free coverage — in many cases total rental prices have increased to include the former CDW charge. The disadvantage of this inclusion is that you probably will not have the option to refuse this coverage, and will end up paying the added charge — even if you already are adequately covered by your own insurance policy or through a credit card company.

Another cost to be added to the price tag is drop-off charges or one-way service fees. The lowest price quoted by any given company may apply only to a car that is returned to the same location from which it was rented. A slightly higher rate may be charged if the car is to be returned to a different location (even within the same city).

Package Tours

 If the mere thought of buying a package for your visit to Chicago conjures up visions of a trip spent marching in lockstep through the city's attractions with a horde of frazzled fellow travelers, remember that packages have come a long way. For one thing, not all packages necessarily are escorted tours, and the one you buy does not have to include any organized touring at all — nor will it necessarily include traveling companions. If it does, however, you'll find that people of all sorts — many just like yourself — are taking advantage of packages today because they are economical and convenient and save an immense amount of planning time. Given the high cost of travel these days, packages have emerged as a particularly wise buy.

In essence, a package is just an amalgam of travel services that can be purchased in a single transaction. A package (tour or otherwise) may include any or all of the following: round-trip transportation, local transportation (and/or car rentals), accommodations, some or all meals, sightseeing, entertainment, transfers to and from the hotel, taxes, tips, escort service, and a variety of incidental features that might be offered as options at additional cost. In other words, a package can be any combination of travel elements, from a fully escorted tour offered at an all-inclusive price to a simple fly/drive booking that allows you to move about totally on your own. Its principal advantage is that it saves money: The cost of the combined arrangements invariably is well below the price of all of the same elements if bought separately, and, particularly if transportation is provided by discount flight, the whole package could cost less than just a round-trip economy airline ticket on a regularly scheduled flight. A package provides more than economy and convenience: It releases the traveler from having to make individual arrangements for each separate element of a trip.

Tour programs generally can be divided into two categories — "'escorted" (or locally hosted) and "independent." An escorted tour means that a guide will accompany the group from the beginning of the tour through to the return flight; a locally hosted tour means that the group will be met upon arrival at each location by a different local host. On independent tours, there generally is a choice of hotels, meal plans, and sightseeing trips, as well as a variety of special excursions. The independent plan is for travelers who do not want a totally set itinerary, but who do prefer confirmed hotel reservations. Whether choosing an escorted or an independent tour, always bring along complete contact information for your tour operator in case a problem arises, although tour operators often have local affiliates who can give additional assistance or make other arrangements on the spot.

To determine whether a package — or more specifically, *which* package — fits your travel plans, start by evaluating your interests and needs, deciding how much and what you want to spend, see, and do. Gather brochures on Chicago tours. Be sure that you take the time to read each brochure *carefully* to determine precisely what is included. Keep in mind that they are written to entice you into signing up for a package tour. Often the language is deceptive and devious. For example, a brochure may quote the lowest prices for a package tour based on facilities that are unavailable during the off-season, undesirable at any season, or just plain nonexistent. Information such as "breakfast included" or "plus tax" (which can add up) should be taken into account. Note, too, that prices quoted in brochures almost always are based on double occupancy: The rate listed is for each of two people sharing a double room, and if you travel alone the supplement for single accommodations can raise the price considerably (see *Hints for Single Travelers,* in this section).

In this age of erratic airfares, the brochure most often will *not* include the price of an airline ticket in the price of the package, though sample fares from various gateway cities usually will be listed separately, to be added to the price of the ground arrangements. Before figuring your actual costs, check the latest fares with the airlines, because the samples invariably are out of date by the time you read them. If the brochure gives more than one category of sample fares per gateway city — such as an individual tour-basing fare, a group fare, an excursion, or other discount ticket — your travel agent or airline tour desk will be able to tell you which one applies to the package you choose, depending on when you travel, how far in advance you book, and other factors.

(An individual tour-basing fare is a fare computed as part of a package that includes land arrangements, thereby entitling a carrier to reduce the air portion almost to the absolute minimum. Though it always represents a saving over full-fare coach or economy, lately the individual tour-basing fare has not been as inexpensive as the excursion and other discount fares that also are available to individuals. The group fare usually is the least expensive fare, and it is the tour operator, not you, who makes up the group.) When the brochure does include round-trip transportation in the package price, don't forget to add the cost of round-trip transportation from your home to the departure city to come up with the total cost of the package.

Finally, read the general information regarding terms and conditions and the responsibility clause (usually in fine print at the end of the descriptive literature) to determine the precise elements for which the tour operator is — and is not — liable. Here the tour operator frequently expresses the right to change services or schedules as long as equivalent arrangements are offered. This clause also absolves the operator of responsibility for circumstances beyond human control, such as avalanches, earthquakes, or floods, or injury to you or your property. While reading, ask the following questions:

1. Does the tour include airfare or other transportation, sightseeing, meals, transfers, taxes, baggage handling, tips, or any other services? Do you want all these services?
2. If the brochure indicates that "some meals" are included, does this mean a welcoming and farewell dinner, two breakfasts, or every evening meal?
3. What classes of hotels are offered? If you will be traveling alone, what is the single supplement?
4. Does the tour itinerary or price vary according to the season?
5. Are the prices guaranteed; that is, if costs increase between the time you book and the time you depart, can surcharges unilaterally be added?
6. Do you get a full refund if you cancel? If not, be sure to obtain cancellation insurance.
7. Can the operator cancel if too few people join? At what point?

One of the consumer's biggest problems is finding enough information to judge the reliability of a tour packager, since individual travelers seldom have direct contact with the firm putting the package together. Usually, a retail travel agent is interposed between customer and tour operator, and much depends on his or her candor and cooperation. So ask a number of questions about the tour you are considering. For example:

- Has the travel agent ever used a package provided by this tour operator?
- How long has the tour operator been in business? Check the Better Business Bureau in the area where the tour operator is based to see if any complaints have been filed against it.
- Is the tour operator a member of the *United States Tour Operators Association* (*USTOA;* 211 E. 51st St., Suite 12B, New York, NY 10022; phone: 212-944-5727)? *USTOA* will provide a list of its members upon request; it also offers a useful brochure called *How to Select a Package Tour.*
- How many and which companies are involved in the package?

■**A word of advice:** Purchasers of vacation packages who feel they're not getting their money's worth are more likely to get a refund if they complain in writing to the operator — and bail out of the whole package immediately. Alert the tour operator to the fact that you are dissatisfied, that you will be leaving for home as soon as transportation can be arranged, and that you expect a refund. They may have forms to fill out detailing your complaint; otherwise, state your case in a letter. Even if the availability of transportation home detains you, your dated, written complaint should help in procuring a refund from the operator.

SAMPLE PACKAGES TO CHICAGO: Following is a list of some of the major tour operators that offer Chicago packages. As indicated, some operators are wholesalers only, and will deal only with a travel agent.

American Express Travel Related Services (offices throughout the US; phone: 800-241-1700 for information and local branch offices). Offers Chicago city packages, as well as independent and escorted tours throughout the US. The tour operator is a wholesaler, so use a travel agent.

Chicago Gray Line (500 S. Michigan Ave.; phone: 312-427-3107). Offers 3-day city packages that include hotel accommodations and a 4-hour motorcoach tour. Half-day and 1-day tours of the city also are available.

Domenico Tours (751 Broadway, Bayonne, NJ 07002; phone: 201-823-8687). Offers air/hotel city packages to Chicago.

Travel Avenue (641 W. Lake St., Suite 201, Chicago, IL 60606-1012; phone: 312-876-1116 in Illinois; 800-333-3335 elsewhere in the US). Known as a net fare source (see *Traveling by Plane,* in this section), this agency also books custom Chicago city packages.

In addition, many of the major air carriers also maintain their own tour departments or subsidiaries to stimulate vacation travel to the cities they serve. In all cases, the arrangements may be booked through a travel agent or directly with the airline. The following airlines, which fly to Chicago, may offer air/hotel city packages.

American Airlines FlyAAway Vacations (Southern Reservation Center, Mail Drop 1000, Box 619619, Dallas/Fort Worth Airport, TX 75261-9619; phone: 800-321-2121).

Continental's Grand Destinations (PO Box 1460, Milwaukee, WI 53201-1460; phone: 800-634-5555).

Delta's Dream Vacations (PO Box 1525, Fort Lauderdale, FL 33302; phone: 800-872-7786).

Northwest Vacations Center (5101 Northwest Dr., St. Paul, MN 55111-3034; phone: 800-692-8687).

TWA Getaway (10 E. Stow Rd., Marlton, NJ 08053; phone: 800-GETAWAY).

Whether visiting Chicago independently or on one of the above city packages, if you would like to include some organized touring, the following tour operators offer 1-day or shorter guided tours of the city.

ArchiCenter (330 S. Dearborn St.; phone: 922-3431). Offers more than 50 architectural tours in and around the city.

Chicago Architecture Foundation (1800 S. Prairie Ave.; phone: 326-1393). Organizes tours of historical buildings and architectural landmarks of Chicago.

Chicago CTA Culture Bus (222 Merchandise Mart Plaza, 7th Floor; phone: 836-7000). Offers a full-day bus tour of the city on Sundays and holidays.

Chicago From the Lake (455 E. Illinois St., Suite 361; phone: 527-2002). Offers a 90-minute architectural cruise on the Chicago River from May through October.

Chicago Motor Coach (750 S. Clinton St.; phone: 922-8919). Offers a 1-hour tour of the city aboard a double-decker bus.

Chicago Supernatural Tours (PO Box 29054, Chicago, IL 60629; phone: 708-499-0300). Offers 5-hour day or night supernatural tours that visit murder sites, haunted pubs, ghost houses, and cemeteries. Each tour is based on a story of historical folklore. There also is a thrilling 2-hour boat cruise from July through August on Sundays from 11 PM to 1 AM.

Historic Pullman Foundation (1111 S. Forrestville; phone: 785-8181). Organizes tours of the historic Pullman area.

Spirit of Chicago (466 E. Illinois St., Suite 461; phone: 836-7899). Offers lunch and dinner cruises on the Chicago River.

■**Note:** Frequently, the best city packages are offered by hotels that are trying to attract guests during the weekends, when business travel drops off, and during other slower periods. These packages are often advertised in the local newspapers and sometimes in the travel sections of big metropolitan papers, such as the *Chicago Tribune.* It's worth asking about packages, especially family and special-occasion offerings, when you call to make a hotel reservation. Calling several hotels can yield a variety of options from which to choose.

Preparing

Calculating Costs

DETERMINING A BUDGET: A realistic appraisal of travel expenses is the most crucial bit of planning before any trip. It also is, unfortunately, one for which it is most difficult to give precise practical advice.

Estimating travel expenses for a vacation in Chicago depends on the mode of transportation you choose and how long you will stay, as well as the kind of trip you are planning.

When calculating costs, start with the basics, the major expenses being transportation, accommodations, and food. For Chicago, that will mean $150 or more a night for a double at an expensive hotel, $85 to $145 for a moderate property, and somewhat under $85 for an inexpensive one. Dinner for two without wine runs to more than $60 at an expensive restaurant, $40 to $60 at a moderate one, and under $40 at an inexpensive one. Then there are breakfast and lunch to consider.

Don't forget such extras as local transportation, shopping, and miscellaneous items like laundry and tips. The reasonable cost of these items often is a positive surprise to your budget.

Other expenses, such as the cost of local sightseeing tours and other excursions, should be included. Tourist information offices and most of the better hotels will have someone at the front desk to provide a rundown on the cost of local tours and full-day excursions in and out of Chicago. Travel agents also can provide this information.

In planning any travel budget, it also is wise to allow a realistic amount for both entertainment and recreation. Are you planning to spend time sightseeing and visiting local tourist attractions? Is tennis or golf a part of your plan? Are you traveling with children who want to visit every site? Finally, allow for the extra cost of nightlife, if such is your pleasure. This one item alone can add a great deal to your daily expenditures.

If at any point in the planning process it appears impossible to estimate expenses, consider this suggestion: The easiest way to put a ceiling on the price of all these elements is to buy a package tour with transportation, rooms, meals, sightseeing, local travel, tips, and a dinner show or two included and prepaid. This provides a pretty exact total of what the trip will cost beforehand, and the only surprise will be the one you spring on yourself by succumbing to some irresistible souvenir.

Planning a Trip

Travelers fall into two categories: those who make lists and those who do not. Some people prefer to plot the course of their trip to the finest detail, with contingency plans and alternatives at the ready. For others, the joy of a voyage is its spontaneity; exhaustive planning only lessens the thrill of anticipation and the sense of freedom.

For most travelers, however, a week-plus trip can be too expensive for an "I'll take my chances" attitude. At least some planning is crucial. This is not to suggest that you work out your itinerary in minute detail before you go, but it's still wise to decide certain basics at the very start: where to go, what to do, and how much to spend. These decisions require a certain amount of consideration. So before rigorously planning specific details, you might want to establish your general travel objectives:

1. How much time will you have for the entire trip, and how much of it are you willing to spend getting where you're going?
2. What interests and/or activities do you want to pursue while on vacation?
3. At what time of year do you want to go?
4. Do you want peace and privacy or lots of activity and company?
5. How much money can you afford to spend for the entire vacation?

You now can make almost all of your own travel arrangements if you have time to follow through with hotels, airlines, tour operators, and so on. But you'll probably save considerable time and energy if you have a travel agent make arrangements for you. The agent also should be able to advise you of alternative arrangements of which you may not be aware. Only rarely will a travel agent's services cost a traveler any money, and they may even save you some (see *How to Use a Travel Agent,* below).

Make plans early. During the summer months and holidays, make hotel reservations at least a month in advance. If you are flying at these times and want to benefit from savings offered through discount fares, purchase tickets as far ahead as possible. Many hotels require deposits before they will guarantee reservations, and this most often is the case during peak travel periods. (Be sure to get a receipt for any deposit or, better yet, charge the deposit to a credit card.)

When packing, make a list of any valuable items you are carrying with you, including credit card numbers and the serial numbers of your traveler's checks. Put copies in your purse or pocket, and leave other copies at home. Put a label with your name and home address on the inside of your luggage for identification in case of loss. Put your name and business address — *never your home address* — on a label on the outside of your luggage. (Those who run businesses from home should use the office address of a friend or relative.)

Review your travel documents. If you are traveling by air, check to see that your ticket has been filled in correctly. The left side of the ticket should have a list of each stop you will make (even if you are stopping only to change planes), beginning with your departure point. Be sure that the list is correct, and count the number of copies to see that you have one for each plane you will take. If you have confirmed reservations, be sure that the column marked "status" says "OK" beside each flight. Have in hand vouchers or proof of payment for any reservation for which you've paid in advance; this includes hotels, transfers to and from the airport, sightseeing tours, car rentals, and tickets to special events.

Although policies vary from carrier to carrier, it's still smart to reconfirm your flight 48 to 72 hours before departure, both going and returning. If you are traveling by car, bring your driver's license, car registration, and proof of insurance, as well as gasoline credit cards and auto service card (if you have them).

Finally, you always should bear in mind that despite the most careful plans, things do not always occur on schedule. If you maintain a flexible attitude and try to accept minor disruptions as less than cataclysmic, you will enjoy yourself a lot more.

How to Use a Travel Agent

 A reliable travel agent remains the best source of service and information for planning a trip, whether you have a specific itinerary and require an agent only to make reservations or you need extensive help in sorting through the maze of airfares, tour offerings, hotel packages, and the scores of other arrangements that may be involved in your trip.

Know what you want from a travel agent so that you can evaluate what you are getting. It is perfectly reasonable to expect your travel agent to be a thoroughly knowledgeable travel specialist, with information about your destination and, even more crucial, a command of current airfares, ground arrangements, and other wrinkles in the travel scene.

Most travel agents work through computer reservations systems (CRS). These are used to assess the availability and cost of flights, hotels, and car rental firms, and through them they can book reservations. Despite reports of "computer bias," in which a computer may favor one airline over another, the CRS should provide agents with the entire spectrum of flights available to a given destination, as well as the complete range of fares, in considerably less time than it takes to telephone the airlines individually — and at no extra charge to the client.

Make the most intelligent use of a travel agent's time and expertise; understand the economics of the industry. As a client, traditionally you pay nothing for the agent's services; with few exceptions it's all free, from hotel bookings to advice on package tours. Any money the travel agent makes on the time spent arranging your itinerary — booking hotels, resorts, or flights, or suggesting activities — comes from commissions paid by the suppliers of these services — the airlines, hotels, and so on. These commissions generally run from 10% to 15% of the total cost of the service, although suppliers often reward agencies that sell their services in volume with an increased commission called an override.

A travel agent sometimes may charge a fee for special services. These chargeable items may include long-distance telephone costs incurred in making a booking, for reserving a room in a place that does not pay a commission (such as a small, out-of-the way hotel), or for special attention such as planning a highly personalized itinerary. A fee also may be assessed in instances of deeply discounted airfares.

Choose a travel agent with the same care with which you would choose a doctor or lawyer. You will be spending a good deal of money on the basis of the agent's judgment, so you have a right to expect that judgment to be mature, informed, and interested. At the moment, unfortunately, there aren't many standards within the travel agent industry to help you gauge competence, and the quality of individual agents varies enormously.

At present, only nine states have registration, licensing, or some other forms of travel agent–related legislation on their books. Rhode Island licenses travel agents; Florida, Hawaii, Iowa, and Ohio register them; and California, Illinois, Oregon, and Washington have laws governing the sale of transportation or related services. While state licensing of agents cannot absolutely guarantee competence, it can at least ensure that an agent has met some minimum requirements.

Perhaps the best-prepared agents are those who have completed the CTC Travel Management program offered by the *Institute of Certified Travel Agents (ICTA)* and carry the initials CTC (Certified Travel Counselor) after their names. This indicates a relatively high level of expertise. For a free listing of CTCs in your area, send a self-addressed, stamped, #10 envelope to *ICTA*, 148 Linden St., Box 82-56, Wellesley, MA 02181 (phone: 617-237-0280 in Massachusetts; 800-542-4282 elsewhere in the US).

An agent's membership in the *American Society of Travel Agents (ASTA)* can be a useful guideline in making a selection. But keep in mind that *ASTA* is an industry organization, requiring only that its members be licensed in those states where required; be accredited to represent the suppliers whose products they sell, including airline and cruise tickets; and adhere to its Principles of Professional Conduct and Ethics code. *ASTA* does not guarantee the competence, ethics, or financial soundness of its members, but it does offer some recourse if you feel you have been dealt with unfairly. Complaints may be registered with *ASTA* (Consumer Affairs Dept., PO Box 23992, Washington, DC 20026-3992; phone: 703-739-2782). First try to resolve the complaint directly with the supplier. For a list of *ASTA* members in your area, send a self-addressed, stamped, #10 envelope to *ASTA,* Public Relations Dept., at the address above.

There also is the *Association of Retail Travel Agents (ARTA),* a smaller but highly respected trade organization similar to *ASTA.* Its member agencies and agents similarly agree to abide by a code of ethics, and complaints about a member can be made to *ARTA*'s Grievance Committee, 1745 Jeff Davis Hwy., Arlington, VA 22202-3402 (phone: 800-969-6069 or 703-553-7777).

Perhaps the best way to find a travel agent is by word of mouth. If the agent (or agency) has done a good job for your friends over a period of time, it probably indicates a certain level of commitment and competence. Always ask for the name of the company *and* for the name of the specific agent with whom your friends dealt, for it is that individual who will serve you, and quality can vary widely within a single agency.

Insurance

It is unfortunate that most decisions to buy travel insurance are impulsive and usually are made without any real consideration of the traveler's existing policies. Therefore, the first person with whom you should discuss travel insurance is your own insurance broker, not a travel agent or the clerk behind the airport insurance counter. You may discover that the insurance you already carry — homeowner's policies and/or accident, health, and life insurance — protects you adequately while you travel and that your real needs are in the more mundane areas of excess value insurance for baggage or trip cancellation insurance.

TYPES OF INSURANCE: To make insurance decisions intelligently, however, you first should understand the basic categories of travel insurance and what they cover. Then you can decide what you should have in the broader context of your personal insurance needs, and you can choose the most economical way of getting the desired protection: through riders on existing policies; with one-time, short-term policies; through a special program put together for the frequent traveler; through coverage that's part of a travel club's benefits; or with a combination policy sold by insurance companies through brokers, automobile clubs, tour operators, and travel agents.

There are seven basic categories of travel insurance:

1. Baggage and personal effects insurance
2. Personal accident and sickness insurance
3. Trip cancellation and interruption insurance
4. Default and/or bankruptcy insurance
5. Flight insurance (to cover injury or death)

6. Automobile insurance (for driving your own or a rented car)
7. Combination policies

Baggage and Personal Effects Insurance – Ask your insurance agent if baggage and personal effects are included in your current homeowner's policy, or if you will need a special floater to cover you for the duration of a trip. The object is to protect your bags and their contents in case of damage or theft at any time during your travels, not just while you're in flight, where only limited protection is provided by the airline. Baggage liability varies from carrier to carrier, but generally speaking, on domestic flights luggage usually is insured to $1,250 — that's per passenger, not per bag. This limit should be specified on your airline ticket, but to be awarded any amount, you'll have to provide an itemized list of lost property, and if you're including new and/or expensive items, be prepared for a request that you back up your claim with sales receipts or other proof of purchase.

If you are carrying goods worth more than the maximum protection offered by the airlines, consider excess value insurance. Additional coverage is available from airlines at an average, currently, of $1 to $2 per $100 worth of coverage, up to a maximum of $5,000. This insurance can be purchased at the airline counter when you check in, though you should arrive early to fill out the necessary forms and to avoid holding up other passengers.

Major credit card companies provide coverage for lost or delayed baggage — and this coverage often also is over and above what the airline will pay. The basic coverage usually is automatic for all cardholders who use the credit card to purchase tickets, but to qualify for additional coverage, cardholders generally must enroll.

Additional baggage and personal effects insurance also is included in certain of the combination travel insurance policies discussed below.

■ **A note of warning:** Be sure to read the fine print of any excess value insurance policy; there often are specific exclusions, such as cash, tickets, furs, gold and silver objects, art, and antiques. Insurance companies ordinarily will pay only the depreciated value of the goods rather than their replacement value. The best way to protect your property is to take photos of your valuables, and keep a record of the serial numbers of such items as cameras, typewriters, laptop computers, radios, and so on. If an airline loses your luggage, you will be asked to fill out a Property Irregularity Report before you leave the airport. Also, report the loss to the police (since the insurance company will check with the police when processing your claim).

Personal Accident and Sickness Insurance – This covers you in case of illness during your trip or death in an accident. Most policies insure you for hospital and doctors' expenses, lost income, and so on. In most cases, it is a standard part of existing health insurance policies (especially where domestic travel is concerned), though you should check with your insurance broker to be sure of the conditions for which your policy will pay. If your coverage is insufficient, take out a separate vacation accident policy or an entire vacation insurance policy that includes health and life coverage.

Trip Cancellation and Interruption Insurance – Most package tour passengers pay for their travel well before departure. The disappointment of having to miss a vacation because of illness or any other reason pales before the awful prospect that not all (and sometimes none) of the money paid in advance might be returned. So cancellation insurance for any package tour is a must.

Although cancellation penalties vary (they are listed in the fine print in every tour brochure, and before you purchase a package tour you should know exactly what they are), rarely will a passenger get more than 50% of this money back if forced to cancel within a few weeks of scheduled departure. Therefore, if you book a package tour, you should have trip cancellation insurance to guarantee full reimbursement or refund should you, a traveling companion, or a member of your immediate family get sick, forcing you to cancel your trip or *return home early.*

The key here is *not* to buy just enough insurance to guarantee full reimbursement for the cost of the package in case of cancellation. The proper amount of coverage should include reimbursement for the cost of having to catch up with a tour after its departure or having to travel home at the full economy airfare if you have to forgo the return flight tied to the package. There usually is quite a discrepancy between an excursion or other special airfare and the amount charged to travel the same distance on a regularly scheduled flight at full economy fare.

Trip cancellation insurance is available from travel agents and tour operators in two forms: as part of a short-term, all-purpose travel insurance package (sold by the travel agent); or as specific cancellation insurance designed by the operator for a specific tour. Generally, tour operators' policies are less expensive, but also less inclusive. Cancellation insurance also is available directly from insurance companies or their agents as part of a short-term, all-inclusive travel insurance policy.

Before you decide on a policy, read each one carefully. (Either type can be purchased from a travel agent when you book the package tour.) Be sure to check the fine print for stipulations concerning "family members" and "pre-existing medical conditions," as well as allowances for living expenses if you must delay your return due to injury or illness.

Default and/or Bankruptcy Insurance – Although trip cancellation insurance usually protects you if *you* are unable to complete — or begin — your trip, a fairly recent innovation is coverage in the event of default and/or bankruptcy on the part of the tour operator, airline, or other travel supplier. In some travel insurance packages, this contingency is included in the trip cancellation portion of the coverage; in others, it is a separate feature. Either way, it is becoming increasingly important. Whereas sophisticated travelers have long known to beware of the possibility of default or bankruptcy when buying a tour package, in recent years more than a few respected airlines have unexpectedly revealed their shaky financial condition, sometimes leaving hordes of stranded ticket holders in their wake. While default/bankruptcy insurance will not ordinarily result in reimbursement in time to pay for new arrangements, it can ensure that you will get your money back, and even independent travelers buying no more than an airplane ticket may want to consider it.

Flight Insurance – US airlines' liability for injury or death to passengers on domestic flights currently is determined on a case-by-case basis in court — this means potentially unlimited liability. But remember, this liability is not the same thing as an insurance policy; every penny that an airline eventually pays in the case of death or injury likely will be subject to a legal battle.

But before you buy last-minute flight insurance from an airport vending machine, consider the purchase in light of your total existing insurance coverage. A careful review of your current policies may reveal that you already are amply covered for accidental death. Be aware that airport insurance, the kind typically bought at a counter or from a vending machine, is among the most expensive forms of life insurance coverage, and that even within a single airport, rates for approximately the same coverage vary widely.

If you buy your plane ticket with a major credit card, you generally receive automatic insurance coverage at no extra cost. Additional coverage usually can be obtained at extremely reasonable prices, but a cardholder must sign up for it in advance.

Automobile Insurance – If you have an accident in a state that has "no fault" insurance, each party's insurance company pays his or her expenses up to certain specified limits. When you rent a car, the rental company is required to provide you with collision protection. In your car rental contract, you'll see that for about $10 to $13 a day, you may buy optional collision damage waiver (CDW) protection.

If you do not accept the CDW coverage, you may be liable for as much as the full retail cost of the rental car if it is damaged or stolen; by paying for the CDW, you are relieved of all responsibility for any damage to the car. Before agreeing to this coverage, however, check with your own broker about your own existing personal auto insurance policy. It very well may cover your entire liability exposure without any additional cost, or you automatically may be covered by the credit card company to which you are charging the cost of your rental. To find out the amount of rental car insurance provided by major credit cards, contact the issuing institutions.

Combination Policies – Short-term insurance policies, which may include any combination or all of the types of insurance discussed above, are available through retail insurance agencies, automobile clubs, and many travel agents. These combination policies are designed to cover you for the duration of a single trip.

The following companies provide such coverage for the insurance needs discussed above:

Access America International: A subsidiary of the Blue Cross/Blue Shield plans of New York and Washington, DC, now available nationwide. Contact *Access America,* 600 Third Ave., PO Box 807, New York, NY 10163 (phone: 800-284-8300 or 212-490-5345).

Carefree: Underwritten by The Hartford. Contact *Carefree Travel Insurance,* Arm Coverage, PO Box 310, Mineola, NY 11501 (phone: 516-294-0220).

NEAR Services: In addition to a full range of travel services, this organization offers a comprehensive travel insurance package. An added feature is coverage for lost or stolen airline tickets. Contact *NEAR Services,* 450 Prairie Ave., Suite 101, Calumet City, IL 60409 (phone: 708-868-6700 in the Chicago area; 800-654-6700 elsewhere in the US and Canada).

Tele-Trip: Underwritten by the Mutual of Omaha Companies. Contact *Tele-Trip Co.,* PO Box 31685, 3201 Farnam St., Omaha, NE 68131 (phone: 402-345-2400 in Nebraska; 800-228-9792 elsewhere in the US).

Travel Assistance International: Provided by Europ Assistance Worldwide Services, and underwritten by Transamerica Occidental Life Insurance Company. Contact *Travel Assistance International,* 1133 15th St. NW, Suite 400, Washington, DC 20005 (phone: 202-331-1609 in Washington, DC; 800-821-2828 elsewhere in the US).

Travel Guard International: Underwritten by the Insurance Company of North America, it is available through authorized travel agents; or contact *Travel Guard International,* 1145 Clark St., Stevens Point, WI 54481 (phone: 715-345-0505 in Wisconsin; 800-826-1300 elsewhere in the US).

Travel Insurance PAK: Underwritten by The Travelers. Contact *The Travelers Companies,* Ticket and Travel Plans, One Tower Sq., Hartford, CT 06183-5040 (phone: 203-277-2319 in Connecticut; 800-243-3174 elsewhere in the US).

Wallach & Co.: This organization offers two health insurance plans as well as other coverage. Contact *Wallach & Co.,* 243 Church St. NW, Suite 100-D, Vienna, VA 22180 (phone: 703-281-9500 in Virginia, 800-237-6615 elsewhere in the US).

WorldCare Travel Assistance Association: This organization offers insurance packages underwritten by Transamerica Occidental Life Insurance Company and Transamerica Premier Insurance Company. Contact *WorldCare Travel Assist-*

ance Association, 605 Market St., Suite 1300, San Francisco, CA 94105 (phone: 800-666-4993 or 415-541-4991).

Hints for Handicapped Travelers

 From 40 to 50 million people in the US alone have some sort of disability, and more than half this number are physically handicapped. Like everyone else today, they — and the uncounted disabled millions around the world — are on the move. More than ever before, they are demanding facilities they can use comfortably, and they are being heard.

PLANNING A TRIP: Collect as much information as you can about your specific disability and facilities for the disabled in Chicago. Make your travel arrangements well in advance and specify to services involved the exact nature of your condition or restricted mobility, as your trip will be much more comfortable if you know that there are accommodations and facilities to suit your needs.

It is also advisable to call the hotel you are considering and ask specific questions. If you require a corridor of a certain width to maneuver a wheelchair or if you need handles on the bathroom walls for support, ask the manager (many large hotels have rooms designed for the handicapped). A travel agent or the local chapter or national office of the organization that deals with your particular disability — for example, the *American Foundation for the Blind* or the *American Heart Association* — will supply the most up-to-date information on the subject.

The following organizations also offer general information on access:

ACCENT on Living (PO Box 700, Bloomington, IL 61702; phone: 309-378-2961). This information service for persons with disabilities provides a free list of travel agencies specializing in arranging trips for the disabled; for a copy send a self-addressed, stamped envelope. It also offers a wide range of publications, including a quarterly magazine ($8 per year; $14 for 2 years) for persons with disabilities.

Direct Link (PO Box 1036, Solvang, CA 93463; phone: 805-688-1603). This company provides an on-line computer service that links the disabled and their families with a wide range of information, including accessibility, attendant care, transportation, and travel necessities.

Disabled Individuals Assistance Line (DIAL) (100 W. Randolph St., Suite 8-100, Chicago, IL 60601; 800-233-DIAL; both voice and TDD). This toll-free hotline provides information about public and private resources available to people with disabilities.

Information Center for Individuals with Disabilities (Fort Point Place, 27-43 Wormwood St., Boston, MA 02210-1606; phone: 800-462-5015 in Massachusetts or 617-727-5540; both voice and TDD). The center offers information on accessibility of the transportation system, cultural sites and other sightseeing; it also provides referral services on disability-related issues, publishes fact sheets on travel agents, tour operators, and other travel resources, and can otherwise help you research your trip.

Mobility International USA (MIUSA; PO Box 3551, Eugene, OR 97403; phone: 503-343-1284; both voice and TDD). This US branch of *Mobility International,* a nonprofit British organization with affiliates worldwide, offers members advice and assistance — including information on accommodations and other travel services, and publications applicable to the traveler's disability. It also offers a quarterly newsletter and a comprehensive sourcebook, *A World of Options for the 90s: A Guide to International Education Exchange, Community Service and Travel for Persons with Disabilities* ($14 for members; $16 for non-members). Membership includes the newsletter and is $20 a year; subscription to the newsletter alone is $10 annually.

National Rehabilitation Information Center (NRIC; 8455 Colesville Rd., Suite 935, Silver Spring, MD 20910; phone: 301-588-9284). A general information, resource, research, and referral service.

Paralyzed Veterans of America (PVA; PVA/ATTS Program, 801 18th St. NW, Washington, DC 20006; phone: 202-416-7708 in Washington, DC; 800-424-8200 elsewhere in the US). The members of this national service organization all are veterans who have suffered spinal cord injuries, but it offers advocacy services and information to all persons with a disability. *PVA* also sponsors Access to the Skies (ATTS). a program that coordinates the efforts of the national and international air travel industry in providing airport and airplane access for the disabled. Members receive several helpful publications, as well as regular notification of conferences on subjects of interest to the disabled traveler.

Society for the Advancement of Travel for the Handicapped (SATH; 26 Court St., Penthouse, Brooklyn, NY 11242; phone: 718-858-5483). To keep abreast of developments in travel for the handicapped as they occur, you may want to join *SATH,* a nonprofit organization whose members include consumers, as well as travel service professionals who have experience (or an interest) in travel for the handicapped. For an annual fee of $45 ($25 for students and travelers who are 65 and older), members receive a quarterly newsletter and have access to extensive information and referral services. *SATH* also offers two useful publications: *Travel Tips for the Handicapped* (a series of informative fact sheets) and *The United States Welcomes Handicapped Visitors* (a 48-page guide covering domestic transportation and accommodations, as well as useful hints for travelers with disabilities); to order, send a self-addressed, #10 envelope and $1 per title for postage.

Travel Information Service (Moss Rehabilitation Hospital, 1200 W. Tabor Rd., Philadelphia, PA 19141-3099; phone: 215-456-9600 for voice; 215-456-9602 for TDD). This service assists physically handicapped people in planning trips and supplies detailed information on accessibility, for a nominal fee.

Blind travelers should contact the *American Foundation for the Blind* (15 W. 16th St., New York, NY 10011; phone: 212-620-2147 in New York State; 800-232-5463 elsewhere in the US) and *The Seeing Eye* (Box 375, Morristown, NJ 07963-0375; phone: 201-539-4425); both provide useful information on resources for the visually impaired.

The following is a list of travel agencies who specialize in handicapped travel and service the Chicago area:

Dahl Good Neighbor Travel Service (535 N. St. Mary's Rd., Libertyville, IL 60048; phone: 708-362-0129 or 708-362-3376). This agency can arrange a full range of services and provide necessities for disabled travelers, including mentally handicapped individuals and those who need kidney dialysis.

Hinsdale Travel (201 E. Ogden Ave., Hinsdale, IL 60521; phone: 708-325-1335 or 708-469-7349). Janice Perkins, the tour leader, has used a wheelchair for years and leads an active lifestyle. She takes groups of handicapped travelers on the road, booking hotels and making whatever special arrangements that are required.

Weston Travel Agency (134 N. Cass Ave., Westmont, IL 60559; phone: 800-633-3725 or 708-968-2513). This agency specializes in travel services for people with cerebral palsy and those who are wheelchair-bound.

For transportation within the Chicago area, you might want to contact *Illinois Medi-Car* (395 W. Lake St., Elmhurst, IL 60126; phone: 708-530-1500). This company provides specially equipped vans to transport handicapped people for a $38 base charge, plus $2.50 per mile.

In addition, there are a number of publications — from travel guides to magazines — of interest to handicapped travelers. Among these are the following:

Access to the World, by Louise Weiss, offers sound tips for the disabled traveler. Published by Facts on File (460 Park Ave. S., New York, NY 10016; phone: 212-683-2244 in New York State; 800-322-8755 elsewhere in the US; 800-443-8323 in Canada), it costs $16.95. Check with your local bookstore; it also can be ordered by phone with a credit card.

The Diabetic Traveler (PO Box 8223 RW, Stamford, CT 06905; phone: 203-327-5832) is a useful quarterly newsletter for travelers with diabetes. Each issue highlights a single destination or type of travel and includes information on general resources and hints for diabetics. A 1-year subscription costs $15. When subscribing, ask for the free fact sheet including an index of special articles; back issues are available for $4 each.

Guide to Traveling with Arthritis, a free brochure available by writing to the Upjohn Company (PO Box 307-B, Coventry, CT 06238), provides lots of good, commonsense tips on planning your trip and how to be as comfortable as possible when traveling by car, bus, train, cruise ship, or plane.

Handicapped Travel Newsletter is regarded as one of the best sources of information for the disabled traveler. It is edited by wheelchair-bound Vietnam veteran Michael Quigley, who has traveled to 93 countries around the world. Issued every 2 months (plus special issues), a subscription is $10 per year. Write to *Handicapped Travel Newsletter,* PO Box 269, Athens, TX 75751 (phone: 214-677-1260).

Handi-Travel: A Resource Book for Disabled and Elderly Travellers, by Cinnie Noble, is a comprehensive travel guide full of practical tips for those with disabilities affecting mobility, hearing, or sight. The book is available for $12.95, plus shipping and handling, from the *Canadian Rehabilitation Council for the Disabled,* 45 Sheppard Ave. E., Suite 801, Toronto, Ontario M2N 5W9, Canada (phone: 416-250-7490; both voice and TDD).

The Itinerary (PO Box 2012, Bayonne, NJ 07002-2012; phone: 201-858-3400). This bimonthly travel magazine for people with disabilities includes information on accessibility, listings of tours, news of adaptive devices, travel aids, and special services, as well as numerous general travel hints. A subscription costs $10 a year.

The Physically Disabled Traveler's Guide, by Rod W. Durgin and Norene Lindsay, rates accessibility of a number of travel services and includes a list of organizations specializing in travel for the disabled. It is available for $9.95, plus shipping and handling, from Resource Directories, 3361 Executive Pkwy., Suite 302, Toledo, OH 43606 (phone: 419-536-5353 in the Toledo area; 800-274-8515 elsewhere in the US).

Ticket to Safe Travel offers useful information for travelers with diabetes. A reprint of this article is available free from local chapters of the *American Diabetes Association.* For the nearest branch, contact the central office at 505 Eighth Ave., 21st Floor, New York, NY 10018 (phone: 212-947-9707 in New York State; 800-232-3472 elsewhere in the US).

Travel for the Patient with Chronic Obstructive Pulmonary Disease, a publication of the George Washington University Medical Center, provides some sound practical suggestions for those with emphysema, chronic bronchitis, asthma, or other lung ailments. To order, send $2 to Dr. Harold Silver, 1601 18th St. NW, Washington, DC 20009 (phone: 202-667-0134).

Traveling Like Everybody Else: A Practical Guide for Disabled Travelers ($11.95, plus shipping and handling), by Jacqueline Freedman and Susan Gersten, offers the disabled tips on traveling by car, cruise ship, and plane, as well as lists of accessible accommodations, tour operators specializing in tours for disabled travelers, and other resources. To order, contact Modan Publishing, PO Box 1202, Bellmore, NY 11710 (phone: 516-679-1380).

Travel Tips for Hearing-Impaired People, a free pamphlet for deaf and hearing-impaired travelers, is available from the *American Academy of Otolaryngology* (One Prince St., Alexandria, VA 22314; phone: 703-836-4444). For a copy, send a self-addressed, stamped, business-size envelope to the academy.

Travel Tips for People with Arthritis, a free 31-page booklet published by the *Arthritis Foundation,* provides helpful information regarding travel by car, bus, train, cruise ship, or plane, planning your trip, medical considerations, and ways to conserve your energy while traveling. It also includes listings of helpful resources, such as associations and travel agencies that operate tours for disabled travelers. For a copy, contact your local *Arthritis Foundation* chapter, or write to the national office, PO Box 19000, Atlanta, GA 30326 (phone: 404-872-7100).

The Wheelchair Traveler, by Douglass R. Annand, lists accessible hotels, motels, restaurants, and other sites by state throughout the US. This valuable resource is available directly from the author. For the price of the most recent edition, contact Douglass R. Annand, 123 Ball Hill Rd., Milford, NH 03055 (phone: 603-673-4539).

A few more basic resources to look for are *Travel for the Disabled,* by Helen Hecker ($9.95), and by the same author, *Directory of Travel Agencies for the Disabled* ($19.95). *Wheelchair Vagabond,* by John G. Nelson, is another useful guide for travelers confined to a wheelchair (hardcover, $14.95; paperback, $9.95). All three are published by Twin Peaks Press, PO Box 129, Vancouver, WA 98666 (phone: 800-637-CALM or 206-694-2462).

PLANE: The US Department of Transportation (DOT) has ruled that US airlines must accept all passengers with disabilities. As a matter of course, US airlines were pretty good about accommodating handicapped passengers even before the ruling, although each airline has somewhat different procedures. Ask for specifics when you book your flight.

Disabled passengers always should make reservations well in advance and should provide the airline with all relevant details of their conditions. These details include information on mobility and equipment that you will need the airline to supply — such as a wheelchair for boarding or portable oxygen for in-flight use. Be sure that the person to whom you speak fully understands the degree of your disability — the more details provided, the more effective help the airline can give you.

On the day before the flight, call back to make sure that all arrangements have been prepared, and arrive early on the day of the flight so that you can board before the rest of the passengers. It's a good idea to bring a medical certificate with you, stating your specific disability or the need to carry particular medicine.

Because most airports have jetways (corridors connecting the terminal with the door of the plane), a disabled passenger usually can be taken as far as the plane, and sometimes right onto it, in a wheelchair. If not, a narrow boarding chair may be used to take you to your seat. Your own wheelchair, which will be folded and put in the baggage compartment, should be tagged as escort luggage to ensure that it's available at planeside upon landing rather than in the baggage claim area. Travel is not quite as simple if your wheelchair is battery-operated: Unless it has non-spillable batteries, it might not be accepted on board, and you will have to check with the airline ahead of time to find out how the batteries and the chair should be packaged for the flight. Usually people in wheelchairs are asked to wait until other passengers have disembarked. If you are making a tight connection, be sure to tell the attendant.

Passengers who use oxygen may not use their personal supply in the cabin, though it may be carried on the plane as cargo when properly packed and labeled. If you will need oxygen during the flight, the airline will supply it to you (there is a charge) provided you have given advance notice — 24 hours to a few days, depending on the carrier.

Useful information on every stage of air travel, from planning to arrival, is provided in the booklet *Incapacitated Passengers Air Travel Guide.* To receive a free copy, write to the *International Air Transport Association* (Publications Sales Department, 2000 Peel St., Montreal, Quebec H3A 2R4, Canada; phone: 514-844-6311). Another helpful publication is *Air Transportation of Handicapped Persons,* which explains the general guidelines that govern air carrier policies. For a copy of this free booklet, write to the US Department of Transportation (Distribution Unit, Publications Section, M-443-2, Washington, DC 20590) and ask for "Free Advisory Circular #AC-120-32."

Access Travel: A Guide to the Accessibility of Airport Terminals, a free publication of the *Airport Operators Council International,* provides information on more than 500 airports worldwide — including the major airports in the US — and offers ratings of 70 features, such as accessibility to bathrooms, corridor width, and parking spaces. For a copy, contact the Consumer Information Center, Dept. 563W, Pueblo, CO 81009 (phone: 719-948-3334).

The following airlines serving Chicago have TDD toll-free lines in the US for the hearing-impaired:

American: 800-582-1573 in Ohio; 800-543-1586 elsewhere in the US
America West: 800-526-8077
Continental: 800-343-9195
Delta: 800-831-4488
Northwest: 800-328-2298
TWA: 800-252-0622 in California; 800-421-8480 elsewhere in the US
United: 800-942-8819 in Illinois; 800-323-0170 elsewhere in the US
USAir: 800-242-1713 in Pennsylvania; 800-245-2966 elsewhere in the US

Chicago's O'Hare International Airport provides a free guide for handicapped travelers that includes information on special parking and drop-off areas and locations of TDD lines for the deaf. Copies are available at the airport or by calling the Chicago Mayor's Office of Inquiry and Information (phone: 744-6671).

GROUND TRANSPORTATION: Perhaps the simplest solution to getting around is to travel with an able-bodied companion who can drive. If you are accustomed to driving your own hand-controlled car and want to rent one, you are in luck. Some rental companies will fit cars with hand controls. *Avis* (phone: 800-331-1212) can convert a car to hand controls with as little as 24 hours' notice, though it's a good idea to arrange for one more than a day in advance. *Hertz* (phone: 800-654-3131) requires a minimum of 4 days to install the controls, and makes the additional stipulation that the car be returned to the office from which it was rented. Neither company charges extra for hand controls, but *Avis* will fit them only on a full-size car, and both request that you bring your handicapped driver's permit with you. Other car rental companies provide hand-control cars at some locations; however, as there usually are only a limited number available, call well in advance.

The *American Automobile Association (AAA)* publishes a useful booklet, *The Handi-*

capped Driver's Mobility Guide. Contact the central office of your local *AAA* club for availability and pricing, which may vary at different branch offices.

TOURS: Programs designed for the physically impaired are run by specialists who have researched hotels, restaurants, and sites to be sure they present no insurmountable obstacles. The following travel agencies and tour operators specialize in making group and individual arrangements for travelers to Chicago with physical or other disabilities:

Access: The Foundation for Accessibility by the Disabled (PO Box 356, Malverne, NY 11565; phone: 516-887-5798). A travelers' referral service that acts as an intermediary with tour operators and agents worldwide, and provides information on accessibility at various locations.

Accessible Journeys (412 S. 45th St., Philadelphia, PA 19104; phone: 215-747-0171). Arranges for medical professional traveling companions — registered or licensed practical nurses, therapists, or doctors (all are experienced travelers). Several prospective companions' profiles and photos are sent to the client for perusal, and if one is acceptable, the "match" is made. The client usually pays all travel expenses for the companion, plus a certain amount in "earnings" to replace wages the companion would be making at his or her usual job.

Accessible Tours/Directions Unlimited (720 N. Bedford Rd., Bedford Hills, NY 10507; phone: 914-241-1700 in New York State; 800-533-5343 elsewhere in the continental US). Arranges group or individual tours for disabled persons traveling in the company of able-bodied friends or family members. Accepts the unaccompanied traveler if completely self-sufficient.

Flying Wheels Travel (143 W. Bridge St., Box 382, Owatonna, MN 55060; phone: 507-451-5005 or 800-535-6790). Handles both tours and individual arrangements.

Guided Tour (613 W. Cheltenham Ave., Suite 200, Melrose Park, PA 19126-2414; phone: 215-782-1370). Arranges tours for people with developmental and learning disabilities and sponsors separate tours for members of the same population who also are physically disabled or who simply need a slower pace. You must be a member to join their tours. Annual membership is $160 with a $30 one-time initiation fee.

Handi-Travel (First National Travel Ltd., Thornhill Sq., 300 John St., Suite 405, Thornhill, Ontario L3T 5W4, Canada; phone: 416-731-4714). Handles tours and individual arrangements.

USTS Travel Horizons (11 E. 44th St., New York, NY 10017; phone: 800-487-8787 or 212-687-5121). Travel agent and registered nurse Mary Ann Hamm designs trips for individual travelers requiring all types of kidney dialysis and handles arrangements for the dialysis.

Whole Person Tours (PO Box 1084, Bayonne, NJ 07002-1084; phone: 201-858-3400). Handicapped owner Bob Zywicki travels the world with his wheelchair and offers a lineup of escorted tours (many conducted by him) for the disabled. *Whole Person Tours* also publishes *The Itinerary,* a bimonthly newsletter for disabled travelers (see the publication source list above).

Travelers who would benefit from being accompanied by a nurse or physical therapist also can hire a companion through *Traveling Nurses' Network,* a service provided by Twin Peaks Press (PO Box 129, Vancouver, WA 98666; phone: 800-637-CALM or 206-694-2462). For a $10 fee, the client receives the names of three nurses who can be contacted directly; for a $125 fee, the agency will make all the hiring arrangements for the client. Travel arrangements also may be made in some cases — the fee for this further service is determined on an individual basis.

A similar service is offered by *MedEscort International* (ABE International Airport,

PO Box 8766, Allentown, PA 18105; phone: 800-255-7182 in the continental US; elsewhere, call 215-791-3111). Clients can arrange to be accompanied by a nurse, paramedic, respiratory therapist, or physician through *MedEscort*. The fees are based on the disabled traveler's needs. *MedEscort* also can assist in making travel arrangements.

Hints for Single Travelers

Just about the last trip in human history on which the participants were neatly paired was the voyage of Noah's Ark. Ever since, passenger lists and tour groups have reflected the same kind of asymmetry that occurs in real life, as countless individuals set forth to see the world unaccompanied (or unencumbered, depending on your outlook) by spouse, lover, friend, companion, or relative.

The truth is that the travel industry is not very fair to people who vacation by themselves. People traveling alone almost invariably end up paying more than individuals traveling in pairs. Most travel bargains, including package tours, accommodations, resort packages, and cruises, are based on *double occupancy* rates. This means that the per-person price is offered on the basis of two people traveling together and sharing a double room (which means they each will spend a good deal more on meals and extras). The single traveler will have to pay a surcharge, called a single supplement, for exactly the same package. In extreme cases, this can add as much as 30% to 50% to the basic per-person rate.

Don't despair, however. Throughout the US, there are scores of smaller hotels and other hostelries where, in addition to a cozier atmosphere, prices still are quite reasonable for the single traveler.

The obvious, most effective alternative is to find a traveling companion. Even special "singles' tours" that promise no supplements usually are based on people sharing double rooms. Perhaps the most recent innovation along these lines is the creation of organizations that "introduce" the single traveler to other single travelers. Some charge fees, while others are free, but the basic service offered is the same: to match an unattached person with a compatible travel mate. Among such organizations are the following:

Jane's International (2603 Bath Ave., Brooklyn, NY 11214; phone: 718-266-2045). This service puts potential traveling companions in touch with one another. No age limit, no fee.

Partners-in-Travel (PO Box 491145, Los Angeles, CA 90049; phone: 213-476-4869). Members receive a list of singles seeking traveling companions; prospective companions make contact through the agency. The membership fee is $40 per year and includes a chatty newsletter (6 issues per year).

Travel Companion Exchange (PO Box 833, Amityville, NY 11701; phone: 516-454-0880). This group publishes a newsletter for singles and a directory of individuals looking for travel companions. On joining, members fill out a lengthy questionnaire and write a small listing (much like an ad in a personal column). Based on these listings, members can request copies of profiles and contact prospective traveling companions. It is wise to join well in advance of your planned vacation so that there's enough time to determine compatibility and plan a joint trip. Membership fees, including the newsletter, are $36 for 6 months or $60 a year for a single-sex listing; $66 and $120, respectively, for a complete listing. Subscription to the newsletter alone costs $24 for 6 months or $36 per year.

In addition, a number of tour packagers cater to single travelers. These companies offer packages designed for individuals interested in vacationing with a group of single travelers or in being matched with a traveling companion. Among the better established of these agencies are the following:

Odyssey Network (118 Cedar St., Wellesley, MA 02181; phone: 617-237-2400). Originally founded to match single female travelers, this company now includes men in its enrollment. *Odyssey* offers a quarterly newsletter for members who are seeking a travel companion and makes independent arrangements for them. A newsletter subscription is $50.

Travel in Two's (239 N. Broadway, Suite 3, N. Tarrytown, NY 10591; phone: 914-631-8409). For city programs, this company matches up solo travelers and then customizes programs for them. The firm also puts out a quarterly *Singles Vacation Newsletter,* which costs $7.50 per issue or $20 per year.

A good book for single travelers is *Traveling On Your Own,* by Eleanor Berman, which offers tips on traveling solo and includes information on trips for singles. Available in bookstores, it also can be ordered for $12.95, plus postage and handling, from Random House, Order Dept., 400 Hahn Rd., Westminster, MD 21157 (phone: 800-733-3000).

Single travelers also may want to subscribe to *Going Solo,* a newsletter that offers helpful information on going on your own. Issued eight times a year, a subscription costs $36. Contact Doerfer Communications, PO Box 1035, Cambridge, MA 02238 (phone: 617-876-2764).

Those interested in a particularly cozy type of accommodation should consider going the bed and breakfast route. Though a single person will likely pay more than half of the rate quoted for a couple even at a bed and breakfast establishment, the prices still are quite reasonable, and the homey atmosphere will make you feel less conspicuously alone.

Another possibility is the *United States Servas Committee* (11 John St., Room 407, New York, NY 10038; phone: 212-267-0252), which maintains a list of hosts around the world who are willing to take visitors into their homes as guests. *Servas* will send an application form and a list of interviewers at the nearest locations for you to contact. After the interview, if you are accepted as a *Servas* traveler, you'll receive a membership certificate. The membership fee is $45 per year for an individual, with a $15 deposit to receive the host list, refunded upon its return.

Hints for Older Travelers

Special discounts and more free time are just two factors that have given Americans over age 65 a chance to see the world at affordable prices. Senior citizens make up an ever-growing segment of the travel population, and the trend among them is to travel more frequently and for longer periods of time.

PLANNING: When planning a vacation, prepare your itinerary with one eye on your own physical condition and the other on your interests. One important factor to keep in mind is not to overdo anything and to be aware of the effects that the weather may have on your capabilities.

Older travelers may find the following publications of interest:

Discount Guide for Travelers Over 55, by Caroline and Walter Weintz, is an excellent book for budget-conscious older travelers. It is available for $7.95, plus shipping and handling, from Penguin USA (Att. Cash Sales, 120 Woodbine St., Bergenfield, NJ 07621); when ordering, specify the ISBN number: 0-525-48358-6.

International Health Guide for Senior Citizen Travelers, by Dr. W. Robert Lange, covers such topics as trip preparations, food and water precautions, adjusting to weather and climate conditions, finding a doctor, motion sickness, jet lag, and so on. The book also includes a list of resource organizations that provide medical assistance for travelers. It is available for $4.95 postpaid from Pilot Books, 103 Cooper St., Babylon, NY 11702 (phone: 516-422-2225).

Mature Traveler is a monthly newsletter that provides information on travel discounts, places of interest, useful tips, and other topics of interest for travelers 49 and up. To subscribe, send $21.95 to GEM Publishing Group, PO Box 50820, Reno, NV 89513 (phone: 702-786-7419).

Senior Citizen's Guide to Budget Travel in the US and Canada, by Paige Palmer, provides specific information on economical travel options for senior citizens. The book can be ordered for $3.95, plus postage and handling, from Pilot Books (address above).

Travel Easy: The Practical Guide for People Over 50, by Rosalind Massow, discusses a wide range of subjects — from trip planning, transportation options, and preparing for departure to avoiding and handling medical problems en route. It's available for $6.50 to members of the *American Association of Retired Persons (AARP),* and for $8.95 to non-members; call about current charges for postage and handling. Order from *AARP* Books, c/o Customer Service, Scott, Foresman & Company, 1900 E. Lake Ave., Glenview, IL 60025 (phone: 708-729-3000).

Unbelievably Good Deals & Great Adventures That You Absolutely Can't Get Unless You're Over 50, by Joan Rattner Heilman, offers travel tips for older travelers, including discounts on accommodations and transportation, as well as a list of organizations for seniors. It is available for $7.95, plus shipping and handling, from Contemporary Books, 180 N. Michigan Ave., Chicago, IL 60601 (phone: 312-782-9181).

HEALTH: Pre-trip medical and dental checkups are strongly recommended. In addition, be sure to take along any prescription medication you need, enough to last *without a new prescription* for the duration of your trip; pack all medications with a note from your doctor for the benefit of airport authorities. If you have specific medical problems, bring prescriptions and a "medical file" composed of the following:

1. A summary of your medical history and current diagnosis
2. A list of drugs to which you are allergic
3. Your most recent electrocardiogram, if you have heart problems
4. Your doctor's name, address, and telephone number

DISCOUNTS AND PACKAGES: Since guidelines change from place to place, it is a good idea to inquire in advance about discounts on accommodations, transportation, tickets to theater and concert performances and movies, entrance fees to museums, national monuments, and other attractions. For instance, the National Park Service has a Golden Age Passport, which entitles people over 62 (and those in the car with them) to free entrance to all national parks and monuments (available by showing a Medicare card or driver's license as proof of age at any national park).

Many hotel chains, airlines, cruise lines, bus companies, car rental companies, and other travel suppliers offer discounts to older travelers. For instance, *United* offers senior citizen coupon books — with either four or eight coupons each — that can be exchanged for tickets on domestic flights of up to 2,000 miles. These coupons are good 7 days a week for travel in all 50 states, although some peak travel periods are omitted. Other airlines also offer discounts for passengers age 60 (or 62) and over, which may be applicable to one traveling companion per senior. Among the airlines that often offer such discounted airfares are *American, America West, Continental, Delta,* and *Northwest.* For information on current prices and applicable restrictions, contact the individual carriers.

Some discounts, however, are extended only to bona fide members of certain senior citizens' organizations. Because the same organizations frequently offer package tours to both domestic and international destinations, the benefits of membership are twofold: Those who join can take advantage of discounts as individual travelers and also reap the savings that group travel affords. In addition, because the age requirements for some of these organizations are quite low (or nonexistent), the benefits can begin to accrue early. In order to take advantage of these discounts, you should carry proof of your age (or eligibility). A driver's license, membership card in a recognized senior citizens organization, or a Medicare card should be adequate. Among the organizations dedicated to helping older travelers see the world are the following:

American Association of Retired Persons (*AARP;* 1909 K St. NW, Washington, DC 20049; phone: 202-872-4700). The largest and best known of these organizations. Membership is open to anyone 50 or over, whether retired or not; dues are $5 a year, $12.50 for 3 years, or $35 for 10 years, and include spouse. The *AARP* Travel Experience program, available through *American Express Travel Related Services,* offers members tours and other travel programs designed exclusively for older travelers. For example, it offers an independent Chicago program that can be bought by the night. Members can book these services by calling *American Express* at 800-927-0111 for land and air travel.

Mature Outlook (Customer Service Center, 6001 N. Clark St., Chicago, IL 60660; phone: 800-336-6330). Through its *TravelAlert,* tours, cruises, and other vacation packages are available to members at special savings. Hotel and car rental discounts and travel accident insurance also are available. Membership is open to anyone 50 years of age or older, costs $9.95 a year, and includes a bimonthly newsletter and magazine, as well as information on package tours.

National Council of Senior Citizens (1331 F St., Washington, DC 20005; phone: 202-347-8800). Here, too, the emphasis is on keeping costs low. This nonprofit organization offers members a different roster of package tours each year, as well as individual arrangements through its affiliated travel agency *(Vantage Travel Service).* Although most members are over 50, membership is open to anyone (regardless of age) for an annual fee of $12 per person or couple. Lifetime membership costs $150.

While at the moment tour operators that specialize in the senior market generally are not offering city programs, they and many travel agencies, particularly the larger ones, are delighted to make presentations to help a group of senior citizens design a trip. A local chamber of commerce should be able to provide the names of such agencies. Large groups usually get the best breaks.

Hints for Traveling with Children

 What better way to encounter the ethnic and cultural kaleidoscope of Chicago than in the company of the young, wide-eyed members of your family? Their presence does not have to be a burden or an excessive expense. The current generation of discounts for children and family package deals can make a trip together quite reasonable.

Chicago brings members of the younger generation face to face with a varied world of vibrant cultural heritages that are different from their own, which will leave a sure memory that will be among the fondest you will share with them someday. Their insights will be refreshing to you; their impulses may take you to unexpected places with unexpected dividends. The experience will be invaluable to them at any age.

PLANNING: Here are several hints for making a trip with children easy and fun:

1. Children, like everyone else, will derive more pleasure from a trip if they know something about their destination before they arrive. Begin their education about a month before you leave. Using maps, travel magazines, and books, give children a clear idea of where you are going and how far away it is.
2. Children should help to plan the itinerary, and where you go and what you do should reflect some of their ideas. If they already know something about the city and the sites they will visit, they will have the excitement of recognition when they arrive.
3. Give children specific responsibilities: The job of carrying their own flight bags and looking after their personal things, along with some other light travel chores, will give them a stake in the journey.
4. Give each child a travel diary or scrapbook to take along.

Children's books about Chicago and its place in the history of our country provide an excellent introduction and can be found at children's bookstores, many general bookstores, and in libraries. Also look for the Chicago volume of the "Kidding Around" series on US cities, published by John Muir Publications. It starts with an overview of the city, along with some interesting background information, and then it is divided into areas, with descriptions of the various attractions in the general order in which you might encounter them. The book can be ordered for $9.95, plus shipping, from John Muir Publications, PO Box 613, Santa Fe, NM 87504, or by calling 800-888-7504 or 505-982-4087.

And for parents, *Travel With Your Children* (*TWYCH;* 80 Eighth Ave., New York, NY 10011; phone: 212-206-0688) publishes a newsletter, *Family Travel Times,* that focuses on families with young travelers and offers helpful hints. An annual subscription (10 issues) is $35 and includes a copy of the "Airline Guide" issue (updated every other year), which focuses on the subject of flying with children. This special issue is available separately for $10.

Another newsletter devoted to family travel is *Getaways.* This quarterly publication provides reviews of family-oriented literature, activities, and useful travel tips. To subscribe, send $25 to *Getaways,* Att. Ms. Brooke Kane, PO Box 11511, Washington, DC 20008 (phone: 703-534-8747).

Also of interest to parents traveling with their children is *How to Take Great Trips With Your Kids,* by psychologist Sanford Portnoy and his wife, Joan Flynn Portnoy. The book includes helpful tips from fellow family travelers, tips on economical accommodations and touring by car, as well as more than 50 games to play with your children en route. It is available for $8.95, plus shipping and handling, from Harvard Common Press, 535 Albany St., Boston, MA 02118 (phone: 617-423-5803).

Another book on family travel, *Travel with Children* by Maureen Wheeler, offers a wide range of practical tips on traveling with children. It is available for $10.95, plus shipping and handling, from Lonely Planet Publications, Embarcadero West, 112 Linden St., Oakland, CA 94607 (phone: 510-893-8555).

Finally, parents arranging a trip with their children may want to deal with an agency specializing in family travel such as *Let's Take the Kids* (1268 Devon Ave., Los Angeles, CA 90024; phone: 800-726-4349 or 213-274-7088). In addition to arranging and booking trips for individual families, this group occasionally organizes trips for single-parent families traveling together. They also offer a parent travel network, whereby parents who have been to a particular destination can evaluate it for others.

PLANE: Begin early to investigate all available family discount flights, as well as any package deals and special rates offered by the major airlines. When you make your reservations, tell the airline that you are traveling with a child. Children ages 2 through 11 generally travel at about a 20% to 30% discount off regular full-fare adult ticket prices on domestic flights. This children's fare, however, usually is much higher than the excursion fare, which may be used by any traveler, regardless of age. An infant under 2 years of age usually can travel free if it sits on an adult's lap. A second infant without a second adult would pay the fare applicable to children ages 2 through 11.

Although some airlines will, on request, supply bassinets for infants, most carriers encourage parents to bring their own safety seat on board, which then is strapped into the airline seat with a regular seat belt. This is much safer — and certainly more comfortable — than holding the child in your lap. If you do not purchase a seat for your baby, you have the option of bringing the infant restraint along on the off-chance that there might be an empty seat next to yours — in which case some airlines will let you use that seat at no charge for your baby and infant seat. However, if there is no empty seat available, the infant seat no doubt will have to be checked as baggage (and you may have to pay an additional charge), since it generally does not fit under the seat or in the overhead racks.

The safest bet is to pay for a seat — this usually will be the same as fares applicable to children ages 2 through 11, although it usually is less expensive to pay for an adult excursion rate than the discounted children's fare.

Be forewarned: Some safety seats designed primarily for use in cars do not fit into plane seats properly. Although nearly all seats manufactured since 1985 carry labels indicating whether they meet federal standards for use aboard planes, actual seat sizes may vary from carrier to carrier. At the time of this writing, the FAA was in the process of reviewing and revising the federal regulations regarding infant travel and safety devices — it was still to be determined if children should be *required* to sit in safety seats and whether the airlines will have to provide them.

If using one of these infant restraints, you should try to get bulkhead seats, which will provide extra room to care for your child during the flight. You also should request a bulkhead seat when using a bassinet — again, this is not as safe as strapping the child in. On some planes bassinets hook into a bulkhead wall; on others it is placed on the floor in front of you. (Note that bulkhead seats often are reserved for families traveling with small children.) As a general rule, babies should be held during takeoff and landing.

Request seats on the aisle if you have a toddler or if you think you will need to use the bathroom frequently. Carry onto the plane all you will need to care for and occupy your children during the flight — formula, diapers, a sweater, books, favorite stuffed animals, and so on. Dress your baby simply, with a minimum of buttons and snaps, because the only place you may have to change a diaper is at your seat or in a small lavatory.

You also can ask for a hot dog or hamburger instead of the airline's regular dinner if you give at least 24 hours' notice. Some, but not all, airlines have baby food aboard, and the flight attendant can warm a bottle for you. While you should bring along toys from home, also ask about children's diversions. Some carriers have terrific free packages of games, coloring books, and puzzles.

When the plane takes off and lands, make sure your baby is nursing or has a bottle, pacifier, or thumb in its mouth. This sucking will make the child swallow and help to clear stopped ears. A piece of hard candy will do the same for an older child.

Parents traveling by plane with toddlers, children, or teenagers may want to consult *When Kids Fly,* a free booklet published by Massport (Public Affairs Department, 10 Park Plaza, Boston, MA 02116-3971; phone: 617-973-5600), which includes helpful information on airfares for children, infant seats, what to do in the event of overbooked or canceled flights, and so on.

■ **Note:** Newborn babies, whose lungs may not be able to adjust to the altitude, should not be taken aboard an airplane. And some airlines may refuse to allow a pregnant woman in her 8th or 9th month to fly. Check with the airline ahead of time, and carry a letter from your doctor stating that you are fit to travel — and indicating the estimated date of birth.

Things to Remember

1. If you are visiting many sites, pace the days with children in mind. Break the trip into half-day segments, with running around or "doing" time built in.
2. Don't forget that a child's attention span is far shorter than an adult's. Children don't have to see every sight or all of any sight to learn something from their trip; watching, playing with, and talking to other children can be equally enlightening.
3. Let your children lead the way sometimes; their perspective is different from yours, and they may lead you to things you would never have noticed on your own.
4. Remember the places that children love to visit: aquariums, zoos, amusement parks, beaches, nature trails, and so on. Among the activities that may pique their interest are bicycling, boat trips, visiting planetariums and children's museums, and viewing natural habitat exhibits. Several perennial Chicago attractions for children are the *John G. Shedd Aquarium,* the *Field Museum of Natural History,* and the *Adler Planetarium.*

Staying Healthy

The surest way to return home in good health is to be prepared for medical problems that might occur en route. Below, we've outlined everything about which you need to think before you go.

FIRST AID: Put together a compact, personal medical kit including Band-Aids, first-aid cream, antiseptic, nose drops, insect repellent, aspirin or non-aspirin pain reliever, an extra pair of prescription glasses or contact lenses (and a copy of your prescription for glasses or contact lenses), sunglasses, over-the-counter remedies for diarrhea, indigestion, and motion sickness, a thermometer, and a supply of those prescription medicines you take regularly.

In a corner of your kit, keep a list of all the drugs you have brought and their purpose, as well as duplicate copies of your doctor's prescriptions (or a note from your doctor). As brand names may vary in different parts of the US, it's a good idea to ask your doctor for the generic name of any drugs you use so that you can ask for their equivalent should you need a refill.

It also is a good idea to ask your doctor to prepare a medical identification card that includes such information as your blood type, your social security number, any allergies or chronic health problems you have, and your medical insurance information. Considering the essential contents of your medical kit, keep it with you, rather than in your checked luggage.

These precautions will not guarantee an illness-free trip, but should minimize the risk. As a final hedge against economic if not physical problems, make sure your health insurance will cover all eventualities while you are away. If not, there are policies designed specifically for travel. Many are worth investigating. As with all insurance, they seem like a waste of money until you need them. For more information, also see *Insurance* and *Medical and Legal Aid,* both in this section.

HELPFUL PUBLICATIONS: Practically every phase of health care — before, during, and after a trip — is covered in *The New Traveler's Health Guide* by Drs. Patrick J. Doyle and James E. Banta. It is available for $4.95, plus postage and handling, from Acropolis Books Ltd., 13950 Park Center Rd., Herndon, VA 22071 (phone: 800-451-7771 or 703-709-0006).

The *Traveling Healthy Newsletter,* which is published six times a year, also is brimming with healthful travel tips. For an annual subscription, which costs $24, contact Dr. Karl Neumann (108-48 70th Rd., Forest Hills, NY 11375; phone: 718-268-7290). Dr. Neumann also is the editor of the useful free booklet, *Traveling Healthy,* which is available by writing to the *Travel Healthy Program* (PO Box 10208, New Brunswick, NJ 08906-9910; phone: 215-732-4100).

On the Road

Credit Cards and Traveler's Checks

It may seem hard to believe, but one of the greatest (and least understood) costs of travel is money itself. So your one single objective in relation to the care and retention of your travel funds is to make them stretch as far as possible. When you do spend money, it should be on things that expand and enhance your travel experience, with no buying power lost due to carelessness or lack of knowledge. This requires more than merely ferreting out the best airfare or the most charming budget hotel. It means being canny about the management of money itself. Herewith, a primer on making money go as far as possible while traveling.

TRAVELER'S CHECKS: It's wise to carry traveler's checks while on the road instead of (or in addition to) cash, since it's possible to replace them if they are stolen or lost; in the US, you usually can receive partial or full replacement funds the same day if you have your purchase receipt and proper identification. Issued in various denominations, with adequate proof of identification (credit cards, driver's license, passport), traveler's checks are as good as cash in most hotels, restaurants, stores, and banks. Don't assume, however, that restaurants, small shops, and other establishments are going to be able to change checks of large denominations. More and more establishments are beginning to restrict the face amount of traveler's checks they will accept or cash, so it is wise to purchase at least some of your checks in small denominations — say, $10 and $20.

Every type of traveler's check is legal tender in banks around the world, and each company guarantees full replacement if checks are lost or stolen. After that the similarity ends. Some charge a fee for purchase, while others are free; you can buy traveler's checks at almost any bank, and some are available by mail. Most important, each traveler's check issuer differs slightly in its refund policy — the amount refunded immediately, the accessibility of refund locations, the availability of a 24-hour refund service, and the time it will take you to receive replacement checks. For instance, *American Express* offers a 3-hour replacement of lost or stolen traveler's checks at any *American Express* office; other companies may not be as prompt. (Note that *American Express*'s 3-hour policy is based on the traveler's being able to provide the serial numbers of the lost checks — without these numbers, refunds can take much longer.)

We cannot overemphasize the importance of knowing how to replace lost or stolen checks. All of the traveler's check companies have agents throughout the US, both in their own name and at associated agencies (usually, but not necessarily, banks), where refunds can be obtained during business hours. Most of them also have 24-hour toll-free telephone lines, and some will even provide emergency funds to tide you over on a Sunday.

Be sure to make a photocopy of the refund instructions that will be given to you by the issuing institution at the time of purchase. To avoid complications should you need to redeem lost checks (and to speed up the replacement process), keep the purchase receipt and an accurate list, by serial number, of the checks that have been spent or cashed. You may want to incorporate this information in an "emergency packet," also including the numbers of the credit cards you are carrying, and any other bits of information you shouldn't be without. Always keep these records separate from the checks and the original records themselves (you may want to give them to a traveling companion to hold).

Several of the major traveler's check companies charge 1% for the acquisition of their checks; others don't. To receive fee-free traveler's checks you may have to meet certain qualifications — for instance, *Thomas Cook* checks issued in US currency are free if you make your travel arrangements through its travel agency; *American Express* traveler's checks are available without charge to members of the *American Automobile Association (AAA)*. Holders of some credit cards (such as the *American Express Platinum* card) also may be entitled to free traveler's checks. The issuing institution (e.g., the particular bank at which you purchase them) may itself charge a fee. If you purchase traveler's checks at a bank in which you or your company maintains significant accounts (especially commercial accounts of some size), the bank may absorb the 1% fee as a courtesy.

American Express, Bank of America, Citicorp, MasterCard, Thomas Cook, and *Visa* all offer traveler's checks. Here is a list of the major companies issuing traveler's checks and the numbers to call to report lost or stolen checks throughout the US:

> *American Express:* 800-221-7282
> *Bank of America:* 800-227-3460
> *Citicorp:* 800-645-6556
> *MasterCard:* 800-223-9920
> *Thomas Cook MasterCard:* 800-223-7373
> *Visa:* 800-227-6811

CREDIT CARDS: Some establishments you may encounter during the course of your travels may not honor any credit cards and some may not honor all cards, so there is a practical reason to carry more than one. The following is a list of credit cards that enjoy wide domestic and international acceptance:

> *American Express:* Cardholders can cash personal checks for traveler's checks and cash at *American Express* or its representatives' offices in the US up to the following limits (within any single 21-day period): up to $1,000 for *Green* and *Optima* cardholders; $5,000 for *Gold* cardholders; and $10,000 for *Platinum* cardholders. Check cashing also is available to cardholders who are guests at participating hotels in the US and Canada (up to $250), and for holders of airline tickets, at participating airlines (up to $50). Free travel accident, baggage, and car rental insurance if ticket or rental is charged to card; additional insurance also is available for additional cost. For further information or to report a lost or stolen *American Express* card, call 800-528-4800 throughout the continental US.
>
> *Carte Blanche:* Free travel accident, baggage, and car rental insurance if ticket or rental is charged to card; additional insurance also is available at additional cost. For medical, legal, and travel assistance, call 800-356-3448 throughout the US. For further information or to report a lost or stolen *Carte Blanche* card, call 800-525-9135 throughout the US.
>
> *Diners Club:* Emergency personal check cashing for cardholders staying at participating hotels and motels in the US (up to $250 per stay). Free travel accident, baggage, and car rental insurance if ticket or rental is charged to card; additional insurance also is available for an additional fee. For medical, legal, and travel

assistance, call 800-356-3448 throughout the US. For further information or to report a lost or stolen *Diners Club* card, call 800-525-9135 throughout the US.

Discover Card: Offered by a subsidiary of Sears, Roebuck & Co., it provides cardholders with cash advances at numerous automatic teller machines and Sears stores throughout the US. For further information or to report a lost or stolen *Discover* card, call 800-DISCOVER throughout the US.

MasterCard: Cash advances are available at participating banks worldwide. Check with your issuing bank for information. *MasterCard* also offers a 24-hour emergency lost card service; call 800-826-2181 throughout the US.

Visa: Cash advances are available at participating banks worldwide. Check with your issuing bank for information. *Visa* also offers a 24-hour emergency lost card service; call 800-336-8472 throughout the US.

SENDING MONEY: If you have used up your traveler's checks, cashed as many emergency personal checks as your credit card allows, drawn on your cash advance line to the fullest extent, and still need money, have it sent to you via one of the following services:

American Express (phone: 800-543-4080). Offers a service called "Moneygram," completing money transfers in as little as 15 minutes. The sender can go to any *American Express* office in the US and transfer money by presenting cash, a personal check, money order, or credit card — *Discover, Mastercard, Visa,* or *American Express Optima* (no other *American Express* or other credit cards are accepted). *American Express Optima* cardholders also can arrange for this transfer over the phone. The minimum transfer charge is $10, which rises with the amount of the transaction; the sender can forward funds of up to $10,000 per transaction (credit card users are limited to the amount of their pre-established credit line). To collect at the other end, the receiver must show identification (driver's license or other picture ID) at an *American Express* branch office. The company's offices in Chicago are located at 33 N. Clark St. (phone: 263-6617), 111 N. State St. (phone: 781-4477), and 122 S. Michigan Ave. (phone: 435-2595).

Western Union Telegraph Company (phone: 800-325-4176 throughout the US). A friend or relative can go, cash in hand, to any *Western Union* office in the US, where, for a *minimum* charge of $11 (it rises with the amount of the transaction), the funds will be transferred to a centralized *Western Union* account. When the transaction is fully processed — generally within 30 minutes — you can go to any *Western Union* branch office to pick up the transferred funds; for an additional fee of $2.95 you will be notified by phone when the money is available. For a higher fee, the sender may call *Western Union* with a *MasterCard* or *Visa* number to send up to $2,000, although larger transfers will be sent to a predesignated location. *Western Union* has about 30 branches in Chicago; downtown offices include 3477 N. Broadway (phone: 348-4701) and 770 N. LaSalle St. (phone: 642-0220).

CASH MACHINES: Automatic teller machines (ATMs) are increasingly common throughout the US. If your bank participates in one of the international ATM networks (most do), the bank will issue you a "cash card" along with a personal identification code or number (also called a PIC or PIN). You can use this card at any ATM in the same electronic network to check your account balances, transfer monies between checking and savings accounts, and — most important for a traveler — withdraw cash instantly. Network ATMs generally are located in banks, commercial and transportation centers, and near major tourist attractions.

Some financial institutions offer exclusive automatic teller machines for their own customers only at bank branches. At the time of this writing, ATMs that *are* connected generally belong to one of the following two international networks:

Cirrus: Has over 55,000 ATMs in more than 22 countries, including over 35,000 locations in the US and about 300 in Chicago. *MasterCard* holders also may use their cards to draw cash against their credit lines. For a free booklet listing the locations of these machines and further information on the *Cirrus* network, call 800-4-CIRRUS.

Plus System: Has over 30,000 automatic teller machines worldwide, including over 20,000 locations in the US and about 130 in Chicago. *MasterCard* and *Visa* cardholders also may use their cards to draw cash against their credit lines. For a free directory listing the locations of these machines and further information on the *Plus System* network, call 800-THE-PLUS.

Information about these networks also may be available at member bank branches. A recent agreement between these two companies permit banking institutions to join both networks, allowing users of either system to withdraw funds from participating *Cirrus* or *Plus System* ATMs.

Time Zone and Business Hours

TIME ZONE: Chicago is in the central time zone and observes daylight saving time beginning on the first Sunday in April and continuing until the last Sunday in October.

BUSINESS HOURS: Chicago maintains business hours that are fairly standard throughout the country: 9 AM to 5 PM, Mondays through Fridays.

Banks generally are open weekdays from 9 AM to 3 PM, and 24-hour "automatic tellers" or "cash machines" are increasingly common (for information on national networks, see *Credit Cards and Traveler's Checks,* in this section).

Retail stores usually are open from 9:30 or 10 AM to 5:30 or 6 PM, Mondays through Saturdays. Most of the large department stores are open from 10 AM to 7 or 8 PM on weekdays and to 6 or 7 PM on Saturdays. Sunday hours are from noon until 5 or 6 PM.

Mail, Telephone, and Electricity

MAIL: The main post office is downtown at 433 W. Van Buren St. (phone: 765-3210). It is open weekdays from 7 AM to 9 PM, with a self-service section open 24 hours for weighing packages and buying stamps.

Stamps also are available at most hotel desks. There are vending machines for stamps in drugstores, transportation terminals, and other public places. Stamps cost more from these machines than they do at the post office.

For rapid, overnight delivery to other cities, *Federal Express* can be useful. The phone number to call for pick-up in Chicago is 559-9000, while convenient drop-off addresses include 1 Illinois Center, Suite 20; 111 E. Wacker Dr.; 205 N. Michigan Ave.; the Prudential Building, 130 E. Randolph St.; 34 S. Michigan Ave.; and the John Hancock Building, 975 N. Michigan Ave.

TELEPHONE: Public telephones are available just about everywhere — including transportation terminals, hotel lobbies, restaurants, drugstores, libraries, post offices, and other municipal buildings, as well as major tourist centers.

The Chicago area code is 312; the adjoining suburbs are in the 708 area code.

Although you can use a telephone company credit card number on any phone, pay phones that take major credit cards (*American Express, MasterCard, Visa,* and so on) are increasingly common, particularly in transportation and tourism centers. Also now available is the "affinity card," a combined telephone calling card/bank credit card that can be used for domestic and international calls. Cards of this type include the following:

AT&T/Universal (phone: 800-662-7759).
Executive Telecard International (phone: 800-950-3800).
Sprint Visa (phone: 800-446-7625).

Similarly, *MCI VisaPhone* (phone: 800-866-0099) can add phone card privileges to the services available through your existing *Visa* card. This service allows you to use your *Visa* account number, plus an additional code, to charge calls on any touch-tone phone.

You first must dial 1 to indicate that you are making a long-distance call. The nationwide number for information is 555-1212. If you need a number in another area code, dial 1 + the area code + 555-1212. (If you don't know the area code, simply dial 0 for an operator who will tell you.)

Long-distance rates are charged according to when the call is placed: weekday daytime; weekday evenings; and nights, weekends, and holidays. Least expensive are the calls you dial yourself from a private phone at night and on weekends and major holidays. It generally is more expensive to call from a pay phone than it is to call from a private phone, and you must pay for a minimum 3-minute call. If the operator assists you, calls are more expensive. This includes credit card, bill-to-a-third-number, collect, and time-and-charge calls, as well as person-to-person calls, which are the most expensive. Rates are fully explained in the front of the white pages of every telephone directory.

Hotel Surcharges – Before calling from any hotel room, inquire about any surcharges the hotel may impose. These can be excessive, but are avoidable by calling collect, using a telephone credit card (see above), or calling from a public pay phone. (Note that when calling from your hotel room, even if the call is made collect or charged to a credit card number, some establishments still may add on a nominal line usage charge — so ask before you call.)

Emergency Number – As in most cities, 911 is the number to dial in the event of an emergency in Chicago. Operators at this number will get you the help you need from the police, fire department, or ambulance service. It is, however, a number that only should be used for real emergencies.

■**Note:** An excellent resource for planning your trip is *AT&T's Toll-Free 800 Directory,* which lists thousands of companies with 800 numbers, both alphabetically (white pages) and by category (yellow pages), including a wide range of travel services — from travel agents to transportation and accommodations. Issued in a consumer edition for $9.95 and a business edition for $14.95, both are available from *AT&T Phone Centers* or by calling 800-426-8686. Other useful directories for use before you leave and on the road include the *Toll-Free Travel & Vacation Information Directory* ($4.95 postpaid from Pilot Books, 103 Cooper St., Babylon, NY 11702; phone: 516-422-2225) and *The Phone Booklet* (send $2 to *Scott American Corporation,* Box 88, West Redding, CT 06896).

ELECTRICITY: All 50 US states have the same electrical current system: 110 volts, 60 cycles, alternating current (AC). Appliances running on standard current can be used throughout the US without adapters or converters.

Medical and Legal Aid

MEDICAL AID: Nothing ruins a vacation or business trip more effectively than sudden injury or illness. You will discover, in the event of an emergency, that most tourist facilities are equipped to handle the situation quickly and efficiently. All hospitals are prepared for emergency cases, and many hospitals also have walk-in clinics to serve people who do not really need emergency service but have no place to go for immediate medical attention.

Before you go, be sure to check with your health insurance company about the applicability of your hospitalization and major medical policies while you're away. If your medical policy does not protect you while you're traveling, there are comprehensive combination policies specifically designed to fill the gap. (For a discussion of medical insurance and a list of inclusive combination policies, see *Insurance,* in this section.)

If a bona fide emergency occurs, dial 911, the emergency number, and immediately state the nature of your problem and your location. If you are able to, another alternative is to go directly to the emergency room of the nearest hospital. A major medical institution with top emergency facilities is *Rush-Presbyterian St. Luke's Medical Center* (1653 W. Congress Parkway; phone: 942-5000). Another top emergency room is at *Michael Reese Hospital & Medical Center* (Lakeshore Drive at 31st St.; phone: 791-3545).

If a doctor is needed for something less than an emergency, there are several ways to find one. If you are staying in a hotel, ask for help in reaching a doctor or other emergency services, or for the house physician, who may visit you in your room or ask you to visit an office. You also can call the *Chicago Medical Society* (phone: 670-2550), which operates a physician referral service. When you check in at a hotel, it's not a bad idea to include your home address and telephone number; this will facilitate the process of notifying friends, relatives, or your own doctor in case of an emergency.

For other medical emergencies, 24-hour pharmacies include *Walgreen Drug Stores.* Locations include 757 N. Michigan Ave. (phone: 664-4000) and 1601 N. Wells (phone: 642-4008).

If you need to refill a prescription from your own doctor, you should be aware that in some states pharmacists only will fill prescriptions made out by a doctor licensed to practice in that state, so you may have to have a local doctor rewrite a prescription. Even in an emergency — such as a diabetic needing insulin — a traveler more than likely will be given only enough of a drug to last until a local prescription can be obtained. Generally, a hospital emergency room or walk-in clinic can provide a refill from its pharmaceutical department or a prescription that can be filled at a nearby pharmacy.

Emergency assistance also is available for travelers who have chronic ailments or whose illness requires them to return home. If you have a health condition that may not be readily perceptible to the casual observer — one that might result in a tragic error in an emergency situation — the *Medic Alert Foundation* (2323 N. Colorado, Turlock, CA 95380; phone: 800-ID-ALERT or 209-668-3333) offers identification emblems specifying such conditions. The foundation also maintains a computerized central file from which your complete medical history is available 24 hours a day by phone (the telephone number is clearly inscribed on the emblem). The one-time membership fee (between $25 and $45) is based on the type of metal from which the emblem is made — the choices range from stainless steel to 10K gold-filled.

> ■ **Note:** Those who are unable to take a reserved flight due to personal illness or who must fly home unexpectedly due to a family emergency should be aware that airlines may offer a discounted airfare (or arrange a partial refund) if the traveler can demonstrate that his or her situation is indeed a legitimate emergency. Your inability to fly or the illness or death of an immediate family member usually must be substantiated by a doctor's note or the name, relationship, and funeral home where the deceased will be buried. In such cases, airlines often will waive certain advance purchase restrictions or you may receive a refund check or voucher for travel at a later date. Be aware, however, that this bereavement fare may not necessarily be the least expensive fare available and, if possible, it is best to have a travel agent check all possible flights through a computer reservations system (CRS).

LEGAL AID: The best way to begin looking for legal aid in an unfamiliar area is to call your own lawyer. If you don't have, or cannot reach, your own attorney, most cities offer legal referral services (sometimes called attorney referral services) maintained by county bar associations. In Chicago, contact the *Chicago Bar Association* (321 S. Plymouth Court; phone: 554-2000). Such referral services see that anyone in need of legal representation gets it. (Attorneys also are listed in the yellow pages.) The referral service is almost always free. If your case goes to court, you are entitled to court-appointed representation if you can't get a lawyer or can't afford one.

In the case of minor traffic accidents (such as fender benders), it is often most expedient to settle the matter before the police get involved. If you get a traffic or parking ticket, pay it. For most minor violations, you usually will receive a citation, and may be required to appear in court on a specified date.

Drinking and Drugs

DRINKING: As in all 50 states, the legal drinking age in Illinois is 21. Liquor may be served in Chicago restaurants, bars, and lounges from 8 AM until about 2 AM, depending on the license, but drinking establishments close as early as 11 PM. On Sundays, no liquor may be sold before noon.

For retail purchases, liquor, wine, and beer are sold at liquor stores as well as some convenience stores.

DRUGS: Despite the US government's intensified and concerted effort to stamp out drugs, illegal narcotics still are prevalent in the US, as elsewhere. Enforcement of drug laws is becoming increasingly strict throughout the nation, however, local narcotics officers are renowned for their absence of understanding and lack of a sense of humor.

Possession of marijuana is a misdemeanor in Illinois, while being caught with cocaine or heroin brings exposure to a felony charge, with conviction leading to up to 2 years in jail for possession and up to 10 years for selling the drugs. It is important to bear in mind that the quantity of drugs involved is of minor importance. The best advice we can offer is this: Don't carry, use, buy, or sell illegal drugs.

To avoid difficulties during spot luggage inspections at the airport, if you carry medicines that contain such controlled drugs as codeine or codeine derivatives, be sure to bring along a current doctor's prescription.

Tipping

While tipping is at the discretion of the person receiving the service, 50¢ is the rock-bottom tip for anything, and $1 is the current customary minimum for small services. In restaurants, tip between 10% and 20% of the bill. For average service in an average restaurant, a 15% tip to the waiter is reasonable, although one should never hesitate to penalize poor service or reward excellent and efficient attention by leaving less or more.

Although it's not necessary to tip the maître d' of most restaurants — unless he or she has been especially helpful in arranging a special party or providing a table (a few extra dollars *may,* however, get you seated sooner or procure a preferred table) — when tipping is appropriate, the least amount should be $5. In the finest restaurants, where a multiplicity of servers are present, plan to tip 5% to the captain in addition to the gratuity left for the waiter. The sommelier (wine waiter) is entitled to a gratuity of approximately 10% of the price of the bottle of wine.

In allocating gratuities at a restaurant, pay particular attention to what has become the standard credit card charge form, which now includes separate places for gratuities for waiters and/or captains. If these separate boxes are not on the charge slip, simply ask the waiter or captain how these separate tips should be indicated. In some establishments, tips indicated on credit card receipts may not be given to the help, so you may want to leave tips in cash.

In a large hotel, where it is difficult to determine just who out of a horde of attendants actually performed particular services, it is perfectly proper for guests to ask to have an extra 10% to 15% added to their bill. If you prefer to distribute tips yourself, leave the hotel maid at least $1 a day. Tip the concierge and hall porter for specific services only, with the amount of such gratuities dependent on the level of service provided. For any special service you receive in a hotel, a tip is expected — $1 being the minimum for a small service.

Bellhops, doormen, and porters at hotels and transportation centers generally are tipped at the rate of $1 per piece of luggage, along with a small additional amount if a doorman helps with a cab or car. Taxi drivers should get about 15% of the total fare.

Miscellaneous tips: Sightseeing tour guides should be tipped. If you are traveling in a group, decide together what you want to give the guide and present it from the group at the end of the tour. If you have been individually escorted, the amount paid should depend on the degree of your satisfaction, but it should not be less than 10% of the tour price. Museum and monument guides also are usually tipped a few dollars. Coat checks are worth about 50¢ to $1 a coat, and washroom attendants are tipped — there usually is a little plate with a coin already in it suggesting the expected amount. In barbershops and beauty parlors, tips also are expected, but the percentages vary according to the type of establishment — 10% in the most expensive salons; 15% to 20% in less expensive establishments. (As a general rule, the person who washes your hair should get a small additional tip.)

Tipping always is a matter of personal preference. In the situations covered above, as well as in any others that arise where you feel a tip is expected or due, feel free to express your pleasure or displeasure. Again, never hesitate to reward excellent and efficient attention and to penalize poor service. Give an extra gratuity and a word of thanks when someone has gone out of his or her way for you. Either way, the more personal the act of tipping, the more appropriate it seems. And if you didn't like the service — or the attitude — don't tip.

Religion on the Road

 The surest source of information on religious services in an unfamiliar community is the desk clerk of the hotel or resort in which you are staying; the local tourist information office or a church of another religious affiliation also may be able to provide this information. For a full range of options, joint religious councils often print circulars with the addresses and times of services of other houses of worship in the area. These often are printed as part of general tourist guides provided by the local tourist and convention center, or as part of a "what's going on" guide to the city. Many newspapers also print a listing of religious services in their area in weekend editions.

You may want to use your vacation to broaden your religious experience by joining an unfamiliar faith in its service. This can be a moving experience, especially if the service is held in a church, synagogue, or temple that is historically significant or architecturally notable. You almost always will find yourself made welcome and comfortable.

Sources and Resources

Tourist Information

 The Chicago Tourism Council's Visitor Information Center is located in the historic Water Tower (806 N. Michigan Ave. and Pearson St., Chicago, IL 60611; phone: 280-5740). For other local tourist information, see *Local Sources and Resources* in THE CITY.

For More Information

BOOKS AND BOOKSTORES: The variety and scope of books and other travel information in and on the United States today are astounding. Every city and region is represented, and before you leave on your journey, you can prepare by perusing books relevant to your special travel interests. These can usually be found in bookshops devoted to travel, among them the following:

Book Passage (51 Tamal Vista Blvd., Corte Madera, CA 94925; phone: 415-927-0960 in California; 800-321-9785 elsewhere in the US). Travel guides and maps to all areas of the world. A free catalogue is available.

The Complete Traveller (199 Madison Ave., New York, NY 10016; phone: 212-685-9007). Travel guides and maps. A catalogue is available for $2.

Forsyth Travel Library (PO Box 2975, Shawnee Mission, KS 66201-1375; phone: 800-367-7984 or 913-384-3440). Travel guides and maps, old and new, to all parts of the world. Ask for the "Worldwide Travel Books and Maps" catalogue.

Gourmet Guides (2801 Leavenworth Ave., San Francisco, CA 94133; phone: 415-771-3671). Travel guides and maps, along with cookbooks. Mail-order lists available on request.

Phileas Fogg's Books and Maps (87 *Stanford Shopping Center,* Palo Alto, CA 94304; phone: 800-533-FOGG or 415-327-1754). Travel guides, maps, and language aids.

Tattered Cover (2955 E. First Ave., Denver, CO 80206; phone: 800-833-9327 or 303-322-7727). The travel department alone of this enormous bookstore carries over 7,000 books, as well as maps and atlases. No catalogue is offered (the list is too extensive), but a newsletter, issued three times a year, is available on request.

Thomas Brothers Maps & Travel Books (603 W. Seventh St., Los Angeles, CA 90017; phone: 213-627-4018). Maps (including road atlases, street guides, and wall maps), guidebooks, and travel accessories.

Traveller's Bookstore (22 W. 52nd St., New York, NY 10019; phone: 212-664-0995). Travel guides, maps, literature, and accessories. A catalogue is available for $2.

If you are interested in tracing your family's heritage during your trip — an excellent way to bring some historical perspective to your travels — you should send for the free catalogue of the Genealogical Publishing Company (1001 N. Calvert St., Baltimore, MD 21202-3897; phone: 301-837-8271), which includes numerous titles on ancestral sleuthing.

MAGAZINES: As sampling the regional fare is likely to be one of the highlights of any visit, you will find reading about local edibles worthwhile either before you go or after you return. *Gourmet,* a magazine specializing in food, often carries articles on food and restaurants in the US, although its scope is much broader than domestic fare alone. It is available at newsstands nationwide for $2.50 an issue or for $18 a year from *Gourmet,* PO Box 53780, Boulder, CO 80322 (phone: 800-365-2454).

There are numerous additional magazines for every special interest available; check at your library information desk for a directory of such publications, or look over the selection offered at a well-stocked newsstand.

NEWSLETTERS: One of the very best sources of detailed travel information is *Consumer Reports Travel Letter.* Published monthly by Consumers Union (PO Box 53629, Boulder, CO 80322-3629; phone: 800-999-7959), it offers comprehensive coverage of the travel scene on a wide variety of fronts. A year's subscription costs $37; 2 years, $57.

In addition, the following travel newsletters provide useful up-to-date information on travel services and bargains:

> *Entree* (PO Box 5148, Santa Barbara, CA 93150; phone: 805-969-5848). A monthly newsletter, for which a year's subscription costs $59. Subscribers also have access to a 24-hour hotline providing information on restaurants and accommodations around the world. This newsletter caters to a sophisticated, discriminating traveler with the means to explore the places mentioned.

> *The Hideaway Report* (Harper Assocs., PO Box 50, Sun Valley, ID 83353; phone: 208-622-3193). This monthly source highlights retreats — including domestic idylls — for sophisticated travelers. A year's subscription costs $90.

> *Romantic Hideaways* (217 E. 86th St., Suite 258, New York, NY 10028; phone: 212-969-8682). This newsletter leans toward those special places made for those traveling in twos. A year's subscription to this monthly publication costs $65.

> *Travel Smart* (Communications House, 40 Beechdale Rd., Dobbs Ferry, NY 10522; phone: 914-693-8300 in New York; 800-327-3633 elsewhere in the US). This monthly newsletter covers a wide variety of trips and travel discounts. A year's subscription costs $44.

COMPUTER SERVICES: Anyone who owns a personal computer and a modem can subscribe to a database service providing everything from airline schedules and fares to restaurant listings. Two such services to try:

> *CompuServe* (5000 Arlington Center Blvd., Columbus, OH 43220; phone: 800-848-8199 or 614-457-8600). It costs $39.95 to join, plus hourly usage fees of $6 to $12.50.

> *Prodigy Services* (445 Hamilton Ave., White Plains, NY 10601; phone: 800-822-6922 or 914-993-8000). A month's subscription costs $12.95, plus variable usage charges.

■ **Note:** Those considering using any computer bulletin board service — particularly open-access databases, which may be available at no charge — should be sure to take precautions to prevent downloading of a computer "virus." These destructive programs can be passed on inadvertently by other users of the service and usually are invisible — until they start to destroy the files on your computer. Programs designed to screen out such nuisances are available; consult your local software vendor.

Cameras and Equipment

 Vacations (and even business trips) are everybody's favorite time for taking pictures and home movies. After all, most of us want to remember the places we visit — and to show them off to others. Here are a few suggestions to help you get the best results from your travel photography or videography.

BEFORE THE TRIP

If you're taking your camera or camcorder out after a long period in mothballs or have just bought a new one, check it thoroughly before you leave to prevent unexpected breakdowns or disappointing pictures.

1. Still cameras should be cleaned carefully and thoroughly, inside and out. If using a camcorder, run a head cleaner through it. You also may want to have your camcorder professionally serviced (opening the casing yourself will violate the manufacturer's warranty). Always use filters to protect your lens while traveling.
2. Check the batteries for your camera's light meter and flash, and take along extras just in case yours wear out during the trip. For camcorders, bring along extra Nickel-Cadmium (Ni-Cad) batteries; if you use rechargeable batteries, a recharger will cut down on the extras.
3. Using all the settings and features, shoot at least one test roll of film or one videocassette, using the type you plan to take along with you.

EQUIPMENT TO TAKE ALONG

Keep your gear light and compact. Items that are too heavy or bulky to be carried comfortably on a full-day excursion will likely stay in your hotel room.

1. Invest in a broad camera or camcorder strap if you now have a thin one. It will make carrying the equipment much more comfortable.
2. A sturdy canvas, vinyl, or leather camera or camcorder bag, preferably with padded pockets (not an airline bag), will keep your equipment organized and easy to find. If you will be doing much shooting around the water, a waterproof case is best.
3. For cleaning, bring along a camel's hair brush that retracts into a rubber squeeze bulb. Also, take plenty of lens tissue, soft cloths, and plastic bags to protect equipment from dust and moisture.

FILM AND TAPES: If you are concerned about airport security X-rays damaging rolls of undeveloped still film (X-rays do not affect processed film) or tapes, store them in one of the lead-lined bags sold in camera shops. This possibility is not as much of a threat as it used to be, however. In the US, incidents of X-ray damage to unprocessed film (exposed or unexposed) are few because low-dosage X-ray equipment is used virtually everywhere. If you're traveling without a protective bag, you may want to ask to have your photo equipment inspected by hand. One type of film that should never be subjected to X-rays is the very high speed ASA 1000 film. The walk-through metal detector devices at airports do not affect film, though the film cartridges may set them off.

You should have no problem finding film or tapes in Chicago. When buying film, tapes, or photo accessories the best rule of thumb is to stick to name brands with which you are familiar. The availability of film processing labs and equipment repair shops will vary.

THE CITY

CHICAGO

Ask a resident if Chicago has a soul, and you're likely to be greeted with a laugh. The third-largest city in the country (the city proper has more than 3 million people; the metropolitan area, more than 7 million), ninth-largest in the world, Chicago carries a long-standing reputation as a tough meat-and-potatoes town. "Hog Butcher to the World," Carl Sandburg sang; yet it is one of the world's great cities. Despite its greatness, however, Chicago suffers from an inferiority complex, one that stems from the endless, inevitable comparisons to New York and, more recently, to Los Angeles, which has wrested away its "Second City" title.

In fact, there is a unique allure to Chicago. It is a vibrant, hip smorgasbord of theaters, award-winning restaurants, blues bars, museums, after-hours clubs, and world class hotels that stretch like a long, beckoning finger north along Lake Michigan, from the Loop past Lincoln Park. It has inspired a Broadway musical, scores of stories and poems, countless popular songs, and has been the subject of endless numbers of Hollywood films. All of which may seem especially ironic if you consider that nobody really knows whether the Indian word *checagou* means "great and powerful," "wild onion," or "skunk." This long-standing linguistic controversy did not, however, inhibit the composers who created that legendary tribute to "Chicago, that toddling town."

Chicago spreads along 29 miles of carefully groomed lakeshore. Respecting Lake Michigan, the people of Chicago have been careful not to destroy the property near the water with heavy manufacturing or industry. The lake is a source of water, as well as a port of entry for steamships and freighters coming from Europe via the St. Lawrence Seaway. More than 82 million tons of freight are handled by Chicago's ports every year. The city also is the world's largest railroad center. The Chicago Board of Trade is the nation's most important grain market, and O'Hare International, its busiest airport.

Nuclear research and the electronics industry came of age here. In 1942, the world's first self-sustaining nuclear chain reaction was achieved at the University of Chicago. Half the radar equipment used during World War II was made here, too. Chicago is *Second City,* the comedy club that spawned John Belushi, Joan Rivers, Shelley Long, and Bill Murray, among others. Chicago is *Wrigley Field* and the long-suffering *Chicago Cubs.* Chicago is the *Goodman Theater* and the *Hubbard Street Dance Company* and the symphony and bold Helmut Jahn architecture. It is barbecued ribs and stuffed pizza, David Mamet and John Malkovich, Mike Royko and Oprah Winfrey. It is Buddy Guy wailing the blues.

People from all over the world have come here to live. In 1890, 80% of all Chicago residents were immigrants or children of immigrants. There are more Poles in Chicago than in any Polish city except Warsaw, as well as sizable contingents from Germany, Italy, Sweden, and Ireland. People talk about "ethnic Chicago," which means you can find neighborhoods that will make you think you're in a foreign country.

Chinatown stretches along Wentworth Avenue. Vietnamtown occupies several blocks of Argyle Street, and Koreatown fills West Lawrence Avenue. Enclaves of Ukrainians and Sicilians live in West Chicago. The Greeks can be found on South Halsted and West Lawrence; Irish and Lithuanians around Bridgeport and Marquette Park; Latinos in Pilsen; Italians in an area bounded by the University of Illinois at Chicago, the Eisenhower Expressway, and the West Side Medical Center. Polonia, which looks like a set for a 1930s Polish version of *West Side Story,* is mostly along Milwaukee. Nearly every nationality has a museum, and at least some of its customs have become public domain as well. There's a splendid array of inexpensive ethnic restaurants where you can get a whole meal for the price of an appetizer in a ritzier joint.

This cosmopolitan center had unprepossessing beginnings. Marquette and Joliet, the French explorers who provided the first record of the area, knew it as the Chicago Portage, one landmark on their route to the Chicago River from the Mississippi. A trading post was established in 1679. In the 1812 Fort Dearborn Massacre, 53 people were killed by Indians. Eighteen years later, the first parcels of land were sold — $40 to $60 per 15,000-square-foot plot. The city, incorporated in 1837, began to look as if it might amount to something when the *Union Pacific Railroad* connected it to San Francisco in 1869; 2 years later, on October 8, 1871, it was in ashes. Burning at the rate of 65 acres per hour ($125,000 damage per minute) and aided by a furious southwest wind, the Great Fire melted 15,000 water service pipes, took 250 lives, made 90,000 homeless, and left 1,688 acres in rubble. The total damage was estimated at $196 million.

Like San Francisco after its 1906 earthquake, Chicago simply began to rebuild. And in the process, in the course of the following 50 years, a new urban architecture was born. Building quickly and furiously upon 4 square miles of charcoal, and abetted by simple clients whose aesthetics derived from their interests in the profits to be gained from efficient buildings rather than the glory to be garnered from neo-classical palaces, the Chicago architects *invented* the skyscraper; Frank Lloyd Wright pioneered the ground-hugging, prairie-style houses that became the prototypes for the suburban, single-family dwelling units we know today. In 1909, architect Daniel Burnham laid out a plan for the city's parks. Today, 561 of them stretch across 7,332 acres, not to mention 32 clean public beaches and 66,993 acres of trail-crossed forest preserves on the outskirts.

That the beaches are still clean and the forest acreage still pretty much unspoiled is a credit to the city planners, who have, over the years, managed to keep Chicago alive and vibrant even as other downtown areas around the country have declined. While buildings elsewhere were pulled down to make way for parking lots, Chicago got a handful of skyscrapers set on pedestrian plazas studded with magnificent pieces of sculpture by Alexander Calder, Marc Chagall, Pablo Picasso, Claes Oldenburg, Joan Miró, and others. Lively lunchtime programs keep the plazas thronged with sightseers and Loop office workers alike in the summer.

In the same vein is the renovation of the venerable Marquette Building and the completion of the federally and municipally funded $17-million modernization of the State Street shopping area. So if you haven't seen Chicago for a while, you're likely to be astounded. Cars have been banned and only buses are permitted on State Street — what's left of it. Sidewalks have been widened to nearly 50 feet and covered with hexagonal, battleship-gray paving blocks; open-air cafés have sprouted; and modern bus stops, subway entrances, light poles, and newsstands have been constructed of Cor-Ten steel. As part of the general face-lifting, even *Carson Pirie Scott,* the turn-of-the-century department store designed by the celebrated Louis Sullivan, has restored its interior to match the rococo splendor of its well-cared-for façade. Chicago has also been experiencing an architectural renaissance with the construction of major new office buildings, such as One Park Place, 333 Wacker Drive, One Magnificent Mile, and Helmut Jahn's State of Illinois Building (see *Walk 2: The Loop's Alfresco Museum* in DIRECTIONS.

If Chicago's modern face has improved with age, the same cannot be said of local politics. The successors to Mayor Richard J. Daley have not been able to maintain Chicago's old reputation as "the city that works," and municipal discord has become much more the order of the day. In 1989, Richard M. Daley, the first son of the late mayor, was elected to the office his father held for 21 years. Citing improvement of the troubled public school system and a war against crime as top priorities, Daley sends a message far different than any heard from his father. But although he has promised to "set a positive tone" for Chicagoans, his critics doubt that he can bind a racially polarized, divided city.

Still, Chicago is quite a city, even if you consider just the snazzy Gold Coast and all those magnificent apartment buildings along the shore of Lake Michigan; the lecture programs at the University of Chicago; the program of choral works at the neo-Gothic Rockefeller Chapel; the Rush Street bars; and the Magnificent Mile — broad Michigan Avenue, lined with shops and galleries. There are the *Chicago Symphony Orchestra,* the *Lyric Opera,* and the *Art Institute,* with its world-famous collection of Impressionist and post-Impressionist paintings. There's jazz and blues until the wee hours of the morning. And if it's the kind of place that makes you want to sing — well, you won't be the first.

CHICAGO AT-A-GLANCE

SEEING THE CITY: The 110-story Sears Tower (Wacker and Adams Sts.; phone: 875-9696) maintains a Skydeck on the 103rd floor (check out the Calder *Universe* sculpture and see the ground-floor audiovisual show about Chicago before heading skyward). Open daily from 9 AM to midnight. Admission charge. For a view from the north, visit the John Hancock Building (fifth-tallest in the world), fondly nicknamed "Big John." On the 95th floor are a bar and restaurant (closed Saturday lunch and Sunday dinner; 875 Michigan Ave.; phone: 751-3681). Observation deck open daily, from 9 AM to midnight. Admission charge.

For an aerial view of Chicago, there are helicopter tours, including sunset flights, run by *Head West Sky Operations* (at Waukegan Regional Airport; phone: 708-336-6446). At street level, try a "Culture Bus" tour (phone: 836-7000) or the Chicago Architecture Foundation's bus tour past important architectural sites (phone: 922-3432). Several private firms offer bus tours around Chicago; call *American Sightseeing Tours* (phone: 427-3100); *Chicago Motor Coach Company* (phone: 989-8919); or *Gray Line* (phone: 346-9506). If a horse and buggy ride strikes your fancy, contact *J.C. Cutters;* they have a carriage stand at the corner of Chicago and Michigan (phone: 664-6014); or *Antique Coach and Carriage* at 346 W. Division (phone: 735-9400).

For a river view, *Wendella Sightseeing* (400 N. Michigan Ave.; phone: 337-1446) offers boat trips on the Chicago River and Lake Michigan daily from May to mid-October. A charter craft, *Engine Company #41,* runs sightseeing excursions on a 92-foot fireboat; call the *Chicago Fire Boat Cruise Company* (phone: 855-0664). The *Star of Chicago* offers dinner and cocktail cruises year-round (phone: 644-5914); the *Spirit of Chicago,* at Navy Pier, has dining, dancing, and moonlight cruises, as well as narrated tours (455 E. Illinois St.; phone: 836-7899).

For a custom-designed tour of Chicago in your own car, contact Charlotte Kirshbaum (399 Fullerton, Chicago, IL 60614; phone: 477-6509). Or set off on your own following the walking tours in this guide outlined in DIRECTIONS.

 SPECIAL PLACES: A sophisticated public transport system makes it easy to negotiate Chicago's streets. You can explore the Loop, the lakefront, and suburbs by El train, subway, and bus (fare: $1.25).

THE LOOP

The Loop generally refers to Chicago's business district, which is encircled by the elevated train known as the "El."

ArchiCenter – The *Exhibition Gallery* has changing shows that span a wide range of architectural topics. The *ArchiCenter* also offers a variety of tours. Guided walking tours of the Loop (and other neighborhoods) are conducted daily, May through November; Fridays through Mondays at 1 PM the rest of the year. The Chicago Highlights bus tour is available on Saturdays year-round. Fees range from $6 to $17. 330 S. Dearborn, 1st Floor (phone: 922-3431).

Art Institute of Chicago – Founded as an art school in 1879, the *Art Institute* houses an outstanding collection of Impressionist and post-Impressionist paintings, Japanese prints, Chinese sculpture and bronzes, and Old Masters. In the Columbus Drive Addition, is the reconstructed trading room of the old Chicago Stock Exchange. On the west wall of the upper-level McKinlock Court Galleries are Chagall's stained glass *American Windows.* The $23-million Rice Building houses Edward Hopper's *Nighthawks,* Grant Wood's *American Gothic,* Vincent van Gogh's *Bedroom at Arles,* and Toulouse-Lautrec's *Ballet Dancers,* as well as exhibitions of European and American decorative arts and sculpture. Open daily. Admission charge except on Tuesdays. Michigan Ave. at Adams St. (phone: 443-3600 or 443-3500 for recorded information).

Auditorium Theater – Brilliant Chicago architect Louis Sullivan died penniless, but this 103-year-old landmark, one of his most important works, still stands. Designed by Sullivan and Dankmar Adler in 1889 after the Great Fire, the 4,000-seat theater was built as a combination opera house, hotel, and office center. Hand-painted murals and gold leaf abound here, and the interior features 55 million pieces of mosaic tile. The recently restored theater doesn't have a bad seat in the house. Now used for a variety of cultural functions, from stage plays to pop singers, the theater's recent offerings have included such blockbusters as the *Phantom of the Opera* and *Les Misérables*. Tours are offered for groups of 10 or more, but individuals can join, if space is available. There's a charge for the tours. 50 E. Congress Pkwy. (phone: 922-4046 or 902-1919 for performance information).

Chicago Board of Trade – The largest grain exchange in the world, this Art Deco treasure was built in 1930 and, half a century later, gained a new trading floor to accommodate expanding markets. Stand in the visitors' gallery and watch traders gesticulating on the floor, runners in colored jackets delivering orders, and an electronic record of all the trades displayed overhead. Open weekdays, from 8 AM to 2 PM. Explanations begin at 9:15 AM; movies at 10 and 11 AM, noon and 12:30 PM. No admission charge. 141 W. Jackson Blvd. at La Salle St. (phone: 435-3590).

Chicago Mercantile Exchange and International Monetary Market – The spectacle is much the same as at the Board of Trade, only here you can sit down. Opened in 1898 as the Butter and Egg Board, today more than 4,000 traders and staff crowd the trading floor daily. Visitors can watch the auction from a fourth floor gallery that is open weekdays from 7:30 AM to 3:15 PM. Trading does not stop suddenly. Each commodity has its own opening and closing time. Free tours at 9 and 10:30 AM and noon. No admission charge. 30 S. Wacker St. (phone: 930-8249).

Chicago Public Library Cultural Center – This 1897 Italian Renaissance-style building has impressive interiors of green and white marble, elaborate mosaics, and a Louis Tiffany stained glass dome. It is a fitting background for a continuous schedule of dance performances, concerts, art exhibits, photography shows, lectures, and films. The city presents more than 500 free programs and exhibits here annually. 78 E. Washington St. (phone: 346-3278 for recorded message; 744-6630 for general information).

Grant Park – A favorite spot for summer music festivals, the park, located south of Randolph Street (bordered by Randolph Street, Lake Shore Drive, Michigan Avenue, and Roosevelt Drive), offers an incredible view of the Chicago skyline. At the corner of Columbus Avenue and Congress Street, stop by the Buckingham Fountain, the world's largest lighted fountain — with a computerized 135-foot-high water display that spouts daily from May to October. The fountain was modeled after the Latona Fountain at Versailles, but it is twice the size; the formal gardens are just steps away. Between S. Michigan Ave. and Lake Shore Dr., south of Randolph St. (phone: 294-2307).

Halsted Street – If you have time to get to know only one street, make it Halsted, where locals claim you can live an entire lifetime without ever leaving. Spanning 20 miles of metropolitan Chicago — from 3766 North to 12961 South and on through West Pullman and Calumet — it boasts hundreds of restaurants, bars, nightclubs, 30 churches, 50 liquor stores, and offbeat shops you won't find on Michigan Avenue. West of the Loop on Halsted is Chicago's Greektown area with restaurants such as *Neon Greek Village* offering ethnic food — and even belly dancing. Theaters also line some blocks of Halsted, as do jazz and blues bars. For more information see *Walk 13: Halsted — The World on One Street* in DIRECTIONS.

Marshall Field – Chicago's most famous department store. When it was built in 1892 — before electric lighting was common — it was designed in sections, with shopping areas on balconies overlooking a skylit central courtyard. Later, the skylights were covered, one with a vivid blue and gold Louis Tiffany mosaic visible by entering on the corner of Washington and State Streets. The *Crystal Palace,* on the third floor, serves unbelievable ice cream sundaes. Frango mint ice cream (a subtle mix of coffee, chocolate, malt, and mint) is a tradition, as are its chocolates. Open Mondays through Saturdays and the first Sunday of every month. Wabash, State, Randolph, and Washington Sts. (phone: 781-1000).

Museum of Broadcast Communications – This facility traces the city's role in the broadcasting industry using an extensive tape library and exhibits. In the museum's *Kraft Television Theatre,* visitors can watch old commercials and vintage prime time shows. Weekends visitors to the museum's news center can "anchor" a newscast, then watch it on video (call ahead to reserve camera time). The museum's shop, *Commercial Break,* sells ABC Sports jackets and David Letterman T-shirts, along with other media-related items. Open Wednesdays through Fridays and Sundays from noon to 5 PM; Saturdays from 10 AM to 5 PM. Admission charge. 800 S. Wells, River City (phone: 987-1500).

NEAR SOUTH SIDE

Adler Planetarium – Exhibitions on everything from surveying and navigating instruments to modern space exploration devices, plus a real moon rock and an antique instrument collection that is the best in the Western Hemisphere and one of the top three in the world. You can see it all before or after the sky show, which is the reason that most people come. There are new shows every 3 months, one for adults and one for children 5 years old and younger. Open daily, 9:30 AM to 4:30 PM Mondays through Thursdays, until 9 PM Fridays, and until 5 PM weekends. Admission charge for the sky shows only. 1300 S. Lake Shore Dr. on Museum Point (phone: 322-0304).

Field Museum of Natural History – Of this museum's endless exhibitions on anthropology, botany, zoology, and geology, one of its most famous attractions is the pair of fighting elephants in the Main Hall. Other standouts include the hands-on Place for Wonder, where youngsters can touch a fish skeleton from the dinosaur age and try on ethnic masks; the Plants of the World Hall, with reproductions of about 500 plants from around the globe; the renovated Gem Hall; the full-scale model of a Pawnee earth lodge, where there are daily programs on Indian life; a full-size, 3-level ancient Egyptian tomb; and an exhibition called Maritime Peoples of the Northwest Coast. The Hall of Chinese Jade and the display of Japanese lacquerware are also outstanding. Open daily. Admission charge except on Thursdays. S. Lake Shore Dr. at Roosevelt Rd. (phone: 922-9410).

Hull House – Social welfare pioneer Jane Addams founded Hull House as a community service organization working for political reform, to improve garbage collection, to end sweatshops, and to protect abused children. Some of the original Hull House buildings still exist, with exhibits commemorating Addams, a peace activist, humanitarian, and the first North American woman to win the Nobel Peace Prize, as well as her associates, and the neighborhood they served. Open Mondays through Fridays from 10 AM to 4 PM; Sundays from noon to 5 PM. Closed Saturdays. No admission charge. 800 S. Halsted St. (phone: 413-5353).

Prairie Avenue Historic District – This area of 19th-century mansions, along Prairie Avenue, between 18th and Cullerton Streets, is where Chicago's wealthy citizens once lived. The buildings that remain have been restored to their former elegance, while other historic buildings have been moved here. Standouts are the Glessner House (1800 S. Prairie Ave.), built by architect H.H. Richardson in 1886, and the city's oldest building, the Henry B. Clark House, built in 1836. The Chicago Architecture Foundation (phone: 326-1393) runs general tours of the area every Saturday from March through the end of November. On weekdays and at other times of the year, neighborhood or architectural tours are irregularly scheduled.

Printer's Row – Architecture buffs will find a haven among the restored buildings, jazz and blues clubs, bookstores, and galleries just south of the Loop on S. Dearborn and S. Plymouth Court. The *Printer's Row Printing Museum* (open Saturdays and Sundays; 731 S. Plymouth Ct.; phone: 987-1059) is a 19th-century print shop with demonstrations of century-old presses; the museum shop sells prints and cards. The *Morton* hotel (formerly the *Omni Morton*), housed in a building on the National

Historical Register, is a new addition to the area. Every year, outside *Sandmeyer's Book Store* (down S. Dearborn from the *Morton*) there is a 2-day *Printer's Row Fair,* with exhibits dedicated to all aspects of printing and publishing. While in the neighborhood, stop for a drink at the *Printer's Row* restaurant, or have a snack at the *Upfront* — everything you always wanted in a sports bar and more, including a ticket service for local sporting events. This spacious wood-floored jazz spot has pool, darts, and softball leagues, all housed in the elegant Patten Building. For more information see *Printer's Row and South Loop* in DIRECTIONS.

John G. Shedd Aquarium – The largest aquarium in the world, this one has more than 200 fish tanks and a collection of over 7,000 specimens: sturgeon from Russia, Bahamian angelfish, Australian lungfish, and a coral reef where divers feed the fish several times a day. Last year marked the opening of the *Oceanarium,* doubling the size of the museum and creating a Pacific Northwest coastal exhibit with whales, seals, dolphins, and penguins (phone: 939-2438). Open from 9 AM to 5 PM daily, March through October, 10 AM to 5PM daily through February, closed *Christmas* and *New Year's Day.* Admission charge. Museum Point at 1200 S. Lake Shore Dr. (phone: 939-2426).

NEAR NORTH SIDE

Chicago Academy of Sciences – This museum features particularly lively exhibitions about the natural history of the Great Lakes area; the reconstruction of a 300-million-year-old forest that once stood near the present site, complete with gigantic insects and carnivorous dragonflies is especially interesting. There also are a "walk-through" cave and canyon. Open daily. Admission charge except on Mondays. In Lincoln Park at 2001 N. Clark St. (phone: 549-0606).

Chicago Children's Museum – This hands-on museum for youngsters has an observation deck for viewing the city's skyline and a kid-size perspective of the city where children can learn about architecture, try out a fully equipped mini-kitchen, and climb, ride, and fly — all at the same time — in a "Fantasy Vehicle." There is one room filled with nothing but Lego building blocks. Open Thursdays from 5 to 8 PM and weekends from 10 AM to 4:30 PM. Closed Mondays. Admission charge. 435 E. Illinois St., North Pier (phone: 527-1000).

Chicago Historical Society – Pioneer crafts demonstrations and a Chicago Fire slide show make this one of Chicago's most fascinating museums. New galleries focus on the city's beginnings and explore 19th-century American life through furniture and decorative objects. Open daily. Admission charge except on Mondays. Clark St. and North Ave. (phone: 642-4600).

Chicago Maritime Museum – This museum opened in 1989 in what was an old shipping terminal at the North Pier. It has a number of exhibits dedicated to the history of the Great Lakes and the shipping industry — including artifacts raised from sunken vessels — and changing exhibits. Open Tuesdays through Sundays from noon to 5 PM; closed Monday. No admission charge. 435 E. Illinois St. (phone: 836-4343).

Chicago Theater – This theater, restored to its 1920s splendor, offers live performances against a baroque backdrop of marble and crystal chandeliers. Even if you aren't going for the show, stop by for a look at its interior. 175 N. State St. (phone: 559-1212).

International College of Surgeons Hall of Fame – This museum is full of medical curiosities: old examining tables, artificial limbs, a set of amputation tools from the Revolution, a "bone crusher" used for correcting bow legs between 1918 and 1950 (!). Finally, there's a fascinating display of prayers and oaths taken by doctors in different countries. Open from 10 AM to 4 PM Tuesdays to Saturdays, 11 AM to 5 PM Sundays; closed Mondays. No admission charge. 1524 N. Lake Shore Dr. (phone: 642-3555).

Lincoln Park Conservatory – This botanical delight features changing floral displays and a magnificent permanent collection that includes orchids, a 50-foot African fiddle-leaf rubber tree with giant leaves, fig trees, and more ferns than you could ever imagine. Open daily. No admission charge. In Lincoln Park, Stockton Dr. at Fullerton (phone: 294-4770).

Lincoln Park Zoo – The best thing about this zoo is that it has the largest group of great apes in captivity, now in a renovated Great Ape House. The renovated Lion House reopened in 1990, and the Bird House made its debut last year. There are the standard houses of monkey, tiger, lion, bear, and bison, plus the zoo's popular farm. Next door, a building restored to its early 20th-century charm now houses the *Café Brauer* (phone: 294-4660), with its fine view of the park and the Chicago skyline, as well as an office for bike and skate rentals, a small cafeteria, and the *Ice Cream Shoppe,* which dishes out old-fashioned ice cream creations. Open daily from 9 AM to 5 PM. No admission charge. 2200 Cannon Dr., Lincoln Park (phone: 294-4660).

Museum of Contemporary Art – This small museum offers lively changing exhibitions, both retrospectives of contemporary artists and surveys of 20th-century art movements and avant-garde phenomena. The museum also features shows by Chicago artists, symposia, and other special events. Closed Mondays. Admission charge except on Tuesdays. 237 E. Ontario (phone: 280-2660).

Peace Museum – The only one of its kind in the US, it features exhibits and special programs on issues related to war, peace, and nonviolence. Recent expositions have included a study of war refugees. Open daily from noon to 5 PM, Thursdays until 8 PM. Admission charge. 430 W. Erie (phone: 440-1860).

Terra Museum of American Art – The permanent collection here reads like a Who's Who in American Art over the past 2 centuries and includes the works of Mary Cassatt, Winslow Homer, John Singer Sargent, William Merritt Chase, Samuel F.B. Morse, Edward Hopper, and Andrew Wyeth. Morse, inventor of the Morse code, painted the *Gallery of the Louvre,* a huge canvas recreating dozens of paintings from the *Louvre.* One of the few museums in the country dedicated solely to American art and artists, it also has visiting exhibits. Open Tuesdays from noon to 8 PM, Wednesdays through Saturdays from 10 AM to 5 PM and Sundays from noon to 5 PM; closed Mondays. Admission charge. 666 N. Michigan Ave. (phone: 664-3939).

Water Tower – Now a landmark, this survivor of the Great Fire of 1871 serves as a visitors' center. Across the street at the Water Tower Pumping Station is a multimedia show about the city. Open daily except holidays. 803 N. Michigan Ave. (phone: 467-5308).

Water Tower Place – This incredible, vertical shopping mall gets busier and better every year. Asymmetrical glass-enclosed elevators shoot up through a 7-story atrium, past shops selling dresses, books, and gift items, plus restaurants and a movie theater. Branches of *Marshall Field, FAO Schwarz,* and *Lord & Taylor* are here, along with the lovely *Ritz-Carlton* hotel, stretching 20 stories above its 12th-floor lobby in the tower. Its skylit *Greenhouse* is great for tea or cocktails after a hard day of shopping. Michigan Ave. at Pearson St.

Wrigley Building – This 1920s-era structure on the Magnificent Mile was modeled after the Giralda Tower of Spain's Seville cathedral. The clock tower, ornamental details, and white terra cotta façade are illuminated by banks of floodlights in the evening. The world headquarters for Wrigley chewing gum features an archive filled with gum wrappers; unfortunately, visitors are not allowed inside, but the building is worth viewing if just from the outside. 400 N. Michigan Ave. (phone: 923-8080).

NORTH SIDE

Biograph Theatre – A legend, although not as a theater, it was here in 1934 that the Lady in Red (Anna Sage) turned bank robber John Dillinger over to federal agents, ending a massive manhunt for the FBI's "Public Enemy No. 1." For many years, on July 22, the date Dillinger was gunned down by G-men outside the *Biograph,* the movie house showed *Manhattan Melodrama* — the film that was playing when Elliot Ness caught up with Dillinger — for the same 25¢ admission charge. That tradition has been discontinued, but the theater still shows foreign and contemporary films. 2433 N. Lincoln Ave. (phone: 348-1350).

Graceland Cemetery – Buried here are hotel barons, steel magnates, architects Louis Sullivan and Daniel Burnham — enshrined in tombs and miniature temples, and overlooking islands, lakes, hills, and other scenic views. The ranks of Chicago's rich and famous interred here also include George Pullman, inventor of the sleeper railcar, Cyrus McCormick, who invented the harvester, and merchant Marshall Field. The Getty Tomb, designed by Sullivan, is a must stop. On most Sundays in August, September, and October, the Chicago Architecture Foundation sponsors 2-hour tours of the cemetery starting at 2 PM. Cost is $5. Call CAF in advance for details (phone: 922-3431).

Lill Street – With more than 40 professional potters working in dozens of studios, this is the largest ceramics center in the Midwest. Visitors can watch the artisans or even buy some of their work. *Lill Street* potters offer classes, including a 1-day family clay workshop. 1021 W. Lill St. (phone: 477-6185).

SOUTH SIDE

Museum of Science and Industry – Some 2,000 exhibits explain the principles of science in such a lively way that the museum is Chicago's number one attraction. The newest draw is the *Omnimax Theater,* which has an admission charge. Longtime favorites: Colleen Moore's fairy castle of a dollhouse with real diamond "crystal" chandeliers, the cunning Sears circus exhibit, a working coal mine, a walk-through human heart, and a captured German submarine. Open daily except *Christmas,* but it's a madhouse on weekends. No admission charge. S. Lake Shore Dr. at 57th St. (phone: 684-1414).

Oriental Institute Museum – This collection of art, archaeological artifacts, and textiles from the ancient Near East boasts a colossal statue of Tutankhamen and a winged bull with a human head from Assyria. Run by the University of Chicago, the museum offers guided tours and free films on Sunday afternoons. Open Tuesdays through Saturdays from 10 AM to 4 PM, Sundays from noon to 4 PM; closed Monday. 1155 East 58th St. (phone: 702-9521).

Pullman Community – Founded by George Pullman in 1880 as the nation's first company town, this early example of comprehensive urban planning is now a city, state, and national landmark. Walking tours conducted on the first Sunday of the month from May through October tell the story in detail; at other times, find the Green Stone Church and other important sites on maps available at the *Florence* hotel, a Pullman-era structure that serves as a visitors' center of sorts (and provides lunch on weekdays, breakfast and lunch on Saturdays, and brunch on Sundays). A number of the many privately owned row houses are open for special tours held annually on the second weekend in October. West of the Calumet Expy. between 111th and 115th Sts. (phone: 785-8181). For more information see *Walk 16: Pullman Historic District* in DIRECTIONS.

University of Chicago – Guided walking tours of this illustrious university, founded in 1892 by John D. Rockefeller, include a stop at the Robie House (5757 S. Woodlawn Ave.), a fine example of the Prairie School of architecture, designed by Frank Lloyd Wright (as was its furniture) in 1909. The campus also has a marker commemorating the site of the world's first controlled atomic test in 1942 and Rockefeller Chapel, where anecdotes invariably involve famous statesmen, politicians, and celebrities. Campus tours are conducted Mondays through Saturdays at 10 AM; call in advance for the meeting place. The campus is in Hyde Park, bounded by Cottage Grove Ave., 5th St., Dorchester Ave., and 61st St. (phone: 702-8360). No charge for the tour.

WEST SIDE

Garfield Park Conservatory – Here are 4½ acres under glass. The Palm House alone is 250 feet long, 85 feet wide, and 65 feet high; it looks like the tropics. There's a fernery luxuriant with greenery, mosses, and pools of water lilies. The Cactus House has 85 genera, 400 species. At *Christmas,* poinsettias bloom; in February, azaleas and camellias; at *Easter,* lilies and bulb plants; and in November, mums. Open daily, 9 AM to 5 PM. No admission charge. 300 N. Central Park Blvd. (phone: 533-1281).

Mexican Fine Arts Museum – The first Mexican museum in the Midwest, and the largest in the country, pays tribute to the wide and varied Mexican culture with exhibits, theatrical performances, and workshops. The museum's gift shop specializes in Mexican folk art and multilingual publications. Open Tuesdays through Sundays, 10 AM to 5 PM; closed Mondays. 1852 W. 19th St. (phone: 738-1503).

OUTSKIRTS

Brookfield Zoo – Some 200 acres divided by moats and natural-looking barriers make this one of the most modern zoos in the country. There is an indoor rain forest, special woods for wolves, a bison prairie, a replica of the Sahara, and a dolphin show. The Tropic World features South American, Asian, and African birds, primates, and other animals. Open daily. Admission charge except on Tuesdays. 1st Ave. at 31st St. in Brookfield, 15 miles west of the Loop. Take Rte. 290 or I-55 to 1st Ave. Exit (phone: 708-242-2630).

Chicago Botanic Garden – This 300-acre collection of plants, trees, and shrubs from around the world is open year-round — except *Christmas Day* — from 8 AM until sunset. Its special attractions include a three-island Japanese garden, a rose garden, 10 education greenhouses, and a mile-long nature trail. There also is a tram tour of the gardens, an exhibit hall, a library, the *Museum of Floral Arts,* a gift shop, and a café. Half a mile east of the Edens expressway at Lake-Cook Road in Glencoe (phone: 708-835-5440).

Frank Lloyd Wright Home and Studio – Designed by Frank Lloyd Wright (who else?), this was the birthplace of the so-called Prairie School of architecture and is a fine example of that style. At the center of the home is a fireplace around which the rest of the rooms are spread. Wright, who was self-taught, also designed the furniture — perhaps in his 2-story, octagon-shaped, cantilevered drafting room. Intricate ceiling grilles add a special touch. Guided tours are available from 11 AM to 3 PM Mondays through Fridays, 11 AM to 4 PM weekends. 951 Chicago Ave., Oak Park (phone: 708-848-1500).

Lizzadro Museum of Lapidary Art – The collection of Oriental jade carvings is one of the most extensive in the US. About 150 exhibits show off cameos, gemstones, minerals, and fossils. Closed Mondays. Admission charge except on Fridays. 220 Cottage Hill, Elmhurst (phone: 708-833-1616).

Oak Park – Twenty-five buildings in this suburb, most of them remarkably contemporary looking, show the development of Frank Lloyd Wright's Prairie style of architecture. The architect's residence/workshop and Unity Temple are open to the public, and there are daily tours (except on holidays). Admission charge. Edgar Rice Burroughs's and Ernest Hemingway's homes are here, too, along with numerous gingerbread and turreted Queen Anne mansions. The Oak Park Tour Center, based in the Frank Lloyd Wright Home and Studio, operates most area walking tours as well as a visitors' center (at 158 N. Forest), where you can see photo exhibitions and take in an orientation program. At the *Wright Plus Festival,* the third Saturday in May, ten private homes are open to the public. For more information, call the Oak Park Visitor Center (phone: 708-848-1500).

O'Hare International Airport – Opened in 1955, the world's busiest airport was named for Congressional Medal of Honor recipient Edward O'Hare, a navy pilot killed at the Battle of Midway during World War II. In 1987, the addition of a new high-tech *United Airlines* terminal brought lavish praise from architects who described the building as "elegant and exciting." Nearly 57 million passengers pass through here annually. There are free 90-minute group tours of the airport terminals and taxi-ways daily; for tour information, call the Chicago Department of Aviation (phone: 686-2200).

Six Flags Great America – An extravagant roller coaster and a double-tiered carousel are the highlights of this theme park featuring more than 130 rides, shows, and attractions. Musical shows are performed throughout the season, and there's a special giant participatory play area for kids, complete with merry-go-rounds and rides. It also is home to the world's largest motion picture experience. Open daily beginning the week before *Memorial Day* through *Labor Day;* weekends May through September. Admission charge. I-94 at Rte. 132 in Gurnee (phone: 708-249-1776 or, for recorded information, 708-249-2020).

■**EXTRA SPECIAL:** You don't have to go very far from downtown to reach the North Shore suburbs. Follow US 41 or I-94 north. US 41 takes you past Lake Forest, an exquisite residential area, and Lake Bluff, site of the Great Lakes Naval Station. In Waukegan, *Mathon's* seafood restaurant has been delighting crustacean addicts since before World War II (2 blocks east of Sheridan Rd. near the lake on Clayton St.; phone: 708-662-3610; closed Mondays). Heading inland from Waukegan on Route 120 leads directly to lake country, past Gages Lake and *Brae Loch* golf course (Rte. 45, Wildwood; phone: 708-223-5542), Grays Lake, and Round Lake, where Route 120 becomes Route 134, continuing on to Long Lake, Duck Lake, and the three large lakes — Fox, Pistakee, and Grass, near the Wisconsin border. All of these lakes offer water sports, fishing, golf, and tennis. On the northern border with Wisconsin, the 4,900-acre Chain O'Lakes State Park has campsites and boat rental facilities. Pick up Wilson Road north at Long Lake, then take Route 132 past Fox Lake. This leads to US 12, which runs to Spring Grove and the state park (phone: 708-587-5512).

LOCAL SOURCES AND RESOURCES

TOURIST INFORMATION: The Chicago Tourism Council's Visitor Information Center, in the historic Water Tower (806 N. Michigan Ave. and Pearson St., Chicago, IL 60611; phone: 280-5740) distributes a downtown map that pinpoints major attractions and hotels. Chicago Visitor Eventline gives taped information on theater, sports, and special events (phone: 225-2323). Also get copies of these Chicago Transit Authority brochures: the *Chicago Street Directory,* which locates streets by their distance from State or Madison; the *CTA Route Map* of bus, subway, and El routes; and the *CTA Downtown Transit Map.* These are available at El and subway stations. For details, contact the Illinois Travel Information Center (310 S. Michigan Ave.; phone: 793-2094). Contact the Illinois state hotline (phone: 800-223-0121) for maps, calendars of events, health updates, and travel advisories.

A 24-hour hotline is available for quick and up-to-date information on restaurants, nightclubs, hotels, sports, comedy clubs, special events, and more (phone: ITS-CHGO, or 800-747-CHGO, from out-of-town). For information on flights arriving and departing O'Hare International Airport, delays, and even baggage carousel information, call 900-786-8686; the cost is 75¢ per minute.

The Chicago Architecture Foundation (CAF) conducts about 50 different architectural tours of the city. CAF Saturday bus tours cost $17 and leave at 9 AM from the Water Tower (806 N. Michigan Ave.) or 9:30 AM from the ArchiCenter (330 S. Dearborn St.; phone: 922-3431). The 4-hour tours may be booked in advance, although walk-in visitors are accepted if space is available. CAF also sponsors boat tours of the Chicago River from May through October. Days and times vary and some weekday tours are included, so it is best to call for a schedule (phone: 527-1977). The 90-minute tours cost $15 and leave from the North Pier's *Boat Club.* Recorded ArchiTour information is available by calling 782-1776.

For a listing of special events around the city, call the Mayor's Office of Special Events at 744-3315.

The best local guidebook is *Chicago Magazine's Guide to Chicago* (Chicago Guide; $8.95), an insider's look at the city for residents and visitors alike. For self-guided walking tours, see Ira J. Bach's architecturally oriented *Chicago on Foot* (Chicago Review; $14.95).

Local Coverage – *Sun-Times,* morning daily; *Tribune,* morning daily; *Reader,* weekly; *Chicago* magazine, monthly.

Television Stations – WBBM Channel 2–CBS; WMAQ Channel 5–NBC; WLS Channel 7–ABC; WGN Channel 9–superstation; WTTW Channel 11–PBS; WFLD Channel 32–Fox.

Radio Stations – AM: WMAQ 670 (news); WGN 720 (talk/sports); WBBM 780 (news); WLUP 1000 (rock). FM: WBEZ 91.5 (public radio for Chicago); WNUA 95.5 (smooth jazz); WBBM 96.3 (talk/news); WLUP 97.9 (rock); WFMT 98.7 (classical); WKQX 101.1 (classic rock); WGCI 107.5 (pop/rap).

Chicago also has four 24-hour Spanish language stations: WOJO 105.1 FM and AM stations WIND 560, WOPA 1200, and WTAQ 1300.

Food – *The New Good (But Cheap) Chicago Restaurant Book* by Jill and Ron Rohde (Ohio University Press; $4.95) and *Chicago* magazine's section of restaurant reviews.

GETTING AROUND: Bus, Subway, and El – *Chicago Transit Authority* operates bus, subway, and El services. For information, call 836-7000. There's also a do-it-yourself tour on public transport. One good round trip by public transportation starts in the Loop, goes through Lincoln Park, past the Historical Society, and into New Town on the No. 151 bus. When you've ridden enough, get off and catch the same bus going in the opposite direction. On Sundays and holidays, there also is a "Culture Bus," which stops at the *Art Institute,* the *Field Museum,* the *Shedd Aquarium,* the *Adler Planetarium,* the *Museum of Science and Industry,* the *Oriental Institute,* and the *DuSable Museum of African-American History.* It operates every half-hour from 11 AM to 5 PM, May through September.

Car Rental – All major national firms are represented. For further information about renting a car, see GETTING READY TO GO.

Taxi – Cabs can be hailed in the street or picked up at stands in front of the major hotels. You also can call one of Chicago's taxi services: *Yellow* and *Checker Cabs* (phone: 829-4222); *Flash Cab* (phone: 561-1444); *American United* (phone: 248-7600).

Train – *METRA* offers commuter service between the city and its suburbs. Trains depart from the Chicago and Northwestern Station (500 W. Madison) to the north and northwest suburbs, from Union Station (210 S. Canal) to the west and southwest suburbs, and from the Randolph Street (151 E. Randolph) and La Salle Street stations for the south suburbs (phone: 322-6777, 836-7000, or 800-972-7000). *Amtrak* (phone: 800-872-7245) departs from the Union Street Station. *American European Express* (phone: 226-5558) offers luxury overnight rail service 2 days a week between Chicago and Washington, DC, fashioned after Europe's *Orient Express.* The oversize presidential cabin ($829 per person, one way, double occupancy) has side-by-side lower berths, a private shower, a vanity, access to a club car decorated with hand-tooled leather-covered walls and hand-painted ceiling, plus first-rate dining with fine china and crystal goblets. Pricey, but fun; the west (Chicago) to east (DC) direction offers the best scenery during daylight hours.

LOCAL SERVICES: Audiovisual Equipment – *Audio Visual Systems* (phone: 733-3370); *Audio Visual Techniques* (phone: 527-0050).

Baby-sitting – Check at your hotel or contact the following: *America Child Care,* with licensed and insured baby-sitters who will care for children in a hotel suite or accompany youngsters over the age of 12 to museums and parks (505 N. Lake Shore Dr., Suite 210; phone: 644-7300); *Nursefinders* offers certified nurse's aides to care for adults with special needs or children for periods ranging from 4 hours and up (8 S. Michigan Ave., Suite 1500; phone: 263-1477); and *Nanny's Sitting Service* charges hourly for child care at hotels or in homes (103 Fern, Island Lake; phone: 708-526-2853).

Barbers – *Just Haircuts,* a male-only spot for haircuts (in the Monadnock Building at the corner of Van Buren and Federal Sts.; phone: 922-0904); *Truefitt & Hill,* the gentlemen's barber (900 N. Michigan Ave., 6th Floor; phone: 337-2525).

Business Services – *International Office Centers* (203 N. La Salle, Suite 2100; phone: 346-2030); *Express One* for rental of portable phones by the day, week, or month (phone: 800-CELL-ONE).

Carryout – *Room Service* takes phone orders for restaurants then sends the orders by fax to the kitchens of any of 14 North Side restaurants serving a variety of ethnic and standard food. Delivery vans with refrigerators and ovens speed the meal to customers within 70 minutes (or there is no charge). A $4 surcharge per order is added to the menu list price. Oprah Winfrey and Christie Hefner are among its celebrity customers (phone: 707-9300 and 737-8423).

Dry Cleaners – *Downtown Cleaners* (311 S. La Salle; phone: 939-3718; 1011 S. State; phone: 922-1011; and 407 S. Peoria; phone: 433-8174); *King Cleaners & Tailors* (16 E. Delaware; phone: 337-3896); *Pronto One-Hour Cleaners* (1700 W. Madison; phone: 666-8943); *Sewing Express Cleaners & Alterations* (803 W. Randolph; phone: 226-3110).

Eyeglass Repair/Replacement – The following usually offer same-day service and have optometrists on duty: *American Vision Center* (10 N. Michigan; phone: 346-0222; and 540 N. Michigan; phone: 6444-0885); *Dean Optical* (22 W. Monroe; phone: 332-4461); *Eyelines* (300 W. Washington; phone: 236-6460); *Ipco Optical* (28 W. Madison; phone: 782-7918) and at Chicago and North Western Atrium Center (500 W. Madison; phone: 930-5033); *LensCrafters* (205 N. Michigan Ave.; phone: 819-0205); *Pearle Vision Center* (134 N. La Salle; phone: 372-3204; 346 N. Michigan Ave.; phone: 726-8255; and 242 S. State; phone: 663-9122).

Limousine – *Airport Express Limousine Service,* 24 hours (phone: 227-1000).

Medical Emergency Service – *Northwestern Memorial Hospital,* Superior St. and Fairbanks Court (phone: 908-5222).

Messenger Services – *Cannonball Messenger Service* (phone: 829-1234); *Chicago Messenger Service* (phone: 666-6800).

Mechanics/Road Service – *Amoco* station (665 N. Dearborn; phone: 787-8164); *Automotive Towing Service* (895 N. Milwaukee; phone: 243-0600); *B's Brothers Service Station* (1940 N. Hayne; phone: 342-9215); *D'Agostino Standard* (841 W. Irving Park; phone: 528-1950); *First Alert Towing* (720 W. Grand; phone: 421-1449); *North & LaSalle Service* (140 W. North; phone: 944-9388).

National/International Courier – *Federal Express* (phone: 559-9000); *DHL Worldwide Courier Express* (phone: 708-456-3200).

Pharmacy – *Walgreen Drugs* is open from 7 AM to midnight, 1130 N. State St. (phone: 787-7035).

Photocopies – *Aims Copy Services* (69 W. Washington; phone: 332-2604); *Modern Impressions* (105 W. Madison St.; phone: 368-8445).

Photofinishing – The following do passport photos in an hour or less: *Fromex One Hour Photo System* (188 W. Washington; phone: 853-0067); *Magic 30 Minute Photo Lab* (320 W. Madison; phone: 630-0154); *Magna One-Hour Photo* (540 N. Michigan Ave.; phone: 527-0776); *Moto Photo* (500 W. Madison Ave.; phone: 707-8662); *One Hour Photo Hut* (141 W. Jackson; phone: 461-9497); *The Photo Center* (lower concourse John Hancock Center; phone: 337-4272); *Photo Pro One-Hour Lab* (204 N. Michigan Ave.; phone: 641-1133); *Photo 60* (212 W. North; phone: 787-6607).

Post Office – The main office is at 433 W. Van Buren St. (phone: 765-3210). Other branches are located at 211 S. Clark St. (phone: 427-4225) and 227 E. Ontario (phone: 642-7697).

Professional Photographer – *Photo Ideas* (phone: 666-3100); *Stuart-Rodgers-Reilly Photographers* (phone: 787-8696).

Secretary/Stenographer – *A Avenue Typing Service* (phone: 329-1223); *International Office Center* (phone: 346-2030 and 714-8222).

Shoe Repair – *Bee Hive Shoe Works* (1 N. Dearborn; phone: 236-4837; 11 N. Wells; phone: 263-4888; 320 N. Michigan Ave.; phone: 419-8444; and 79 E. Madison; phone: 419-1660); *Brooks Shoe Service* (55 E. Washington; phone: 372-2504); *Lupo's Shoe Repair* (401 N. Michigan Ave.; phone: 661-0111; and 303 E. Ohio; phone: 320-0173); *Sam the Shoe Doctor* (162 W. Van Buren; phone: 939-9571; 132 S. Franklin; phone: 332-9390; 101 W. Adams; phone: 332-8528; Sears Tower, lower level at Franklin St.; phone: 876-9001; and 173 N. Clark; phone: 283-8256).

Shoeshine – *Just Haircuts* (corner of Van Buren and Federal Sts.; phone: 922-0904); *Truefitt & Hill* (900 N. Michigan Ave., 6th Floor; phone: 337-2525).

Tailoring – *Lupo's Shoe Repair,* 401 N. Michigan Ave. (phone: 661-0111).

Translations – *Chicago-Europe Language Center* (208 S. La Salle, Suite CM-285; phone: 276-6683) arranges multilingual tours and other translation services. Check at your hotel for reliable services.

Teleconference Facilities – *Bismarck, Drake, Palmer House,* and *Sheraton-Plaza* hotels (see *Best in Town,* below).

Translator – *Berlitz* (phone: 782-6820); *Joan Masters & Sons* (phone: 787-3009).

Typewriter Rental – *Benbow Office Machines,* 2-week minimum (phone: 427-5969); *Mid-City Typewriter Exchange,* 1-week minimum (phone: 666-0745).

Western Union/Telex – Many locations around the city (phone: 800-325-6000).

Other – *A.S.A.P. Word Processing* (phone: 558-9333); *Business Center,* desk space and typewriters, conference rooms, photocopying, in the *O'Hare Hilton* (phone: 686-8000); *H.Q. Headquarters Company* (phone: 372-2525 or 642-5100), word processing, telex, facsimile, conference rooms; *Woodstock Conference Center,* modern facilities for groups of up to 50 in an 80-acre rustic setting, 50 miles from O'Hare and equidistant from Chicago, Milwaukee, and Madison (in Woodstock, Illinois; phone: 815-338-3600).

 SPECIAL EVENTS: Chicago still boasts a large Irish population and on *St. Patrick's Day,* even those who have no roots in the "Auld Sod" don green and become Irish for a day. The official *St. Patrick's Day Parade,* which starts at Dearborn Avenue and runs from Wacker to Van Buren is held on the Saturday closest to March 17. For details, phone: 263-6612; but on the saint's day itself, there is a separate *South Side Irish St. Patrick's Day Parade* (phone: 238-1969). Chicago plunges wholeheartedly into this holiday; even the Chicago River is dyed green for the occasion.

Summertime is festival time. In June, rhythm and blues fills the air at the *Chicago Blues Festival* in Grant Park (phone: 744-3315). A week earlier is the 2-day *Gospel*

Festival, also at Grant Park (phone: 744-3315). Later in June is the *Old Town Art Fair* at Lincoln Park and to close out the month, millions of hungry Chicagoans and visitors turn out for the week-long *Taste of Chicago,* at which city restaurants set up booths and offer samples of the Windy City's best — and most ethnically diverse — cooking; the culinary festivities end with a rousing *Fourth of July* celebration. Late July marks the annual Chicago–to–Mackinac Island yacht race with boats leaving from Monroe Street Harbor (phone: 861-7777).

In September, *"Viva! Chicago,"* a 2-day celebration of Latin music, attracts lovers of salsa, merengue, mambo, and samba to Grant Park to listen and dance to the music of such internationally known musicians as Tito Puente and Mongo Santa Maria. For information, call 744-3315. Chicago's *Jazz Festival,* which started in 1978, is the city's longest running free lakefront festival. Past lineups of performers at the 4-day jazz festival have included Ray Charles, Miles Davis, Ella Fitzgerald, Dave Brubeck, George Benson, Sarah Vaughn, and B.B. King (phone: 744-3370).

Oktoberfest, in mid-September, is sponsored by the *Berghoff* restaurant and is held on Adams Street from State to Dearborn. During the last weekend in September, the *Latino Film Festival* offers 10 days of films at theaters around the city. For locations and film listings, call 431-1330 or 935-5744. September also brings former *Chicago Tribune* columnist Mike Royko's annual *Ribfest* — the largest spareribs-cooking competition in the country — at Grant Park, north of the *Field Museum of Natural History.*

Since 1965, Chicago has hosted an international film festival, a tradition that continues during 2 weeks every October. Various theaters on the city's north side screen the long list of films; a schedule is available by calling 644-FILM.

Other musical events include the *Chicago Folk Festival,* sponsored by the University of Chicago in early February and featuring folk music, arts, and crafts and food (phone: 702-9793), as well as the *Ravinia Festival,* a series of outdoor concerts by the *Chicago Symphony Orchestra* held throughout the summer in Highland Park (phone: RAVINIA).

In August, the *Western Open Golf Tournament* is played at *Butler National Golf Club* in Oakbrook. The *Arlington Million,* the world's richest thoroughbred race, is held the last week of August at *Arlington Park.*

 MUSEUMS: Chicago is paradise if you like going to museums. Those described in *Special Places* have plenty of company, including the following:
Balzekas Museum of Lithuanian Culture – Has dolls, textiles, folk art, antique weapons and a hands-on children's museum. 6500 S. Pulaski Rd. (phone: 582-6500).

Chicago Sports Hall of Fame – Everything you ever wanted to know about the Windy City's teams and athletes — and more. 227 W. Ontario St. (phone: 943-3086).

Museum of Holography – More than 75 three-dimensional images created by lasers are displayed. 1134 W. Washington Blvd. (phone: 226-1007).

Polish Museum of America – Offers 350 paintings by Polish and Polish-American artists, costumes and a 30,000-volume library. 984 N. Milwaukee Ave. (phone: 384-3352).

Spertus Museum of Judaica – Special Holocaust exhibit along with a collection that spans 3,500 years of Jewish history. 618 S. Michigan Ave. (phone: 922-9012).

Swedish-American Museum – Historic documents plus works of famous Swedish artists, including Carl Larson and Anders Zorn; at *Christmas,* there is a traditional Swedish *Festival of Lights* complete with candles, *Christmas* decorations, and songs. 5211 N. Clark Ave. (phone: 728-8111).

Ukrainian National Museum – A large collection of folk art, including Ukrainian ceramics, *Easter* eggs, and costumes. 2453 W. Chicago (phone: 384-6482).

Vietnam Museum – Right in the Argyle (New Chinatown) District, this tiny — and poorly marked — museum has exhibits featuring military, civilian, and cultural war memorabilia from 1954 to 1980. 5002 N. Broadway (phone: 728-6111).

Great sculpture and art also can be seen in the plazas of downtown skyscrapers: Bertoia's spellbinding *Sounding Sculpture,* at the Standard Oil Bldg. (200 E. Randolph); *Flamingo,* a stabile by Alexander Calder, at Federal Center Plaza (Adams and Dearborn); Calder's gaily colored mobile *Universe,* in the Sears Tower lobby (Wacker and Adams); sculptor Claes Oldenburg's 101-foot-high baseball bat, *Batcolumn* (600 W. Madison); and Chagall's *Four Seasons* mosaic, at First National Plaza (Monroe and Dearborn). For more information see *Walk 2: The Loop's Alfresco Museum* in DIRECTIONS.

And don't miss the roof art. There are four wind-powered sculptures, each weighing more than a ton, atop the city's new $30 million *Sporting Club* (211 North Stetson Dr. near the *Fairmont* hotel). *Children of the Sun,* the 17-foot-tall rotating sculpture by Japanese artist Susumu Shingu, is made of stainless steel pipe and punched metal.

■ **Note:** If you're at First National Plaza at noon, you might catch a free concert. *Chicago's Picasso* (its formal title because no one could agree on a name), a giant sculpture, is at the Richard J. Daley Plaza (on Washington and Clark near the Chagall). There are free concerts at the plaza every weekday, weather permitting. Joan Miró's *Chicago* sculpture mural is across the street from Daley Plaza. Buckingham Fountain, a Chicago landmark in Grant Park at Congress Parkway, is illuminated from May to September.

MAJOR COLLEGES AND UNIVERSITIES: Although far too big to be called a college town, Chicago has many fine universities. The University of Chicago, known for its economics and social science departments, has its main entrance at 5801 S. Ellis Ave. (phone: 753-1234); De Paul University (25 E. Jackson and in Lincoln Park at 2323 N. Seminary; phone: 341-8000); Illinois Institute of Technology (3300 S. Federal; phone: 567-3000); Lake Forest College (Sheridan Rd., Lake Forest; phone: 708-234-3100); Loyola University (820 N. Michigan; phone: 670-3000; and 6525 Sheridan Rd.; phone: 274-3000); Northwestern University (Chicago Ave. and Lake Shore Dr.; phone: 908-8649; and in Evanston; phone: 708-491-5000); Roosevelt University (430 S. Michigan Ave.; phone: 341-3500); University of Illinois at Chicago (601 S. Morgan; phone: 996-3000).

SHOPPING: Some of Chicago's best sights are indoors, along the aisles of the city's many shops and department stores. While Los Angeles boasts Rodeo Drive and New York has Fifth Avenue, in Chicago the chic shopping district is known as the Magnificent Mile, the blocks along North Michigan Avenue between the Chicago River and Oak Street. Along the Magnificent Mile is *900 N. Michigan,* an enclosed mall of elegant stores; a block away is *Water Tower Place,* another elegant indoor mall; *Chicago Place,* a new 8-level enclave of upscale shops is at 700 N. Michigan Avenue. Oak Street just west of Michigan is lined with international designer shops. There also is a gallery of shops in the renovated industrial buildings at 1800 N. Clybourn and the *Atrium Mall* in the State of Illinois Center (100 W. Randolph, level 2). For Chicagoans, the traditional shopping area is State Street, where local favorites like *Marshall Field* and *Carson Pirie Scott* are found.

North Pier Chicago, a renovated multi-use building that was formerly a shipping terminal, has 3 floors filled with dozens of unusual shops and restaurants as well as museums and gamerooms. Locals looking for fine jewelry at good prices head for the *Mallers Building* (5 N. Wabash St.), which features 16 floors of retail and wholesale jewelry stores. And Hyde Park, a neighborhood near the University of Chicago, is the place for bookworms.

And for flea market aficionados, every Sunday, the Italian neighborhood of Market Street turns into Chicago's largest outdoor bargain spot. Get here early — the good stuff is gone by 10 AM — for everything from used clothes to antiques. There are strolling musicians and stands serving good ethnic food. Open 6 AM to noon. Maxwell at 1300 S. Halsted.

Accent Chicago – Every item in stock has "Chicago" imprinted on it — and we mean everything. *Water Tower Place,* level 7 (phone: 944-1354).

Alfred Dunhill – Men's clothes with a corporate look and a British touch (even some of the salespeople are British). *Water Tower Place,* level 2 (phone: 467-4455).

Archicenter – Although this is actually the museum/office for the Chicago Architecture Foundation, it also has one of the most complete gift shops for those seeking architecture-theme souvenirs of their visit, including children's gifts. Its book collection is especially impressive. 350 S. Dearborn (phone: 922-3431/2).

Ark Thrift Shop – Three floors packed with furniture, pictures, clothes, and collectibles, run by the Jewish Federation of Chicago. 3345 N. Lincoln (phone: 248-1117).

Avventura – Some of the showiest men's shoes anywhere, plus more traditional footwear, ties, and belts. It's worth a trip here just to see the giant black cowboy boots with the red bull on front and No. 23 on back, custom designed for Michael Jordan. *Water Tower Place,* level 4 (phone: 337-3700).

Banana Republic – The chain that prepares you for the urban jungle has great sales. Try on the safari gear for an exotic escape. *Water Tower Place,* level 4 (phone: 642-7667).

Bang & Olufsen – The thinnest of the thin in new electronic equipment; for the minimalist crowd. 15 E. Oak St. (phone: 787-6006).

Beauty & the Beast – A stuffed toy animal jungle with everything from a life-size tiger to a talking parrot. *Water Tower Place,* level 7 (phone: 944-7570).

Benkendorf Collection – Fine antique clocks, including English and French timepieces from the 17th and 19th centuries. *900 N. Michigan,* level 1 (phone: 951-1903).

Bloomingdale's – The Midwest flagship store for this legendary New York retailer has 6 floors of merchandise plus 4 spas and 2 restaurants. The Art Deco touches are a plus. *900 N. Michigan* (phone: 440-4460).

Bottega Veneta – Fine Italian leather items, carefully crafted and tastefully displayed. Everything from luggage to desk accessories, plus a small selection of women's shoes and scarves. 107 E. Oak St. (phone; 664-3220).

Burberry's – Classic trench coats and other weatherproofs are the tradition here; also a wide range of men's and women's fair-weather apparel and accessories. 633 N. Michigan Ave. (phone: 787-2500).

Carson Pirie Scott – The more than 130-year-old tradition of the Windy City has 7 floors of fashion and furnishings. Even if you aren't in a spending mood, stop by to see the elegant building, designed by architect Louis Sullivan. Corner of Madison and State Sts. (phone: 744-2000).

Cartier – The Midwest outpost of the fine French jeweler. 630 N. Michigan Ave. (phone: 266-7440).

Cashmere Cashmere – As the name implies, everything here is cashmere. *900 N. Michigan,* level 4 (phone: 337-7558).

C.D. Peacock – This landmark, founded the same year Chicago became a city, has silver, crystal, jewelry, and fine china. 101 S. State St. (phone: 630-5700).

Chanel – Classic clothes and accessories from this world-famous name. 940 N. Michigan Ave. (phone: 787-5500).

City – Avant-garde furniture. 361 W. Chestnut St. (phone: 664-9581).

City of Chicago – The place for memorabilia and souvenirs, this store carries everything from tote bags to a Chicago manhole cover, including posters, sculpture, books, street banners, calendars, T-shirts, crafts — and the ever-popular Chicago street signs. Pick up one in stock for $35 or special order a custom-made sign for $40. 174 W. Randolph St. (phone: 332-0055).

Custom Shop Tailors – Custom-fit shirts, ties, suits, slacks, overcoats, and blazers for men. Also made-to-order blouses for women. *Water Tower Place,* level 3 (phone: 943-0444) and *900 N. Michigan,* level 2 (phone: 337-7979).

The Disney Store – Every Mickey Mouse memento imaginable — and those of his Disney pals as well. *Water Tower Place,* level 4 (phone: 280-1199).

Eddie Bauer – Come here for rugged sportswear and accessories like Ray-Ban sunglasses, canvas lunch bags, and great compasses. *Water Tower Place,* level 6 (phone: 337-4353) and 123 N. Wabash Ave. (phone: 263-6005).

Famous Fido's – Just about everything for dogs and cats, including the "Famous Fido's Doggie Deli" with a dining area and carryout of all-natural dog food, pet treats, and cakes. 1533 W. Devon Ave. (phone: 973-3436).

Fannie May – Chicago's favorite chocolates for more than 7 decades are sold in more than 100 shops around the city although its best-known outlets are at *Water Tower Place* (phone: 664-0420) and *North Pier* (phone: 527-9372).

FAO Schwarz – Kiddie heaven, with dolls, stuffed animals, and video games galore. Grownups don't have a bad time here, either. *Water Tower,* level 2 (phone: 787-8894).

Feline Inn – A celebration of cats, packed with everything you can imagine — from clothes to coat hangers — with felines emblazoned on each item. 1445 N. Wells (phone: 943-2230).

Furniture Tronics – A futuristic boutique of electronic items. *900 N. Michigan,* level 5 (phone: 664-9292).

Gianni Versace – This Italian designer's 2-story boutique is stocked with the latest of his European fashions. 101 E. Oak St. (phone: 337-1111).

Godiva Chocolatier – Belgian chocolates packaged in classy gold wrappers, plus cappuccino and espresso. 845 N. Michigan Ave. (phone: 280-1133).

The Goldsmith – Custom-designed jewelry, plus a great selection of antique gems — and a repair service. *Water Tower Place,* level 2 (phone: 751-1986).

Hammacher Schlemmer – Everything imaginable in classy and unique gifts, ranging from heated pet beds to a personalized Wurlitzer jukebox, along with a wide variety of kitchen and electronic gadgets. 618 N. Michigan Ave. (phone: 664-9292).

Hermès – The ultimate in scarves and leather goods from the fine French designer. 110 E. Oak St. (phone: 787-8175).

Illinois Artisans Shop – A wide array of items made by the state's top craftspeople. 100 W. Randolph St. (phone: 814-5321).

Isis – Unusual fashions for women, all in one-size-fits-all, including hand-painted items, fringed jackets, and parachute-silk skirts. 38 E. Oak St. (phone: 664-7076).

Marshall Field – Everything from rare books and Frango mints to wardrobe coordinators and foreign language translators at the two downtown stores of this Chicago landmark. At press time the flagship store (111 N. State St.; phone: 781-1000) was undergoing the largest renovation in retailing history. The second downtown location is at *Water Tower Place* (phone: 781-1234).

Neiman Marcus – Designer clothes, furs, perfume, and jewelry are just some of the goodies available in one of the trendiest stops along the Miracle Mile. 737 N. Michigan Ave. (phone: 642-5900).

Network – The NBC Tower also is home to a shop that carries NBC memorabilia, plus T-shirts emblazoned with the names of your favorite TV shows. 455 N. Columbus Dr. (phone: 836-5555).

North Beach Leather – Trendy leather fashions for men and women; repair service, too. *Water Tower Place,* level 3 (phone: 280-9292).

Nuts on Clark – Gourmet nuts, coffee, wine, exotic teas, fruit, and chocolate are featured at this 30,000-square-foot store, just 2 blocks north of *Wrigley Field.* Open Mondays through Saturdays 9 AM to 6 PM, Sundays 10 AM to 2 PM. 3830 N. Clark (phone: 549-6622).

Pavo Real Boutique – Sweaters from Peru and Bolivia plus handmade jewelry crafted by local and international artists. *Water Tower Place,* level 7 (phone: 944-1390).

Pea in the Pod – Wearer-friendly maternity fashions from classic work suits to flashy sportswear, 46 E. Oak St. (phone: 337-6604).

Pompian – Pricey designer togs (like a $470 silk T-shirt) for women from around the world. 57 E. Oak St. (phone: 337-6604).

Reckless Records – Selections of alternative rock, imports, and independent music artists. The shop claims to have the largest selection of used albums in the city. 3157 N. Broadway (phone: 404-5080).

Rizzoli – Best sellers, plus a wide array of art, architecture, history, and children's books; an extensive paperback section; European magazines; CDs; stationery; and cassettes. *Water Tower Place,* level 3 (phone: 642-3500).

Saks Fifth Avenue – Apparel and accessories are complemented by a good beauty salon at the store known for its personalized service. 700 N. Michigan Ave. (phone: 944-6500).

Stuart Chicago – Italian imports for men ranging from sportswear to formal attire. 102 E. Oak St. (phone: 266-9881).

Sugar Magnolia – African-print skirts, funky children's clothes, and silk-screened ties. 34 E. Oak St. (phone: 944-0885).

Terri D – One of the standouts on Oak Street, with merchandise ranging from whimsical toy-inspired jewelry to sequin jackets and classic dresses. 59 E. Oak St. (phone: 787-9600).

Theodora – Unusual boutique offering everything from hand-crocheted skirts to 1950s paisley shirts, 50 E. Oak St. (phone: 266-2285).

Tiffany & Co. – The Midwest branch of the place where Audrey Hepburn breakfasted. 715 N. Michigan Ave. (phone: 944-7500).

Ultimo – Men's designer fashions; plus women's apparel, shoes, and jewelry. 114 E. Oak St. (phone: 787-0906).

A Unique Presence – Exceptional crafts and gifts in a year-round art fair atmosphere. Unusual items from more than 175 North American artists, including ceramics, blown glass, wood, handmade paper, leather, and an array of handmade jewelry. 212 N. Clybourn (phone: 929-4292).

Women & Children First – The only truly feminist bookstore in the city offers regular book signings and special events linked to feminism in literature. 5233 N. Clark St. (phone: 769-9299).

■ **Note:** If you don't want to traipse, but still want to take advantage of Chicago's chic stores, call any of the city's major department stores for personal shoppers. At *Carson Pirie Scott,* it's mainly a catalogue-type affair, but personal shoppers at *Neiman Marcus* even make house (or hotel) calls. *Bloomingdale's* has separate personal shopper services for men and women.

 SPORTS AND FITNESS: Plenty of major-league action in town.

Baseball – The *White Sox* play at the new *Comiskey Park* (35th and Shields, off the Dan Ryan Expy.; phone: 924-1000). Seating 43,500 spectators, this state-of-the-art park is equipped with more efficient escalators and elevators, plus numerous services and concessions for the fans. The *Cubs* play at *Wrigley Field* (Addison and Clark; phone: 281-5050), now occasionally at night.

Basketball – The 1991 NBA champion *Bulls* play at *Chicago Stadium,* 1800 W. Madison (phone: 733-5300).

Bicycling – Chicago has a glorious bike path along the shore of Lake Michigan, running from the Loop to the North side — about 6 miles. You can rent bikes in summer from the concession at Lincoln Park.

Bocce – Remember how good Marlon Brando looked playing this Italian bowling game in *The Godfather?* The almost 400 members of the *Highland Bocce Club* gather at *Highwood Bocce Court,* beneath an Italian deli and the train tracks, to play in good weather. 440 Bank Lane (phone: 708-432-9804). There also are bocce courts at three city parks: McGuane Park (290 S. Poplar Ave.), Riis Park (6110 W. Fullerton Ave.), and Smith Park (2526 W. Grand Ave.).

Bowling – Turn back the clock 35 years and try *Leo and Ella's Southport Lanes,* where Leo and Ella Beitz still employ pin boys for their four alleys. *Inside Chicago* magazine's readers rate this as the best of its kind. 3325 N. Southport (phone: 472-1601).

Cricket – Games sponsored by the United Cricket Conference are played Sundays at noon until mid-September in Washington Park (55th St. and King Dr.); also at James Park (Oakton and Dodge Sts. in Evanston). For schedule information, call 768-7515.

Fishing – After work, people flock to the rocks along the shore, casting nets for smelt. The rocks around Northwestern University at Evanston are especially popular. There's also an artificial island, accessible by footbridge, near Northwestern.

Fitness Centers – *Body Elite* (445 W. Erie; phone: 664-5710) and *Combined Fitness Centre* (1235 N. La Salle; phone: 787-8400) both allow non-members for a fee.

Football – The NFL *Bears* (phone: 663-5100) play at *Soldier Field.*

Golf – Chicago has 18 public golf courses, some along the lakeshore. The most accessible municipal course is *Waveland* in Lincoln Park. *Brae Loch* in Wildwood (phone: 708-223-5542) is mentioned under *Special Places.* The Chicago Park District offers golf instruction. For information, call 294-2274. There also is a new indoor golf facility, *Klubs Golf* (behind the *Sofitel* hotel, 5551 Milton Pkwy. in Rosemont, west of River Rd. at Bryn Mawr), with putting greens, practice sand traps, professionals on hand, a pro shop, and videotape lessons (phone: 708-671-5858).

Hiking – *Windy City Grotto,* the Chicago Chapter of the *National Speleological Society,* organizes frequent field trips to cave country in southern Indiana and Missouri. For information, contact *Windy City Speleonews* (c/o Bill Mixon, 5035 N. South Drexel, Chicago, IL 60615). *Chicago Mountaineering Club* organizes weekend expeditions and teaches safe climbing techniques. They meet at the *Field Museum* every second Monday. For information, write to them (PO Box 1025, Chicago, IL 60690). The *Sierra Club* (53 W. Jackson; phone: 431-0158) also organizes outings.

Hockey – The NHL *Black Hawks* play in *Chicago Stadium* from September through April (phone: 733-5300).

Horse Racing – Horses race at four tracks in the Chicago area:

Arlington Park, Euclid Ave. and Wilke Rd., Arlington Heights (phone: 708-255-4300)

Hawthorne, 3501 S. Laramie, Cicero (phone: 708-780-3700)

Maywood Park, North and 5th Aves., Maywood (phone: 708-626-4816)

Sportsman's Park, 3301 S. Laramie, Cicero (phone: 708-242-1121)

Ice Skating – Once temperatures dip below 45F, ice skating begins at Daley Bicentennial Plaza (337 E. Randolph St.; phone: 294-4790). Skate rentals are available at the plaza. There also is ice skating year round at the indoor rink at *McFetridge Sports Center* (3843 N. California Ave.; phone: 478-0211). Call in advance for skating hours.

Jogging – Run along Lake Shore Drive to Lincoln Park; there is a 5-mile track inside the park. Or simply do as many Chicagoans do and jog along the lakefront, accessible via numerous pedestrian walkways.

Polo – Summers at the *Oak Brook Polo Club* (3500 Midwest Ave., Oak Brook;

phone: 708-325-5566); during winter you can play indoors at the *Chicago Armory* (Chicago Ave. and Fairbanks).

Sailing – Lake Michigan offers superb sailing, but as experienced sailors can tell you, the lake is deceptive. Storms with winds of up to 40 knots can blow in suddenly. Check with the Coast Guard before going out (phone: 219-949-7440). You can rent boats and take sailing lessons from *City Sailors* (phone: 975-0044). There are a few marinas between the Loop and Evanston and others along suburban shores. Highland Park is one of the most popular city marinas.

Skiing – There are more than 50 ski clubs in the Chicago area. For information, contact the *Chicago Metro Ski Council,* PO Box 7926, Chicago, IL 60680 (phone: 346-1268).

Soccer – Montrose, with 4 fields, is *the* soccer place. Walk up the 32-foot Cricket Hill for a bird's-eye view of the games. The *International Soccer League* plays on Sundays; the less popular, though equally enthusiastic, *Central American Soccer League* plays Saturdays. Weekend games start in the summer and run all day from 8 AM to 6 PM through October.

Swimming – Beaches line the shore of Lake Michigan. Those just to the north of the Loop off Lake Shore Drive are the most popular and often the most crowded. Oak Street Beach along the Gold Coast is the most fashionable beach. If you go farther north, you'll find fewer people. The Chicago Park District offers swimming lessons at some of the 72 city pools. The best are at Wells Park and Gill Park. For information, call 294-2333.

Tennis – The city has 708 outdoor municipal courts. The best are at Randolph and Lake Shore Drive, just east of the Loop (phone: 294-4792). For other tennis information, call 294-2314.

Tobogganing – The Cook County Forest Preserve District operates 14 slides at five locations from 10 AM to 10 PM daily when the weather allows. Equipment rentals are available. Call 261-8400 for details.

 THEATERS: For schedules and ticket information, check the publications listed in "Tourism Information" in GETTING READY TO GO or visit a League of Chicago Theatres' *Hot Tix* booth (24 S. State St.; in Evanston, at the Sherman Ave. garage between Church and Davis Sts.; and in Oak Park, at *Lake Theatre,* 1020 Lake St.) selling full-price, advance sale tickets and half-price day-of-sale tickets for cash only Mondays through Saturdays. (Half-price Sunday tickets are sold the day before). The League of Chicago Theatres also runs a 24-hour phone information line with performance schedules (phone: 977-1755). *THEATRE TIX* takes phone orders for full-price, advance sale tickets (phone: 902-1919).

The main Chicago theaters are the *Shubert* (22 W. Monroe; phone: 977-1700); *Civic* (20 N. Wacker Dr.; phone: 346-0270); the *Blackstone* (60 E. Balbo; phone: 977-1700); and the *Apollo Theater Center* (2540 N. Lincoln; phone: 935-6100). The *Goodman Theatre,* a tradition since 1925, stages new plays and contemporary productions (200 S. Columbus; phone: 443-3800).

Off-Loop houses are new theaters and converted warehouses and garages, mostly on the near north side. Productions here have gone on to Broadway or network TV. Chicago's Off-Loop district includes the *Steppenwolf Theatre* (1650 N. Halsted; phone: 385-1650), with an internationally acclaimed company that moved down Halsted Street last year to a larger 500-seat complex. This company has grown considerably since its start in a suburban garage in the 1970s. Other thriving Off-Loop theaters are *Organic* (3319 N. Clark; phone: 327-5588); *Victory Gardens,* dedicated to the works of Chicago playwrights — Steve Carter and Jane Sherman are particular favorites (2257 N. Lincoln; phone: 549-5788); *Wisdom Bridge* (1559 W. Howard; phone: 743-6442); and *Body Politic* (2261 N. Lincoln; phone: 871-3000).

Dinner theaters include *Drury Lane South* (2500 W. 95th, Evergreen Park; phone: 779-4000); *Pheasant Run* (Pheasant Run Lodge, Rte. 64, St. Charles; phone: 584-1454); and the *Candlelight Playhouse,* the nation's first dinner theater (5620 S. Harlem Ave. in Summit; phone: 496-3000).

Experimental theater is staged by the *Pegasus Players* at various locations (phone: 271-2638) and *Next Theatre Company* (927 Noyes St. in Evanston; phone: 708-475-1875). Fans of the extreme cutting edge head to *Theater Oobleck* (3829 N. Broadway; phone: 384-3346). The *Latino Chicago Theater Company* performs at *The Firehouse* (1625 N. Damen; phone: 486-5120).

Chicago's arts and theater community in recent years has given more attention to poets with innovative forums called "Poetry Slams." In best beat tradition, these gatherings feature Chicago's top performance poets who listen, read, and compete at the nationally recognized *Uptown Poetry Slam,* held Sundays at the *Green Mill* cocktail lounge (4802 N. Broadway; phone: 878-5522); the open mike starts at 7 PM, performance poets come on an hour later, and the slam competition begins at 9 PM. The *West Side Poetry Slam* is geared toward a more genteel audience, which is encouraged to participate on Tuesdays at *Fitzgerald's* (6615 W. Roosevelt Rd. in Berwyn; phone: 708-788-2118).

Fans of classic, foreign, or art films will find them at *Facets Multimedia* (555 W. Belden; phone: 281-9075), the *Film Center of the Art Institute* (Columbus Dr. at Jackson Blvd.; phone: 443-3737), and *Fine Arts Theater* (418 S. Michigan Ave.; phone: 939-3700). For a golden-age film experience, try the *Music Box,* with its mammoth screen, sky ceiling with winking stars and moving clouds, dramatic lobby — and great popcorn. Films shown here are Hollywood standards, foreign fare, and some independents (3733 N. Southport Ave.; phone: 871-6604). The *Biograph,* where John Dillinger was gunned down, also still shows films (2433 N. Lincoln; phone: 348-4123).

MUSIC: Chicago isn't the musical desert that the Midwest once was thought to be. Good music (and lots of it) can be heard all over the place. The world-renowned *Chicago Symphony Orchestra,* under the baton of Daniel Barenboim, can be heard from late September until early June at *Orchestra Hall,* a National Landmark Building (220 S. Michigan Ave.; phone: 435-6666). The orchestra also plays at the *Ravinia Festival* outside the city in Highland Park from late June through August (1575 Oakwood Ave. at Lake-Cook and Green Bay Rds.; phone: 708-433-8800). Don't miss the *Grant Park Symphony,* which plays four times weekly in the summer under the stars along Lake Michigan. Concerts are free; audiences usually pack picnic dinners and sit out on the lawn. Another favorite is the *Chicago Sinfonietta,* a professional orchestra that performs classical, romantic, and contemporary music (7900 W. Division in River Forest; phone: 366-1062).

Some of the hottest tickets in town from September to February are for performances of the *Chicago Lyric Opera,* which stages classics and new productions at the *Civic Center for Performing Arts* (20 N. Wacker Dr.; phone: 346-0270). *Chamber Music Chicago* (phone: 242-6237) performs at *Orchestra Hall* and the *Blackstone Theatre* (60 E. Balbo; phone: 362-8455). A new company, the *Chicago Opera Theatre* (phone: 663-0048), has been receiving good reviews and is attracting a growing number of supporters. Its performances (which are in English) can be seen at various locations, including the *Athenaeum Theatre* (2936 N. Southport St.; phone: 525-0195), from February through the end of May.

As for dance, the newly formed *Ballet Chicago* presents classical ballet, the *Hubbard Street Dance Company* and the *Joel Hall Dance Company* are known for jazz, modern dance is the forte of the *Joseph Holmes Dance Company,* and the *Chicago Repertory Dance Ensemble* stages classical and modern dance. For up-to-date listings of dance performances and their locations, check the Friday and Sunday editions of the *Chicago*

Tribune and *Chicago Sun-Times;* the *Reader; Chicago* magazine or call the *Dance Hotline* (phone: 419-8383).

 NIGHTCLUBS AND NIGHTLIFE: Don't leave the Windy City without taking in some of its fine blues, jazz, reggae, and folk music; you can listen or dance. Or try an offbeat bar, a neighborhood sports pub, or a comedy club in one of the few Midwest cities where nightlife lasts until dawn.

Chicago's blues tradition is a revered one, and some of the country's finest blues performers can be found in a handful of clubs around the city. *Blue Chicago* is the newest and is convenient for both the after-work crowd and out-of-towners staying in the Loop. This bar books big-time acts and its prices are reasonable (937 N. State St.; phone: 642-6261). Crowded *B.L.U.E.S.* is built around solid blues acts and a lively environment (2519 N. Halsted; phone: 528-1012) and a sister club, the roomy *B.L.U.E.S. Etcetera,* appeals to people who think they don't like blues but who can be drawn by such favorites as Bo Diddley and Albert King (1124 W. Belmont Ave.; phone: 525-8989). At *Buddy Guy's Legends,* in the former home of Chess Records, bluesman Guy holds court over new and veteran acts (754 S. Wabash; phone: 427-0333). But Chicago's standout jazz club is *Kingston Mines,* where local blues musicians — and celebrities — go after other clubs have closed for music that goes on until the wee hours (2548 N. Halsted St.; phone: 477-4646).

As strong as the city's blues legacy is its love of jazz. At *Andy's Lounge,* patrons dressed in anything from T-shirts to suits, enjoy an array of jazz from 5 to 8:30 PM weeknights (11 E. Hubbard St.; phone: 642-6805). The *Cotton Club* (1710 S. Michigan Ave.; phone: 341-9787), with its photos of the stars of the original *Harlem* club, has an open mike on Mondays that attracts novices and old hands alike (1710 S. Michigan Ave.; phone: 341-9787). Joe Segal's *Jazz Showcase* at the *Blackstone* hotel (636 S. Michigan Ave.; phone: 427-4300) is another favorite for live jazz, as is the *Get Me High Lounge,* an understated spot beside a railway overpass (1758 N. Honore; phone: 252-4090). *Green Mill* cocktail lounge looks like the Al Capone haunt it once was, with an ornate interior and live jazz 6 nights a week (4802 N. Broadway; phone: 878-5552). The *Jazz Hotline* provides information on performers and where they'll appear (phone: 427-3300).

Jazz also reigns supreme at *The Vic* (3145 N. Sheffield; phone: 472-0366) and *Byfields* (in the *Omni Ambassador East* hotel, 1301 N. State Pkwy.; phone: 787-6433). *Pops for Champagne* (2934 N. Sheffield Ave.; phone: 472-1000) is an unusual jazz nightclub with a formal French garden and a grand variety of champagnes to sip while you relax. *Toulouse* (49 W. Division St.; phone: 944-2606) has an intimate piano bar where Cole Porter's or Noël Coward's songs are heard; and *Yvette* (1206 N. State St.; phone: 280-1700) has enthusiastic twin piano duets.

Reggae is making inroads and it's always steamy at the *Wild Hare,* which features regional bands and touring Caribbean acts 7 nights a week (3530 N. Clark; phone: 327-0800). At the *Equator Club,* the in-crowd comes late for reggae, Afro-beat, calypso, soca, and hip-hop played by musicians from around the globe (4715 N. Broadway; phone: 728-2411).

Other nightspots include the *David Adler Cultural Center,* a suburban folk music mainstay with an open stage jam session most Fridays (1700 N. Milwaukee, Libertyville; phone: 708-367-0707). At *Earl's Pub,* for the price of a drink, patrons get amazing talent — as they have for the past 25 years (2470 N. Lincoln Ave.; phone: 929-0660), and at *No Exit,* chess, espresso and music — including folk, blues, and jazz — are heard (6970 Glenwood; phone: 743-3355). The *Old Town School of Folk Music,* a recently remodeled landmark, features a top-flight concert hall and is a cutting-edge outlet for traditional and world beat music (909 W. Armitage; phone: 525-7793).

Music isn't just an exhibition sport in the Windy City, where dance clubs abound.

Alcazar (2828 N. Broadway; phone: 929-7111) is where the cream of the city's art community go to dance. And at *Baja Beach Club* (404 E. Illinois; phone: 222-1992) even the staff gets into the act. Good alternative tunes draw a serious dance crowd onto the spacious floor at *Club 950-Lucky Number* (950 Wrightwood; phone: 929-8955). The *Shelter* (564 W. Fulton; phone: 648-5500) draws the radically chic, who flock here in hopes of spotting celebrities like *Aerosmith,* who drop by when in town. *Outtakes* is a cozy, upscale dance bar where the glass-topped bar doubles as a giant aquarium (16 W. Ontario; phone: 951-7979). *Avalon* is three clubs in one with alternative music, rock, and more relaxed cabaret fare from which to choose (959 W. Belmont; phone: 472-3020). *Jukebox Saturday Night* (2251 N. Lincoln; phone: 525-5000) is the place to dance to vintage 1950s and 1960s rock 'n' roll.

More informal pubs and taverns include *Johann's Wine Bar,* a European style wine bar with live classical music (10 E. Delaware Place; phone: 642-1170) and *John Barleycorn Memorial Pub,* where classical music soothes patrons trying any of 30 imported beers against a backdrop of prints of famous paintings and sculptures; in the summer, it has the city's most attractive outdoor beer gardens (658 W. Belden; phone: 348-8899). *Lucky's* is the trendy hangout of the young and beautiful, most of whom show up in something expensive and black (213 W. Institute Pl.; phone: 751-7777). Sports bars are also plentiful: *Gamekeepers* (345 W. Armitage; phone: 549-0400); *George & Valentina's* sports bar (3456 N. Damen; phone: 248-1173); *Justin's* with two satellite dishes and six TV sets (3358 N. Southport; phone: 929-4844); and *McGee's,* where the folks behind the bar say you can request any game you want on the projection TV set in the back room (corner of Harrison and Wells; phone: 554-1991).

■**COMIC RELIEF:** The biggest news for after-hours people has been an explosion of comedy clubs. Chicago has been a comedy center since the 1959 founding of *Second City,* whose graduates include Joan Rivers, David Steinberg, the Belushi brothers and much of the cast of *Saturday Night Live. Second City* and its spin-off, *Second City E.T.C.,* perform at 1608 and 1616 N. Wells St. (phone: 337-3992). Meanwhile, the *Comedy Womb* is a star-making club above the *Pines* restaurant (8030 W. Ogden in Lyons; phone: 708-442-5755) and *Second Zanies* play the best of the locals as well as such national talent as Jay Leno and Sam Kinnison (1548 N. Wells; phone: 337-4027). The *Improv* (504 N. Wells; phone: 782-6387), with 400 seats, is the largest comedy club in the Midwest and the top local spot for national talent. Comedians on the way to becoming household names are also found at *Catch A Rising Star* (1151 E. Wacker Dr.; phone: 565-4242) and *Funny Firm* (318 W. Grand; phone: 321-9500).

BEST IN TOWN

CHECKING IN: There are quite a number of interesting hotels in Chicago, varying in style from the intimate clubbiness of the *Tremont* and *Whitehall* to the supermodern elegance of the *Ritz-Carlton.* Unless otherwise noted, all listed here have at least one restaurant; the choice of eating places normally increases with the price of a room and the size of the hotel. Big hotels have shops, meeting places, and nightly entertainment. Rates in Chicago are higher than in most other midwestern cities: Expect to pay $150 to $220 for doubles in expensive hotels; $85 to $145 in those classified as moderate; and from $40 to $85 in those listed as inexpensive. If money is no object, ask for a room with a view. "Near North Side" hotels are close to New Town, Lincoln Park, and *Water Tower Place;* Loop locations (about

10 minutes away by taxi) are convenient to businesses and the fine old downtown department stores. For bed and breakfast accommodations, contact *Bed and Breakfast Chicago* (PO Box 14088, Chicago, IL 60614; phone: 951-0085).

The city government, in conjunction with dozens of hotels, offers special winter rates from September through March. The Chicago Office of Tourism can provide a list of hotels with reduced rates or special packages for visitors during the winter (or off season). There also is a new alternative to hotels. You can rent homes and apartments while their owners are away. Units are available in the downtown, Near North, Lakeshore, Lincoln Park, and nearby neighborhoods at prices starting at $50 per person per night. For more information contact the Chicago Department of Tourism (phone: 280-5740). All telephone numbers are in the 312 area code unless otherwise indicated.

Chicago Hilton and Towers – In 1985, about $150 million — the most ever spent on a hotel renovation — transformed this 30-story landmark building into a good-looking, modern property. The former *Conrad Hilton* now features 1,543 rooms, the most lavish of which is the 2-story Conrad Hilton Suite for $4,000 a night. Restored to their 1927 grandeur are the Great Hall and the Versailles-inspired Grand Ballroom. Facilities include a fitness center with an indoor running track, sun deck, exercise equipment, swimming pool, saunas, and whirlpool baths; there also is a computerized business center. Sometimes large groups of enthusiastic convention goers make it difficult to feel comfortable without a name tag. The Tower rooms are the most elegantly furnished, and have the added convenience of their own registration and checkout desk (on the 24th floor) — not an insignificant bonus when the hordes line up at the lobby cashier each AM. Check out *Kitty O'Shea's Pub* for good, simple fare (see *Eating Out*). There's a 140,000-square-foot convention center, a self-parking garage, and 21 rooms equipped for handicapped guests. For a fee, a telephone answering machine can be hooked up to your room phone. Amenities include 24-hour room service, concierge, 46 meeting rooms, secretarial services, A/V equipment, photocopiers, computers, CNN, and express checkout. 720 S. Michigan Ave. (phone: 922-4400; Fax: 312-922-5240; Telex: 62975566). Expensive.

Drake – A 535-room institution, with a graciousness not often found in hotels these days. The *Cape Cod Room* is Chicago's finest seafood eatery (see *Eating Out*). The hotel has 24-hour room service, concierge, 19 meeting rooms, secretarial services, A/V equipment, photocopiers, computers, CNN, and express checkout. Near North Side. N. Michigan Ave. at Lake Shore Dr. and Walton Pl. (phone: 787-2200; Fax: 312-787-1431; Telex: 27028). Expensive.

Embassy Suites – Located in downtown Chicago, this link in the all-suite hotel chain offers spacious "apartment-type" accommodations with all the service and convenience of a first-rate hotel. Suites have living room and dining areas, a small work area, kitchen (complete with microwave oven), bedroom, and bath; other amenities include an indoor fitness center and pool. There is valet service, complimentary morning newspaper, meeting/banquet space for groups of up to 30 people, and express checkout. 600 N. State St. (phone: 943-3800). Expensive.

Fairmont – Opulent and sophisticated, its 700 rooms and suites look out at the city skyline and Lake Michigan, and feature such appointments as marble bathrooms equipped with a TV set, telephone, and lighted dressing table. The hotel's supper club, *Moulin Rouge,* features top-name entertainment. There's also a bank of 12 meeting rooms with teleconference facilities and a spectacular penthouse boardroom with a panoramic view of the lake. Amenities include 24-hour room service, concierge, A/V equipment, photocopiers, computers, CNN, and express checkout. 200 N. Columbus Dr. (phone: 565-8000; Fax: 312-856-9020; Telex: 936092). Expensive.

Four Seasons – One of the city's newest luxury hotels occupies 19 floors of a stunning high-rise that also is home to the local branch of *Bloomingdale's*. There are 343 rooms (more than a third boast separate sitting rooms), an opulent Presidential Suite, and 16 residential apartments in this member of what is arguably the best managed hotel group in the world. Guest facilities include two-line telephones, lighted makeup mirrors, a spa, sauna, and indoor swimming pool. Other amenities are 24-hour room service, concierge, 12 meeting rooms, secretarial services, A/V equipment, photocopiers, computers, CNN, and express checkout. This is a luxury hotel worth the adjective. 120 E. Delaware Pl. (phone: 280-8800 or 800-332-3442; Fax: 312-280-9184; Telex: 00214923). Expensive.

Guest Quarters – This 345-suite complex, just east of Michigan Avenue, has a 30th-floor health club that offers panoramic views of the city and Lake Michigan, along with a pool, sauna, whirlpool bath, and exercise room. The *Cityside Bistro & Bar* offers live entertainment Mondays through Saturdays and dining at *Grille 198*. 198 E. Delaware Pl. (phone: 800-424-2900 or 664-1100). Expensive.

Hyatt Regency Chicago – The 2,000 rooms in its two ultramodern towers recently underwent a $20-million refurbishing. Conveniently located between the Loop and N. Michigan Ave. Fine dining at *Truffles*. Amenities include 24-hour room service, concierge, 102 meeting rooms, secretarial services, A/V equipment, photocopiers, computers, CNN, and express checkout. 151 E. Wacker Dr. (phone: 565-1000, 800-233-1234, or 800-228-9000; Fax: 312-565-2966; Telex: 256237). Expensive.

Hyatt Regency O'Hare – Ideal for a comfortable overnight stop between planes. There are 1,100 rooms and a health club. Amenities include 24-hour room service, concierge, 48 meeting rooms, secretarial services, A/V equipment, photocopiers, computers, CNN, and express checkout. South River Rd. exit off Kennedy Expy. (phone: 708-696-1234, 800-233-1234, or 800-228-9000; Fax: 708-696-1418; Telex: 282503). Expensive.

Hyatt Regency Suites – In the heart of downtown, this 347-suite link in the Hyatt chain has luxury amenities offered in an apartment-like setting. 676 N. Michigan Ave. and Huron (phone: 800-882-1234 or 337-1234). Expensive.

Inter-Continental – Two year's worth of restoration enhanced the sophisticated Biedermeier-style rooms and suites that distinguished the old *Medinah Athletic Club*. Built during the crash of 1929, the club has been transformed into a 337-room hotel overlooking Michigan Avenue. Butlers serve afternoon tea in a lobby sitting room. There is a concierge desk, as well as 11 meeting rooms, secretarial services, A/V equipment, photocopiers, computers, and express checkout. 505 N. Michigan Ave. (phone: 944-4100 or 800-327-0200; Fax: 312-944-3050; Telex 62654670). Expensive.

Mayfair Regent – Unlike most of the new high-rise hotels opening these days, this one is small enough to offer the ultimate in comfort and style — the ratio of employees to guests is 1 to 1. Dinner here is an elegant affair: The rooftop *Ciel Bleu* offers classic French food and romantic views of Lake Michigan (particularly pleasant at breakfast); the *Palm,* on the ground floor, has steaks as prime as those served by its New York counterpart (see *Eating Out*). Amenities include 24-hour room service, concierge, 4 meeting rooms, secretarial services, A/V equipment, photocopiers, computers, and express checkout. 181 E. Lake Shore Dr. (phone: 787-8500; 505-243-6466, collect, from Alaska; 800-545-4000 elsewhere in the US; Fax: 312-664-6194; Telex: 256266). Expensive.

Le Meridien Chicago – There are 247 rooms, 35 suites, and 6 penthouse suites in this new property (formerly *21 East*). Rooms have compact-disc players, VCRs, and remote-control TV sets. Guests requesting transportation to The Loop each morning are obliged in a stretch BMW. Health club facilities are available nearby. 21 E. Bellevue Place (phone: 800-443-2100 or 266-2100). Expensive.

Midland – Recently renovated and restored to its European elegance, this 260-room property has combined a number of its smaller rooms and created executive class suites for its primarily business clientele. There are phones in some bathrooms and non-smoking rooms are available. A vocalist performs Friday nights in the *Ticker Tape* bar and grill. This is an excellent location, within walking distance of museums, theaters, the Sears Tower, and Grant Park. Guests can use the nearby *Randolph Tower Fitness Center* at reduced rates. Facilities include a swimming pool, sauna, and tanning booth. 172 W. Adams at La Salle (phone: 800-621-2360 or 332-1200). Expensive.

Morton – A National Historical Register building in the Printer's Row District (and formerly the *Omni Morton*), now a member of the Hyatt chain, it has an elegant green-and-black lobby, 161 rooms and suites, lounges, meeting areas, an exercise room and gym, plus the first-rate *Prairie* restaurant (see *Eating Out*). 500 S. Dearborn St. (phone: 800-843-6678 or 663-3200). Expensive.

Nikko Chicago – This elegant, 425-room hotel overlooking the Chicago River was built by Nikko Hotels International, Japan's largest hotel chain. Japanese touches abound — landscaped indoor gardens, native artwork, even Japanese suites with tatami sleeping rooms. A 3-floor amenity area includes a 2-story executive lounge, a business center with computer terminals, a business library, and a health club. Other pluses are 24-hour room service, concierge, 6 meeting rooms, secretarial services, A/V equipment, photocopiers, computers, CNN, and express checkout. 320 N. Dearborn St. (phone: 744-1900; Fax: 312-527-2650; Telex: 276536). Expensive.

Omni Ambassador East – Now part of the Omni Classic chain, this lovely old hotel hasn't lost an ounce of charm. It still houses the famous *Pump Room* restaurant (see *Eating Out*), a Chicago institution whose entryway is lined with photos of famous guests, who always dine in booth one. Convenient location in the Gold Coast area, close to Lincoln Park, Rush Street, and the Magnificent Mile of Michigan Avenue. (Not affiliated with the *Ambassador West*, across the street.) Amenities include 24-hour room service, concierge, 9 meeting rooms, secretarial services, A/V equipment, photocopiers, computers, CNN, and express checkout. 1301 N. State Pkwy. (phone: 787-7200; Fax: 312-787-4760; Telex: 9102212120). Expensive.

Palmer House – A busy, 1,800-room giant, this is another Chicago tradition. The sumptuous *Empire Room* is a visual delight. You also can dine here at the *Palmer Steak House* and *Trader Vic's*. Amenities include a concierge desk, 38 meeting rooms, secretarial services, A/V equipment, photocopiers, computers, CNN, and express checkout. In the Loop on the State Street mall. Monroe St. between State and Wabash (phone: 726-7500; Fax: 312-917-1735; Telex: 382182). Expensive.

Park Hyatt – Small, with 255 elegant rooms and suites, and as convivial as it is convenient to N. Michigan Ave. and the historic Water Tower. The hotel offers 24-hour room service, concierge, 4 meeting rooms, secretarial services, A/V equipment, photocopiers, computers, and express checkout. 800 N. Michigan Ave. (phone: 280-2222; Fax: 312-280-1963; Telex: 256216). Expensive.

Ritz-Carlton – Contemporary and chic, this beautifully appointed 432-room luxury establishment, a member of the fine Four Seasons chain, rises 20 stories above its 12th-floor lobby. In the spectacular *Water Tower Place* complex, it has all the accoutrements of elegance, including a fine health club and skylit indoor swimming pool. Amenities include 24-hour room service, concierge, 6 meeting rooms, secretarial services, A/V equipment, photocopiers, computers, CNN, and express checkout. Near North Side. 160 E. Pearson (phone: 266-1000; Fax: 312-266-1194; Telex: 00206014). Expensive.

Sheraton-Plaza – The 233 rooms and 100 suites at this gem recently were remodeled and offer a residential decor with such in-room amenities as refreshment centers, coffee machines, and complimentary cable channels. Facilities include a rooftop outdoor swimming pool, health club privileges at a nearby private facility, plus a lobby-level restaurant and bar. Business pluses are a concierge desk, 10 meeting rooms, secretarial services, A/V equipment, photocopiers, computers, CNN, and express checkout. Just off Michigan Avenue. 160 E. Huron St. (phone: 787-2900; Fax: 312-787-6093). Expensive.

Swissôtel – This 625-room property boasts spectacular views of the Chicago River and Lake Michigan, along with spacious guestrooms (among the largest in the country at 450 square feet) complete with marble bathrooms. Despite the hotel's distinctly European flavor (more than 20% of the staff and close to half the guests are European), *Land of Plenty,* its signature dining room, emphasizes American cooking. Amenities include 34 function and conference rooms, a 60-seat theater, and a business center with a stock-market quotation board, newswire, and business library. 323 E. Wacker Dr. at Illinois Ctr. (phone: 565-0565 or 800-65-GRAND). Expensive.

Tremont – The paneled lobby, with its elaborate moldings and chandeliers, is more like a private sitting room than a public foyer. The 139 rooms offer traditional elegance. The hotel, which changed ownership from John B. Coleman to Rank North America, also is the home of *Cricket's,* one of Chicago's best restaurants (see *Eating Out*). Amenities include 24-hour room service, concierge, 4 meeting rooms, secretarial services, A/V equipment, photocopiers, computers, CNN, and express checkout. 100 E. Chestnut (phone: 751-1900 or 800-621-8133; Fax: 312-280-1304). Expensive.

21 East Kempinski – This Magnificent Mile hostelry boasts an elegant 4-story atrium lobby and 247 rooms, including 6 duplex penthouse suites, overlooking the city and Lake Michigan. There is a piano bar and formal dining in *Café 21,* which serves Southwestern fare. Amenities include 24-hour room service, concierge, 6 meeting rooms, secretarial services, A/V equipment, photocopiers, computers, CNN, and express checkout. 24 E. Bellevue Pl. (phone: 266-2100; Fax: 312-266-2103). Expensive.

Westin Chicago – This deluxe, near–North Side hotel has 742 rooms and a health club with sauna and steam room. The *Chelsea* restaurant serves continental fare and the *Lion Bar* is a popular spot that's generally crowded with businesspeople. Amenities include 24-hour room service, concierge, 18 meeting rooms, secretarial services, A/V equipment, photocopiers, CNN, and express checkout. Near the *Drake* and the Hancock Center. N. Michigan Ave. at Delaware (phone: 943-7200; Fax: 312-943-9347; Telex: 206593). Expensive.

Whitehall – Devoted to detail and known for its elegance and its careful, courteous service. Its excellent restaurant is open only to members and registered guests. Its 223 rooms are decorated in the style of an English country manor. Amenities include 24-hour room service, concierge, 6 meeting rooms, secretarial services, A/V equipment, photocopiers, computers, and express checkout. 105 E. Delaware Pl. (phone: 944-6300; Fax: 312-280-1304). Expensive.

Richmont – A somewhat moderately priced alternative near the Magnificent Mile. There are 193 guestrooms, a meeting room, and the *Rue St. Clair* lobby bar, which looks like a French bistro but serves American fare. Amenities include A/V equipment, photocopiers, and CNN. 162 E. Ontario St. (phone: 787-3580 or 800-621-8055; Fax: 312-787-1299). Expensive to moderate.

Allerton – Close to museums and shopping on Michigan Avenue, 10 minutes from the Loop. The 380-room property is an economical but quite pleasant choice — and a steal in this location. There's also a good restaurant, *L'Escargot* (see *Eating Out*). Amenities include 10 meeting rooms, secretarial services, A/V equipment, and photocopiers. 701 N. Michigan Ave. (phone: 440-1500; Fax: 312-440-1819). Moderate.

Bismarck – There are 525 rooms and some nice suites. Amenities include 19 meeting rooms, secretarial services, A/V equipment, photocopiers, and express checkout. The *Walnut Room* serves breakfast and lunch, and the *Chalet* is where guests go for dinner. 171 W. Randolph at La Salle (phone: 236-0123; Fax: 312-236-3177). Moderate.

Congress – Not as large as the nearby *Palmer House* (800 rooms), but this unit of the Best Western chain has a well-deserved reputation for personal attention. It also boasts fine views of Lake Michigan and Grant Park. The hotel offers 24-hour room service, 22 meeting rooms, A/V equipment, and photocopiers. 520 S. Michigan Ave. (phone: 427-3800; Fax: 312-427-3972; Telex: 4330281). Moderate.

Claridge – With 172 rooms and 6 suites, (three with wood-burning fireplaces), it's just steps away from art galleries, jazz clubs, and fine stores. Health club facilities are available nearby. In-room amenities include Frango mints from *Marshall Field* and a beer that is brewed locally. 1244 North Dearborn Pkwy. (phone: 800-245-1258 or 787-4980). Moderate.

Days Inn Lake Shore Drive – The best things about this 586-room property are its setting opposite the lake and Navy Pier and its relatively low rates, which are even more reasonable considering the outdoor pool. Amenities include 5 meeting rooms, A/V equipment, photocopiers, CNN, and express checkout. 644 N. Lake Shore Dr. (phone: 943-9200; Fax: 312-649-5580; Telex: 4973443). Moderate.

Essex – A dinner-theater playhouse is one of the attractions at this 225-room, 55-suite property. There's also an outdoor swimming pool in the summer and guests have access to nearby health/gym facilities. Although not high-tech, this is a pleasant place to stay and the staff is friendly. 800 S. Michigan Ave. (phone: 800-621-6909 or 939-2800). Moderate.

Executive House – Recently renovated, it has 415 rooms and 60 suites, all with wonderful city views. Conference and meeting rooms are available; the *LaSalle* restaurant offers fine continental cooking; the use of nearby health club facilities also is available. Attracting members of the international business community, it offers a special telephone system that allows guests to access dialing and travel instructions in various foreign languages. Valet parking. 71 East Wacker Dr. (phone: 800-621-4005 or 346-7100). Moderate.

Forum – This place offers 517 rooms, a restaurant, meeting rooms, and access to a gym and pool. 525 N. Michigan Ave. (phone: 800-628-2112 or 944-0055). Moderate.

Holiday Inn City Centre – Architecturally more interesting than you might expect. Swimming pools and a health club, indoor tennis courts, racquetball, and free parking make this establishment's 500 rooms almost a bargain. Amenities include a concierge desk, 11 meeting rooms, A/V equipment, photocopiers, CNN, and express checkout. 300 E. Ohio (phone: 787-6100; Fax: 312-787-6259). Moderate.

Holiday Inn of Elk Grove – Convenient to O'Hare. With 159 rooms and a domed indoor pool, it's an economical choice for an overnight stop. Small pets are welcome. Amenities include 5 meeting rooms, A/V equipment, photocopiers, CNN, express checkout, and transportation to the airport. 1000 Busse Rd. (phone: 708-437-6010; Fax: 708-806-9369). Moderate.

Oxford House – All 175 rooms and 24 suites have wet bars; guests can use health club facilities (including a pool) nearby. Conveniently located just a few blocks from Grant Park and the Magnificent Mile shopping area, it has a restaurant, *Café Angelo* and 2 lounges, *Cheers* and *The Winery*. 225 N. Wabash (phone: 800-344-4111 or 346-6585). Moderate.

Avenue – This budget motel has only 78 rooms and few amenities, but it's close to town. 1154 S. Michigan Ave. (phone: 427-8200). Inexpensive.

Grove – An outdoor pool and low (for Chicago) prices make this 40-room motel a real find. Restaurant nearby. A half-hour drive from the Loop (longer in rush hour). 9110 Waukegan Rd., Morton Grove (phone: 708-966-0960). Inexpensive.

 EATING OUT: The city's restaurant business is booming, and some of the finest cooking in America can be found here. Expect to pay from $60 and up for two at those restaurants we've noted as expensive; between $40 and $60, for moderately priced meals; and under $40 at our inexpensive choices. Prices do not include drinks and wine, tips or taxes. All telephone numbers are in the 312 area code unless otherwise indicated.

Ambria – Everything about this place charms, from the comfortable setting to the menu's sophisticated variations on nouvelle cuisine. Dinner might begin with a salad of sliced duck, pine nuts, and fresh pears with red currant dressing, or a tropical lobster salad. Desserts are simply remarkable. There's also a *dégustation* dinner for 4 or more with samplings of many dishes. Closed Sundays. Reservations necessary. Major credit cards accepted. 2300 N. Lincoln Park W. (phone: 472-5959). Expensive.

Biggs – In a restored Victorian mansion. The prix fixe menu changes every day, but the selection often includes beef Wellington, duck à l'orange, roast rack of lamb *persillade,* fettuccine with lobster and scallops, and tenderloin tips sautéed with fresh mushrooms and served on wild rice. There's an extensive wine list. Open daily for dinner. Reservations necessary. Major credit cards accepted. 1150 N. Dearborn (phone: 787-0900). Expensive.

Café Provençal – An intimate room on a quiet north suburban Evanston street. It offers some of the most painstakingly prepared French dishes in the area — the Wisconsin pheasant with rosemary-honey glaze and the New York foie gras with Cortlandt apples are particularly recommended. Closed Sundays. Reservations advised. Major credit cards accepted. 1625 Hinman St., Evanston (phone: 708-475-2233). Expensive.

Charlie Trotter's – The menu changes daily in this adventuresome, 2-room nouvelle cuisine restaurant, the civilized home of some of the city's most imaginative dishes. Appetizers range from caviar-topped sea scallops to sweetbreads with pancetta, radicchio, shredded potato, sweet peppers, and sharp cilantro butter presented in a crisp potato shell. Entrées are equally varied: tender venison and smoked quail with hazelnuts. Service is excellent; the wine list is extensive. Closed Sundays and Mondays. Reservations necessary. Major credit cards accepted. 816 W. Armitage (phone: 248-6228). Expensive.

Le Ciel Bleu – Overlooking the Oak Street beach and the Lake Michigan shoreline, this delightful eating establishment in the *Mayfair Regent* hotel (see *Checking In*) favors a menu with dishes from Provence and Northern Italy. The seafood soup *niçoise* and angel hair pasta with wild mushrooms and thyme are not to be missed. Open daily. Reservations necessary. Major credit cards accepted. 181 E. Lake Shore Dr. (phone: 951-2864). Expensive.

Cricket's – In the style of the old *"21" Club* in New York, with red-checkered tablecloths, bare floors, low ceilings, and walls festooned with corporate memorabilia, and a menu that includes chicken hash Mornay and various daily specials. A very good choice for Sunday brunch. Open daily. Reservations necessary. Major credit cards accepted. *Tremont Hotel,* 100 E. Chestnut (phone: 280-2100). Expensive.

Everest Room – An elegant French restaurant with a commanding view from atop

LaSalle Street, Chicago's Wall Street. The cornucopia of original dishes reflect the chef's Alsatian roots. Try the roast filet of sea bass wrapped in crisp shredded potatoes. Closed Sundays and Mondays. Reservations necessary. Major credit cards accepted. 440 S. La Salle (phone: 663-8920). Expensive.

Le Français – For years, Jean Bouchet made this one of America's finest French restaurants. Today the kitchen is in the hands of Roland and Mary Beth Liccioni, and the still-excellent fare has a somewhat lighter touch to it. The pastries are superb! Closed Sundays. Reservations necessary. Major credit cards accepted. 269 S. Milwaukee, Wheeling; take Kennedy Expy. to Rte. 294 north, Willow exit (phone: 708-541-7470). Expensive.

Gene and Georgetti – In an old, wood-frame building near the Merchandise Mart, hearty sirloin, T-bone steaks, and animated conversation mingle. This eatery also dishes up popular Italian dishes and huge salads. Closed Sunday. Reservations unnecessary. Major credit cards accepted. 500 N. Franklin (phone: 527-3718). Expensive.

Gordon – When Gordon Sinclair's culinary imagination ignites, his clientele is happy to eat the superlative results. Grilled Norwegian salmon with Chinese mustard glaze or charred lamb with minted couscous and eggplant and garlic are beautifully balanced by such desserts as lemon soufflé with warm caramel sauce. Open daily. Reservations advised. Major credit cards accepted. 500 N. Clark St. (phone: 467-9780). Expensive.

Jackie's – An intimate 50-seat neighborhood spot, serving some of the finest nouvelle cooking in the city. Consider delicate orange-honey-glazed squab served with Chinese vermicelli and cabbage garnished with cashews and cloud-ear mushrooms. Closed Sundays and Mondays. Reservations necessary. Major credit cards accepted. 2478 N. Lincoln (phone: 880-0003). Expensive.

Jimmy's Place – Opera fans can experience the glory of Verdi, Puccini, and Mozart while dining on medaillons of veal, spicy shrimp ragout in sesame crêpes, and veal sweetbreads atop grilled, smoked leeks. Closed Sundays. Reservations advised. Major credit cards accepted. 3420 N. Elston Ave. (phone: 539-2999). Expensive.

Morton's of Chicago – Another fine steak-and-potatoes establishment whose loyal returnees gulp down everything from kosher hot dogs to chicken in the pot to fabulous cheesecake. Open daily. Reservations advised. Major credit cards accepted. 1050 N. State St. (phone: 266-4820). Expensive.

Nick's Fishmarket – The number of choices on the menu is bewildering, but the work of choosing is worth the effort. The cold appetizer assortment of shellfish is always a good bet, and try the pan-fried whole baby salmon or an abalone dish for an entrée. Closed Sundays. Reservations necessary. Major credit cards accepted. First National Plaza, Monroe St. (phone: 621-0200). Expensive.

95th – For food with a view, this is your best bet. An American regional cuisine menu that changes seasonally. Open daily for lunch and dinner; dinner only on Saturdays; brunch and dinner Sundays. Reservations advised. Major credit cards accepted. 95th Floor, John Hancock Center, 172 E. Chestnut St. (phone: 787-9596). Expensive.

Palm – Owned by the same people who run the well-known New York restaurants called *Palm* and *Palm, Too,* this eatery has a similar decor of sawdust-covered floors and walls hung with drawings of regular patrons. Also like its East Coast counterparts, the kitchen here specializes in producing great steaks and lobsters. Closed Sundays. Reservations necessary. Major credit cards accepted. *Mayfair Regent Hotel,* 181 E. Lake Shore (phone: 944-0135). Expensive.

Le Perroquet – Subtle, sumptuous; one of the best dining places around. Expect a parade of delectable wonders such as *moules* or a *soufflé de crevettes Madras* as hors d'oeuvres; salmon mousseline, venison filet, or quail as entrées; pastries to follow. Closed Sundays. Reservations necessary. Major credit cards accepted. 70 E. Walton (phone: 944-7990). Expensive.

Pump Room – A winning formula of fine food, diligent service, and lovely decor have made this a legend among Chicago restaurants. Continental dishes are the mainstays, but there are some nouvelle cuisine specialties; both are complemented by the restaurant's good wine list. Open daily. Reservations necessary. Major credit cards accepted. 1301 N. State Pkwy. (phone: 266-0360). Expensive.

Rust Belt Café – This comfortable coffeehouse with reggae background music claims to serve "post-industrial cuisine" — which translates to American food with Italian and French accents. Try the mixed grill, a trio of veal tenderloin, quail marinated in hazelnut pesto, and homemade Tuscan sausage with raisins and pine nuts. For dessert, sample the rich, but light, chocolate truffle torte. Lunch is served Tuesdays through Saturdays; brunch on Sundays. Dinner is served Tuesdays through Sundays. Closed Mondays. Reservations advised. Major credit cards accepted. 2747 N. Lincoln (phone: 880-7878). Expensive.

Seasons – This opulent, urbane room features some of the most inventive nouvelle preparations in the city. Try the quail with game-sausage stuffing or the venison. Open daily. Reservations necessary. Major credit cards accepted. *Four Seasons Hotel,* 120 E. Delaware (phone: 280-8800). Expensive.

Spiaggia – Expertly prepared Northern Italian food — including unique pasta dishes, veal, and a grilled fish of the day — served in a beautiful setting. Open daily except Sunday lunch. Reservations advised. Major credit cards accepted. 980 N. Michigan (phone: 280-2750 or 280-2764). Expensive.

Printer's Row – Chef Michael Foley awakens sluggish palates with his delicious fare. Choose to dine in the snug wine library, an intimate room lined with bookcases (including Michael's cookbooks), another cozy room decorated with a hunting motif, or the main dining area. The roast pheasant with *jus au naturel* and five kinds of onions, as well as the grilled salmon with a basil cream sauce and sun-dried tomato pasta, are true standouts. Chocoholics should dive into the chocolate terrine studded with fresh raspberries or the white and dark chocolate cheesecake with amaretto sauce. Closed Sundays. Reservations advised. Major credit cards accepted. 550 S. Dearborn St. (phone: 461-0780). Expensive to moderate.

T'ang Dynasty – The spectacular decor in this dining place across from *Bloomingdale's* is the backdrop for authentic Mandarin dishes and genteel service. The house specialty is Beggar's Hen, rock cornish hen with black mushroom stuffing. There is a buffet weekdays. Major credit cards accepted. Reservations necessary. Lunch and dinner daily. 100 E. Walton (phone: 664-8688). Expensive to moderate.

Arnie's – The star of the show is the prime rib, tender as a cloud and sliced nearly 2 inches thick, also everything from ribs to scallops. Calm your sweet tooth with divinely inspired white chocolate mousse. Live music Fridays through Sundays. Sunday brunch, lunch Tuesdays through Fridays and dinner every evening. Reservations advised. Major credit cards accepted. 1030 N. State (phone: 266-4800). Moderate.

Arun's – One of the city's most elegant Thai dining spots, it offers such daily specials as quilted shrimp with fried rice cracker and curry sauce, prawns with garlic-lime sauce, and catfish curry. End the meal with fragrant layered rice custard and Thai iced coffee. Open for dinner Tuesdays through Sundays. Reservations advised. Major credit cards accepted. 4156 N. Kedzie (phone: 539-1909). Moderate.

Bando – With enough glitz to fill a Las Vegas lounge and some dishes as hot as the Nevada desert, this Korean eatery has black enamel tables equipped with grills for the house specialty: you-cook meats. Adventurous diners should try the fiery octopus in red sauce or spicy fish stews. Appetizers, such as the pan-fried oysters dipped in batter, are generous enough to double as entrées. Open daily for lunch and dinner. Reservations advised. Major credit cards accepted. 2200 W. Lawrence (phone: 728-0100). Moderate.

Bukhara – This Indian place claims its recipes go back 1,000 years. The focus is on marinated fresh seafood, poultry, beef, and lamb roasted in tandoors (hollow clay ovens). Try the tandoori chicken in pomegranate juice or the shish kebab with cumin-flavored lamb. Finish with a pudding of dates, almonds, and milk. Lunch and dinner daily. Reservations advised. Major credit cards accepted. 2 E. Ontario St. (phone: 943-0188). Moderate.

Butcher Shop Steakhouse – A unique dining experience, where you have your steak and cook it, too. In this latest, growing trend, guests select a filet or T-bone and pop it on the grill themselves. For those who prefer full service, the kitchen happily will oblige (there's an additional $2 charge if you leave the cooking to them). Open daily. Reservations advised. Major credit cards accepted. 358 W. Ontario (phone: 440-4900). Moderate.

Cape Cod Room – An institution, this seafood spot serves reliable fresh pompano, lobster, and other finny fare. Closed *Christmas*. Reservations necessary. Major credit cards accepted. *Drake Hotel*, 140 E. Walton (phone: 787-2200). Moderate.

Chestnut Street Grill – The Frank Lloyd Wright and Louis Sullivan ornamentation are as distinctive as the house specialty, grilled seafood. Try the swordfish or the tuna. The desserts are sinful, especially the cappuccino-candy ice cream. Open daily. Reservations advised. Major credit cards accepted. Mezzanine level, *Water Tower Place* (phone: 280-2720). Moderate.

The Eccentric – *Chicago Bears* Coach Mike Ditka was the first Chicago celebrity to open a successful restaurant. Sportscaster Harry Carey was next. This one is Oprah Winfrey's. It lives up to its name: lots of wild colors, paintings by local artists, an amalgam of French, English, American, and Italian cooking styles, and such dishes as cold fruit soup with chili peppers. Don't pass up Oprah's lumpy mashed potatoes with horseradish. Open daily. No reservations. Major credit cards accepted. 159 W. Erie (phone: 787-8390) Moderate.

L'Escargot – Unpretentious and pleasant, with an emphasis on provincial French cooking, including a cassoulet — white beans, sausage, pork, and goose. There's always fresh fish and homemade pastries on the menu. Open daily. Reservations advised. Major credit cards accepted. *Allerton Hotel*, 701 N. Michigan (phone: 337-1717). Moderate.

Hatsuhana – Delicious sushi and sashimi; tables as well as counter seating available. Open daily. Reservations advised. Major credit cards accepted. 160 E. Ontario (phone: 280-8287). Moderate.

Lawry's The Prime Rib – The specialty here is prime ribs, served in three thicknesses with Yorkshire pudding and a big fresh salad with Lawry's special Famous French dressing and Lawry's seasoned salt. Open daily for dinner; weekdays for lunch. Reservations necessary. Major credit cards accepted. 100 E. Ontario (phone: 787-5000). Moderate.

Lou Mitchell's – For those who consider the idea of awakening before noon a barbaric proposal, make an exception and head for this outstanding breakfast spot. The doors open at 5:30 AM. Freshly squeezed orange juice is followed by perfectly prepared pancakes, omelettes served in the pan, freshly baked biscuits, and fantastic coffee. Formica tabletops, eccentric waitresses, and a low-key clientele complete the picture. Closed Sundays. Reservations advised. Major credit cards accepted. 563 W. Jackson Blvd. (phone: 939-3111). Moderate.

Prairie – Quite possibly where the term Midwestern cooking was coined, this intimate dining spot offers fine regional fare. The decor is elegant and uncluttered, à la Frank Lloyd Wright, and the open kitchen is a fine place to pick up on new cooking techniques as you watch your food in transit between the cutting board and your plate. Whitefish smothered with onions, crisp bacon, puréed squash, and smoked whitefish caviar is just one of the thoughtfully prepared entrées, and those willing to chance an extra pound should try the warm carrot raisin cake with bourbon glaze and sugarplums. Closed Sundays. Reservations advised. Major credit cards accepted. 500 S. Dearborn (phone: 663-1143). Moderate.

Salvatore's – Diners at this handsome Italian restaurant may sit in a garden atrium or in one of two dining rooms. The menu features 14 kinds of homemade pasta and fresh fish specials that change daily, but the kitchen is most proud of its *castelle di vitello* (roasted milk-fed veal) and *fettuccine alla Caroline* (green noodles with pine nuts, mushrooms, spinach, and cheese). Among the choices on the wine list are 114 varieties from Italy. Open daily. Reservations advised. Major credit cards accepted. 525 W. Arlington Pl. (phone: 528-1200). Moderate.

Scoozi – A cavernous former garage that's been turned into a smashing gathering place with evocative period decor. Besides the chef's daily specials, the unusually large menu includes provincial Italian specialties such as a 3-foot-long pizza served on a wooden plank (calorie counters, fear not; they do come smaller), osso buco (braised veal shanks), and pheasant that is smoked on the premises and served with a choice of soft, baked, or sautéed polenta (the Italian version of grits). Open weekdays for lunch, daily for dinner. Reservations for lunch only. Major credit cards accepted. 410 W. Huron (phone: 943-5900). Moderate.

Shaw's Crab House – A mammoth, immensely popular pre–World War II–style seafood house. Don't miss the stone or soft-shell crabs if they're in season. The pecan pie may be Chicago's best. Open daily. Reservations for lunch only. Major credit cards accepted. 21 E. Hubbard (phone: 527-2722). Moderate.

La Strada – An Italian place with a reputation for its tableside preparation of such specialties as veal *forestiera,* rich with mushrooms and artichokes in wine sauce. Other highlights include eggplant *involtini* and carpaccio. Closed Sundays. Reservations advised. Major credit cards accepted. 151 N. Michigan (phone: 565-2200). Moderate.

Terczaki's – Traditional American food just like mom used to make. Open nightly. Reservations advised on weekends. Major credit cards, *except* American Express, accepted. 2635 N. Halsted (phone: 404-0171). Moderate.

Szechwan House – The hot and sour soup and the crispy duck are just as appetizing as the chef's more unusual dishes, such as snails in spicy sauce and deep-fried ground shrimp wrapped in seaweed. Open daily. Reservations advised. Major credit cards accepted. 600 N. Michigan (phone: 642-3900). Moderate to inexpensive.

Tania's – Elegant Caribbean and Latin American decor and dim lights make this a romantic spot on weeknights, but this Cuban eatery hops on weekends when local Latinos flock here to eat and dance the night away. Seafood dishes are the house specialty, but don't overlook the meat. The wine list is mostly Spanish but includes such South American offerings as Chilean Concha y Toro Casillero del Diablo. Throw the diet out the window and finish off your meal with a flaming Caribbean coffee spiked with Kahlua and Pampero rum. Reservations (and dress code) necessary on weekends. Open daily. Major credit cards accepted. 2659 N. Milwaukee (phone: 235-7120). Moderate to inexpensive.

Taste of Morocco – Waiters in fezzes and flowing *djellabas* serve up exotic and pleasing fare in this modest storefront posing as a richly colored Moorish tent. A succulent appetizer is the *bisteya* pastry — filo dough layered with almonds, chicken, egg, cinnamon, and sugar. Mediterranean-style salads and couscous are vegetarian options. There's a moderately priced wine list. Major credit cards accepted. Closed Mondays; open only for dinner the rest of the week. 3255 N. Halsted (phone: 327-6100). Moderate to inexpensive.

Ann Sather's – There actually are two: The original institution may be the world's only Swedish restaurant in a former funeral home. It is on West Belmont Avenue near a couple of other Chicago institutions: *Wrigley Field* and the *Steppenwolf Theatre*. The menu varies from time-honored Swedish dishes to hearty American fare: pork sausage patties and rich country gravy, beefsteak and eggs with cinnamon rolls. Brunch is particularly good. Open daily. Reservations unnecessary. MasterCard and Visa accepted. 929 W. Belmont Ave. (phone: 348-2378) and 5207 N. Clark St. (phone: 271-6677). Inexpensive.

Army & Lou's – This hangout for Chicago aldermen serves the best soul food in the city. Try the greens and neck bones, the Northern beans with ham hocks, the smothered chicken and corn bread dressing, or better yet, the $30 Taste of Soul, which includes everything from chicken to catfish to chitlins and more ham hocks. Closed Tuesdays. Reservations advised. Major credit cards accepted. 422 E. 75th (phone: 483-6550). Inexpensive.

Beau Thai – One of Lincoln Park's fine collection of Southeast Asian eateries. Specialties include *pad thai,* a warm noodle dish; duck Beau Thai, cooked with cashews and vegetables; and sweet, creamy cold Thai coffee for dessert. Closed Mondays. Reservations accepted on weekends only. Major credit cards accepted. 2525 N. Clark (phone: 348-6938). Inexpensive.

Berghoff – Another Chicago tradition. Although the service is rushed, the meals are bountiful and the selection wide-ranging: ragout, Wiener schnitzel, steaks, and seafood. Closed Sundays. Reservations accepted for five or more. Major credit cards accepted. 17 W. Adams (phone: 427-3170). Inexpensive.

Billy Goat Tavern – Every newspaper town has to have a bar where reporters and editors congregate for inexpensive drinks and greasy fries. For Chicagoans, this home of juicy thick burgers is the place. The walls of the sub-ground bar are decorated with memorabilia collected by the owner, whose goatee allegedly inspired the name; and though its decor won't win any *Architectural Digest* awards, it's a lively lunchtime spot with newsmen, dock workers, and bankers. Newspaper columnist Mike Royko is a regular here. Open daily. No reservations; no credit cards. 430 N. Michigan (phone: 222-1525). Inexpensive.

Bizzoni's Brown Bag – Locals say Mama B.'s Italian beef sandwiches may be the juiciest in town — and that's just the beginning. Heading the list of sandwiches are a herculean sub made of hand-rolled meatballs and bathed in Mama Bizzoni's secret vinaigrette recipe. The service here is fast. Open 7 days a week for lunch and dinner. No reservations; no credit cards. 1056 W. Webster St. (phone: 549-3082). Inexpensive.

Blue Mesa – Southwestern cooking is one of this city's latest dining crazes, and Santa Fe style reigns in this comfortable room of whitewashed adobe and bleached pine. Lovers of wonderfully pulpy guacamole and steaks smothered in green chilies and onions will be quite content. Open daily. Reservations necessary for parties of 8 or more. Major credit cards accepted. 1729 N. Halsted (phone: 944-5990). Inexpensive.

Bub City – A rollicking, mammoth, down-home Texas eating house, featuring shrimp and crab barbecue and "Big Easy" bayou music to wash it all down. This is one loud, entertaining joint. Wear denim. Open daily. No reservations. Major credit cards accepted. 901 W. Weed (phone: 266-1200). Inexpensive.

Café Ba-Ba-Reeba! – A boisterous, informal Spanish *tapas* restaurant/bar with an authentic feel. Dining here involves tossing back dry sherry with bites of hot and cold *tapas.* The tender squid, stuffed with its own ground meat and crunchy pistachios, is especially good. Open Tuesday through Saturday for lunch, daily for dinner. Reservations accepted for lunch only. Major credit cards accepted. 2024 N. Halsted (phone: 935-5000). Inexpensive.

Carson's – Probably the best spareribs in the city. Salads with a creamy, anchovy-flavored dressing and tangy au gratin potatoes are the other lures. Don't dress up because bibs (supplied) are essential. Open daily. No reservations, so expect to wait. Major credit cards accepted. 612 N. Wells St. (phone: 280-9200). Inexpensive.

Dick's Last Resort – Right on the Chicago River, this establishment offers buckets of ribs, shrimp, catfish, and crab legs along with 74 kinds of beer. Live Dixieland jazz 7 nights a week at a bar that advertises that it has no cover charge — and no taste. In fact, this spots bills itself as the restaurant that is the "shame of Chicago and an embarrassment to any neighborhood." Tacky, but it's fun. Open for lunch and dinner daily; until 4 PM on weekends. Entertainment from 5 PM on. Open daily. Reservations advised. Major credit cards accepted. 435 E. Illinois in the basement level of *North Pier* (phone: 836-7870). Inexpensive.

Dixie Que – This former gas station offers fill ups of such down home, southern-style roadhouse specialties as barbecued spaghetti and Caesar salad topped with smoked chicken, red pepper strips, and mixed pecans. For dessert, there's old-fashioned banana pudding. Lunch and dinner daily. Major credit cards accepted. Reservations unnecessary. 2001 W. Fullerton (phone: 252-5600). Inexpensive.

Ed Debevic's – The creation of Rich Melman, king of Chicago restaurateurs — a 1950s diner that has crowds lining up outside. Burgers, chili, malts, fries, and a rollicking *American Graffiti* atmosphere. Open daily. No reservations or credit cards accepted. 640 N. Wells (phone: 664-1707). Inexpensive.

Febo's – A real "old neighborhood" restaurant where the Northern Italian cooking tastes as if it came out of a family kitchen. Try the antipasto, followed by linguine Alfredo, cannelloni, tortellini, or chicken Alfredo in mushrooms and lemon-herb wine sauce. Closed Sundays. Reservations necessary on weekends. Major credit cards accepted. 2501 S. Western (phone: 523-0839). Inexpensive.

Frontera Grill and Topolobampo – A pair of upscale Mexican dining rooms. *Frontera* specializes in tempting appetizer platters of guacamole, deep-fried chicken taquitos, and ceviche. *Topolobampo* offers, among other treats, roast pork loin with red-chili apricot sauce and pumpkin purée. Closed Sundays and Mondays. Reservations advised. Major credit cards accepted. 445 N. Clark St. (phone: 661-1434). Inexpensive.

Geja's Café – This restaurant has good food — from fondue to seafood — and a romantic atmosphere, with flamenco and classical guitar played here every night of the week. Reservations advised. Major credit cards accepted. 340 W. Armitage (phone: 281-9101). Inexpensive.

Gennaro's – A real mom-and-pop operation, the atmosphere is cozy and the Italian food is among Chicago's best. Seasoned Italian bread complements the fresh homemade pasta and a red sauce made from a recipe that dates back three generations. Dinner Thursdays through Sundays. Reservations advised. No credit cards. 1352 W. Taylor St. (phone: 243-1035). Inexpensive.

Greek Islands – You can find thoughtfully prepared dishes such as gyros, squid, lamb, and fresh broiled red snapper at this simple eatery. The decor isn't elegant, but the food is delicious. Open daily. Reservations unnecessary. Major credit cards accepted. 200 S. Halsted (phone: 782-9855). Inexpensive.

Hard Rock Café – Yes, Chicago has one, too. The walls of this hip hamburger emporium are covered with an assortment of rock music artifacts and declarations of world peace. Chili and grilled burgers lead the menu. Wash it all down with a fruit and honey "health shake." At the very least, a good addition to any trendy

T-shirt collection. Open daily. Reservations unnecessary. Major credit cards accepted. 63 W. Ontario (phone: 943-2252). Inexpensive.

Hecky's in Highwood – Arguably the best ribs in all of Illinois, New Orleans native Hecky Powell opened his corner take-out in suburban Evanston 6 years ago and popular demand required that he expand to a second ramshackle barbecue shack. There is indoor seating for about 40 and another 50 or so diners are accommodated on the lawn in good weather. The place is filled with photos of Powell's family and a host of jazz greats, some of whom show up for summer weekend jam sessions. The all-you-can-eat buffet includes ribs, chicken, hot links, greens, red beans and rice, coleslaw, corn bread, and the silkiest sweet potato pie around. You can bring your own beer; soft drinks and coffee are available. Restaurant open Fridays and Saturdays; takeout available every night except Mondays from 5 PM on. No reservations; no credit cards. 1902 Green Bay Rd., Evanston (phone: 708-433-6180). Inexpensive.

Helmand – Come here for savory Afghan baby pumpkin and lamb Kabuli in an exotic, attractive setting. Top off the meal with baklava baked with ground pistachios, cheese-like burfee, and coffee or spiced tea. The service is as good as the food. Open for dinner Mondays through Saturdays. Reservations advised. Major credit cards accepted. 3201 N. Halsted (phone: 935-2447). Inexpensive.

Jerome's – The room is warmly decorated and the service draws little complaint, but the food is the real attraction. In addition to a regular selection of meat, poultry, and fish, the kitchen turns out fresh bread and desserts and six to eight special dishes every day. Open daily. Reservations advised. Major credit cards accepted. 2450 N. Clark (phone: 327-2207). Inexpensive.

Kitty O'Shea's Pub – Kilkenny-born manager Eamonn Brady's connections bring in a range of lively Irish music groups to play nightly in this dimly lit, Dublin-style spot in the *Chicago Hilton* (see *Checking In*). The menu consists of simple food but there is a great potato-leek soup and some good deep-fried appetizers such as chicken wings coated in a Guinness ale batter. Guinness and Harp beer are drawn from antique taps. Open for lunch and dinner daily. Reservations advised. Major credit cards accepted. 403 W. Belmont (phone: 929-7500). Inexpensive.

Parthenon – This eatery has been a Greektown institution for more than 2 decades, and offers good food in comfortable, though slightly worn, surroundings. The extensive menu runs from chicken shish kebabs to Greek sausage to baked lamb's head. Juicy gyros and wine-marinated octopus are among bite-size appetizers, and for dessert, try the moist almond-honey cake. There also is an 11-course, family-style meal available. Open daily. Reservations advised for groups of six or more. Major credit cards accepted. 314 S. Halsted (phone: 726-2407). Inexpensive.

Pasteur – This attractive, recently remodeled corner storefront is among the best of some 2 dozen Vietnamese restaurants in the city. Recommended entrées are whole fried red snapper topped with sweet-salty spicy sauce with scallions and lime or the charming nest of crispy fried egg noodles filled with seafood and vegetables. Open for lunch Tuesdays to Sundays; dinner daily. Reservations unnecessary. Major credit cards accepted. 4759 N. Sheridan (phone: 271-6643). Inexpensive.

Three Happiness – Get a group together and head out early to avoid a wait at Chinatown's favorite dim sum spot. It's big, crowded, noisy, and dirty but you'll feast for $10 per person. Skip the regular menu, wait for the carts from the kitchen laden with steamed dumplings and buns, deep-fried pastries, plates of cold meats, scrumptious sweets, and other exotic fare that comprises the traditional Cantonese tea lunch. Open daily for lunch only. No reservations. Major credit cards accepted. 2130 S. Wentworth (phone: 791-1228). Inexpensive.

Tulpe – This Lithuanian haven with only eight tables exemplifies the best in neighborhood restaurants, offering hearty honest cooking at low prices in unpretentious surroundings. Most meals include a well-stocked bread basket, homemade soup, salad or slaw, entrée, dessert, and beverage. There is no menu; guests choose from among the 12 to 16 daily specials posted above the five-seat lunch counter. Meat-stuffed dumplings, juicy pork chops, roast chicken, and homemade sausage are fine options. The staff is cheerful and friendly. During warm weather, there is outdoor dining on weekends. Open for breakfast, lunch and an early dinner (until 8 PM) 7 days a week. No liquor; no reservations; no credit cards. 2447 W. 69th St. (phone: 925-1123). Inexpensive.

Yak-Zies – Unless you like spicy food, beware of the buffalo wings in this dimly lit, subterranean-style eatery — or order them in their milder versions. Better yet, stick to the juicy 8-ounce wine-marinated burger which, like all sandwiches here, comes with crunchy curly fries. Salty popcorn boosts beer sales for *Bulls* game watchers. Open every day for lunch and dinner, until 5 AM on Saturdays. Reservations unnecessary. No credit cards. 506 W. Diversey Pkwy. (phone: 327-1717). A second location is at 3710 N. Clark St. (phone: 525-9200). Inexpensive.

■ **Hot Dog!:** If all of the above fail to seduce your culinary sensibilities, the *Wieners Circle* is a terrific alternative for those with the I-can't-get-a-good-hot-dog blues. The special (and novel) concoction of the house is the "chardog," a half pound of spicy beef on a soft bun with onions, tomatoes, cucumbers, pickles, mustard, relish, and perhaps the kitchen sink. Ignore the seedy atmosphere and utter lack of decor, and concentrate on the perfect french fries and charcoal-broiled cheddar burgers. Open daily. Reservations unnecessary. No credit cards. 2622 N. Clark St. (phone: 477-7444).

Finally, a visit to this city's eating establishments wouldn't be complete without a taste of Chicago's famous deep-dish pizza — layer upon layer of toppings baked in a deep-dish pan. The pioneer of this pizza fit for Goliath was *Pizzeria Uno* (29 E. Ohio St., phone: 321-1000), a place whose food more than makes up for its lack of atmosphere. Also in the area is *Pizzeria Due* (619 N. Wabash Ave.; phone: 943-2400), serving the same hearty pizza. *Gino's East* (160 E. Superior St.; phone 943-1124) uses cornmeal crusts to vary the flavor. Two other places to try this local delicacy are *Giordano's of Lincoln Park* (1840 N. Clark St.; phone: 944-6100) and *Eduardo's Natural Pizza* (9300 Skokie Blvd., Skokie; phone: 708-674-0008). The latter eatery also serves the latest fad in pizza-noshing, stuffed pizza — a thick, gooey pie-like creation. Both are open daily. Reservations unnecessary. Major credit cards accepted.

DIVERSIONS

For the Experience

Quintessential Chicago

 Proud Chicagoans not only can readily point to their "city that works" as home to the skyscraper, but also as home of one of the country's first golf courses, deep-dish pizza, the flaming Greek cheese dish saganaki, jazz and blues, and celebrated writers who captured the city's spirit and the world's imagination. Chicago boasts an impressive list of native sons and daughters who shaped the development of the nation, invented new social and educational institutions, or left their imprint on the city's cultural scene.

A city of superlatives, Chicago is home to the world's tallest buildings, widest range of diverse ethnic communities, and greatest concentration of Nobel Prize winners. Past and present, the city has spawned merchants and mobsters, lawyers and longshoremen, musicians and politicians, moguls of commerce and visionary thinkers — and is proud of them all.

JAZZ AND BLUES: Say "blues" and you have to say Chicago — the city brought the world such musical legends as Muddy Waters, Bo Diddley, and singer Alberta Hunter. Starting with the Depression, Chicago was a magnet, attracting hundreds of thousands of blacks from the Deep South who migrated northward in search of jobs. They brought the blues of the Mississippi Delta to the funky, run-down bars and nightclubs of Chicago's black ghettos; it was here that the music of the Deep South — gritty, rhythmic, and elemental in its imagery — was transformed by the addition of the electric guitar into what became known as the Chicago blues. By the 1960s, a generation of white kids had discovered and fallen in love with the sound. Today, the blues is still an integral part of Chicago's musical signature, and the city is a place where only the best blues musicians survive and flourish.

One of the city's most respected "sweet home Chicago" joints is the tiny (and appropriately named) *B.L.U.E.S.* (2519 N. Halsted St.; phone: 528-1012), across the street from the somewhat more grungy *Kingston Mines* (2548 N. Halsted St.; phone: 477-4646). Both offer live music 7 nights a week, along the strip affectionately known as "the street" to the blues musicians who come here — and jam until dawn once the clubs have closed for the night. Not to be forgotten is *Buddy Guy's Legends* (754 S. Wabash Ave.; phone: 427-0333), the club owned and operated by the blues guitarist who influenced dozens of major musicians, from Eric Clapton to Jimi Hendrix. In June, the *Petrillo Music Shell* in Grant Park is the setting for a 3-day Chicago blues festival featuring headliners from across the country.

Jazz, that other great American popular musical form, also has a long history in this town. For many historians, the seeds of Chicago's colorful musical legacy were sown in 1893 at the *World's Columbian Exposition,* which drew 26 million visitors to the city, including a large number of black musicians who came to see and play at the event. Jazz may have originated in New Orleans, but Chicago was one of the principal conduits for spreading it throughout the country and eventually the world. There are some who even claim that the term "jazz" came from turn-of-the-century Chicago musician Jasbo Brown, whose improvisational music style prompted his audiences to yell, "More, Jas!"

Jazz erupted in the smoky speakeasies of the Prohibition years. In the 1930s, the *Savoy Ballroom* was where Louis Armstrong belted out high Cs on his trumpet; Duke Ellington, Ella Fitzgerald, Dizzy Gillespie, and Benny Goodman also were regulars. Chicago clubs hosted a veritable "Who's Who" of jazz: Pianist Dorothy Donegan, drummer Buddy Rich, Billie Holiday, Earl "Fatha" Hines, master clarinetist Jimmy Noone, Gene Krupa, Tommy Dorsey, and other legendary greats regularly appeared in the city's nightclubs and ballrooms.

For many years, clubs such as *London House* and the *Blue Note Club* helped keep jazz flourishing in Chicago. The *Playboy* clubs, with their practice of featuring a jazz trio, also played a part in helping keep jazz alive.

Another Chicago phenomenon is the so-called Austin High Gang — jazz musicians who went to school at, or who were associated with, Austin High School. Cornet player Jimmy McPartland and top sax stylist Bud Freeman attended Austin, and Benny Goodman was an acknowledged member of the gang, even though he didn't go to school at Austin. Gene Esposito, a leading light of Chicago's contemporary jazz scene, who is spearheading a drive to preserve jazz as an art form by establishing a Center for Jazz Arts, is another Austin alumnus.

Now the *Savoy* is gone, so are many of Chicago's jazz and blues pioneers, but their musical tradition remains. In Chicago nightclubs and concert halls today fans can hear everything from wrenching blues to swing, from Dixieland to bebop to avant-garde jazz.

One of Chicago's great after-work jazz spots is *Andy's Lounge* (11 E. Hubbard St.; phone: 642-6805). The club's nightly "Jazz at Five" program (weekdays from 5 to 8:30 PM) rotates five regular groups through a weekly schedule of performances. This is a dark, cozy spot to sit with a beer and a sandwich or thin-crust pizza and listen to many of Chicago's top jazz musicians. In contrast, *Pop's For Champagne* (2934 N. Sheffield Ave.; phone: 472-1000) is an elegant, romantic place, offering more than 100 different types of bubbly, but also serving up some good low-key jazz. There is live music nightly (except Tuesdays) and a Sunday jazz-and-champagne brunch. As its name suggests, the *Gold Star Sardine Bar* (680 N. Lake Shore Dr.; phone: 664-4215) is ultra-tiny, but somehow it has developed a penchant for attracting big names — Woody Herman, Buddy Rich, and Count Basie all have appeared here. For jazz in the afternoon — specifically Tuesday afternoons from early June through early September from 4 to 7:30 PM — plan to be at the *McKinlock Court Garden* restaurant (at the *Art Institute*, Michigan Ave. at E. Adams St.; phone: 443-3530) for a jazz quartet and an alfresco meal. And for jazz in the wee hours, head for *Ace's Diner* (4801 N. Broadway; phone: 878-8118), where the music runs from 3 to 7 AM and, yes, you can order breakfast to go with the music. Across the street from *Ace's* is the *Green Mill* (4802 N. Broadway; phone: 878-5552), a traditional Chicago jazz club and once a favorite haunt of Al Capone. Now it's better known for its Saturday late-night jam sessions. The *Cotton Club* (1710 S. Michigan Ave.; phone: 341-9787) is a re-creation of a Harlem club of the 1920s, and sports a celebrity wall of fame of that era. This swanky, upscale club has separate rooms for jazz and disco. Probably Chicago's most glamorous spot for jazz is Joe Segal's *Jazz Showcase* in the *Blackstone* hotel (636 S. Michigan Ave.; phone: 427-4300). Attracting an impressive roster of world class performers, it hosts Charlie Parker Month in August, when musicians who worked with, or were influenced by, the legendary "Yardbird" take the stage. This also is a lively spot during the annual *Chicago Jazz Festival* (held over *Labor Day* weekend), especially for impromptu late-night jam sessions.

CHICAGO LEGENDS: Chicago isn't known as the "Windy City" because of the stiff breezes that whip off the lake (although they'll definitely chill you in February). The nickname was bestowed upon the city by East Coast journalists in honor of the blow-hards and boosters who convinced the US Congress that Chicago, not New York City, was the most appropriate site for the 1893 *World's Columbian Exposition,* which celebrated the 400th anniversary of Europe's discovery of the Americas. Chicago was a year late getting the exposition off the ground, but once it did, the city put on quite a big show; in numbers, one of every three Americans visited here.

The lake aside, Windy City residents have plenty of which to be proud: poets (Carl Sandburg, Eugene Field), architects (Frank Lloyd Wright, Louis Sullivan), Nobel Prize winners (Milton Friedman, James Cronin), educational innovators (John Dewey, William Rainey Harper), legal minds (Clarence Darrow), social reformers (Jane Addams, Ida B. Wells, Frances Willard), merchants (Marshall Field), mail order kings (A. Montgomery Ward, Richard Sears), butchers for the masses (Philip Armour, Gustavus Swift), and writers (Theodore Dreiser, Finley Peter Bonne, George Ade, Ben Hecht).

At the turn of the century, Chicago further distinguished itself by producing such writers as Sherwood Anderson (*Winesburg, Ohio*), Edgar Lee Masters (*Spoon River Anthology*), Hamlin Garland (*Son of the Middle Border*), and L. Frank Baum (*The Wizard of Oz*), whose classic is every bit as popular today as it was 53 years ago. There also were writers and muckrakers like Upton Sinclair, whose *The Jungle* created a national sensation and galvanized efforts to regulate the meat-packing industry. Thanks to James T. Farrell, Studs Lonigan was born in Chicago. And Saul Bellow, Nobel Prize winner and the city's best-known current literary resident, writes about people from Chicago and those who have passed through it.

Those who more recently have distilled Chicago and made art of it operate in different media. The great oral historian and radio personality Studs Terkel represents a Chicago point of view, but in the words of others. The crusty and quick-witted columnist Mike Royko has made himself rich poking fun at Chicago's politicos, plodders, and pretenders. In the performing arts, David Mamet served his apprenticeship in the city's small experimental theaters, then went on to become a Pulitzer Prize–winning playwright and screenwriter; in film, John Hughes has brought his version of Chicago's suburbs to the movies. The mystery novel, too, is a burgeoning local art form, exemplified by novelist Sara Paretsky, who uses the city and its haunts as the backdrop for her crime stories.

In recent years, as often in the past, Chicago's major celebrities have been its architects: Helmut Jahn the most controversial, Stanley Tigerman the most cerebral, and the various members of Skidmore, Owings & Merrill the most celebrated. But it is for its politicians that Chicago is most widely known, most particularly in the person of the late Richard J. Daley, one of the last of the old-style big-city power brokers. "Boss" of the city for more than 20 years, he let few things happen without his approval. Through a vast network of personal contacts, he made sure the streets were swept and the garbage picked up (at least in the precincts that voted for him); what money changed hands in the process he didn't want to know about. The city was stunned by his death and for a decade struggled to pull itself together. Harold Washington, the city's first black mayor, seemed on the brink of bringing the city into line until he, too, died of a heart attack. After another year of floundering and political wrangling, the city opted for what it thought was a known quantity, Richard M. Daley, the Boss's son. But he is a different man in a different time; the patronage system through which his father ran Chicago has been dismantled by court decrees. The jury is still out on this Daley.

And then there's Oprah. Chicago's answer to Phil Donohue has gained national prominence as a television personality (the *Oprah Winfrey Show*), actress (*The Color Purple*), and shrewd business manager. And she has ignored the lure of Hollywood, demonstrating a commitment to Chicago with investments like her popular restaurant, the *Eccentric,* and Harpo Studios, where she tapes her show and produces others.

Last, but far from least, there's the dark side. Like Chicago's heroes, its cads and buffoons operated on a larger-than-life scale: There were market manipulators who lost millions of dollars of other people's money (Samuel Insull, Charles Yerkes), politicians who left the city a reputation it still hasn't lived down (Bathhouse John Coughlin, Hinky Dink Kenna, William Hale Thompson, Long John Wentworth), madames (the Everleigh sisters), and mobsters (Alphonse Capone, John Dillinger).

No discussion of gangsters can begin or end without mentioning Al Capone, who started in Chicago as a bodyguard to the mobster-owner of a nightclub and rapidly moved up the ranks in an infamous reign of terror. "Scarface" was one of the flashiest gang rulers; always dressed in spats and a boutonniere, he defied the law and outwitted fellow mobsters until he was nailed by the federal government on, of all things, tax evasion. Capone's own excesses actually brought about his downfall. A battle for supremacy between bootleggers, the Irish group on the North Side and the Italian one, led by Capone, on the South Side, resulted in the 1929 St. Valentine's Day Massacre, in which members of Bugsy Moran's North Side gang were gunned down by Capone's men posing as police officers. Even though Capone was sent to prison in 1931, mob fighting continued, some of it still under his control.

It is possible to relive those "good old days" — and get to see some of Chicago's less well-known neighborhoods — by taking a trip with *Untouchable Tours* (phone: 881-1195). Guides dressed as mobsters and wielding harmless Tommy guns pile their audience into a black, bullet-riddled bus and drive them past defunct breweries, the site of the nightclub where Capone got his start; the tottering *Lexington* hotel, from which Scarface ran his empire; and the grassy lot where the St. Valentine's Day Massacre took place. Other famous "hit" spots also are on the itinerary. In the evening, gangland lives on at *Tommy Gun's Garage* (1237 S. State St.; phone: 728-2828), a steak-and-potatoes restaurant (boasting Depression-era prices) under the El just south of the Loop. A sinister-looking doorman guards the entrance; women dressed as flappers serve drinks; and men decked out in dark, double-breasted suits provide the entertainment. Guests are given good 5¢ cigars and garlic cloves. (Gangsters supposedly rubbed garlic on their bullets before firing; if the shot didn't kill the victim, garlic-induced blood poisoning would.) Memorabilia at *Tommy Gun's* includes the armrest John Dillinger allegedly used at the *Biograph* theater before his fateful exit. (Some of the *Untouchable Tours'* junkets are offered in conjunction with an evening at *Tommy Gun's*.)

PIZZA AND RIBS: On *Christmas Day* in 1865, the Union Stock Yard opened on Chicago's South Side. During its heyday it was the world's largest meat-packing district, a complex that included a bank, a hotel, and a daily newspaper devoted to the meat-packing industry. Although the stockyard and its famous restaurant, the *Stock-yard Inn,* closed in 1971, Chicago's tradition as a meat town remains — there's not much that can beat a thick Chicago cut of prime aged beef or a rack of the city's famous finger-licking ribs saturated in barbecue sauce. Although the city's long list of restaurants now ranges from ethnic eateries to world class temples of haute cuisine, Chicago still is *the* place to tie on a bib and settle down with a messy but hearty slab of ribs. It also is the spot to test authentic deep-dish pizza, which Chicagoans claim as one of their city's major contributions to American gastronomy. Whether you try regular deep-dish or stuffed pizza, you'll be getting a piece of pie at least an inch thick, loaded with cheese and combinations of sausage, green peppers, onions, mushrooms, ground beef, bacon, anchovies, and almost any other topping imaginable. Deep-dish (or "Chicago-style") pizza traces its roots to the landmark pizza parlor *Pizzeria Uno* (29 E. Ohio St.; phone: 321-1000), which opened in Chicago in 1943. The pizza dished out there drew such crowds that 12 years later a sister restaurant, *Pizzeria Due* (619 N. Wabash Ave.; phone: 943-2400), opened; both still do a rousing business. *Gino's East* (160 E. Superior St.; phone: 943-1124), which didn't invent deep-dish but certainly has worked on perfecting it, is another pizza-lover's paradise. Part of the fun is standing in line with hungry Chicagoans and tourists, waiting to see if the pizza lives up to its reputation. It does.

MAGNIFICENT MILE: Twenty-five years ago, real estate developer Arthur Rubloff turned the area along Michigan Avenue between Oak Street and the Chicago River, an elegant stretch of unusual and predominantly exclusive shops and restaurants known mainly to natives, into the Magnificent Mile, one of the world's classiest shopping centers. At its head, Oak Street now rivals Rodeo Drive with its list of luxury emporiums: *Ultimo* and *Marilyn Miglin,* plus imports like *Hermès, Bottega Contessa, Giorgio Armani, Gianni Versace,* and *Rodier,* to name a few. Although a hefty budget is necessary to shop here, browsing among the elegant fittings is free, and who knows? Maybe that dress of your dreams has been marked down. But regardless of whether you shop or just stop, don't miss this elegant, extravagant expanse.

LAKE MICHIGAN: Chicago owes its existence to Lake Michigan and the Chicago River, the link between the Great Lakes and the Mississippi River. The city's first permanent resident, Jean Baptiste Point du Sable, opened a trading post here in 1781 (Marquette and Joliet came in 1679 but didn't stay). By the 1880s, Chicago had grown to become the nation's busiest port. Ships laden with grain, lumber, and ore arrived at the crowded docks along the Chicago River; raw materials were made into manufactured goods, then shipped cross-country on the railroads that quickly made the city a transcontinental hub.

When the course of the river was reversed in the 1890s and the Port of Chicago moved south to Lake Calumet, a farsighted group of businessmen (organized as the Commercial Club) commissioned architect Daniel Burnham to draw up a Plan of Chicago. Published in 1909, the plan was the first attempt at comprehensive urban planning by any major US city. It called for an unobstructed waterfront as part of a citywide system of parks and boulevards that began at the lakeshore in Jackson Park, on the South Side, ran through the city's core, and ended in Lincoln Park, on the North Side. Burnham's legacy lives on in Chicago's waterfront today; 29 miles of publicly owned and accessible shoreline, with 31 public beaches and a number of harbors, lagoons, and parks. "Make no small plans," Burnham advised, "they have no magic to stir men's souls." His generation of Chicagoans, at least, heeded his advice.

Believed by many to be Chicago's quintessential urban resource, the lakeshore offers sunbathing, golf, tennis, and outdoor concerts, as well as jogging and biking on miles of lakefront paths. On the water, there's swimming, sailing, cruising, and fishing for trout and salmon. In mid-August, yacht clubs and boaters decorate all manner of colorfully lit craft that sail down the lakefront on *Venetian Night.* Sightseeing excursions sail aboard the *Wendella* (phone: 337-1446), the *Mercury* (phone: 332-1353), or the 175-foot *Odyssey* (phone: 639-7739), the newest of the group. The starkly modern-looking *Odyssey* offers lunch and dinner cruises complete with music and dancing, as well as brunch on Sundays, and moonlight sails Fridays and Saturdays. Costs range from $24 to $65 per person. The boat departs from Navy Pier; make reservations in advance.

SUMMERS IN THE CITY: Summer in Chicago means different things to different people: baseball fans (or fanatics) flock to *Wrigley Field* or *Comiskey Park* to watch either the *Cubs* or the *White Sox;* music lovers head for the expanse of lawn at *Ravinia,* summer home to the *Chicago Symphony Orchestra* and venue for all manner of pop, classical, and jazz concerts (audience members sit on the grass, many of them with lavish picnics spread out on white linen tablecloths, china, silverware, and crystal), and still others try to plan a visit around the *Taste of Chicago,* an 8-day celebration of alfresco gluttony.

Comiskey Park, home to the *White Sox* and the newest of the city's ballfields (the first ball was thrown into play in April 1991), is a $150 million high-tech environment for a determinedly low-tech game ("refreshingly antiseptic," says a critic) that is drawing new fans to an old team. Over on the north side of town, the ever-hopeful *Cubs* try to swing their way into the *World Series* at *Wrigley Field*. Here there are singles and suburbanites, stockbrokers and surgeons, drawn more by the lovely old ballpark than by a winning team. "The Cubbies, they love to break your heart," says a fan (the last time the team won a *World Series* was in 1908), but the scoreboard is not neon yet, the ivy is real, and you needn't know anything about the game to relish an afternoon here.

If Chopin and champagne are more your style, pack a picnic and head for *Ravinia,* in suburban Highland Park 25 miles north of the Loop. All you need is the $7 admission fee and a blanket. A train from Northwestern Station stops at its gates; call RAVINIA (728-4642).

From decorum on the grass to gluttony in Grant Park (along Columbus Drive, 1 block east of Michigan): *Taste of Chicago* is the city's annual picnic, except no one brings their own food. Instead, dozens of Chicago restaurants offer their varied specialties — ribs from *Arnie's,* cheeseburgers from the *Billy Goat Grill, Gino's* pizza, *Harry Caray's* fried calamari, hot dogs from *Fluky's, Mike Ditka's* fried ice cream, and *Eli's* famous cheesecake. In addition, there's almost continuous music in the *Petrillo Bandshell.* It all begins the last weekend in June and lasts through the *Fourth of July;* on the night of July 3 it draws the biggest crowds, when the *Grant Park Orchestra* performs the *1812 Overture* and the city puts on what it contends is the nation's most spectacular (after all this is Chicago) fireworks display out over the lake. Even more amazing is how Chicago moves a million people in and out of a mile-square area in a few hours. Don't plan on driving, the trains are on a special schedule. Calmer times to enjoy *Taste of Chicago* are at lunch and in the early evening. Buy what you want and meander over to Buckingham Fountain or the lakeshore; there's no way to eat it all, so you might walk up and down the aisles to survey the offerings before making any choices.

Chicago's Best Hotels

 In the past decade, the number of hotel rooms in Chicago, particularly those on the elegant side, has more than doubled — a sign of the city's continued prominence as a convention center and increasing recognition as an international tourist attraction. For years, hotels like the *Drake* at the top of Michigan Avenue, and the *Ambassador East,* home of the famed *Pump Room* restaurant, have been included on lists of nationally noted hostelries. Noteworthy, too, is the recently refurbished *Hilton & Towers,* among the world's largest hotels. Whether it is sophistication, high-tech amenities, service, or the art of pampering, Chicago hotels rank among the world's finest. Below are some examples.

CHICAGO HILTON & TOWERS: In 1985, a $185 million restoration put the 1927 grandeur back into this 30-story landmark, while adding lavish, modern amenities. The 1,543 rooms include the Towers, with 120 suites. One of these, the $4,000-per-night Conrad Hilton Suite, has its own heliport, plus four private elevators and the services of a maid and butler. The hotel has a fitness center with an indoor track, sun deck, exercise equipment, swimming pool, saunas, and whirlpool baths. The elegantly furnished Towers rooms have their own 24th-floor registration desk, plus a VIP lounge with complimentary cocktails, continental breakfast, and a view of the lake.

The hotel offers executives a computerized business center and 140,000-square-feet of in-house exhibition space; a telephone answering machine can be hooked up to guestrooms. Other pluses include a self-service parking garage, 21 barrier-free rooms for handicapped access, and a computerized concierge — just touch the computer screen to find out about personal services, shopping, dining, and entertainment in the area. *Kitty O'Shea's Pub* is a surprisingly authentic Irish saloon staffed by Irish men and women under a government exchange program. *Buckingham's* restaurant offers a fine menu, plus an impressive selection of 120 single-malt scotch whiskies. Information: *Chicago Hilton & Towers,* 720 S. Michigan Ave. (phone: 922-4400).

CLARIDGE: This 172-room hotel is steeped in pure Chicago. The pillow mints are Frangos from *Marshall Field,* the shampoo and conditioner are from Chicago-based Helene Curtis, the beer is a local brew, and even the elevator music features Windy City musicians. On each of the 12 floors, mini-exhibitions focus on Chicago legend and lore. Completely renovated, this new version of the landmark hotel has six suites, including three with wood-burning fireplaces, a library stocked with works by Chicago writers, and knowledgeable personnel — all of whom have actually attended a workshop in Chicago history. Comfortable and intimate, the *Claridge* is just steps from clubs, art galleries, fine stores, and jazz nightspots. Continental breakfast is included, and there's a limo service to the Loop. Health club facilities are available nearby. Information: *Claridge,* 1244 N. Dearborn Pkwy. (phone: 787-4980 or 800-245-1258).

DRAKE: A fabulous lobby with an ornate marble fountain, rooms with old-fashioned high ceilings, plus a graciousness rare in hotels these days (the elevators even have velvet-covered benches!), set this Hilton property apart. There are 535 rooms (all complete with terry robes, fresh fruit, and a daily newspaper); some suites offer incredible views of Lake Michigan. The nearly 75-year-old grande dame offers a traditional late-afternoon tea in the *Palm Court* with a choice of 14 teas, a selection of pastries, currant buns, and scones, and background music from a harpist. Opened in 1933, the nautically themed *Cape Cod Room* remains among Chicago's finest seafood eateries; try one of a half dozen lobster specialties or a bowl of the famous *Bookbinder's* red snapper soup. Information: *Drake,* N. Michigan Ave. at Lake Shore Dr. and Walton Pl. (phone: 787-2200).

FOUR SEASONS: Afternoon tea and proximity to *Bloomingdale's* (located in the same high-rise) are this well-managed property's draws, as well as an opulent Presidential suite and 16 residential apartments. More than a third of the 343 rooms boast separate sitting rooms. Guest facilities include 24-hour room service, two-line telephones, and well-stocked mini-bars; the hotel also has a health center with an outdoor jogging track. One of Chicago's newest luxury hotels, it is popular with businesspeople. Information: *Four Seasons,* 120 E. Delaware Pl. (phone: 280-8800 or 800-332-3442).

INTER-CONTINENTAL: A meticulous restoration has brought this 338-room Art Deco gem, built in 1929 as the *Medinah Athletic Club,* back to its former splendor. Intricate marble, bronze, brass, painted ceilings, and sculptured details in terra cotta, gold leaf, granite, and fine wood are among the treasures unearthed here. Guestrooms boast lush carpeting, furnishings of fruitwood inlaid with ebony or maple and bedspreads inspired by 19th-century French toile design. Afternoon tea and freshly baked raisin scones served with preserves and thick Devonshire cream are late-day musts. The ornate marble pool on the 14th floor was once used by Johnny Weissmuller, Olympian and movie Tarzan. Information: *Inter-Continental,* 505 N. Michigan Ave. (phone: 944-4100 or 800-327-0200).

MAYFAIR REGENT: Unlike most of the new high-rise hotels, this lakefront property is small enough to offer the ultimate in comfort and style — the ratio of employees to guests is 1 to 1 and service is exemplary. A non-smoking floor is one of its features. Also offered is the ultimate in service, including a maid to help guests unpack, fresh fruit and jasmine tea to refresh them upon arrival, and such in-room amenities as terry robes, slippers, and an umbrella. Dinner here is an elegant affair: The rooftop *Le Ciel Bleu* offers classic French food and romantic views of Lake Michigan (particularly pleasant at breakfast). Tea with finger sandwiches and French service is offered in the *Mayfair Lounge* from 3 to 5 PM daily. *The Palm,* on the ground floor, has steaks as prime as those served by its famous New York counterpart, plus the largest Maine lobsters in town. Information: *Mayfair Regent,* 181 E. Lake Shore Dr. (phone: 787-8500; 505-243-6466, collect from Alaska; 800-545-4000 elsewhere in the US).

LE MERIDIEN CHICAGO: This high-tech hotel boasts rooms with compact-disc players and a selection of CDs, as well as VCRs and remote-control television sets. The 247 rooms, 35 suites, and 6 penthouse suites have deep-soak bathtubs and glass-encased showers. Guests have access to nearby health club facilities and the hotel operates two oversize BMWs for free shuttle service to the Loop each morning. The stylishly Art Deco *Laurent* restaurant offers first-rate French fare and a bountiful Sunday brunch; with its huge picture windows overlooking Rush Street, it's a romantic spot from which to watch the world go by. Information: *Le Meridien Chicago,* 21 E. Bellevue Pl. (phone: 266-2100 or 800-443-2100).

MIDLAND: Recently renovated, this 260-room property is located close to the heart of Chicago's business and financial district. Facilities include a fitness center and meeting rooms; there are three non-smoking floors. Guests can take advantage of free transportation provided by a chauffeur-driven English cab, plus complimentary cocktail hour, buffet breakfast, and daily newspaper. The *Exchange* restaurant offers continental fare, and at the *Ticker Tape Bar and Grill* a vocalist performs Wednesday through Friday evenings. This Art Deco landmark is ideally located within walking distance of museums, theaters, the Sears Tower, and Grant Park. Information: *Midland,* 172 W. Adams at La Salle (phone: 332-1200 or 800-621-2360).

NIKKO CHICAGO: This elegant 425-room hotel overlooking the Chicago River was built by Nikko Hotels International, Japan's largest hotel chain. Japanese touches abound — landscaped indoor gardens, Asian artwork, even two Japanese-style suites, each with tatami sleeping rooms, a private rock garden, and a deep-soak tub. Four "Nikko floors" are served by a lounge offering complimentary hors d'oeuvres and continental breakfast. A center within the hotel has computer terminals and a business library. The health club offers a sauna, bicycles, treadmills, rowing machines, and weights. Daily exercise garb is provided. A jazz trio is featured in the *Hana Lounge* nightly (except Sundays). Breakfast is served in the award-winning *Les Célébrités* restaurant, which has river views and such creative treats as ginger flapjacks with blueberries and shirred eggs with wild-game sausage. For authentic Japanese food, the *Benkay* has teppanyaki tables, a sushi bar, and private tatami rooms. Information: *Nikko Chicago,* 320 N. Dearborn St. (phone: 744-1900).

OMNI AMBASSADOR EAST: Convenient to Oak Street Beach, the shopping along North Michigan Avenue, and the Lincoln Park Zoo, this landmark hotel, listed on the National Register of Historic Places, now is part of the Omni Classic chain. The 275 rooms and 52 suites in this lovely hostelry have not lost an ounce of charm; there's an "Author's Suite" — temporary home to writers on promotional tours — that has bookcases filled with signed volumes. The hotel is still home to the famous *Pump Room* restaurant, a Chicago institution — and a great place for sighting celebrities. The entryway is lined with photos of famous guests — from Bogie and Bacall to Frank Sinatra and Queen Elizabeth II — all of whom have dined in booth No. 1. It also features live entertainment: dancing to a three-piece band, and standard (but well-prepared) fare such as roast duck, prime ribs, and double-cut lamb chops. Information: *Omni Ambassador East,* 1301 N. State Pkwy. (phone: 787-7200).

PARK HYATT: If you want pampering, this elegant 255-room hostelry across from the historic Water Tower is the place to be. Indulgences and little "extras" here include fresh fruit and candy in guestrooms; a suite with an 1898 Steinway piano, three-times-a-day maid service, complimentary car wash (if you've driven here), and a fleet of courtesy cars that includes a 1965 Rolls-Royce Silver Cloud III. Afternoon tea is served in the lobby lounge, and there's elegant dining in the acclaimed *La Tour* restaurant, a champagne bar, weekend caviar bar, and a classical guitarist in the lounge. Information: *Park Hyatt,* 800 N. Michigan Ave. (phone: 280-2222).

RITZ-CARLTON: Shoppers love this Magnificent Mile location, connected as it is by elevator to *Water Tower Place,* and celebrities (this is the choice of many) appreciate its high level of comfort and its attentive and discreet service. The huge 12th-floor atrium lobby, with its plush seating and the restful sound of its fountain, has to be one of the most tranquil spots in town. All of its 432 spacious rooms have equally spacious king-size beds. The hotel dining room serves fine French fare and offers an excellent Sunday champagne brunch. Information: *Ritz-Carlton,* 160 E. Pearson St. (phone: 266-1000).

SWISSÔTEL: This 625-room property offers spectacular views of the Chicago River and Lake Michigan, and has a distinct European-business flavor — although *Land of Plenty,* its signature dining room, emphasizes American cooking. Still, there are European-style breakfasts at the *Garden Café* and Swiss-trained bakers at the adjoining *Konditorei* producing fresh-baked breads (try the crack-crust Swiss variety) and pastries to go. More than 20% of the staff and close to half the guests are European. Guestrooms are spacious (among the largest in the country at 450 square feet) and have marble bathrooms with separate glass-enclosed showers. Catering to business needs are 34 function and conference rooms, a 60-seat, state-of-the-art theater, and a business center with a stock-market quotation board, newswire, and business library. Information: *Swissôtel,* 323 E. Wacker Dr. at Illinois Ctr. (phone: 565-0565 or 800-65-GRAND).

Chicago's Best Restaurants

If Chicago's restaurants don't receive as much attention nationally as those on either coast, their quality and innovation are less the reason than is the traditional Midwestern reluctance to toot one's own horn. Culinary distinction hasn't characterized the city for long, however. For decades, this was a steak-and-potatoes town; the epitome of gastronomic excellence was the old *Stockyard Inn.* In the mid 1960s, the now-shuttered *Maxim's* (an exact replica of the Paris original) brought elegant French dining to Chicago. Earlier, at *Pizzeria Uno,* Chicago developed its own style of pizza. But between *Prairie* and *Printer's Row,* an original heartland gastronomy began to develop. The growth of Chicago's native food culture was helped along by Richard Melman, the brains behind Lettuce Entertain You Enterprises, who developed the idea of the theme restaurant and who saw it blossom into an international phenomenon. (See *Ed Debevic's* and *Shaw's Crab House* below). While elegant French restaurants remain on the list of Chicago's best, members of the city's ethnic melting pot have contributed some nominees to the list as well. Below is a sampling of what epitomizes Chicago's variety and excellence.

AMBRIA: Everything is charming about this toney, Lincoln Park restaurant in the *Belden-Stratford* apartment hotel, from the comfortable setting to the menu's sophisticated variations on nouvelle cuisine. Dinner might begin with a salad of sliced duck, pine nuts, and fresh pears with red-currant dressing or a tropical lobster salad. Desserts from the kitchen of chef Gabino Sotelino include a range of pastries, mousses, sorbets, ice cream, and soufflés. For four or more there is a *dégustation* dinner with samples of many dishes. The mood here is formal. Open for dinner; closed Sundays. Major credit cards accepted. Information: *Ambria,* 2300 N. Lincoln Park W. (phone: 472-5959).

ARUN'S: This is the antithesis of the typical basic storefront ethnic eatery. One of the city's most elegant dining rooms, it offers such daily specials as quilted shrimp with fried rice cracker and curry sauce, prawns with garlic-lime sauce, and catfish curry. Fragrant layered rice custard and Thai iced coffee are the perfect finish. Open for dinner Tuesdays through Sundays. Major credit cards accepted. Information: *Arun's,* 4156 N. Kedzie (phone: 539-1909).

CAFÉ PROVENÇAL: This intimate French country-style restaurant, on a quiet street in north suburban Evanston, offers some of the most carefully prepared French dishes in the area — the Wisconsin pheasant with rosemary-honey glaze and the New York foie gras with Cortlandt apples are particularly recommended. The homemade bread here is mouth-watering, and the desserts are heavenly. This is an aromatic spot (it's filled with flowers), dressed with soft lighting, pink tablecloths, and a large fireplace. Open for dinner every day but Sunday. Major credit cards accepted. Information: *Café Provençal,* 1625 Hinman St., Evanston (phone: 708-475-2233).

CAPE COD ROOM: This long-honored seafood restaurant inside the *Drake* hotel serves well-prepared fresh fish such as ahi tuna, trout, halibut, fresh lobster, pompano, and other finny fare. Specialties include a variety of lobster dishes, Norwegian salmon, and *Bookbinder's* red snapper soup. This venerable restaurant has consistently been listed as one of the nation's finest seafood eateries since it opened in 1933; its checkered tablecloths, captain's chairs, copper pots, chowder kettles, and stuffed sailfish decorating the walls make it a cozy spot. Open for lunch and dinner daily except *Christmas Day.* Major credit cards accepted. Information: *Cape Cod Room, Drake Hotel,* 140 E. Walton (phone: 787-2200).

CARSON'S: It's always worth the wait at this busy establishment to feast on the city's most mouth-watering babyback ribs, smoked and prepared with the kitchen's own slightly spicy sauce. You'll need plenty of napkins and a bib (it comes with your meal). In keeping with the city's stockyard heritage, the other offerings here lean heavily toward meat: barbequed chicken, pork, and beef, prime ribs, and steak. There is a single seafood item on the menu. Especially tasty accompaniments include salads with a creamy, anchovy-flavored dressing, and tangy au gratin potatoes. The ambience is lively and friendly, if a bit loud on weekend nights, and the decor — mirrored walls and plenty of comfy booths — is casual. The entrance, lined with autographed photos of politicians, sports figures, and actors, reads like a Chicago hall of fame. Everyone from Mayor Daley to Michael Jordan has eaten here. Open daily. Major credit cards accepted. Information: *Carson's,* 612 N. Wells St. (phone: 280-9200).

ED DEBEVIC'S: Fans of saddle shoes, angora sweaters, and the 1950s-style diner rejoice! *Ed's* is the second coming of the traditional American diner, complete with old-time rock 'n' roll, smart-talking, gum-snapping waitresses, and all-American food. Dobie Gillis would be right at home in this culinary time capsule. Although most of the dishes won't stop traffic, the hamburgers (on freshly baked buns), tangy barbecued pork sandwiches, and generous salads are good bets. Home-style meatloaf with mashed potatoes is the ultimate in comfort food. Dessert pies are traditional and well-made. This is a great spot to dine informally; teens love it. Open for lunch and dinner, 7 days a week. No credit cards. Information: *Ed Debevic's,* 640 N. Wells (phone: 664-1707).

EVEREST ROOM: In a relatively short time, this spectacular restaurant — with a 40th-floor westerly view of the city — has risen (no pun intended) to acclaim as one of Chicago's very finest. The cooking is a combination of traditional French preparations and dishes of chef Jean Joho's native Alsace. Standouts include black squid risotto, salmon soufflé, oxtail terrine with horseradish sauce, and venison with elderberries. Apple strudel is a recommended dessert. There is a special pre-theater menu and a seven-course *dégustation* menu that provides a good sampling of the superb fare. Closed Sundays and Mondays. Major credit cards accepted. Information: *Everest Room,* 440 S. La Salle St. (phone: 663-8920).

LE FRANÇAIS: For years, chef Jean Bouchet made this one of America's finest French restaurants. Today, after Bouchet's death, the kitchen is in the hands of Roland and Mary Beth Liccioni, and the still-excellent fare has a somewhat lighter touch. Standouts include rack of lamb served with tiny fresh vegetables and couscous, stuffed Dover sole, Lyonnaise sausage served en croute with port wine sauce, and crayfish bisque. The between-course sorbets are imaginative and the pastries are superb. Closed Sundays. Major credit cards accepted. Information: *Le Français,* 269 S. Milwaukee, Wheeling; take Kennedy Expy. to Rte. 294 N., Willow exit (phone: 708-541-7470).

FRONTERA GRILL and TOPOLOBAMPO: Offering what is arguably the finest and most authentic Mexican fare in the Midwest, this pair of adjoining restaurants is the creation of Rick and Deann Bayless, whose prolonged travels across Mexico enabled them to appreciate and perfect recipes for regional cooking. Wood-grilled meats and dishes such as chile rellenos are a specialty at *Frontera,* the first of these two restaurants to open (no reservations); the newer, pricier *Topolobampo* does take reservations and offers more elegant fare, such as roasted wild turkey with a *mole poblano* sauce and pork loin roasted with an apricot-red chile sauce. Closed Sundays and Mondays. Major credit cards accepted. Information: *Frontera Grill* and *Topolobampo,* 445 N. Clark St., (phone: 661-1434).

JACKIE'S: An intimate 50-seat neighborhood spot serving some of the finest nouvelle cuisine in the city — fine French food with Oriental highlights. Consider delicate orange-honey-glazed squab served with Chinese vermicelli and cabbage garnished with cashews and cloud-ear mushrooms. Lobster salad is served with rock shrimp and smoked mussels over fettucine flavored with saffron and squid ink. Mousse-filled "chocolate sack" is owner/chef Jackie Shen's signature dessert. Closed Sundays and Mondays. Major credit cards accepted. Information: *Jackie's,* 2478 N. Lincoln (phone: 880-0003).

PIZZERIA UNO: In 1943, Ike Sewell and Rick Ricardo opened this eatery and invented Chicago's famous deep-dish pizza — generous layers of toppings baked with a thick crust in a deep-dish pan. This restaurant just goes to show that sometimes you can't improve on the original. It is always crowded and always frenzied. Cocktails and beer are available to accompany your pizza. The atmosphere may be thin here, but the food more than makes up for it. If *Pizzeria Uno* gets too crowded, try its sister spot, *Pizzeria Due,* same fare and only slightly more elegant surroundings. Both are open daily for lunch and dinner. Major credit cards accepted at both. Information: *Pizzeria Uno,* 29 E. Ohio St. (phone: 321-1000); *Pizzeria Due,* 619 N. Wabash Ave. (phone: 943-2400).

PRAIRIE: This striking split-level building has cathedral ceilings and tall windows, inspired by the architecture of Frank Lloyd Wright, and innovative cooking from America's heartland. Try the Wisconsin buffalo, Lake Superior whitefish, Michigan dried fruits, or Iowa pheasant prepared by chef Stephen Langlois. Finish with apple pie that defines the genre or Indian persimmon pudding. A five-course tasting menu is available, with interesting Midwestern wines to accompany the food. Unfortunately, service can be slow. Breakfast is served every day of the week, with brunch on Sundays; lunch is available on weekdays; dinner is served nightly. Major credit cards accepted. Information: *Prairie,* 500 S. Dearborn in the *Morton* hotel (phone: 663-1143).

SHAW'S CRAB HOUSE: Offering the city's widest selection of oysters — sometimes up to a dozen or so varieties — and the best crab cakes west of Maryland, this restaurant has consistently been one of Chicago's finest seafood houses. Creamy New England–style clam chowder is a good way to start, and a properly tart key lime pie provides an admirable finish. In between, there are seasonal soft-shell and stone crabs, Dungeness crab, and a reliable selection of grilled fish. The adjoining *Blue Crab Lounge* offers a raw bar and more casual dining. Open daily. Major credit cards accepted. Information: *Shaw's Crab House,* 21 E. Hubbard St. (phone: 527-2722).

SPIAGGIA: With picture windows overlooking the Magnificent Mile, this is one of Chicago's most stylish Italian dining places. There's subdued Art Deco lighting and a piano tinkling in the background, and the menu features ambitious pasta dishes, grilled fish, roast chicken, and specialties such as grilled veal chop with fresh sage. Its little sister café across the hall is more casual — yet still stylish and very romantic — and is a good spot to share a thin, blistery pizza or perhaps enjoy an excellent rendition of osso buco. Open daily except Sunday lunch. Major credit cards accepted. Information: *Spiaggia,* 980 N. Michigan Ave. (phone: 280-2750, 280-2764).

T'ANG DYNASTY: *Chicago Sun Times* restaurant critic Don Rose calls this the "most gorgeous Chinese restaurant in town. . .maybe of any persuasion." The spectacular decor in this eatery across from *Bloomingdale's* showcases imported works of art and is the backdrop for authentic Mandarin dishes and genteel service. The specialty is Beggar's Hen, rock cornish hen with black mushroom stuffing that is baked in a moisture-sealing clay casing that is cracked open with a mallet at tableside. Other standouts are stuffed crab claws, prawn fingers, and a superlative version of Peking duck. Open for lunch and dinner daily. Try the lunch buffet weekdays. Major credit cards accepted. Information: *T'ang Dynasty,* 100 E. Walton (phone: 664-8688).

TANIA'S: Festive decorations and dim lights make this a romantic spot on weekdays, but this sleek Latin restaurant club, which grew out of the neighborhood grocery of Cuban émigre Elias Sanchez, hops on weekends, when crowds of local Hispanics flock here to eat and dance the night away. Seafood dishes (including authentic Spanish paella) are the house specialty, but don't overlook the intriguing casseroles or the meat dishes, such as *lechón asada* (roast pork) — or Chicago's best black bean soup. The very good wine list is mostly Spanish, with some select South American offerings, led by the Chilean Concha y Toro Casillero del Diablo. Throw your diet out the window and finish off your meal with Caribbean coffee and Kahlua, Pampero rum, or espresso. Open daily. Major credit cards accepted. Information: *Tania's,* 2659 N. Milwaukee (phone: 235-7120).

A Windy City Shopping Spree

Chicago is the Midwestern haven for shopping fanatics, offering everything from the chicest of the chic European designers to discount stores and second-hand shops. It even has its own *Bloomingdale's,* the first "Bloomies" located away from the Eastern Seaboard. Buy a *Cartier* diamond or an African skirt, a used record or hand-painted jewelry — Chicago has it all. The sleekest shopping district is the Magnificent Mile, the blocks along North Michigan Avenue between the Chicago River and Oak Street; many stores listed below are found there. It boasts three marvelous upscale malls, the 7-story *Water Tower Place* (at Pearson St.), the new *Chicago Place,* and *900 North Michigan.* For Chicagoans, the traditional shopping area is State Street, where such local favorites as *Marshall Field* and *Carson Pirie Scott* are found.

ArchiCenter – The museum/office of the Chicago Architecture Foundation, it also has one of the most complete gift shops for those seeking architecture-linked souvenirs of their visit, including children's gifts. Its selection of architectural books and periodicals is extensive; it also is a good source for maps. Many architectural tours start here. 350 S. Dearborn (phone: 922-3431/2).

Avventura – Some of the showiest men's shoes anywhere, plus more traditional footwear, ties, and belts. And take a look at the giant black cowboy boots (emblazoned with a red bull on the front and No. 23 on back) that were custom-designed for Michael

Jordan, the Chicago *Bulls* basketball great. *Water Tower Place,* level 4 (phone: 337-3700).

Beauty & The Beast – This children's toy store is a jungle of stuffed creatures, with everything from a life-size tiger to a moving, chirping parrot. *Water Tower Place,* level 7 (phone: 944-7570).

Bloomingdale's – The Midwest flagship store for this legendary New York retailer has six floors of merchandise, plus four spas and two restaurants. Its sixth-floor Petrossian counter stocks Caspian caviar, Norwegian smoked salmon, and other delicacies, all of which may be sampled in the adjacent *Petrossian Rendezvous* restaurant. 900 North Michigan (phone: 440-4460).

Bottega Veneta – Fine (and pricey) Italian leather items, carefully crafted and tastefully displayed. Everything from luggage to desk accessories, plus a small selection of shoes and scarves. 107 E. Oak St. (phone: 664-3220).

Burberry's – Classic trench coats and other weatherproofs are the tradition here, but there also is a wide range of men's and women's apparel and accessories. You pay for the name and the cachet of the distinctive plaid, but quality designed to last comes along with the substantial price tag. 633 N. Michigan Ave. (phone: 787-2500).

Carson Pirie Scott – You can't get any more Chicago than this store, whose Windy City tradition stretches back more than 130 years. There are 7 floors of fashions and furnishings here. Even if you aren't in a spending mood, stop by to see the elegant building designed at the turn of the century by architect Louis Sullivan (note the distinctive iron ornamentation on the northwest corner.) 1 S. State St. (phone: 744-2000).

Cartier – The Midwestern outpost for this fine French jewelry chain, this toney shop is as exclusive as its many international counterparts. 630 N. Michigan Ave. (phone: 266-7440).

C.D. Peacock – This Chicago landmark was founded the same year as the city itself, 1837, and has purveyed silver, crystal, jewelry, and fine china to Chicagoans ever since. With chandeliers, fine cabinetry, and bronze peacock doors, it's known for its service (and for its expert repair shop). In the *Palmer House* hotel, State and Monroe Sts. (phone: 630-5700).

Chanel – The French design house's signature clothes, complete with quilted leather bags, ropes of chains and pearls, and classic fashions on the Magnificent Mile. 940 N. Michigan Ave. (phone: 787-5500).

City – This store sells sleek, high-tech leather-and-chrome furniture, mostly European-made. 361 W. Chestnut St. (phone: 664-9581).

City of Chicago – The Chicago lover's stop for memorabilia, it offers a wide range of *real* Windy City artifacts — such as manhole covers, parking meters, and even uprooted traffic lights. Shop for posters, sculptures, books, street banners, tote bags, calendars, T-shirts, and crafts — and the ever-popular Chicago street signs. Pick up one in stock for $35 or order a custom-made sign designating your favorite spot for $40. 174 W. Randolph St. (phone: 332-0055).

Famous Fido's – One-stop shopping for your feline friend or canine companion. This famous department store for dogs and cats has just about everything. Take Spot to lunch at "Famous Fido's Doggie Deli," which has a dining area as well as all-natural dog food, pet treats, and cakes to take out. 1533 W. Devon Ave. (phone: 973-3436).

Fannie May – Chicago's favorite chocolates for more than 7 decades are sold out of more than 100 shops around the city. The best-known outlets are in *Water Tower Place* (phone: 664-0420) and *North Pier* (phone: 527-9372). Also, don't overlook the bargains: "seconds" that are imperfectly shaped (but taste just as delicious) at the outlet store (51 E. Randolph; phone: 782-3224).

Feline Inn – This is the ultimate cat hotel, where owners board their feline companions. But it also is a celebration of cats, with the feline theme emblazoned on watches, earrings, rings, pins, bracelets, and countless other items. Owner Peg O'Boyle also paints figurines and planters devoted to the meow crowd. She also sells pedigree kittens. 1445 N. Wells (phone: 943-2230).

Godiva Chocolatier – For those with a taste for sumptuous sweets, Godiva's chocolates, made from original Belgian recipes and packaged in classy gold-foil wrappers, are the Dom Perignon of chocolates. If chocolate is not your fatal attraction, try the rich cappuccino and espresso at this shop in *Water Tower Place* (phone: 280-1133).

Hammacher Schlemmer – Everything imaginable in classy and unique gifts (plus lots of gadgets and gizmos that you never imagined existed), ranging from heated pet beds to a Wurlitzer jukebox, along with a wide variety of kitchen and electronic gadgets. Offbeat, unusual? How about a tandem bicycle with side-by-side seats, a basketball hoop for the swimming pool, or slippers shaped like dinosaur feet? 618 N. Michigan Ave. (phone: 664-9292).

Illinois Artisans Shop – Located inside the spectacular State of Illinois Center, this store is a showcase for the state's top craftspeople, showcasing the work of more than 400 artists. Included are jewelry, ceramics, prints, weavings, and beautifully wrought quilts. 100 W. Randolph St. (phone: 814-5321).

Mallers Building – This 21-story office building has 16 floors of retail and wholesale jewelers. Here shoppers can buy diamonds, get a watch repaired, sell silver and gold, and have a favorite piece engraved. Stop on the third floor to visit a genuine old-time deli with great cheese blintzes and potato pancakes. 5 N. Wabash St.

Marshall Field – The quintessential Chicago retailer (founded in 1853) — and a pioneer of American department stores — purveys all manner of merchandise, from apparel to rare books to Chicago's favorite Frango mints. Services offered here range from wardrobe coordinators to translators who help overseas visitors hurdle any shopping language barriers. In 1991 the store, which began its retail life with the credo "Give the lady what she wants," was in the throes of a multi-million-dollar renovation, said to be the largest in US retail history. In addition to nearly 150 departments aimed at the latter-day equivalent of the carriage trade, the store has a wonderful assortment of food counters on the seventh floor; tucked away on this floor is the *Bowl & Basket,* a good spot for hearty soup and a sandwich carved from a slab of beef or ham. Afternoon tea is a *Field*'s tradition — as is the huge, beautifully decorated *Christmas* tree that dominates the store each holiday season. 111 N. State St. (phone: 781-1000). There is a second downtown store at *Water Tower Place* (phone: 781-1234).

Maxwell Street – Every Sunday, vacant lots in this Italian neighborhood turn into Chicago's largest outdoor flea market. Get there close to dawn — the good stuff is gone by 10 AM — and be prepared to buy some souvenirs from merchants who hawk everything from used clothes to antiques. Stroll around and listen to musicians who have set up at the market, watch the city's ethnic communities mingle as they haggle over prices, and grab a bite to eat from the food stands — pork-chop sandwiches are legendary. Open 6 AM to noon. At Maxwell and 1300 S. Halsted. Nearby are the vice police headquarters, where exteriors were shot for the "Hill Street Blues" TV show.

Museum Shop of the Art Institute of Chicago – Mobiles, stained glass, books, note cards, calendars, and a variety of high-quality gifts, such as faithful reproductions adapted from artworks in the museum's collection. An extensive stock of jewelry is especially worth inspecting. On *Valentine's Day,* a calligrapher is on hand to personalize cards. Michigan Ave. at Adams St. (phone: 443-3534).

Neiman Marcus – Designer clothes, furs, perfume, and jewelry are just the beginning of what's available in one of the trendiest of the trendy stops along the Magnificent Mile. Designer salons, a fourth-floor epicure shop, a complete beauty salon, and a noted lingerie shop are among the features of this top-of-the-line department store, with a soaring 3-level atrium. 737 N. Michigan Ave. (phone: 642-5900).

Network – The NBC Tower, a new building constructed in Art Deco style, is home to this NBC store where you can pick up all the Peacock Network memorabilia imaginable. Included are T-shirts emblazoned with the names of your favorite television shows. 455 N. Columbus Dr. (phone: 836-5555).

Nuts on Clark – Welcome to 30,000 square feet of delicious nuts, coffee, wine, exotic tea, fruit, and chocolate. Located 2 blocks north of *Wrigley Field.* 3830 N. Clark (phone: 549-6622).

Reckless Records – Vinyl lives — at least in this store, which has an incredible selection of alternative rock, imports, and independent music artists. The shop claims to have the largest selection of used albums in the city. 3157 N. Broadway (phone: 404-5080).

Rizzoli – This is the bookstore extraordinaire, offering best sellers, along with a wide array of art, architecture, history, and children's books, plus an extensive selection of paperbacks, European magazines, compact discs, stationery, and cassettes. Browse in these genteel surroundings as classical music provides a harmonious background. *Water Tower Place,* level 3 (phone: 642-3500).

Saks Fifth Avenue – Apparel and accessories are complemented by beauty-salon ministrations at this store known for service. Anchoring the gleaming new *Chicago Place,* an 8-level specialty retail center, *Saks* specializes in a wide range of women's fashions but also has departments for men, children, and infants, and gifts. 700 N. Michigan Ave. (phone: 944-6500).

Sugar Magnolia – African-print skirts, funky children's clothes, and silk-screened ties are among the worldly fashions found here. Tie-dyes and designer jeans round out the collection. 34 E. Oak St. (phone: 944-0885).

Tiffany & Co. – Perhaps the country's most famous luxury jewelry emporium (thanks to Audrey Hepburn and Truman Capote). In addition to jewelry, there are crystal, porcelain, and timepieces at the Midwestern outpost of this upscale bastion of exquisite quality and design. 715 N. Michigan Ave. (phone: 944-6500).

A Unique Presence – Exceptional artisan crafts and gifts in a year-round art-fair atmosphere. Unusual items from more than 175 North American artists, including ceramics, blown glass, wood, handmade paper, leather, and an array of handmade jewelry. 212 N. Clybourn (phone: 929-4292).

Women & Children First – The only truly feminist bookstore in the city offers regular book signings and special events linked to literature and feminism. 5233 N. Clark St. (phone: 769-9299).

Antiques: Chicago's Best Hunting Grounds

Antiquing is not reserved for weekends in Chicago — any day of the week will do just fine. The city and its suburbs are filled with shops offering antiquarian treasures. The bounty ranges from all manner of Americana to centuries-old European china and clocks to Orientalia and Art Deco. The largest concentration of shops within the city limits is along Belmont Avenue, between 1400 W. Belmont and 2400 W. Belmont.

Benkendorf Collection – Fine 17th- and 19th-century clocks from England and France are featured items here. *900 North Michigan,* level 1 (phone: 951-1903).

Carteaux Jewelers – Tucked among the modern jewelry here are antique pieces for sale. 31 N. Wabash (phone: 782-5375).

Chicago Riverfront Antique Mart – Five floors of imported and early American furniture and antiques. This location also has an auction hall with regularly scheduled antique auctions. 2929 N. Western (phone: 252-2500).

Crete-Beecher Antique Dealers – This clutch of fine antiques shops is in Crete, one of Chicago's far-south suburbs. Spend a few pleasant hours tracking down treasures, then head south to the tiny village of Grant Park and have dinner at the *Bennett-Curtis House,* the antique-filled house of Sam and Charlotte Van Hook. Main St. and Route 1 in Crete (phone: 708-672-8298).

Glen Ellyn Antique Shops – There are 14 stores specializing in antiques in Glen Ellyn, a suburb west of Chicago. The wide range of collectibles includes estate jewelry and hand-painted china. Shops are concentrated at the intersections of Main St. and Crescent and Main St. and Pennsylvania (phone: 708-469-0907).

The Goldsmith – Mixed in with this shop's custom jewelry designs is a selection of antique jewelry. *Water Tower Place,* level 2 (phone: 751-1986).

New York Jewelers – This century-old diamond and jewelry wholesaler carries a large selection of estate jewelry, including antiques. 3 S. Wabash Ave. (phone: 855-0145).

Sassafras – This shop specializes in antique advertising memorabilia. Signs, clocks, and posters inscribed with the names of the products they promoted are just some of the delightful novelties for sale. 2260 N. Lincoln Ave. (no phone).

For the Body

Golf

Home of one of the nation's first 18-hole courses (the *Chicago Golf Club* opened in the western suburb of Wheaton in 1892), Chicago considers its golf courses to be among the best in the country. The city's rolling prairies, woods, and streams adapted well to the design and construction of stunning courses, and the game caught on with the city's elite. By the turn of the century, there were more than a dozen courses in the area, frequented by industrialists, merchants, and professionals. Exclusive golf club membership is still a ticket into Chicago's inner circle; many deals are made on courses like *Bob-O-Link* on the North Shore (which accepts only male members). Early on, the city became the headquarters of the Western Golf Association; for years the *Western Open* was played on Oak Brook's *Butler International*, until it moved to the larger *Cog Hill* course in Lemont in 1991. No less an authority than *Golf Digest* claims that Chicago has eight of the country's best golf courses; several of the leading ones open to the public are listed below. Some of the less expensive and more accessible public courses also are listed; to play requires getting in line before dawn on weekends.

CANTIGNY: Located on the former estate of Robert McCormick, controversial editor and publisher of the *Chicago Tribune,* this club offers a public course in a pampered country-club setting. Designed by Roger Packard, it was listed the best new course in 1989 by *Golf Digest.* It includes an extra 9-hole course in case the full 18 holes are booked, which is most of the time. Reservations are accepted 7 days in advance; greens fees are $45, $55 with a golf cart; closed Mondays. Information: *Cantigny Golf Club,* 27 W. 270 Mack Rd., Wheaton. (phone: 708-668-3323).

COG HILL: One of the nation's best-known courses (it hosted the *1991 Centel Western Open*), it also is the nation's largest public golf facility. The four 18-holers vary in difficulty, the most challenging of which is Dubsdread, the championship course. Near the Palos Forest Preserve, its ample clubhouse serves three full meals a day; the links also have a halfway house. Open 365 days a year. Greens fees are $23 and $27 for the less challenging courses, $65 for Dubsdread; a golf cart is an additional $23 for two. Information: *Cog Hill,* 12294 S. Archer Ave., Lemont (phone: 708-257-5872).

FOREST PRESERVE NATIONAL: Early in this century, city planners began acquiring undeveloped lands in Cook County for a forest preserve system. Many of the area's golf courses are near these preserves of open meadow, woods, and streams; 18-hole *Forest Preserve National* is actually *in* one of them. The Western Golf Association lists it as one of the top 25 courses in the world — the lines that form here long before dawn testify to that fact. Open daily during the season; no reservations. Greens fees are $12 on weekdays, $16 on weekends; golf carts are $16. No phone reservations. Information: *Forest Preserve National,* 163rd and Central Ave., Oak Forest (phone: 708-429-6886).

KEMPER LAKES: This relatively new, well-manicured 18-hole course with bent-grass fairways and large, undulating greens, hosted the *PGA Championship* in 1989 and the *Grand Slam of Golf* for several years. Built around several artificial lakes, water comes into play on nine of its holes. Reservations must be made 1 week in advance; greens fees are $90 per person, including golf cart. Information: *Kemper Lakes,* Old McHenry Rd., Hawthorne Woods (phone: 708-540-3450).

PINE MEADOW: Listed as the best new public course in 1986 by *Golf Digest,* it has remained among the country's 25 best public courses since that time. With 18 holes spread out over 200 acres, it offers a fair test of all golfing abilities; it also includes a lighted practice range. Open daily until November from 5 AM to 10 PM; greens fees are $45; golf cart is $23. Reservations, accepted in advance, must be prepaid with a major credit card. Information: *Pine Meadow,* in far north suburban Mundelein (take I-94), 1 mile north of Rte. 176 on Butterfield Rd. (phone: 708-566-4653).

Several other courses closer to the city proper include the popular and crowded *Waveland,* a 9-hole course in Lincoln Park. On the lakeshore, with the city's skyline as a backdrop, it's hard to play into, but it costs less than $10 to play. To get to *Waveland,* head north on Lake Shore Drive to Irving Park (4400 North), and follow the signs. (For further information call the Chicago Park District at 294-2200 or 294-2274.)

The north suburban villages of Wilmette and Glencoe also maintain good 18-hole courses on the edge of forest preserves. They are open daily, April to November, from dawn to dark. The *Wilmette Golf Course* (near the Lake Street exit on I-94 and Harms Road) takes reservations 1 day in advance for weekdays, 6 days in advance for weekends. Greens fees are $22; a golf cart costs an additional $22 (phone: 708-256-9777). *Glencoe* (a few miles farther north) accepts no phone reservations, but will take them in person for weekday games; on weekends, it's first come, first served. Greens fees are $21 on weekdays, $23 on weekends; $15 for 9 holes or after 4 PM; a cart is $20 extra. To get there, take I-95 (the Edens Expressway) to Dundee Road, head east to the second stoplight, and turn left. The country club is a half mile north, where the road ends, at 621 Westly Rd. (phone: 708-835-0981).

Horsing Around

 There is nowhere within the city's limits to ride horseback (the last stable with access to Lincoln Park was closed in the 1960s, when Sandburg Village was constructed). Happily, there are numerous trails in the Forest Preserve Districts in the six-county metropolitan area, Chicago's magnificent system of greenways that surround the city, mainly along the course of the Skokie, Des Plaines, and Fox rivers.

In Cook County, all riders must be guided, and frequently on weekends there are long waits for mounts. (The city still offers carriage rides, most of which leave from the Water Tower on North Michigan Avenue.) Some of the larger and more accessible public stables are listed below; for information on dozens of others, call the Forest Preserve offices. For Cook County, call 261-8400 or 708-233-3767; for Lake County (north), 708-367-6640; for DuPage County (west), 708-620-3800; for Will County (southwest), 815-727-8700; for Kane County (far west), 708-232-1242.

WILLOW BROOK ACRES: Riders at all levels are welcome here, but they must be guided. Horse and guide can be rented for $15 an hour, plus a $1 licensing fee that's good all year. There's a pleasant jaunt over quaint wooden bridges and through quiet woods frequented by deer and other animals. A special treat here is the 90-minute Sunday ride (from 9:30 to 11 AM), which includes breakfast. Information: *Willow Brook,* 9501 Austin, in north suburban Morton Grove (accessible from Edens Expy.; phone: 708-967-9800).

WEDGEWOOD: Only for experienced riders who must be able to prove their ability to saddle and bridle a horse before they are allowed access to more than 100 miles of trails that wind through the Cook and Lake County forest preserves. Cost is $15 per hour; a trail rider license (cost is $1) also is necessary. Information: *Wedgewood Riding Center,* 699 N. Milwaukee Rd. in north suburban Wheeling (accessible from I-94; phone: 708-537-9610).

HAWTHORNE HILLS: Located in the Lake County Forest Preserve, experienced riders can go out without a guide to ride on its 6 miles of gravel horse trails. Patrolled trails are marked with appropriate gait, and riders must follow these guidelines or risk being ticketed. Children must be 12 years of age or older. The cost is $15 for an hour with a guide, or $20 for 90 minutes without a guide; permit fee is included; reservations are required a day in advance. Information: *Hawthorne Hills,* on Milton Rd. in far northwest suburban Wauconda, 1½ hours north of the city along Route 12 (phone: 708-526-0055).

Where They Bite: Fishing in Chicago

With Lake Michigan as its front yard, there's lots of fishing in Chicago. Since there are high levels of PCBs and other contaminants in the lake, commercial fishing is banned, but that doesn't stop pier-bound anglers, who line the lakefront at dawn when the fish tend to be biting and who have no qualms about eating what they catch. The most popular pier within the city limits is the largest, at Montrose Harbor (4400 North at Lake Shore Drive, at the north end of Lincoln Park). An annual rite of spring is smelt fishing, sometime in April when the tiny silver smelt are running. For devotees, it's an all-night, lantern-lit affair, with lots of beer to ward off the chill. Almost every pier along the lakeshore (there are dozens in the city and suburbs) is loaded with smelt fishers; more dedicated anglers will want to take a charter boat out into the lake. But even for diehard landlubbers, it's great fun to just watch. Below are a few favorite launching pads.

CHICAGO SPORTFISHING ASSOCIATION: A nonprofit association of licensed charter boat captains organized to promote sportfishing (mostly for trout and salmon), this group arranges fishing excursions on Lake Michigan. Each craft is 30 feet long or more and can take up to six anglers. The cost is $395 for 5 hours, $475 for 6 hours, or $635 for 8 hours (plus the city's 4% amusement tax). A $5 fishing license and salmon stamp also are required. The association also will make arrangements for pleasure cruising. Information: *Chicago Sportfishing Association,* in Burnham Harbor, just south of the *Shedd Aquarium* and *Adler Planetarium* on Lake Shore Dr. (phone: 922-1100).

MIDWEST CHARTER BOAT ASSOCIATION: Like the *Chicago Sportfishing Association,* this is a coalition of licensed charter boat captains who take parties out for fishing, pleasure cruises, or diving. Boats can accommodate from four to six passengers. The cost is $365 for 5 hours for six people and $310 for 4 hours; 6- and 8-hour trips also can be arranged. Charters set out from all the city's major harbors: Montrose, Belmont, Diversey, and Burnham. Information: *Midwest Charter Boat Association* (phone: 935-4188).

Freewheeling in Chicago

It's no wonder that cycling is a favorite outdoor pastime in Chicago. The city's vast lakefront and extensive forest preserves not only offer wide-open spaces but also a mainly flat terrain; the only hills are gentle ones, and the woods — even those next to busy thoroughfares — are quiet. Serious cyclists should bring their own bikes; those who are just interested in a casual ride can rent bicycles at the *Village Cycle Center* (1337 N. Wells, just south of North Ave. and close to Lincoln Park; phone: 751-2488). Bicycles cost $7.50 per hour, with a 2-hour minimum, or $25 for a 24-hour period. Come early, especially on weekends. For more information about cycling, call or write the *Chicagoland Bicycle Federation,* PO Box 64396, Chicago, IL 60664 (phone: 427-3325).

LAKEFRONT BIKE PATH: The ride along the lakefront is fairly empty during much of the week. On weekends it can be crowded, particularly along the midsection north of the Loop. The full lakefront bike path runs from 5800 North, at the northern end of Lincoln Park, along Oak Street Beach, and out by Navy Pier; it crosses the river and continues south through Grant and Burnham parks to Jackson Park on the South Side, a ride of nearly 12 miles. There are places to pick up food and drinks along the way.

FOREST PRESERVES: All of Chicago's forest preserves maintain paved or gravel bike paths. For specifics, call individual districts (see the list under *Horsing Around,* above). One path is the 10-mile North Branch Bicycle Trail, which follows the Chicago River's northern branch from Devon Avenue (6400 North) in the city to the *Chicago Botanical Garden* in Glencoe. The well-marked, paved path is frequently crowded on summer Sunday afternoons, but it is delightful in the evenings and the rest of the year; there's a restaurant in the garden. For a map, contact the *Cook County Forest Preserve* at 261-8400 or 708-233-3767.

ILLINOIS PRAIRIE PATH: One of the finest trails in the state, this 45-mile stretch winds along an abandoned railroad track through parts of Cook, Kane, and Du-Page counties. It begins in west suburban Maywood and heads either to southwestern Aurora or west to Batavia and the Fox River. It goes through suburban towns, farmlands, prairie, and meadowlands. A guidebook is available from the nonprofit *Illinois Prairie Path Association,* Box 1086, Wheaton, IL 60187 (phone: 708-665-5310).

Swimming

Other than Rio de Janeiro, Chicago is probably the only city in the world where you can swim with skyscrapers as a backdrop. The Oak Street Beach, at the top of Michigan Avenue, isn't Ipanema (bathing suits are required here), but the people watching is just as fine. For less crowded conditions, there's the North Avenue Beach (1600 North), which also includes a public bathhouse. Both are free. The most accessible public beach outside the city is in north suburban Wilmette; admission is $4 per person.

Tennis

The Chicago Park District maintains two downtown tennis facilities. The better of the two (by far) consists of 12 well-lighted clay courts at Daley Bicentennial Plaza, in the northern end of Grant Park at 337 E. Randolph Street, near several residential high-rises. Courts cost $5 an hour; open weekdays from 7 AM until 10 PM, weekends from 8 AM to 7 PM; reservations are required (phone: 294-4790). There also are several courts farther south in Grant Park, at 9th and Columbus Dr.; reservations are not required.

Sailing Chicago's Waterways

 With that huge lake out there, you'd think that Chicagoans would do a lot of sailing, but powerboats are a lot more popular here. Among sailors though, *the* race is the annual mid-July *Chicago to Mackinaw,* the nation's longest and oldest freshwater regatta. Weekend sailors practice for the *Mac* from May through September, or just go out and race a variety of classes — Stars and J-24s and Solings are popular. Races start from several harbors each weekend: the *Chicago* and *Columbian* yacht clubs at Monroe Street, the *Chicago Yacht Club* branch at Belmont Harbor (3200 North), and *Sheridan Shore* in Wilmette. If you're a sailor, you might try to make friends with a boat owner to get a spot on a crew. For more casual sailing, craft are available for rent from four places in the city (see below) and one in suburban Wilmette. Note: The lake is tricky; you should know heading up from jibbing before you weigh anchor.

CHICAGO PARK DISTRICT: Sailboats can be rented from three Chicago Park District locations. Barnett 14-foot boats and windsurfers cost $10 for 1 hour, $15 for 2 hours; 16-foot HobieCats (a catamaran) cost $15 for 1 hour, $25 for 2; instruction is available for an additional $5; a $20 deposit and driver's license are required. At Burnham Harbor (between the *Adler Planetarium* and McCormick Place), renters must stay within the spacious harbor; open Mondays through Saturdays (phone: 294-2399). At the South Side Cultural Center (6100 South), sailors can venture farther into the lake; open Thursdays through Sundays (phone: 288-1223). From Farwell Avenue (6900 North, near Loyola University), sailors also can go farther out into the lake; closed on Mondays; make reservations a day or two in advance (phone: 262-7377).

BILL GLADSTONE'S SAILING CLUB: For a more challenging time on the water, experienced sailors might want to try a J-22, a 22-foot version of the popular J-24, often raced out of Chicago's harbors. The craft can accommodate up to five people; to be sure you can get a boat (these are popular with regulars), call a week in advance. Boats cost $35 per hour during the week, $40 on weekends; for new customers, there's a $10 check-out charge. At the north end of Belmont Harbor, Lake Shore Dr. at 3200 North (phone: 871-SAIL).

CHARLOTTE ANN: Sailing on this 100-year old, 90-foot, two-masted schooner might be more for the soul than for the body since a five-member crew does most of the work, but the air is fresh and the view superb. It offers brunch cruises on Sundays from 11 AM to 2 PM; there's an evening cruise on Mondays (6:30 to 9:30 PM), with snacks and drinks but no meals; both are $40 per person; capacity is 32 people. The *Charlotte Ann* sails out of Burnham Harbor, south of the *Adler Planetarium* (phone: 643-3400).

WILMETTE PARK DISTRICT: North suburban Wilmette supports one of the loveliest beaches on the North Shore; you can walk along it for nearly a mile. It also is accessible by public transportation; take the Howard Street line as far as it goes, then switch to the Linden Avenue train and ride to the end of the line. The beach is only 4 blocks away; the Baha'i House of Worship is a lakefront landmark. Windsurfers and 14-foot Barnetts are available weekdays for 1 hour for $12, 2 hours for $22; on weekends 1 hour for $17. Weekday HobieCat rental costs $17 for 1 hour, $29 for 2 hours; the weekend charge is $30 for 1 hour, $45 for 2 hours. A $50 deposit is required for all rentals; major credit cards accepted. Reservations are required, and they can be made up to 48 hours in advance (phone: 708-256-9662). If you are driving, take Lake Shore Drive north to Sheridan Road and follow it to the Baha'i House of Worship (you can't miss it) and start looking for a parking place.

For the Mind

Memorable Museums

 Judging by the excellence of its major museums, Chicagoan's take-it-or-leave-it attitude toward culture hardly applies here. In fact, the city is fiercely proud of its museums — and with good reason. Four of them — *Adler Planetarium,* the *Shedd Aquarium,* the *Field Museum of Natural History,* and the *Museum of Science and Industry* — have something practical to offer about the skies, the seas, all of nature, and what people have done with them. They also say something about the city's economic history; the original endowments for each of them came from merchants and mail order kings: Sears, Roebuck for *Adler* and the *Museum of Science and Industry,* Marshall Field for *Shedd* and the *Field.* The *Art Institute of Chicago* also is one of the city's treasures; located at the side of the Loop, it's friendly, familiar, and a fair measure of the city's love of fine art. Several other new museums have opened recently, and some old ones are gaining new popularity. A few of these are mentioned as well.

ADLER PLANETARIUM: Founded in 1930 by Sears, Roebuck executive Max Adler, its major attraction is the narrated sky show, where visitors can sink into deeply cushioned chairs and contemplate the secrets of the universe. In addition to changing shows — a recent one was "New Views of the Solar System" — and the popular holiday favorite, "Star of Bethlehem," there also are numerous exhibits on astronomy, many — like "Beam Me Up" — geared to children. Its founder's intention was educational: bringing an understanding of the heavens down to earth. A research center dedicated to computer-enhanced views of the planets is now under construction. There also is a shop for amateur stargazers — which you'll definitely become after a visit here. Open daily from 9:30 AM to 5 PM year-round and until 9 PM on Fridays, when there also is a late sky show. No admission charge to the planetarium; admission charge to the sky show. Information: *Adler Planetarium,* 900 E. Solidarity Dr., or 1300 South on Lake Shore Dr. (phone: 322-0300).

ART INSTITUTE OF CHICAGO: The illustrious Grant Wood would have been proud that he is included among the august artists whose work hangs in this museum, one of the world's leading art treasure houses. Its extensive collection of French Impressionist and post-Impressionist paintings includes Georges Seurat's *A Sunday Afternoon on the Island of La Grande Jatte,* Edward Hopper's *Nighthawks,* and Grant Wood's *American Gothic,* in addition to artworks that encompass centuries of human creativity from around the world. Its recently rehung 20th-century gallery is awesome, and don't miss the famous Thorne miniature rooms (68 exquisitely decorated period rooms from around the world, built to ¹/₁₂ scale). The institute's "please touch" children's museum has been extensively remodeled, and was scheduled to reopen this spring. (Tours of all the collections are offered free of charge.) After wandering through the museum, check out its shop for some unusual gifts. Open weekdays from 10:30

AM to 4:30 PM, Saturdays from 10 AM to 5 PM, and Sundays from noon to 5 PM. (A Culture Bus, which makes stops at all the major downtown museums, leaves every half hour — May through September — from the front of the *Art Institute.*) Information: *Art Institute of Chicago,* Michigan Ave. at Adams St. (phone: 443-3600; for recorded information, 443-3500).

CHICAGO CHILDREN'S MUSEUM: Previously known as *Express-ways,* this is a place where children can explore architecture via child-size reproductions of Chicago buildings, or dress up like the characters in the historical portraits that hang on the museum's walls. There also is a playroom, where a child can work with building blocks. You might want to avoid the museum on weekends, when it's packed. Thursday evenings (from 5 to 8 PM), a free night for families, also draws large crowds. Closed Mondays; closed Thursdays during the day; other hours are Tuesdays through Sundays from 10 AM to 4:30 PM; admission charge. (While there, you might want to visit the *Chicago Maritime Museum;* phone: 836-4343), which recalls the days when the Great Lakes were more like a busy interstate highway system.) Information: *Chicago Children's Museum,* 435 E. Illinois (phone: 527-1000).

CHICAGO HISTORICAL SOCIETY: Its striking façade — storefront windows offering previews of what's inside (a significant aspect of its recent $15 million expansion) — is designed to draw visitors in, not intimidate them. For more than 130 years, the *CHS* has been documenting the social, cultural, and industrial development of Chicago; its most extensive exhibit ever, "A House Divided: America in the Age of Lincoln," includes the bed in which Lincoln died. The "Chicago Street" and "We the People," as well as dioramas of the city's early history and the Chicago Fire, are major attractions. Its store is well-stocked with memorabilia, and the *Society Café* is a lovely place to eat. Open daily from 9:30 AM to 4:30 PM and Sundays noon to 5 PM; admission charge, except on Mondays. Information: *Chicago Historical Society,* 1601 N. Clark St. at North Ave. (phone 642-4600).

DU SABLE MUSEUM OF AFRICAN-AMERICAN HISTORY: Chicago more than likely is the country's only major city whose first permanent resident was of African descent. This museum — in the South Side's Washington Park, near where many of the city's current residents of African descent live — is named after Jean-Baptiste Point duSable, a fur trader from Haiti who settled on the banks of the Chicago River in 1789. Among the museum's major features are a 10-foot-high carved mahogany mural depicting highlights of African-American history; there also is a large display of African artifacts. Changing displays include depictions of life in the Caribbean, among others. Open Mondays through Fridays from 9 AM to 5 PM, Saturdays and Sundays from 1 to 5 PM; admission charge. Information: *Du Sable Museum of African-American History,* 740 E. 56th St. (phone: 947-0600).

FIELD MUSEUM OF NATURAL HISTORY: No superlatives can adequately describe the contents of this enormous collection, initially endowed by dry goods king Marshall Field. From the great brass elephant and dinosaur skeleton in its grand lobby to the ancient Chinese artifacts on the floor above, from displays of flora and fauna to the Pawnee earth lodge, it is a museumgoers' dream. Recently the museum has been adding to its long list of "biggests" and "bests" with some new, very user-friendly exhibits (designed by the son of renowned pediatrician and author, Benjamin Spock). The most spectacular of them is "Traveling the Pacific," which re-creates a coral island and an island town, placing artifacts in a context that makes it easy for a city child to relate to; even grownups who have actually visited such places will be impressed. A reconstructed Egyptian tomb, complete with mummy, is equally extraordinary. Open daily from 9 AM to 5 PM; admission charge, except on Thursdays. Information: *Field Museum of Natural History,* S. Lake Shore Dr. and McFetridge (phone: 922-9410).

MUSEUM OF BROADCAST COMMUNICATIONS: One of Chicago's newest and most popular museums, this is a favorite among TV fans and media archivists. Private study booths allow visitors to view videotapes of old commercials and television shows. For those with a Walter Mitty fantasy of being a TV news anchor, there is a News Center where technicians will videotape your not-ready-for-prime-time debut. At $19.95, your 15-minute newscast makes a nice souvenir. The gift shop has other fun items linked to the networks and their celebrities. Open Wednesdays through Fridays and Sundays from noon to 5 PM, Saturdays from 10 AM to 5 PM; admission charge. Information: *Museum of Broadcast Communications,* 800 S. Wells in River City (phone: 987-1500).

MUSEUM OF CONTEMPORARY ART: An outpost of the avant-garde, this museum has earned its reputation by showcasing important new artists on the cutting edge in film, conceptual and, or more traditional forms of expression; it also displays the work of more established modern artists. The substantial permanent collection includes the work of artists from around the world, as well as those artists from such Chicago schools as the Imagists of the 1960s. Owing to its cramped quarters, the museum has little of the latter on display; work is under way on a new building, set to open in 1995 near the Water Tower. Daily tours are available. The museum's store has some unusual gifts, and the *Site Café* offers a cozy light lunch. Open Tuesdays through Saturdays from 10 AM to 5 PM, Sundays from noon to 5 PM; no admission charge on Tuesdays, otherwise admission is discretionary. Information: *Museum of Contemporary Art,* 237 E. Ontario (phone: 280-2660).

MUSEUM OF SCIENCE AND INDUSTRY: Affectionately dubbed "the attic" by students at the nearby University of Chicago, this extraordinary museum was founded in the 1920s by Sears, Roebuck head Julius Rosenwald. Books have been written about its contents. Highlights include a working coal mine, a captured World War II German submarine, Colleen Moore's fairy-tale castle, a walk-in model of a space shuttle, a simulated tour of the human brain, and a reproduction of a 19th-century cobblestoned village street. Newer exhibits focus on ways in which money changes hands and how computers work. The circular *Omnimax Theater* and Henry Crown Space Center are other must-sees. Every schoolchild in the city visits here at least once, and most families spend a day. Open daily *Memorial Day* through *Labor Day* from 9:30 AM to 5:30 PM; the rest of the year it is open weekdays from 9:30 AM to 4 PM, weekends from 9:30 AM to 5:30 PM; admission charge (additional charge for the *Omnimax Theater*), except on Thursdays. Information: *Museum of Science and Industry,* 5700 S. Lake Shore Dr. (phone: 684-1414).

SHEDD AQUARIUM: The 90,000 gallon main tank holds 6,000 species of aquatic creatures. The residents of the aquarium's simulated coral reef are fed daily at 11 AM and 2 PM; it's worth planning your visit around these feeding times. Elsewhere, all manner of other fish swim in separate tanks under marine-themed mosaic walls. The *Shedd*'s 170,000-square-foot indoor *Oceanarium* — an ocean on the lake — is surrounded by a walk-through Alaskan coastline teaching exhibit. Dolphin shows are offered daily (these are very popular; you might want to reserve ahead of time), and river otters can be seen at play in a new display on aquatic mammals. Open daily from 9 AM to 6 PM; admission charge. Information: *Shedd Aquarium,* 1200 S. Lake Shore Dr. (phone: 939-2426).

SPERTUS MUSEUM OF JUDAICA: A highlight is the Artifact Center, where children can sift through the sand of a simulated archaeological dig to uncover Middle Eastern artifacts. There is an impressive display of Jewish religious objects, a Holocaust Memorial collection of personal items found at concentration camps, and a range of traveling exhibits. Open Sundays through Thursdays from 10 AM to 5 PM, Fridays from 10 AM to 3 PM; admission charge. Information: *Spertus Museum of Judaica,* 618 S. Michigan, at the Spertus College of Judaica (phone: 922-9012).

Houses of Worship

Chicago boasts some of the nation's most magnificent churches, many filled with fine art and statuary, stained glass windows, and exquisitely carved altars. These houses of worship initially served ethnic groups that emigrated here from predominantly Catholic countries; unfortunately, despite the fact that some churches are architectural treasures, the neighborhoods that housed them changed, and many no longer have a sizeable enough parish to support and maintain them. One, Holy Family on West Roosevelt Road, was recently saved from demolition (and, one hopes, will be restored) by a massive fund-raising effort. Both the Chicago Architecture Foundation (phone: 326-1393) and the Illinois Landmarks Preservation Council (phone: 922-1742) give tours of the city's churches and temples. Below are a few of Chicago's most heavenly spots.

BAHA'I HOUSE OF WORSHIP: This nine-sided, domed structure, listed on the National Register of Historic Places, has delicate concrete filigree, resembling a three-tiered wedding cake, and is surrounded by nine flower gardens and almost as many fountains. The Baha'i faith, which originated in 19th-century Iran, emphasizes the spiritual unity of humanity, and the temple's nine sides represent the world's nine major religions. The interior is equally striking — sun-filled and stark, but restful. The structure took 4 decades (1920 to 1960) to build, while money slowly was raised for its construction. There also is a museum on the ground floor. Services are held every day at 12:15 PM; the church is open to the public from 10 AM to 10 PM. Information: *Baha'i House of Worship,* 100 Linden Ave. in Wilmette (phone: 708-256-4400).

HOLY NAME CATHEDRAL: Though architecturally undistinguished, this Victorian Gothic building (1874) of lemon-colored limestone is the principal church of the Roman Catholic Archdiocese of Chicago. The building, however, is more widely known for its connection with gangland massacres: North Sider Dion O'Banion was murdered in his flower shop across the street by Al Capone's South Side gang in 1924; 2 years later, another mob did in Hymie Weiss (a good Catholic boy), missed three of his compatriots, and nicked the church's front steps. (The bullet holes remained there for decades, until they were discreetly repaired.) Information: *Holy Name Cathedral,* Chicago Ave. and N. State (phone: 787-8040).

NORTH SHORE CONGREGATION ISRAEL: Home of one of the city's oldest and largest Jewish congregations, this imposing building — on a bluff high above Lake Michigan — was designed in 1964 by Minoru Yamasaki, who referred to it as "the architecture of light." Its vaults have amber-tinted skylights, and the side windows open on a vista of trees, lawn, and lake. In 1982, Chicago architect Thomas Beeby added a more intimate chapel, classical in design and cylindrical in shape. Though the addition pays no heed to the original design, it won Beeby an award from the American Institute of Architects. Visitors are welcome weekdays from 9 AM to noon and 2 to 4 PM. Information: *North Shore Congregation Israel,* Sheridan Rd. in north suburban Glencoe (phone: 708-835-0724).

OLD ST. PATRICK'S: The city's oldest church building (built between 1852 and 1856), St. Patrick's survived the Great Chicago Fire (an early parishioner may well have been Mrs. O'Leary, owner of the infamous cow). It also survived the 1959 construction of the Kennedy Expressway, just behind it, which dealt a final blow to the neighborhood. Today, as new housing in the area expands the church's congregation, its pews are full again on Sundays. On the last weekend in July, the church also sponsors "the world's largest block party," with music, dancing, and enough food and drink to bring out the Irish in anyone who partakes. Information: *Old St. Patrick's*, corner of Desplaines and Adams, just west of the Loop (phone: 782-6171).

ROCKEFELLER MEMORIAL CHAPEL: This massive Gothic edifice serves the University of Chicago and is named for John D. Rockefeller, its chief benefactor. It has lovely stained glass windows and a 72-bell carillon that is noted for its exquisite tone. The chapel's high, vaulted ceiling is richly decorated with tiles; banners from the Vatican Pavilion of the 1964 *New York World's Fair* hang in the nave. Appropriately, it is the scene of convocations and numerous concerts, plus some affairs of state: It was here (in 1969) that John D. Rockefeller IV, presidential contender and senator from West Virginia, married Sharon Percy, daughter of another senator and then-presidential contender Charles Percy — a regal setting for such a merger. To learn more about this building and the surrounding campus, join a campus tour; they leave nearby Mondays through Fridays at 10 AM; call in advance for the meeting place. Information: *Rockefeller Memorial Chapel,* 156-80 59th St. (phone: 702-8360).

ST. CHRYSOSTOM'S: For a look at where the Protestant elite lived and worshipped during the early years of this century, visit this Episcopalian church (1894), surrounding a courtyard and the elegant turn-of-the-century homes along here and on State Parkway and Astor Street, just east of it. The interior houses a replica (on canvas) of the 10th-century mosaic of St. John from a church in Constantinople. Information: *St. Chrysostom's,* 1424 N. Dearborn Pkwy. (phone: 944-1083).

ST. JOHN CANTIUS: Once home to the city's largest Polish congregation, this 2,000-seat church now offers the city's only mass in Latin; services frequently include Gregorian chants and orchestral music. Built in 1893, its massive altar of cherry and oak and gilt is said to have been made for the *World's Columbian Exposition,* held the same year. The rest is baroque in every way: faux marble columns, gilt, and paintings and tiles on every surface. Information: *St. John Cantius,* 825 N. Carpenter (phone: 243-7373).

SECOND PRESBYTERIAN CHURCH: A century ago, this neo-Gothic jewel served Prairie Avenue, where the city's wealthiest and most socially prominent families lived. Robert Todd Lincoln, Philip Armour (of packinghouse fame), George Pullman, and Marshall Field were members. Designed by New York architect James Renwick in 1874, it has windows by Louis Tiffany but no steeple — that was lost when lightning struck in 1900 and it never was replaced. As a result of the ensuing fire, however, the interior was remodeled by Chicago's Howard Van Doren Shaw and Frederick Bartlett (founder of the *Art Institute*'s Impressionist collection). After several decades of decline, a refurbishing effort is under way. Information: *Second Presbyterian Church,* 1936 S. Michigan (phone: 225-4951).

UNITARIAN UNITY TEMPLE: Designed by Frank Lloyd Wright in 1905, this was the architect's first public building, and the one he called a "little jewel." Considered one of the nation's great architectural showpieces, it is on the National Register of Historic Places. Made of poured concrete because it was an inexpensive material, the temple contrasted sharply with most other church buildings — and much of Oak Park — at the time. Rather than a traditional steeple pointing heavenward, Unity, with its strong horizontal lines, is very solidly earthbound. Its interior is equally striking: all squares, cubes, and rectangles, with a center pulpit and low-hanging balcony and high windows that flood it with light. In recent years, the church has been restored inside and out, the interior to its original colors of cream, brown, and sea green. Included in the architectural tours of Oak Park, it also is open to the public weekdays from 1 to 4 PM and on weekends from 2 to 4 PM; admission charge for tours. Information: *Unitarian Unity Temple,* 875 Lake St. in Oak Park (phone: 708-848-6225).

A Shutterbug's Chicago

 If you can get it to hold still long enough, Chicago is an exceptionally photogenic city. There is architectural variety, old is juxtaposed with new, ornate with ordinary; there is a skyline bristling with the temples of modern commerce and graced with a 19th-century church spire; and there is the ever-present — and often-photographed — El.

Chicagoans are, by and large, delighted to share their city with others — pose in front of the Water Tower, at the *Art Institute*'s lions, or under *Marshall Field*'s clock and the sidewalk traffic will pause while you click the shutter. For other shots, the city's diversity means that all manner of tableaux will divert the eye: an ornate turn-of-the-century building reflected in the façade of a mirrored-glass skyscraper, women in saris passing a Jewish bakery, sunbathers at the Oak Street Beach against the background of the Magnificent Mile. There are any number of places from which to capture the drama of Chicago's skyline on film, beginning with two of the world's highest vantage points.

Chicago also has natural variety: A column of trees embroiders a park footpath, ivy inches up a colonial red brick building, and a summer sunset sparks the river ablaze. In all, the thriving city, the shimmering lake, the park, the people, and traces of rich history make Chicago a fertile stomping ground for shutterbugs. Even a beginner can achieve remarkable results with a surprisingly basic set of lenses and filters. Equipment is, in fact, only as valuable as the imagination that puts it to use.

Don't be afraid to experiment. Use what knowledge you have to explore new possibilities. At the same time, don't limit yourself by preconceived ideas of what's hackneyed or corny. Because the Sears Tower has been photographed hundreds of times before doesn't make it any less worthy of your attention.

In Chicago, as elsewhere, spontaneity is one of the keys to good photography. Whether it's a sudden shaft of light bursting through the clouds and hitting the river just so, or bathers frolicking in the waters off Oak Street Beach, don't hesitate to shoot if the moment is right. If photography is indeed capturing a moment and making it timeless, success lies in judging just when a moment worth capturing occurs.

A good picture reveals an eye for detail, whether it's a matter of lighting, positioning your subject, or taking time to frame a picture carefully. The better your grasp of the importance of details, the better your results will be photographically.

Patience often is necessary. A rusted old Volkswagen in the center of your Magnificent Mile street scene? Reframe your image to eliminate the obvious distraction. People walking toward a scene that would benefit from their presence? Wait until they're in position before you shoot. After the fact, many of the flaws will be self-evident. The trick is to be aware of the ideal and have the patience to allow it to happen. If you are part of a group, you may well have to trail behind a bit in order to shoot properly. Not only is group activity distracting, but bunches of people hovering nearby tend to stifle spontaneity and overwhelm potential subjects.

The camera not only provides an opportunity to capture Chicago's varied and subtle beauty, but also a chance to interpret it. What it takes is a sensitivity to the surroundings, a knowledge of the capabilities of your equipment, and a willingness to see things in new ways.

LANDSCAPES, WATERSCAPES, AND CITYSCAPES: Chicago's bustling byways and historic buildings most often are visiting photographers' favorite subjects. But the city's green spaces and waterways provide numerous photo possibilities as well. In addition to the lions in front of the *Art Institute,* the Sears Tower, and the Fourth Presbyterian Church on Michigan Avenue, be sure to look for natural beauty: the Grant Park elm trees lining South Michigan Avenue, the well-manicured plots of flowers in the Lincoln Park Conservatory, and the sailboats and motorcraft that ply Montrose Street Harbor are just a few examples.

Color and form are the obvious ingredients here, and how you frame your pictures can be as important as getting the proper exposure. Study the shapes, angles, and colors that make up the scene and create a composition that uses them to best advantage.

Lighting is a vital component in landscapes and waterscapes. Take advantage of the richer colors of early morning and late afternoon whenever possible. The overhead light of midday often is harsh and without the shadowing that can add to the drama of a scene. This is when a polarizing filter is used to best effect. Most polarizers come with a mark on the rotating ring. If you can aim at your subject and point that marker at the sun, the sun's rays are likely to be right for the polarizer to work for you. If not, stick to your skylight filter, underexposing slightly if the scene is particularly bright. Most light meters respond to an overall light balance, with the result that bright areas may appear burned out.

Although a standard 50mm to 55mm lens may work well in some landscape situations, most will benefit from using a 20mm to 28mm wide-angle lens. *Adler Planetarium,* with city skyscrapers looming in the distance, for example, is the type of panorama that fits beautifully into a wide-angle format. Use a detail as a focal point for your shot: A flower, for instance, can be used to set off a view of the Oak Street Garden area, or people can provide a sense of perspective in a shot of the *Art Institute.*

To isolate specific elements of any scene, use a telephoto lens. Perhaps there's a particular carving in a historic church that would make a lovely shot, or it might be the interplay of light and shadow on the Picasso sculpture in Daley Plaza. The successful use of a telephoto lens means developing an eye for detail.

PEOPLE: As with taking pictures of people anywhere, there are going to be times in Chicago when a camera is an intrusion. Your approach is the key: Consider your own reaction under similar circumstances and you get an idea of what would make others comfortable enough to be willing subjects. People often are sensitive to having a camera suddenly pointed at them, and a polite request, while getting you a share of refusals, also will provide a chance to shoot some wonderful portraits that capture the spirit of the city as surely as the scenery does. For candids, an excellent lens is a zoom telephoto in the 70mm-to-210mm range; it allows you to remain unobtrusive while the telephoto lens draws the subject closer. And for portraits, a telephoto can be used effectively as close as 2 or 3 feet.

For authenticity and variety, select a place likely to produce interesting subjects. The Water Tower is an obvious spot for visitors, but if it's local color you're after, visit Little Saigon or one of the *Taste of Lincoln Park* festivals in mid-July, or the *Bud Billiken Day* parade. The area around Buckingham Fountain is a good place for people shots. Aim for shots that tell what's different about Chicago. In portraiture, there are several factors to keep in mind. Morning or afternoon light will add richness to skin tones, emphasizing tans. To avoid the harsh facial shadows cast by direct sunlight, shoot in the shade or in an area where the light is diffused.

SUNSETS: While the sun doesn't set over the lake in Chicago, there are days when the last golden rays reflect off a lone sailboat, or when a fiery light hits the water and the skyline is crowned with magical clouds of pink and lavender, purple and red.

When shooting sunsets, keep in mind that the brightness will distort meter readings. When composing a shot directly into the sun, frame the picture in the viewfinder so that only half of the sun is included. Read the meter, set, and shoot. Whenever there is this kind of unusual lighting, shoot a few frames in half-step increments, both over and under the meter reading. Bracketing, as this is called, can provide a range of images, the best of which may well be other than the one shot at the meter's recommended setting.

Use any lens for sunsets. A wide-angle is good when the sky is filled with color-streaked clouds, when the sun is partially hidden, or when you're close to an object dramatically silhouetted against the sky.

Telephotos also produce wonderful silhouettes, either with the sun as a backdrop or against the palette of a brilliant sunset sky. Bracket again here. For the best silhouettes, wait 10 to 15 minutes after sunset. Unless using a very fast film, a tripod is recommended.

Red and orange filters often are used to accentuate a sunset's picture potential. Orange will help turn even a gray sky into something approaching a photogenic finale to the day, and can provide particularly beautiful shots linking the sky with the sun reflected on the ocean. If the sunset is already bold in hue, the orange will overwhelm the natural colors. A red filter will produce dramatic, highly unrealistic results.

NIGHT: If you think that picture possibilities end at sunset, you're presuming that night photography is the exclusive domain of the professional. If you've got a tripod, all you'll need is a cable release to attach to your camera to ensure a steady exposure (which often is timed in minutes rather than fractions of a second).

For situations such as evening concerts at *Ravinia* or nighttime river cruises, a strobe does the trick, but beware: Flash units often are used improperly. You can't take a view of the skyline with a flash. It may reach out as far as 30 feet, but that's about it. On the other hand, a flash used too close to a subject can cause overexposure, resulting in a "blown out" effect. With most cameras, strobes will work with a maximum shutter speed of 1/125 or 1/150 of a second. If you set the exposure properly and shoot within range, you should come up with pretty sharp results.

CLOSE-UPS: Whether of people or of objects, close-ups can add another dimension to your photography. There are a number of shooting options, one of which is to use a 70mm or a 210mm lens at its closest focusable distance. Unless you're working in bright sunlight, a tripod will be worthwhile. If you are very near your subject and there is a good deal of reflective light, it may pay to underexpose a bit in relation to the meter reading.

If you do not have a telephoto lens, you still can shoot close-ups using a set of magnification filters. Filter packs of one-, two-, and three-time magnification are available, converting your lens into a close-up lens. Even better is a special macro lens designed for close-up photography.

The following are some of Chicago's truly special photograph opportunities.

A SHORT PHOTOGRAPHIC TOUR

SEARS TOWER: Day or night, the view from the 103rd-floor Skydeck Observatory is breathtaking — a wonderful aerial vista for photos. On a clear day, the view from the Skydeck encompasses four states (Illinois, Wisconsin, Indiana, and Michigan). The lake looks almost benign, and the city appears lilliputian, colorful, and orderly; watch the tiny El as it winds its way north. For the best photos, use the slowest color film available for your camera (such as ASA 25) and a tripod. If you haven't got one, steady the camera on a railing or use slightly faster film. Don't use a flash, because it will reflect on the Skydeck window (tickets to the Skydeck are sold until 11:30 PM).

JOHN HANCOCK CENTER: It's not as tall as the Sears Tower, but the view is just as spectacular. From 9 AM to midnight each day you can take your camera up to Hancock Center's 94th-floor observatory and check out the view — on clear days, it stretches 80 miles in every direction. (The same rules for film speed and a tripod apply here as at the Sears Tower.)

MONTROSE HARBOR: For a fabulous view of the Chicago skyline, walk to the end of this harbor at Lincoln Park's northern end. Here a finger of land stretches far out into the lake, affording shots of high-rises and homes. To get there, head north on Lake Shore Drive and keep bearing right. Parking is available and admission is free.

LINCOLN PARK CONSERVATORY: Thousands of varieties of trees, flowers, and vegetation from around the world are on display in this glass-domed indoor facility, also one of the city's most photogenic places. Wander through the 3 acres of carefully tended gardens, perhaps posing storks at play at the fountain sculpture. In Lincoln Park at 2200 North, just south of Fullerton Ave.

MICHIGAN AVENUE BRIDGE: This historic 1919 bridge across the Chicago River offers an excellent vantage point for capturing the vibrant essence of Chicago's powerful urban landscape on film. Sunset lends a stunning play of color to the city's skyscrapers along the river's banks. One of the city's most popular thoroughfares for people and for vehicles, this bridge (and others) is frequently raised and lowered to let passing boats through. If you're lucky enough to be there when it happens, it can make for a super shot.

NAVY PIER: Several mayors and numerous civic groups have debated for decades about a real purpose for this delightful relic of the pre-automobile era — when people boarded boats here to spend a day at the dunes. Now being substantially overhauled to serve as a new exposition space, Navy Pier remains accessible along all its half-mile length, making it another lakeside spot offering an excellent view of the city's skyline and a perfect spot for photographing boats coming and going on the lake. East of Lake Shore Dr. at the end of Grand St.

OLIVE PARK: Just east of Navy Pier, this is where you can shoot bikini-clad bathers with a city skyscraper as a backdrop. This spit of land was built 25 years ago to house a water filtration plant; across the water are apartment buildings along Lake Shore Drive.

SOLIDARITY DRIVE: Named in honor of Chicago's Polish Community, the long drive out to the *Adler Planetarium* is one of Chicago's favorite spots for picture taking (visiting morning TV shows choose this as their outdoor location). And indeed, it's quite a view, with the Loop spread out to the north and the boat-studded Burnham Harbor to the south. To get here, take Lake Shore Drive south to McFetridge (it will be on the left and comes up quickly) behind the *Field Museum*. Solidarity Drive is just a block north, on the right. During the winter, there are lots of places to park.

THE EL: For the least expensive ($1.25) photographic tour of Chicago, take a train. The Ravenswood El winds north from the Loop through what's called Near North, then into upscale Lincoln Park; at Belmont (3200 North), it heads west through Lake View and Ravenswood, old ethnic neighborhoods surrounding former manufacturing districts; then ends where you can get on another train to return. The Howard Street Line comes out of the subway tunnel at Fullerton (2400 North) and heads north to the city's border, through neighborhoods called Uptown, New Town, and Rogers Park. You can get off the train at any stop that's appealing, then aim and shoot. Suggestions are Sedgwick, Armitage, Paulina (on Ravenswood line only); also Addison (*Wrigley Field*), Sheridan, Argyle (Little Saigon), and Morse (Rogers Park). Pick up either train in the Loop.

DIRECTIONS

Introduction

The Second City, City of the Big Shoulders, The Windy City, The City That Works — Chicago seems to have a nickname for every occasion. The only thing it lacks is a nickname that does it justice.

But then, it's hard to sum up a city of such varied appeal. Its skyline is visually stunning, a match for any in the world, and yet it's the city's neighborhoods that give it a flavor all its own. Chicago's culture is sophisticated without being snooty, it has opera and symphony, some of the best, but it also has peerless blues and jazz. People here are accessible, downright friendly for city-dwellers, but they're also shrewd, sharp, and skilled at the art of the deal. And what about that lakefront? It's more playground than working port, but somehow you get the sense that it's the source of the city's wealth. Chicago is the City of...who needs another nickname, Chicago is Chicago.

This is a *big* city; it has more than 3 million residents, stretches 15 miles inland from the lake and 29 miles north to south. Despite those figures, it is astonishingly easy to get around. Not only is it possible to drive to most of the city's major sites, there's often a parking place on the street nearby. If you prefer public transportation, Chicago's efficient CTA (aka the El) zips from Chinatown on the South Side to Little Saigon on the North Side with one change of train, from *Comiskey Park* to *Wrigley Field* in 20 minutes, from *Field*'s on State Street to *Field*'s at *Water Tower Place* in just 5. A hint about traveling the city on public transportation: The basic fare is $1.25 (there are discounts for off-hour trips and for seniors). Packs of 10 tokens are available at most fare booths and cost only $9. Buying 10 tokens at a time can eliminate the need to fish for change on the buses (they require exact fare) or stand in line at the train station.

As if ease of access were not enough, Chicago's grid plan and street numbering system even make it hard to get lost here. State Street is the north-south axis, Madison Street the east-west axis: 1200 North on any street is at Division; 800 West is at Halsted. It's like having a built-in compass. Train stations and highway exits all say what hundred east, west, north, or south they are.

One thing visitors quickly discover is that Chicago is a city of neighborhoods. Traditionally, those enclaves have grown up around a common cultural background, but increasingly, the social cement holding them together is a shared lifestyle. Some of the walks that follow immerse the visitor in the city's cultural stew pot of Chinese, German, Greek, Italian, Swedish, and Vietnamese peoples. Other walks cover such commercial highlights as the Loop and the Magnificent Mile, but residential and historical neighborhoods like Lincoln Park, the Gold Coast, and Pullman are also included. Here, too, are strolls that appeal to distinct interests like sculpture and architecture.

As with any big city, there is a dark underbelly to Chicago. But by taking the usual reasonable precautions (don't carry lots of cash, stay out of dark alleys, etc.), you can avoid an unpleasant element in your visit.

There are many more ways to see Chicago than there is room for here, and many more sites than can conveniently be included in these walks. In some cases, it's possible to split a walk up into two parts or more, allowing you to sample smaller bits of the city in a leisurely manner. If time is at a premium, however, the Wacker Drive tour (Walk 4) offers the best overview of the city and its history. Afterwards, hop the El and ride around the Loop or north to prowl the neighborhoods around Argyle Street, stopping for dinner at a Southeast Asian restaurant. For a more leisurely view of the city, take the Halsted Street tour (Walk 13), getting off the bus (or out of the car) frequently along this city sampler.

Whatever route you choose will offer something to delight the mind, the senses, or both. There is history here as well as culture. There also is great food, greater architecture, and the greatest people (including "The Greatest" himself, Muhammad Ali). Norman Mailer called Chicago "the last great American city," and that may be as close as words can come to identifying this manageable metropolis.

Walk 1: The Loop — A Heritage in Stone and Steel

Long Chicago's vibrant business center, the Loop is still the left ventricle of the heartland, pumping goods and services to the Midwest, the nation, and the world. Though the main shopping district has moved from State Street to North Michigan Avenue, just outside the Loop, the towering buildings within the lariat of elevated track from which the area takes its name still house corporate headquarters of *Fortune* 500 companies, high-powered law firms, and international financial services institutions. These imposing structures are not only a symbol of Chicago's business brawn, they are also a reminder that the talents of architects William Le Baron Jenney, Daniel H. Burnham, John Wellborn Root, and Louis Sullivan made Chicago the birthplace of the modern skyscraper.

Though the very first skyscraper, Jenney's Home Insurance Building, no longer exists, some of the landmarks of modern structural engineering still stand in downtown Chicago. Throughout this century, the Loop's architectural tradition has continued, providing a showcase for the work of such modern giants as Miës van der Rohe, Helmut Jahn, and the firm of Skidmore, Owings & Merrill. Two of the world's tallest skyscrapers are in this city: the Sears Tower and the John Hancock Building. The Loop also is dotted with open-air plazas (many of them settings for sculptures or mosaics by celebrated artists) that add a humanizing touch to the steel-and-glass spires. The mingling of art and commerce here reflects the spirit of a city that takes pride in its tradition of architectural innovation, and in its growing reputation as a cultural center. Indeed, these ideas come together in two structures, the Auditorium Building on South Michigan Avenue and the *Civic Opera House* on Wacker Drive, both of which were conceived with commercial space that would subsidize theaters or cultural areas, a notion that was unheard of in 1890 when the Auditorium was built.

The elevated train, or El, enters the downtown area from the west along Lake Street, curves south on Wabash, swings west at Van Buren, and heads north again and out of downtown along Wells Street. The area now officially known as the Loop generally includes an additional block or two falling just outside of the circumscribing tracks. For those with the energy and sturdy shoes, the best way to see downtown is to hike up and down its streets (the Loop is less than a mile across on the diagonal), looking at the assortment of building designs that represents a century-and-a-quarter of

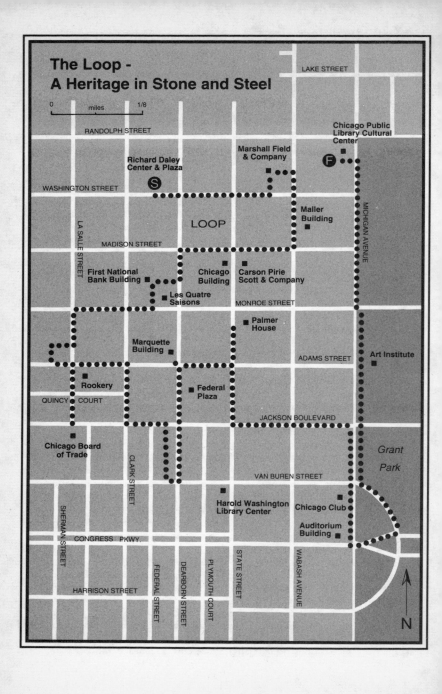

The Loop -
A Heritage in Stone and Steel

0 miles 1/8

LAKE STREET

RANDOLPH STREET

Chicago Public
Library Cultural
Center

F

Marshall Field
& Company

Richard Daley
Center & Plaza

S

WASHINGTON STREET

LOOP

Maller
Building

MICHIGAN AVENUE

LA SALLE STREET

MADISON STREET

First National
Bank Building

Chicago
Building

Carson Pirie
Scott & Company

Les Quatre
Saisons

MONROE STREET

Palmer
House

Marquette
Building

ADAMS STREET

Art Institute

Rookery

QUINCY COURT

Federal
Plaza

JACKSON BOULEVARD

Chicago Board
of Trade

CLARK STREET

Grant
Park

VAN BUREN STREET

SHERMAN STREET

Harold Washington
Library Center

Chicago Club

Auditorium
Building

CONGRESS PKWY.

FEDERAL STREET

DEARBORN STREET

PLYMOUTH COURT

STATE STREET

WABASH AVENUE

HARRISON STREET

N

architectural history. (This entire area was burned to the ground in the Great Chicago Fire of 1871.) This walk hits the highlights of the Loop, beginning at the Richard J. Daley Center and Plaza on Washington Street, between Dearborn and Clark Streets, and ending 3 blocks east at Michigan and Washington.

For all of its sophistication, Chicago also is known to look with low-brow skepticism on highfalutin' ideas of art and architecture. In 1964, when the city's 31-story Civic Center was completed, few words of praise were heard for its ugly, rust-colored Cor-Ten steel cladding. And in 1967, when a 50-foot tall sculpture made of the same steel was plunked down in the plaza in front of the building, indifference grew to downright disdain. Sure it was a Picasso, but what was it? And why was it made out of rusty metal? As time passed, the self-weathering Cor-Ten assumed a handsome reddish-brown patina and the *Chicago Picasso* (the artist never offered any clarification by giving it a name) became a truly civic center, attracting noonday crowds and serving as a landmark for casual meetings. After Richard J. Daley, Chicago's four-term mayor, died in 1976, the building, which housed offices and courtrooms, and its plaza were renamed in his honor. The Loop's first outdoor modern artwork, now a source of pride and an unofficial symbol for the city, went on to precipitate an avalanche of sculpture in the downtown area (see *Walk 2: The Loop's Alfresco Museum*).

During the summer, Daley Plaza is a center for outdoor activity, featuring a popular lunchtime concert series called *Under the Picasso*. From June through September the music (or dance) begins at noon 2 or 3 days a week. Arrive early, it's standing room only by 11:45 AM. For schedule information, call FINE ART (346-3278). On other days the plaza hosts a farmers' market and crafts fair. For information about the market and fair, call the Mayor's Office of Special Events at 744-3370.

From Daley Plaza, stroll east along Washington Street to *Marshall Field* (111 N. State, see *Quintessential Chicago* in DIVERSIONS). This landmark emporium, determined to "give the lady what she wants," has defined service for generations of American retailers and their clients. The famed store is currently undergoing a major renovation that is scheduled to be completed this year. Walk inside to see the newly gold-topped columns on the main floor and the brand-new atrium in the middle of the store. The *Walnut Room,* where generations of elegant young Chicago ladies had their first "lunch" (in white gloves with grandmother) is still serving on the seventh floor.

Across the street from *Field*'s is a vacant lot, a stalled development project. Ironically, the block once held the office building where, according to legend, Louis Sullivan met his partner, engineer Dankmar Adler, and began one of the most fruitful collaborations in American architectural history. This also is hallowed ground for the legal profession: The same building once held the law office of Clarence Darrow. In 1894, long before the famed Scopes trial (in which he argued for the right to teach evolution in schools), he made his reputation locally by defending socialist leader Eugene V. Debs following the bitter Pullman strike. Here, too, were the offices of John Peter Altgeld, the populist Governor of Illinois who was driven from office in 1896 for saving three Haymarket rioters from the gallows. The property is now awaiting construction of twin office towers and a shopping galleria designed by Helmut Jahn.

Walk through *Field*'s to Wabash and go south. Look around at the city under the El tracks; this street once was dark, grubby, and shunned by shopkeepers, but today it has become a cozy retailing area. Among the stores along here are a branch of *Crate & Barrel* (101 N. Wabash), purveyors of china and glassware, and the main store of bookseller *Kroch's & Brentano's* (29 S. Wabash). This stretch of Wabash also is called Jewelers Row, and the Maller Building (5 S. Wabash; see *A Windy City Shopping Spree* in DIVERSIONS) is the district's center.

At Madison (the dividing line between north and south on the city's street grid system), turn right toward State Street and the city's other landmark store, *Carson Pirie Scott* (1 S. State, see *Shopping* in THE CITY). Louis Sullivan's last great commission, the rectilinear upper floors with their characteristic "Chicago windows" (fixed center pane and side panes that open) are offset by the elaborate cast-iron decorations surrounding its elegant rotunda and canopied entrances.

Across the street is the Chicago Building (7 W. Madison). This 1905 gem by Holabird & Roche, one of the city's leading firms, provides a brief course in the defining characteristics of Chicago School architecture as it was developed by Sullivan and his followers: A building should have a bottom or base, a shaft or series of similar stories defining its height, and a distinct top; the exterior of the building should reveal its underlying structure; and the interior should be airy and well lit — hence the Chicago window. Unlike others of its vintage, the Chicago Building also has its cornice, or top, intact. (The building is now largely vacant and threatened by the wrecker's ball, but city and state landmark commissions are seeking a purchaser who will rescue it from oblivion.)

Continue west on Madison to Dearborn and the towering, tapered skyscraper of the First National Bank Building. The 60-story First National is reputed to be the world's tallest bank. On the Monroe Street side of the building, between Dearborn and Clark, is a plaza where hundreds of office workers lunch during the summer in the shadow of Marc Chagall's glass-and-stone mosaic *Les Quatre Saisons* (*The Four Seasons*). This is Chicago's favorite place to sit and watch the workaday world pass by; you might want to do the same.

From the vantage point of the plaza, look up at the stepped-back top of 33 W. Monroe. This building was designed by and houses Skidmore, Owings & Merrill, the renowned architectural firm that has spread Miës van der Rohe's steel-and-glass construction style throughout the world. On the west side of Madison at this corner is the Xerox Center, recognizable by its distinctive rounded façade.

Two blocks west, where Monroe and LaSalle intersect, is the city's financial center and headquarters for three of its banks: Northern Trust, Harris Bank, and LaSalle National Bank. Cross LaSalle and walk south to 190 S. LaSalle, a post-modern office building of pink granite with extruded bronze framing the tall glass entryways. This product of New York architects Philip Johnson and John Burgee has a stunning 5-story lobby sheathed in marble. Amble through it to the Adams Street entrance, pausing to look at the tapestry created by Helena Hernmarck. The hanging depicts one of the most famous illustrations from visionary architect Daniel Burnham's 1909 Plan of Chicago. Burnham, who had created the much-admired master plan for the *World's Columbian Exposition,* was given the task of doing the same for the entire city. The ambitious document that resulted laid out principles of urban planning still being used here.

One block south, on Jackson Boulevard at Quincy Court, stop in the middle of the block and turn to the west. The El station visible from here has been refurbished to look as it did a century ago when the train system was still in its infancy. At the corner is the Federal Reserve Bank (230 S. LaSalle), the government bank that serves the center of the country.

The Chicago Board of Trade Building (141 W. Jackson), a masterpiece of Art Deco architecture, was designed by Holabird & Root. Step inside (the doors are open Mondays through Fridays from 9 AM to 5 PM) for a look at the lobby's sleek curves, styled with machined precision in aluminum and polished granite. If you arrive in the morning, go into the visitors' gallery and watch the frenzied activity on the floor of the world largest commodities futures trading market. The trading here, in grains, timber, pork bellies, silver, and gold, is largely conducted in a unique sign language. (Free tours are offered Mondays through Fridays at 9, 10, 11 AM, and noon; call 435-3620 for information.)

Leaving the Board of Trade, head north, passing by the Continental Bank building. Five years ago, before the federal government had to step in to bail it out to the tune of $4.5 billion, the bank's lobby was lined with rows of tellers' windows; now it houses a variety of clothing shops. A plaque on the Jackson Street side of the building commemorates one of the great achievements of the 19th century. On this spot in 1883 the nation was officially divided into four standard time zones, part of an international agreement to standardize time. Before 1883, local time was determined by the whims of the residents, and wreaked havoc with railroad timetables.

On the corner of Adams Street (the street names are carved in the side of the building) is the Rookery (209 S. LaSalle), an elegant office building designed in 1885 by Burnham & Root. Taking its name from the pigeons that roosted in an earlier building on the site, the Rookery's most recent major renovation is near completion. The Rookery's richly ornamented façade, a city and national landmark, is of terra cotta and brick. Inside is a light-filled atrium that was redesigned by Frank Lloyd Wright in 1905 and a circular stairway that is a must-see.

Walk east on Adams to Clark Street, turn right and go to Jackson, then walk east to the Monadnock Building (53 W. Jackson). Dubbed the world's tallest office building at the time of its construction, the 16-story stone monster is still one of the world's tallest buildings with load-bearing walls (they are 6-feet thick at their base). This engineering marvel of 1891 was produced by Burnham & Root, one of the city's most distinguished firms (the south half, completed by Holabird & Roche in 1893, is slightly different from the north half). A thorough restoration begun a decade ago has brought the building back to its former glory. This is a pleasant place to stop for a bagel or a cold drink or to shop for flowers or a fountain pen in one of the elegant stores. Among the most attractive details of the restoration are the tile floors and the doors and windows. Take a stairway up a flight or two for a sense of what office life was like a century ago.

Exit the Monadnock on the Van Buren side, turn left and walk around the outside of the building and along Dearborn. Across the street is the Fisher Building (343 S. Dearborn). This 1896 Daniel Burnham-designed building is notable mainly for its Gothic details and ornamentation incorporating fish and fanciful sea creatures. Nearby is the *ArchiCenter* (342 S. Dearborn), the Loop center of the Chicago Architecture Foundation. Whether you are a casual explorer of the city's wonders or a serious student, this is the place to indulge a craving for more information about Chicago's buildings. In addition to books, periodicals, and posters, the *ArchiCenter* offers architectural tours of the Loop and other parts of the city (for recorded tour information, call 782-1776).

Continue north on Dearborn past Federal Plaza and the Dirksen and Kluczynski office buildings (to the right and left, respectively) designed by Miës van der Rohe shortly before his death. It's appropriate to pause here a moment and learn something about this admired and influential architect. Ludwig Miës van der Rohe was one of the many talented émigrés from Hitler's Germany. He came to Chicago in 1938 to teach architecture at the Illinois Institute of Technology (then called the Armour Institute of Technology). It was from here that he elaborated and refined the notions of design simplicity that revolutionized urban architecture. His familiar dictum "less is more" is stamped indelibly on Chicago's skyline.

In the center of Federal Plaza is a post office and the delightful coral-colored sculpture *Flamingo,* by Alexander Calder. From the intersection of Adams Street, two distinctly patterned buildings are visible: Ahead to the left, at Clark Street, are the Commonwealth Edison offices; to the right is the Marquette Building (140 S. Dearborn), an 1894 Chicago School masterpiece by Holabird & Roche. Over the Dearborn Street entrance to the Marquette is a bronze plaque depicting the 1637 discovery of the Chicago River by the Jesuit missionary-explorer for whom the building is named. Recently restored Tiffany mosaics illustrating scenes from Father Marquette's travels decorate the lobby.

From the Marquette, return to Adams Street and turn left. The *Berghoff* (17 W. Adams), serving beer and bratwurst since the turn of the century, is a good lunch or refreshment stop. At State, turn left again, cross the street, and walk a half block north to the *Palmer House* (17 E. Monroe; see *Checking In* in THE CITY). Potter Palmer was one of Chicago's more audacious 19th-century businessmen. After building up a multimillion dollar fortune in the dry-goods trade, he sold out to Marshall Field and bought a large parcel of land along State Street, intending to make it the grandest thoroughfare in the city. To seed his investment he built the original *Palmer House,* the most opulent hotel in the city. Unfortunately, only days after it opened in 1871 it burned to the ground in the Great Fire. The current hotel, the third on this site, was built in 1925 and has an exquisite lobby on the second floor.

Two blocks south of the *Palmer House* is the new Harold Washington

Library Center (between Van Buren and Congress), named in fond remembrance of Chicago's first black mayor, who died in 1987. The nation's largest municipal library building features a stunning piece of floor art that incorporates a quotation from Washington's first inaugural address.

At Jackson Street, turn left and go 2 blocks east to Michigan Avenue. Walk south again, passing Van Buren Street and the Chicago Club, an Italian Romanesque fantasy built in 1929. The Fine Arts Building (410 S. Michigan) was built in 1885 to serve as a showroom for Studebaker carriages. Today, it is home to a movie theater (usually showing arty imports) and a bookstore on the ground level; artists' studios, a design school, and recital halls are upstairs. This building has been a refuge for creative people throughout much of its history. One of its most famous residents was Margaret Anderson, who published *The Little Review* here. This literary journal was a forum for many great writers — among the contributors were Sherwood Anderson, Hart Crane, T.S. Eliot, Ernest Hemingway, Aldous Huxley, and Gertrude Stein. Most notorious, however, Ms. Anderson dared to print episodes from James Joyce's *Ulysses,* triggering a censorship battle that lasted 3 years. If it's time for a repast, stop at the *Artist's Café,* where there's outdoor dining in the summer and Greek-inspired dishes all year long.

Next door is the Auditorium Building (430 S. Michigan), a stunning combination of Louis Sullivan's visionary architecture and Dankmar Adler's engineering genius. Conceived as a combination office building, hotel, and opera house, it was once one of the greatest symbols of Chicago's power. Stand in the lobby and admire its marble walls and mosaic floor, or sweep up the grand stairway to the landing that looks out over Grant Park, and imagine what it might have been like to check in here in the hotel's heyday. (The building now belongs to Roosevelt University.)

The crowning achievement of the Sullivan-Adler collaboration is the *Auditorium Theater* on the Wabash side of the building. Frank Lloyd Wright called this acoustically superb, 4,200 seat theater (all seats have unobstructed views) "the greatest room for music and opera in the world." During World War II this wonderful theater was turned into a bowling alley. Fortunately, a major fund-raising effort in the mid-1960s brought about a restoration. For a theater experience of a lifetime, try to get tickets to whatever is playing here. Recent productions have included *Les Misérables* and *Phantom of the Opera.*

Cross Michigan Avenue and go between the monumental bronzes at the entrance to Grant Park. Beyond is Buckingham Fountain (for more information about the statues and the fountain, see *Walk 2: The Loop's Alfresco Museum*). Back from the street, walk along an ornamental balustrade, maneuvering around the cracked masonry and stairway to cross Jackson Street to the *Art Institute of Chicago.* (Unfortunately, planners of the Grant Park Underground Garage neglected to allow for pedestrian crossways at the entrances and exits along here.)

On the way to the *Art Institute,* pause in the museum's refreshing south garden, where Lorado Taft's *Spirit of the Great Lakes* stands. The *Art Institute* (see *Chicago-at-a-Glance* in THE CITY) is one of the world's great museums. Plan to see it, for armor, for Chagall and O'Keefe, for textiles and design objects, and most of all for its renowned collection of Impressionist paintings. It's a day trip by itself. Directly across Michigan from the museum is *Orchestra Hall,* home of the celebrated *Chicago Symphony.*

Cross Michigan Avenue at Monroe Street to get to the *Chicago Public Library Cultural Center* (78 E. Washington), a classic-revival gem of granite and limestone on the outside, marble and mosaic inside. This is a fine example of the beaux arts architecture that Sullivan and Wright rebelled against. When it was built in 1897 it was the main public library and the height of architectural fashion. Walk up the elegant main stairway to Preston Bradley Hall, its Tiffany dome is a splendid setting for the free concerts given here every Wednesday at noon. The center also hosts changing exhibitions of photography, art, and artifacts, most by Chicago artists. Call the city's FINE ART (346-3278) number for information.

The Loop walk ends here. From the Cultural Center's Randolph Street entrance it's just a 3-block stroll east to Daley Plaza where the tour began. If you still want more, wander east along Randolph, enjoying the area's panoramic views of the city skyline, and south across Grant Park to Buckingham Fountain. The 40-story Prudential Building (130 E. Randolph) was the city's tallest when it was built in 1955. North of the Prudential is the State of Illinois Center, a multi-building complex designed by Helmut Jahn. Farther east are several new apartment towers. North on Michigan Avenue toward the Chicago River are more striking structures, mainly built during the 1920s, among them is the Carbide and Carbon Building (230 N. Michigan), an elegant Art Deco concoction of black granite, green terra cotta, and gold-plated decoration. (To connect with another walk, see *Walk 2: The Loop's Alfresco Museum.*)

Walk 2: The Loop's Alfresco Museum

Chicago is a city of public art, and dozens of murals and sculptures enhance its buildings and plazas, particularly in and around the Loop. Since 1978 alone, the Chicago Office of Fine Arts and the Department of Public Works have commissioned some 30 new pieces, and many additional works have been privately sponsored. The Office of Fine Arts even publishes a *Loop Sculpture Guide*. (To obtain a copy, stop at the Department of Cultural Affairs, 78 E. Washington, or at *Kroch's and Brentano's* branches. The guide costs $1.)

The walking tour that follows goes past some 2 dozen works of modern urban art, including the extraordinary gallery of sculptures by 20th-century masters Jean Dubuffet, Pablo Picasso, Joan Miró, Marc Chagall, Alexander Calder, and Henry Moore, which graces the area between the State of Illinois Building and the Federal Center. The entire walk takes 2 to 3 hours.

Start in what has been dubbed the New East Side at the northeast corner of the intersection of North Michigan Avenue and Randolph Street. Head east on Randolph toward Lake Michigan and the Standard Oil Building (200 E. Randolph). In the building's plaza, one wall of which is a waterfall, is a lovely reflecting pool. The 11 rods that rise out of the pool constitute Harry Bertoia's untitled abstract "musical" sculpture (1975). Bertoia is an Italian-born metal-working artist who designs furniture as well as sculpture. The reed-like forms are of copper-beryllium and brass and they sit in a granite base. When the wind is blowing, which is less often than the appellation "The Windy City" would lead one to expect, the rods sway, causing them to chime.

Just west of the plaza is Stetson Street, one of the Loop's quieter streets. Turn right and cross to the west side. Just ahead, atop the turrets of the *Sporting Club*, are four wind sculptures by Asamu Shingu. The *Children of the Sun* (1990), as they are called, turn and twist in the shifting breeze.

At Stetson and Lake, turn left (headed west), passing the newly landscaped Prudential Plaza. Beaubien Court was named for Mark Beaubien, one of Chicago's earliest settlers and the first to build a stone structure, a hotel. Beaubien was an enterprising innkeeper; according to legend he would give his guests a blanket to bed down on only to snatch it back when they were asleep and give it to the next customer. (Not surprisingly, there was always a bed available at his hotel.) Cross Beaubien to Boulevard Towers Plaza at Michigan Avenue. Here Jerry Peart's *Splash* (1986), a brightly colored 21-foot sculpture, enlivens a plaza framed by buildings designed by associates of Miës van der Rohe. The kinetic sinuosity of *Splash* suggests

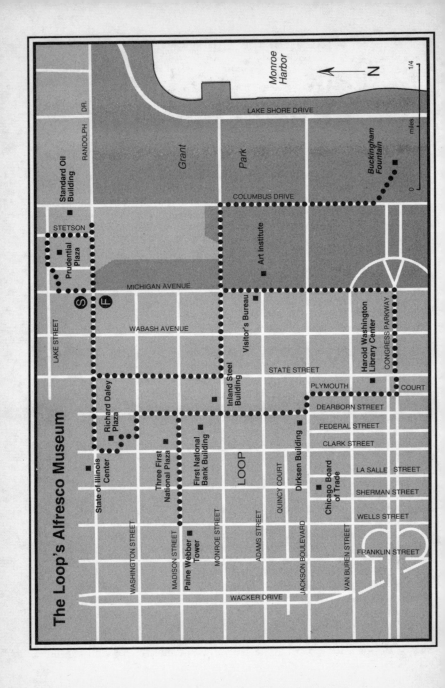

The Loop's Alfresco Museum

Monroe Harbor

N

1/4

0 miles

LAKE SHORE DRIVE

RANDOLPH DR.

Standard Oil Building

Grant

Park

Buckingham Fountain

COLUMBUS DRIVE

STETSON

Prudential Plaza

Art Institute

MICHIGAN AVENUE

LAKE STREET

Ⓢ Ⓕ

WABASH AVENUE

Visitor's Bureau

Harold Washington Library Center

STATE STREET

CONGRESS PARKWAY

Richard Daley Plaza

Inland Steel Building

PLYMOUTH

COURT

DEARBORN STREET

State of Illinois Center

Three First National Plaza

First National Bank Building

FEDERAL STREET

CLARK STREET

LA SALLE STREET

LOOP

Dirksen Building

Chicago Board of Trade

SHERMAN STREET

QUINCY COURT

WELLS STREET

WASHINGTON STREET

MADISON STREET

Paine Webber Tower

MONROE STREET

ADAMS STREET

JACKSON BOULEVARD

VAN BUREN STREET

FRANKLIN STREET

WACKER DRIVE

breaking waves, and is a vivid counterpoint to the severe lines of its surroundings.

Exit the plaza on Michigan Avenue, cross to the west side, and turn left, walking 1 block south. At Randolph (across Michigan from where the tour began) is Israeli artist Yaacov Agam's column *Communication X9* (1983). Its 360 statues in one are all a matter of perspective. As you walk around this op-art piece, forms and colors shift and change in almost dizzying fashion.

Turn right on Randolph and walk 4 blocks (crossing Wabash, State, and Dearborn Streets) to the blue-glass State of Illinois Center at Clark and Randolph. The abstract sculpture with graffiti-like designs in front of the building is *Monument with Standing Beast* (1984) by French artist Jean Dubuffet. This artwork is meant to be walked through. Its four fiberglass elements seem to represent an animal, a tree, a gateway, and a tower, no doubt a reference to the skyscraper city. The artist had genuine affection for Chicago, and this is one of only three US commissions he completed. He died only a year after this piece was unveiled.

Don't pass up this opportunity to go into Helmut Jahn's State of Illinois Center (100 W. Randolph) behind the Dubuffet sculpture. The dazzling atrium features an untitled sculpture by John Henry at its entrance, as well as other works of art. The State of Illinois Gallery is on the second floor, and downstairs is a food court and shops selling Chicago souvenirs and items created by Illinois artisans.

Leave the center and turn right. Walk half a block south on Clark Street to the Richard J. Daley Plaza, facing Washington between Clark and Dearborn. Beyond the fountain is what Chicagoans call "The Picasso." This gift to the city from Pablo Picasso is the work that started the city's outdoor museum of modern sculpture. When it was unveiled in 1967, controversy swirled around this head of a woman, but it has since become a popular landmark.

Facing the Picasso, in a small plaza on the other side of Washington Street, is a work by Picasso's friend, rival, and countryman, Joan Miró. This figure of a woman, simply called *Miró's Chicago* (1981), recalls ancient sculptures of Mediterranean goddesses. Look for the star in one of the ceramic tile insets and for the Braille label with a miniature of the figure. Miró, like Picasso, gave his design to the city as a gift, and also like the Picasso, money was raised locally to construct the large piece from the artist's model.

Few architects (and even fewer engineers) are honored by a public work of art. However, at the back of this plaza (69 W. Washington) is a bronze relief (1988) by another Spanish artist, Carlos Marinas, honoring Fazlur Khan. Khan was the engineering partner at Skidmore, Owings & Merrill whose structural innovations made many of the firm's skyscrapers possible, including the Sears Tower.

Leave the plaza and turn right on Washington to get to Dearborn Street, a few steps away. Turn right and go south for 1 block, then take another right and go west on Madison. In the atrium of Three First National Plaza (mid-block) is Henry Moore's *Large Upright Internal/External Form* (1983). Since the sculptor is best known for his reclining figures, the verticality of this piece comes as a surprise. Moore never lost interest in the human figure, and this sculpture suggests the sheltering protectiveness of one human being for another. The interior form also exists as a separate work in the *Art Institute*'s north garden.

Two-and-a-half blocks west on Madison, at Wells Street, is *Dawn Shadows* (1983). Artist Louise Nevelson said the black steel work was inspired by the area's nickname, the Loop. It's necessary to see this 30-foot-high piece from all sides to appreciate it. The nearby El platform provides a dramatic view of *Dawn Shadows* and its reflections in the mirrored façade of the building behind it.

Diagonally across the street from the Nevelson sculpture is the Paine Webber Tower. In its Madison Street lobby are two vividly colored metal wall pieces by Frank Stella. Cross LaSalle Street on the way back to Dearborn and look to the right (south). A shiny aluminum sculpture of *Ceres* (1930), the Greek goddess of grain and harvest, tops the building that closes LaSalle Street. The building is the Chicago Board of Trade, where grain futures are traded, and the Art Deco figure is by Chicago-born John Storrs. If you would like a closer look, the artist's maquette (model) of the statue is on view at the *Art Institute of Chicago,* as is the maquette for the Picasso. (If you want to skip the Nevelson and this part of the tour, leave the Three First National Plaza atrium and walk east a half block to the First National Bank Building.)

From *Dawn Shadows,* walk 2½ blocks east and go south on Dearborn, passing the First National Bank Building to the building's plaza. Marc Chagall's mosaic *The Four Seasons* (1974) is perhaps the city's best-loved public artwork. Made from hand-chipped stone and glass fragments, as well as bits of Chicago bricks, the wall depicts the four seasons of the year and the four seasons of humankind, from infancy to old age. The colorful work also includes Chicago's skyline and sailboats on Lake Michigan. The sunken plaza below the mosaic is in the exact center of the Loop and is one of the city's most popular gathering spots.

When you leave the Chagall, cross Dearborn to the lobby of the Inland Steel Building at the corner of Dearborn and Monroe (30 W. Monroe). Inside is *Radiant I* (1958) by Richard Lippold, a sculpture of wire and plate that celebrates the aesthetic possibilities of steel technology.

Stay on the east side of Dearborn and walk south another block to Alexander Calder's *Flamingo* (1974), painted a red he used so often it was nicknamed Calder red. Like the Dubuffet sculpture, this artwork should be explored from every angle. The giant red loops of the bird figure add color and liveliness to the three federal buildings designed by Miës van der Rohe that form its cage.

The mid-size structure across Dearborn at Jackson Boulevard is the Dirksen Building. Walk around it to the other side, where a painted aluminum relief sculpture nearly 8 stories high graces the brick wall of a building across from the Dirksen. This Sol Lewitt wall project is formally titled *Lines in Four Directions* (1985). Throughout the day, light plays off its white slats, creating patterns and shadows that change as the sun runs its course.

Go back to Jackson Boulevard and walk south 1 block on Plymouth Court to explore the richly ornamented Harold Washington Library Center (which opened in October 1991). The library's design is a clear example, on a grand scale, of the classicism of the new modernist architects of the current generation.

Return to Michigan Avenue via Congress Parkway. At the intersection of the two streets are *The Bowman* and *The Spearman* (1928), two equestrian bronze statues at the entrance to Grant Park. The Yugoslavian artist Ivan Mestrovic felt the sculptures not only honored Native Americans but celebrated the energy of the "Chicago spirit." After viewing the dramatic figures, walk north to the corner of Jackson and Michigan.

At this corner is the *Art Institute*'s south garden, where you will find Lorado Taft's *Fountain of the Great Lakes* (1913). The fountain's five classically robed female figures hold giant shells and pour water from one to another in allegorical imitation of the five Great Lakes. Taft, a Chicago native and prolific artist, supervised the installation of all the sculpture at the 1893 *World's Columbian Exposition.*

Walk past the museum to see its lions, which were sculpted by Edward Kemeys, one of the many artists who worked at the 1893 fair. Among the many plaster animal figures Kemeys created to decorate bridges and building entrances were a pair of lions guarding the Palace of Fine Arts, now the *Museum of Science and Industry.* Those statues were studies for the *Art Institute*'s bronze felines, which were installed the following year. (If you look closely, you'll see that the lions are in similar, though not identical, poses.) In 1969, the museum itself became a piece of sculpture when Christo, the international artist known for creating works on a gigantic scale, wrapped the entire building in canvas, securing it with several miles of rope.

On the far side of the museum, enter the north garden, where there are two contemporary works. Henry Moore liked his sculptures to be seen outdoors against the sky and trees; here in the garden is the *Large Interior Form* (1975) he gave to the *Art Institute* in 1983. Across from Moore's bronze is *Flying Dragon,* another of Calder's red stabiles. Like Moore, Calder always makes references to natural forms, in this case a dragonfly.

To continue exploring the area around the *Art Institute,* walk east on Monroe Street to the museum's Columbus Drive side. There, in the east garden, is an architectural fragment posing as sculpture: Dankmar Adler and Louis Sullivan's arched entrance to the Chicago Stock Exchange, which was completed in 1894 and demolished in 1972. The rich terra cotta ornament surrounding the entrance was salvaged and installed here in 1977.

South of the Columbus Drive entrance to the museum is the *Celebration of the 200th Anniversary of the Founding of the Republic* by Isamu Noguchi, another 20th-century master. The tall, columnar form with 50 panels, one for each of the states, fuses the artist's Japanese heritage and his American sensibilities. Noguchi asserts its stainless-steel and rainbow granite will last forever.

If the weather is nice you might opt at this point to take a little side trip down Columbus Drive to Buckingham Fountain and Grant Park's formal gardens. The fountain, a prominent feature of the lakefront, was bestowed on the city in 1927 by Kate Buckingham in honor of her brother, a former director of the *Art Institute.* The fountain was modeled after one at Versailles but at twice the size. A computer controls the flow of a million and a half gallons of water, and once an hour the central geyser shoots 135 feet into the air.

Return to Monroe Street and head west to get to State Street, where there are two more contemporary sculptures. At State and Monroe, turn right and walk to Madison. During its heyday the intersection of State and Monroe was the world's busiest corner. Here, if you haven't already done so, take a moment to study Louis Sullivan's splendid bronze ornamentation on the curved entrance of the *Carson Pirie Scott* store. On the other side of Madison, on the north end of the CTA shelter, is Bruce Nauman's circular neon *Human Nature/Life Death* (1986). Every few seconds it flashes one of four different brightly colored messages: life-death, love-hate, pleasure-pain, and human nature-animal nature.

A block north, at the corner of Washington, is another circular sculpture, a large work called *Being Born,* by Virginio Ferrari. The sculpture's two stainless-steel elements fit together with precision, symbolizing the exacting standards of the tool-and-die industry that commissioned it. The reflecting pool at the base is set in a granite ring, a favorite seat for summer lunching. A block ahead is Randolph; turn right and follow it back to your starting point at Columbus Drive.

Walk 3: Printer's Row and South Loop

Variously known as the South Loop, Printer's Row, Burnham, or Dearborn Park, the area immediately south of Congress Expressway has been transformed in the past decade. During that time, the aging manufacturing district has been reinvigorated with luxurious loft apartments, architects' offices, bookstores, taverns, and coffeehouses. Though a derelict and dangerous area for many years before its rebirth, at the turn of the century Printer's Row was as much a center of the nation's publishing business as New York was. The buildings that now house luxury loft apartments were sturdy enough to withstand the steady pounding of big printing presses, and nearby Dearborn Street Station, now a struggling mall, was one of the nation's major rail terminals.

Start this walk though Printer's Row from the Loop, heading south on Dearborn Street. At Harrison, the next street south, is *Printer's Row* (550 S. Dearborn; see *Eating Out* in THE CITY), an estimable (and pricey) restaurant featuring distinctly midwestern cooking. Other, less expensive eateries are abundant in this neighborhood, among them are an *Edwardo's* pizza (Congress across from the *Hyatt*), *La Margarita* (Dearborn Station at Polk), and *Taste of Siam* (across from Dearborn Station).

This district is almost as architecturally rich as the Loop, and since most of the old buildings are still standing, it offers an even better picture of what Chicago looked like while it was inventing American architecture. Particularly notable are the Old Franklin Building (525 S. Dearborn), the oldest on this block, the Terminals Building (537 S. Dearborn), with a heavy limestone base and arched entrance, and the Pontiac Building (542 S. Dearborn), with projecting bays and tripartite Chicago windows.

Cross Harrison to the Transportation Building (600 S. Dearborn). This shallow, 22-story structure, dating from 1911, offers great views of the area. Across the street is Grace Place (637 S. Dearborn), a church in a loft. (If it's open, check out the sanctuary's rough-hewn timbers and sheet-metal cross.) The façade of the 1912 Franklin Building (720 S. Dearborn) is decorated with colorful tiles depicting scenes of the printer's trade as it existed before the advent of computerized typesetting. *Sandmeyer's Bookstore* is worth a visit for its strong collection of books on art and the region. Across the street is the *Prairie Avenue Bookshop* (711 S. Dearborn), which boasts the nation's largest collection of books on architecture.

Thirsty? Stop in at *Kasey's Tavern* (701 S. Dearborn), and if it's lunchtime, drop in at *Moonraker,* an outdoor café a few doors south. At Polk Street is Dearborn Street Station. Dating from 1885, the imposing Romanesque-revi-

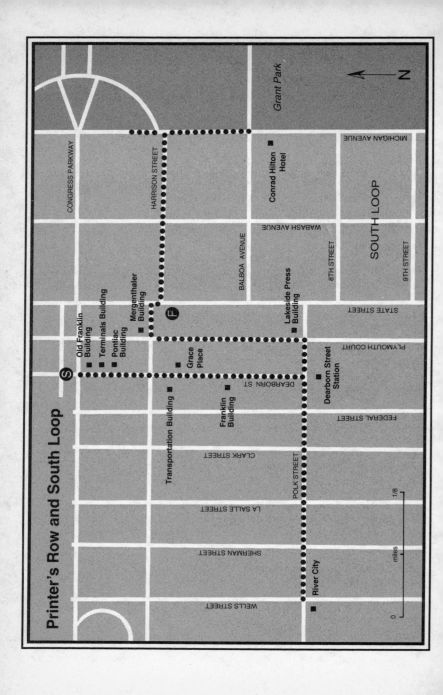

Printer's Row and South Loop

val red brick depot is the oldest railroad station in the city. Though it was exquisitely restored in the late 1980s and set up to be a retail center, it has yet to attract the commercial tenants its developers anticipated. Inside there's a hardware store and a bank to serve the neighborhood's growing residential population.

Behind Dearborn Station is Dearborn Park, a pleasant and growing residential community of apartments and townhouses built where railroad tracks once led out of the city. Two decades ago, none of this existed, now it's expanding southward to include more single-family houses. The community includes a grade school, as well as housing for senior citizens. Not far from here, on Michigan Avenue at Balbo, is the *Conrad Hilton* hotel (see *Checking In* in THE CITY). It was in front of the *Hilton* and in Grant Park beyond that Chicago police, perhaps antagonized by the flamboyant antics of hippies, yippies, and other radicals, attacked a large group of student protesters during the 1968 Democratic convention. The ensuing "police riot," as it has come to be called, overshadowed the events at the convention that nominated Hubert Humphrey and, according to some, diminished Mayor Richard J. Daley's power.

From Dearborn Station, detour 2 blocks west on Polk Street to River City (800 S. Wells), a futuristic creation of architect Bertrand Goldberg, who also designed Marina City on the Chicago River. Walk inside to see the unusual serpentine atrium. Also stop at the *Museum of Broadcast Communications* (see *Memorable Museums* in DIVERSIONS), which has exhibits about Chicago's role in the radio and television industries.

Return to Polk and Dearborn in front of the station and go 1 very short block east to Plymouth Court. At the corner is the Lakeside Press Building (731 S. Plymouth Court), built by R.R. Donnelley in 1897 to house part of Lakeside Press's growing operations. Now, like most of the other buildings in the area, it's full of loft apartments. In its basement is the *Printer's Row Printing Museum,* a working 19th-century letterpress print shop that offers courses and tours.

Walk back to Harrison along the narrow Plymouth Court. On the corner is the Mergenthaler Building (531 S. Plymouth Court), an 1886 structure that's been cleverly adapted for office and residential use. Wedge-shape bays on the south wall extend the space, there's a neon address sign above the door, and at the northeast corner are the remnants of *Tom's Grill* — ivy now grows where hamburgers once fried.

To extend this walk, go back into the Loop or along Harrison Street to Michigan Avenue, where the Pacific Garden Mission (646 S. State) stands. At Michigan and Balbo (1 block south of Harrison) is the *Blackstone* hotel, site of numerous presidential nominating conventions. The totally renovated *Chicago Hilton* also is on this corner. At Harrison and Michigan are the *Spertus Museum of Judaica* and the *Center for Contemporary Photography at Columbia College* (see *Chicago at-a-Glance* in THE CITY).

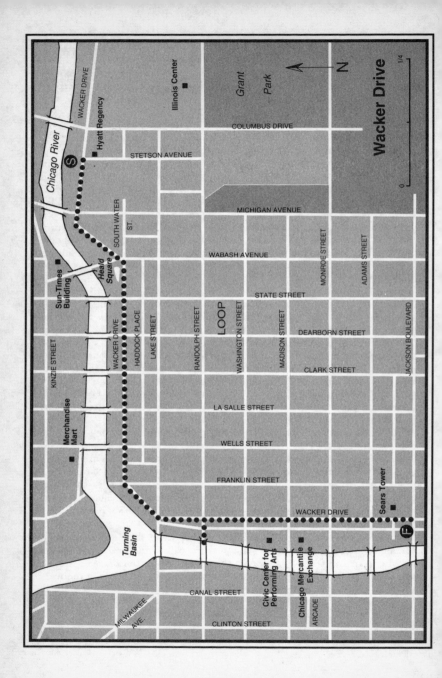

Wacker Drive

Walk 4: Wacker Drive

Wacker Drive runs along the south bank of the Chicago River from Lake Michigan to where the river splits, following the south branch to the Sears Tower. Because the city first grew along the banks of the river, this is one of the oldest parts of Chicago. A century ago, this thoroughfare was called South Water Street and it was lined with a jumble of street vendors and stalls clustered around the city's busy docks. Marshall Field got his start in retailing near here, and it's where Potter Palmer started acquiring real estate.

The riverbank began to change after 1910. It was then that silver-haired civic-improver Charles H. Wacker was appointed head of the Chicago Plan Commission. The group was responsible for implementing the 1909 Plan of Chicago, an elegant and innovative attempt to bring reason and order to a city that had grown too fast, and Wacker did it with gusto. As a result of the 1909 Plan, two major railroad stations were moved west of the river, sending traffic away from the city's core, and taking the market with it to Randolph Street. The road along the river, formerly lined with a motley collection of warehouses and aging docks (the Port of Chicago had already moved south to Lake Calumet), was renamed in his honor.

Like many other cities, Chicago has recently rediscovered the river in its own back yard. While the city effectively turned its back on the Chicago River when the buildings along Wacker Drive were constructed, it now wants to incorporate the waterway again, making it a new center of activity. To that end, a pedestrian walkway along the edge of the river is in the planning stages.

Though the planned "riverwalk" has yet to be realized, a stroll along Wacker Drive goes close to the water and high enough to appreciate the city's majesty. It's easy to get to the starting point of this walk; Wacker is at Illinois Center, 1 block east of Michigan. Our tour follows the direction of the river's flow, from Columbus Drive west. What's wrong with this picture? The river should flow west to east, not the other way around. It is another of Chicago's engineering marvels that the city was able to reverse the flow of the river in 1889 to better serve its sanitation needs.

To begin the walk, stand on the narrow pedestrian strip on the upper level of Wacker across from the *Hyatt Regency* hotel at Illinois Center. To the east, on the opposite bank of the river, is a fountain that shoots a jet of water across the river once an hour on the hour. The fountain was erected in 1989 by the Metropolitan Water Reclamation District in celebration of its 100th anniversary. It was this agency that built the lock at the mouth of the river to reverse its flow. By doing so, they were able to send waterborne diseases out of the city via a sanitary canal rather than sending them into the lake.

Illinois Center was begun nearly 30 years ago as an effort to redevelop the area occupied by the abandoned, century-old Illinois Central Railroad terminal. Miës van der Rohe created a master plan that included many of the buildings on the site shortly before his death in 1969. (The plan, which violates the city's grid system, is now criticized by planners, but it was state-of-the-art at the time.) Two hotels, an apartment building, and several office towers now stand on the site.

At Michigan Avenue is a quartet of impressive buildings. The two on the other side of the river are the Tribune Tower and the Wrigley Building. On this side, the one east of Michigan (333 Michigan) is in the 1920s style called Moderne, the building on the west side of the street with the curved entrance (360 Michigan) is neo-classical. All four are particularly striking because they can be seen full-length.

Cross Michigan Avenue, staying on the river side of Wacker, and continue west. Continue along the river, passing the Heald Square Monument in the middle of the intersection with Wabash. The last work by Lorado Taft, one of Chicago's favorite sculptors, this 1941 statue shows George Washington with Robert Morris and Hyam Solomon, two men who helped finance the Revolutionary War. Funds for the construction of the monument were raised by Barnet Hodes, a lawyer and alderman whose Polish-Jewish background was similar to that of Solomon. The low-profile Sun-Times Building is visible across the river from here, as are Miës van der Rohe's IBM Plaza, and Marina City, the pioneering urban living concept designed by Bertrand Goldberg, who worked in Miës's studio as a young man.

Along Wacker Drive, 17 bridges cross the Chicago River and its south branch. In the early days of the city, each bridge had a bridge tender whose job was to raise the bridge for river traffic. Since the river is a critical link between the Great Lakes and the Mississippi River (via the Illinois River), that meant considerable work. Today, boat owners cooperate by coming down the river in groups. When a batch is scheduled to go through, two pairs of bridge tenders man the bridges. They work in pairs on consecutive spans and open and close the bridges one at a time. When a team finishes its bridge, the tenders get into their cars and drive up or down the river (they have special parking privileges) and prepare to open the next bridge in the sequence.

At the Clark Street intersection is a plaque memorializing Chicago's worst maritime disaster. On July 24, 1915, nearly 4,000 employees of the Western Electric Company's Hawthorne Works in Cicero were boarding the *Eastland* when the ship capsized. Eight hundred and twelve people who had been headed for a day's outing at the dunes met their deaths instead. Whole families were wiped out; children who stayed home were orphaned; the firm was decimated. (In 1989, students at the Illinois Math and Science Academy in Aurora, thinking this sad episode of Chicago history was nearly forgotten, organized an effort to have this plaque installed.)

The Merchandise Mart, across the river from LaSalle Street, is the world's largest wholesaling complex. It was built in 1929 — just before the market crash — as a new home for Marshall Field's wholesale business, but it was never used for its intended purpose. During the 1930s, it was bought at a bargain price by Joseph Kennedy, patriarch of Boston's Kennedy clan. Still a source of the family's wealth, it houses showrooms for the interior design trade and has a shopping mall on its lower two floors. Just beyond the

Merchandise Mart's newly restored façade is the Apparel Center, which provides showrooms for clothing designers.

Cross Wells Street, pass under the El tracks, and pause to look at the handsome curving sheet of green glass ahead on the east side of Wacker. This dramatic 1983 building, designed by New York's Kohn Pederson Fox and executed by Chicago's Perkins & Will, takes its shape from the curve of the river. If the building is open, walk into its lobby; the *Chicago Athenaeum* has a gallery here that features exhibitions on design topics.

Follow the drive as it curves south. At Randolph, cross Wacker again and walk to the bridge. To the west is the new Morton International Building, headquarters for the firm that mines salt and makes rubber rings for space shuttle engines, among other things. Rather than having its back to the river, as do the older buildings along here, this structure not only faces but embraces the waterfront.

Return to Wacker Drive and cross it again to get a better view of the *Civic Center for Performing Arts* (20 N. Wacker; see *Music* in THE CITY). Behind this complex of theaters lies another of Chicago's remarkable tales of big business. Samuel Insull, who had been a secretary to Thomas Edison, came to Chicago to run one of the city's many electric companies and eventually established himself as the only electric company in town. He used the wealth from that enterprise to buy up railroads and further enhance his power. When he commissioned the *Civic Center for Performing Arts,* perhaps as a gift for his wife (a former actress who wanted to return to the stage), he was at the pinnacle of his career. Unfortunately, the *Center,* for which Insull had heavily mortgaged his business, opened shortly before the stock market crash of 1929. Though Insull's Commonwealth Edison company survived on loans for several years, his tottering empire eventually collapsed. The power mogul fled Chicago and died of a heart attack on a subway platform in Paris. He was penniless but well dressed; he was identified by the "SI" embroidered on his shirt cuffs.

At Madison Street look to the south side of Wacker again. The building at 10 S. Wacker is headquarters for the Chicago Mercantile Exchange, where boisterous traders buy and sell options on all manner of futures, from pork bellies to interest rates. For a guided tour, stop by between 7:30 AM and 3:15 PM weekdays. It's free and it's fun (phone: 930-8249).

The final stop on this tour is the Sears Tower (233 S. Wacker, see *Chicago at-a-Glance* in THE CITY), between Adams and Jackson. Its entrance is actually on Franklin Street, but it's easier to see how the building sits in the plaza from here. The arched glass entryway was constructed nearly 10 years after the building was completed, and generated another of Chicago's seemingly endless architectural controversies. Some thought the plaza too stark without the addition; others, particularly architectural purists, thought it glitzed up a building that made a strong enough statement on its own. The tower is 1,454 feet tall and has the world's fastest elevator (it travels more than 20 miles per hour and takes only 55 seconds to get to the 103rd floor). Take a trip to the Skydeck (after all, it is the world's tallest building) and get a bird's-eye view of the City that Works. It's open from 9 AM to midnight 7 days a week (phone: 875-9696).

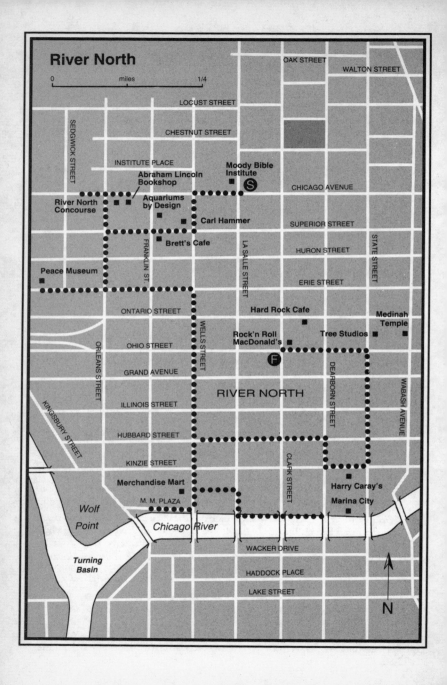

Walk 5: River North

Originally a manufacturing and warehouse district, River North began to decline after the Second World War, when factories moved out and urban blight moved in. In the mid 1970s, gallery owners discovered the large loft spaces and bargain rents and began trekking over from North Michigan Avenue. Today, the neighborhood not only has been reborn, it has become so populated with trendy restaurants, pricey shops, and designers' studios that some of the art galleries have crossed the Chicago River into a new district called River West. Now the area boasts the nation's largest concentration of galleries outside New York City's SoHo.

It's easy to reach this area; several buses run on State and LaSalle Streets; others, going south only, run on Clark. Both the El (at Chicago and Franklin or the Merchandise Mart at Wells and the river) and the subway (at Chicago and State or Grand and State) stop in the neighborhood. If you have a car, there are several parking garages in the area. Start this walk at LaSalle and Chicago, and note the Moody Bible Institute on the northwest corner. There's a bookstore here and a lovely interior courtyard behind the institute (accessible from LaSalle Street).

Go west 1 block to Wells, then south 1 block to Superior and you'll be at the beginning of Chicago's art gallery district. Start at *Carl Hammer* (200 W. Superior) on the corner of Superior and Wells; walk in (browsers are always welcome) and pick up a copy of the *Gallery Guide* (it's free, and it's available in all the area's galleries. Many of the River North galleries are on street level, but some are upstairs (banners hang from their windows). Either consult the *Gallery Guide* for what's where or just walk west for the next 2 blocks, stopping where the spirit moves you. Most galleries are open from 10 AM to 5 PM, Tuesdays through Saturdays; many have openings on Friday evenings except during the summer. Wine and munchies are served, the streets are crowded, and anyone can come. Again, the *Gallery Guide* is your source for what's happening when.

The heaviest concentration of galleries is on Superior between Wells and Orleans. You might want to make a circle tour, or hop back and forth across the street. For refreshments, *Brett's Café*, a charming hole-in-the-wall with good food, is at the southeast corner of Franklin and Superior. If the kids are along, stop at *Aquariums By Design* (740 N. Franklin), a subterranean shop visible from the street, just a half block north of *Brett's*. Walking past it is like looking into a dark ocean with neon-hued fish flashing around. Browsers are just as welcome as buyers. A half block north of this shop, at Franklin and Chicago, is the *River North Café*, an Art Deco spot offering coffee, pastries, and deli sandwiches.

Continue west on Superior to Orleans and cross the street, turn right and go 1 block toward Chicago Avenue. *River North Concourse* (750 N. Orleans) is a warehouse-turned-emporium featuring several galleries and shops. On the first floor is *Chiaroscuro* (phone: 988-9253), a funky gallery with papier-mâché sculpture, functional ceramics, painted furniture, and the like. Across the hall is the *Gallery Vienna,* a 2-story trove of Viennese furniture from 1890–1930, the period called Jugenstyl. Upstairs are several more galleries.

Also visit the *Abraham Lincoln Book Shop* (around the corner at 357 Chicago Ave.; phone: 944-3085); ring the bell to enter. This warm and inviting store, lined floor to ceiling with glass-doored bookcases, is more like a museum, displaying Lincoln-related art, books, and documents, and attracting Civil War and Lincoln history buffs from around the country. Proprietor Daniel Weinberg is frequently called upon to authenticate Lincoln memorabilia. He is glad to share his interests, even if you are only browsing. There is parking near the bookstore.

Across the street and 1 block west, the Cabrini-Green housing project begins. Along Chicago, some of these buildings are well-tended; however, the upper floors of the high-rises beyond are empty, burned out or boarded up. From the south side of Chicago, look west, where a large red sign announces the headquarters of *Montgomery Ward.* From its warehouse on the river, goods used to be moved by boat to the railroads and then around the nation.

Walk back to Orleans and head south. At Superior is *Café el Lago,* once a working class diner, it is now frequented by artists and art dealers. At Huron and Superior is the *Green Door,* a popular bar and restaurant in a somewhat rickety-looking structure that was one of the first buildings to go up after the Chicago Fire; the food here is good and the ambience terrific. Between these two establishments is a block-long parking lot. Until a disastrous fire in April 1989, the block contained an 1880s building that was the center of the River North gallery district. Continue 2 more blocks south along Orleans to Erie; turn right and walk 1 block to the *Peace Museum* (430 W. Erie; phone: 440-1860), the nation's only museum dedicated exclusively to peace issues and the impact of war.

Retrace your steps back along Erie Street, cross Orleans and Franklin to former Chicago *Bear* Walter Payton's *America's Bar* (phone: 915-5986). Across the street is Flair House, a restored dairyman's house now housing an advertising agency. Across Erie is Oprah Winfrey's *Eccentric* (159 W. Erie; phone: 787-8390), a restaurant and watering hole. The entrance to *Ed Debevic's* (see *Eating Out* in THE CITY), the quintessential diner, complete with wisecracking waitresses in saddle shoes and bobby socks, is 1 block south on Wells, facing Ontario. One block west is Mike Ditka's restaurant, *City Lights* (223 W. Ontario; phone: 280-1790), where the lines are long and the steaks are thick.

Continue south along Wells, past 3 blocks of elegant shops between Ohio and Hubbard. Among the stores here are *Rita Bucheit Limited,* featuring Austrian antiques and artifacts; *Mario Vilas* for decorative items; and *Arryelle* for the ultimate in bedding.

On Wells between Hubbard and the Chicago River is the 1929 Merchandise Mart, the world's largest commercial building. The showrooms (featuring interiors and furnishings) are open mainly to dealers and decorators; the first two floors are undergoing a massive renovation for retail space that was scheduled to open late last year. Walk around to the building's riverfront side to see the recently restored façade. The Merchandise Mart has mounted several large bronze busts of prominent American businessmen, including F. W. Woolworth and Edward Filene, on the outer walls, in a display that it likes to refer to as a merchandising Hall of Fame. Enjoy the panoramic view east and south across the river, and west toward the Apparel Center (wholesale clothing) at Wolf Point, where the Chicago River divides into north and south branches.

If you walk through the parking lot behind *Roche-Bobois,* a store at 333 N. Wells, cross La Salle and go a half block west to the river, you'll find a city office building with a river walk, offering a marvelous view of the Loop, along its southern façade. The river walk continues between Clark and Dearborn, behind the Quaker Oats Building and the *Nikko* hotel. Between Dearborn and State is the plaza of Marina City, the nation's first mixed-use downtown project. Sadly, this building, dating from the early 1960s, has been allowed to deteriorate, but look up to see the corn-cob-shape double tower, with patioed apartments above several levels of parking. Beneath the plaza is the marina that gave the complex its name.

Retrace your steps back to the Merchandise Mart and head east on Hubbard Street to Dearborn, from which the northern façades of the buildings described above can be seen. At Dearborn, go south 1 block to Kinzie Street and *Harry Caray's,* a restaurant in a Dutch-inspired commercial building (33 W. Kinzie). This popular local Italian-American spot is named after the *Cubs'* beloved announcer; you can see its huge "Holy cow!" banner (Caray's favorite expression) from blocks around.

Continue east on Kinzie for 1 more block to State Street. Turn left, passing by *Gold Coast Dogs* (418 N. State), which serves up the ultimate Chicago hot dog. Between Grand and Illinois, on the right side of State, is the spanking-new, triangle-shape glass-and-steel American Medical Association headquarters, designed by Japanese architect Kenzo Tange and completed in 1990. Continue north along State to Ohio and note the charming 2-story Tree Studios, running the full block to Ontario on the east side of the street. Built in 1894 as studio space for artists, it still is home to many modern Calder wannabes. East of the Tree Studios (facing Wabash) is the moorish-style Medinah Temple, headquarters for the Chicago Shriners, their annual circus, and the quadrennial Friday-night-before-the-election rally for the Democratic presidential candidate.

From Tree Studios, the golden arches of the *Rock 'n' Roll McDonald's* (600 N. Clark at Ohio) are visible across a parking lot. Before ending the River North tour, this is a must-see: Its funky decor includes life-size Beatles, Archie and Betty in a red Corvette, and a wondrous collection of wacky artifacts. It has the usual reliable menu and is one of the busiest *McDonald's* in the world.

On the way to *McDonald's,* pause at Dearborn and look 1 block north to Ontario to see the imposing, fortress-like structure that once housed the

Chicago Historical Society and is now home to *Excalibur*, a huge nightclub and bar that features music from the 1950s to the 1970s. In the middle of the block, between Dearborn and Clark, facing Ontario, is Chicago's *Hard Rock Café*, across a parking lot. Wander over to its front door, if that suits you.

To return to the start of the walk, go 5 short blocks north to Chicago, then 1 block west to La Salle.

Walk 6: North Michigan Avenue

Though the soul of Chicago is still the Loop, the city's spirit has gradually been moving across the Chicago River to North Michigan Avenue. Until *Water Tower Place* was built in 1974, Michigan Avenue was a tree-lined boulevard of individually owned shops, office buildings, and art galleries; its commerce was more cultured than that of the bustling Loop. Now "Boul Mich" has more law firms than art dealers; family-run shops are giving way to classy, high-end stores, many of them branches of international chains. Once a street of stately and modestly-scaled graystone buildings, North Michigan has become an exhibition of architectural one-upmanship. Yet, though the street is said to have the world's densest concentration of upscale retailing, happily the Magnificent Mile still retains some of the quiet elegance that earned it its nickname.

Our walk begins at the intersection of Michigan and Wacker. On this spot stood Fort Dearborn, the trading outpost that grew into the city. Until 1835, when all the area's Native Americans were required by treaty to move west of the Mississippi, this post primarily traded with the tribes that lived along the lakeshore. Stroll across the river on the Michigan Avenue Bridge. To the north and on the left is the Wrigley Building, the skyscraper that chewing gum built; on the right is the Tribune Tower, home of the *Chicago Tribune.* Behind the bright, white Wrigley towers is the Sun-Times Building (and a pleasant terrace with a *McDonald's*).

Cross the avenue to Pioneer Court, just south of the Tribune Tower. This Gothic tribute to the power of the press was designed by the firm of Hood & Howells, who won a 1923 competition for the commission. Some of America's greatest journalists have worked out of this building. Also from here came *Dick Tracy, L'il Orphan Annie,* and the "Dewey Beats Truman" headline.

Walk between the Tribune Tower and the modern Equitable Building to the Channel Gardens, the recently completed pedestrian entrance to the new (1989) NBC Building. Walk through the new garden-centered street known as CityFront Place and look east toward the lake. From here the Navy Pier is visible. This 1916 structure extends a half mile out into the lake and is the site of Chicago's annual *International Art Expo* and numerous other exhibitions and festivals. Also visible is Lake Point Tower, a 70-story cloverleaf-shape apartment building, said to be the world's tallest purely residential building.

For a pleasant (though hardly brief) detour, go through the NBC Building and walk a half block north to Illinois Street, and then 4 blocks east to

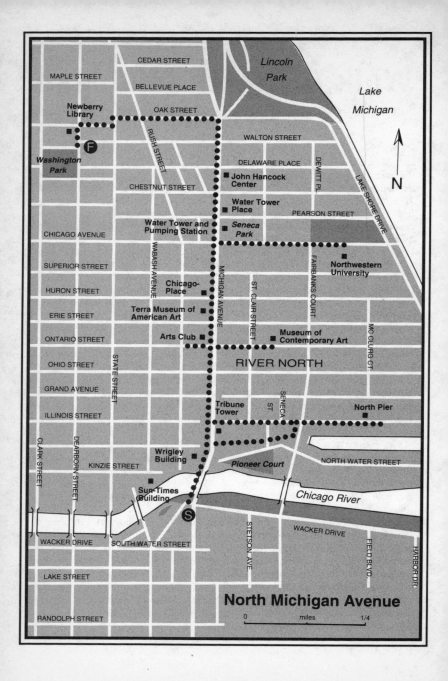

North Michigan Avenue

0   miles   1/4

North Pier (435 E. Illinois). This former riverside warehouse has been transformed into several floors of delightful shops and restaurants. It also has *BattleTech Center,* a state-of-the-art "virtual reality" video game parlor. On a warm, sunny day, there's no better place for a cool beer or soft drink than one of the numerous spots along the water's edge at *North Pier,* looking back on the city. Ice cream and more substantial fare are available as well.

If you didn't take the detour, follow CityFront Place behind the Tribune Tower until it turns west at upper Illinois Street. On the right is the recently restored *Inter-Continental* hotel (see *Checking In* in THE CITY). This architectural fantasy, built in 1929 to house the *Medinah Athletic Club,* moves from Assyrian to Renaissance themes, incorporating a little Moorish here, a bit of Celtic there, and touch of Byzantine just for good measure. The restoration was exquisitely done. If it's a chilly afternoon, stop in the lobby for afternoon tea (or find another excuse to see it before returning to Michigan Avenue).

Take in the street scene while strolling north on Michigan. For an interesting side trip, take any one of the staircases down to Lower Michigan Avenue. News junkies might want to stop at the *Billy Goat Tavern* (430 N. Michigan at Illinois), where reporters (including venerable columnist Mike Royko) hang out. The hamburgers are greasy, but the beer is cold, the ambience authentic, and the curse on the *Cubs* is worth asking about.

Along this stretch of Michigan there are several office buildings, the *Chicago Marriott* hotel (540 N. Michigan), a branch of *Kroch's and Brentano's* bookstore (516 N. Michigan), plus a choice of chi-chi cookie and yogurt stores. Three blocks north of Illinois is Ontario Street. From the east side of the avenue, take a brief detour to the *Museum of Contemporary Art* (237 E. Ontario; see *Memorable Museums* in DIVERSIONS) or just look around at the interesting mix of old townhouses and modern office towers standing side by side. From the west side of the street, walk a half block west to the *Arts Club of Chicago* (109 E. Ontario). This is a private club, but visitors are allowed inside to look at its showpiece, an elegant stairway designed by Miës van der Rohe.

At the corner of Erie and Michigan is the spanking-new and ultra-clean flagship *Crate & Barrel* store. Its modest 5 stories, in glass and white aluminum, buck the trend toward overpowering Michigan Avenue with towers. Take a trip on the store's escalator and try to resist buying something.

After that, head north, passing the *Terra Museum of American Art* (see *Chicago at-a-Glance* in THE CITY). *Stuart Brent Books* (670 N. Michigan) is another Chicago institution and a store for serious bibliophiles. It was founded by its namesake, an iconoclastic chum of Nelson Algren and Studs Terkel.

On the next block is *ChicagoPlace,* the newest of the city's vertical malls. *Saks Fifth Avenue* has moved here from its graystone dowager premises across Michigan. At the entrance to *ChicagoPlace,* be sure to notice the 2-story murals on either side. Mrs. O'Leary's cow (peeking out from behind the prairie grass) is just one of the symbols of Chicago's past depicted in this delightful artwork. Prairie style architectural details abound throughout this multi-story mall. In the eighth-floor food court there's a garden, a waterfall, and a wall sculpture based on an Indian headband, plus about anything imaginable in the fast-food category.

Outside again, continue walking north toward the arched, rose-colored granite entrance to *Neiman Marcus* (737 N. Michigan), on the east side of the street. Behind the store and facing Chicago Avenue (which is the next street north) is a 63-story condominium tower, one of downtown's most elegant addresses. For another side trip, wander east on Chicago for 2 blocks to Northwestern University's downtown campus. Its medical center and law school are here; headquarters for the American Dental Association and the American Hospital Association (after Washington, DC, Chicago is the nation's association capital) are nearby.

The curious-looking castle with the tower poking up in the middle is the Water Tower (it's visible all the way up the avenue). This building and the matching Pumping Station (across Michigan), are the only downtown survivors of the Great Chicago Fire. The tower masks a 135-foot-tall standpipe. The first floor of the building now houses the Chicago Office of Tourism. A pleasant park surrounds it, and horse-drawn carriage rides leave from here. (Rides cost about $35 a half hour. For further information, ask any driver.) If it's time for lunch, try *Bistro 110* (110 E. Pearson), which is right across the street.

At the Pumping Station is *Here's Chicago,* a sound-and-light show in which Abe Lincoln, who began his political career in Illinois, introduces some of the city's other notables and narrates a magnificent helicopter tour of the city's skyscrapers. Right outside the Pumping Station is *Untouchable Tours,* a 2-hour bus ride through neighborhoods once frequented by the likes of Frank Nitti, Earl "Little Hymie" Weiss, and Dion O'Banion, as well as the most notorious of them all, Al Capone. (In winter, tours are only held on weekends; phone: 881-1195).

Though the vertical mall at *Water Tower Place* beckons, take a roundabout route to it by walking south on Michigan to Chicago Avenue, turning left behind the Pumping Station. A little beyond the most charming fire station in the city is Seneca Park, a great rest stop. The park's lovely play lot is named for the late restaurateur who concocted *Eli's* cheesecake (the establishment he founded is across Chicago Avenue), and was built with money raised by the community. Grown-ups might want to sit a while and meditate on Deborah Butterfield's *Horse* (1990).

Now it's time for *Water Tower Place,* a site nearly everyone who comes to Chicago visits at least once. *Water Tower Place* pioneered the concept of the vertical shopping mall in Chicago. Since 1988, two others have sprung up in town, but this is still the king. The staff at the information desk can guide you to *Field*'s or *Lord & Taylor,* to *Rizzoli* or *Accent Chicago,* to places selling shoes or ships or sealing wax; there's almost nothing that isn't available here. The mall also has several places to eat and a movie theater, and the building is open until long after the stores close.

Just north of the Water Tower is "Big John," the John Hancock Center. Once the world's tallest building, it is now shadowed by Sear's Tower and New York's World Trade Center. The Hancock, however, is the only one of the three that has residential apartments. For a peak dining experience (with prices to match), try the *95th Restaurant.* From the ground, note the giant steel braces that rise diagonally up the sides of the building until they seem to disappear into the clouds.

Across Michigan from "Big John" is the Fourth Presbyterian Church (126 E. Chestnut), a Gothic-revival structure built in 1912. During the summer, the church offers concerts in its cloistered garden. If the church is open, visit the sanctuary for a harmonious retreat from glass and steel amid the carved wood and stained glass.

Mammon reigns north of the church at the shops at *900 N. Michigan,* the most elegant and upscale of the avenue's malls. *Bloomingdale's* anchors this one, and there are numerous other shops (many of them European imports) in which to indulge. Across the street is the Playboy Building (919 N. Michigan), from which Hugh Hefner ran his bunny empire. (Now his daughter, Christie, is in charge, and she moved Playboy Corp. to Lake Shore Drive.)

Between Walton and Oak on Michigan is a composition of three hexagonal granite and glass tubes called One Magnificent Mile. Twenty-five years ago, it was developer Arthur Rubloff who gave North Michigan the nickname memorialized here. The building houses shops, offices, a movie theater, and apartments, as well as *Spiaggia* (980 N. Michigan; see *Eating Out* in THE CITY), one of city's most pricey and intriguing restaurants.

From One Magnificent Mile, you can either walk west on Oak Street, Chicago's intimate street of one-of-a-kind shops, or connect with the walk through the exclusive Gold Coast neighborhood (see *Walk 7: The Gold Coast*).

Oak Street offers a delightful collection of shops selling an assortment of goods from leather to linens, fur to feathers. For a movie, try the recently restored 1937 *Esquire Theater* (53 E. Oak). The building's clean Art Deco streamlining was a marked contrast to the Moorish palace-style movie houses that preceded it. Oak Street's shopping area ends at Rush Street, where it intersects with State Street. Either get a downtown-bound bus here or walk 1 block farther to Dearborn and 1 block south (both very short blocks) to Walton. A public elementary school is on one side of the street; on the other is the 1892 Newberry Library, keeper of maps and genealogical and historical archives. The library faces Washington Square (also known as Bughouse Square), the city's first public park and long a forum for orators and rhetoricians of all political persuasions. To get back downtown from here, either hail a cab or walk back to State Street and catch a bus.

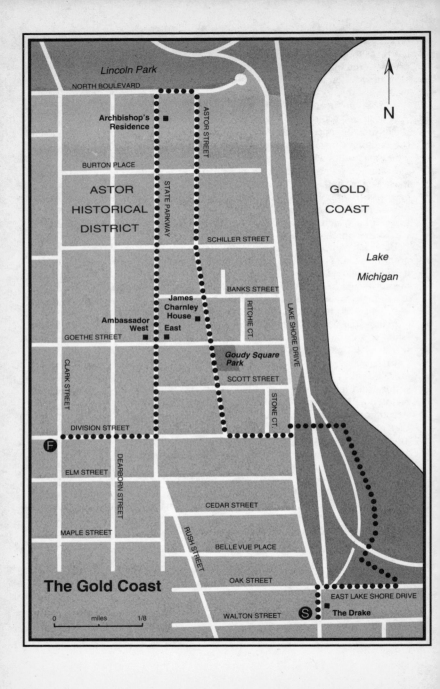

Walk 7: The Gold Coast

The Gold Coast is a mere wedge of land 6 blocks long and 3 blocks deep, but the amount of wealth concentrated here in the neighborhood's heyday was nothing short of stupefying. Potter Palmer was the first of Chicago's businessmen to build here, and his presence drew many others. Though millionaire fur trader John Jacob Astor never lived here, the most attractive street in the area was named for him. As time goes on, the Gold Coast mansions are increasingly hemmed in by the high-rise luxury apartments of the city's envious nouveaux riches, but the grand old homes that made this *the* place to live are undiminished by the comparison.

This walk begins, appropriately, at the grande dame of Chicago hostelries, the *Drake* (140 E. Walton Place; see *Checking In* in THE CITY). Since its opening in 1921, it has provided lodgings for many dignitaries, among them Queen Elizabeth. If it happens to be mid-afternoon, stop in for tea at the *Oak Terrace* before strolling down block-long E. Lake Shore Drive, the most exclusive of Chicago addresses. The gazebo and landscaping are recent additions to the park (which also boasts very inviting benches) on the street's north side.

Amble along the lakeshore north toward Division Street. On the west side of Lake Shore Drive are the apartment buildings that form a sort of front-yard fence for the Gold Coast. Two blocks north of Oak, mansions begin to appear amid the apartment towers. Once, the drive was lined with such magnificent houses.

Turn left at Division Street to get to the heart of the Gold Coast. Walk past Stone Court to Astor Street and turn right. This tranquil, 6-block-long street is lined with marvelously well-maintained private residences, many of them dating from the turn of the century. At 1308-12 Astor is an ivy-covered residence designed by John Root (who lived at 1310) of the architectural firm Burnham and Root.

A little farther along, at 1335 Astor, is where Irna Phillips lived. So who's Irna Phillips? She was the writer who created television's first soap operas, "The Guiding Light," "As the World Turns," and "Young Dr. Malone." Nearby is *Court of the Golden Hands* (1349-53 Astor), where the door knockers are in the shape of a delicate hand holding an apple.

The James Charnley House (1364 Astor) was designed by Louis Sullivan, with an assist from his young protégé, Frank Lloyd Wright. While Sullivan's decorative hand has adorned the building's façade, Wright's influence can be seen in the roofline of the 3-story house. Its appearance is a sharp contrast to the other houses on the street, which were built around the same time.

Continue walking along Astor until it ends at the southernmost end of Lincoln Park, and then turn left on North Boulevard to North State Parkway. Lincoln Park is the largest oasis in Chicago, covering 1,200 acres of lakefront property. It also is the location of the *Chicago Historical Society* (near the corner of North and Park) and the *Lincoln Park Zoo.*

At State, turn south again. On the left is the Queen Anne–style Archbishop's Residence (1555 N. State Parkway), the oldest building in the Astor Historical District. Since 1885 it has been the home of the Roman Catholic Archbishop of Chicago. On a more secular note, 1340 N. State Parkway was once the Playboy mansion, home of Hugh Hefner. It now belongs to the *Art Institute.*

At the corner of Goethe, the *Ambassador East* and *Ambassador West* hotels face each other. Booth One in the *Ambassador East*'s restaurant, the *Pump Room* (see *Eating Out* in THE CITY), once was the most important place to be seen in Chicago. Some who sat at the booth to the right of the bar were Gertrude Lawrence (setting a record at 90 consecutive nights), Frank Sinatra, Salvador Dali, David Bowie, and even Morris the Cat. The restaurant serves continental food with a price tag appropriate to the neighborhood.

Walk south 2 blocks to get back to Division Street. Quick-change artist that the city is, it has gone from elegance and tranquillity to the honky-tonk of Division Street's bars in 2 short blocks. If you didn't dine in Booth One, try *P.J. Clarke's* (1204 N. Clark), popular with singles and owned by a man said to "run" Near North (the only thing he really runs is an insurance agency by that name). *Yvette* (next door) is a tad tonier; pizza, the Chicago standby, is available at *Edwardo's* (1212 N. Dearborn). Buses down State Street are readily available from here, and there's a subway stop at Clark and Division.

Walk 8: Lincoln Park

Lincoln Park is one of Chicago's most affluent neighborhoods, and it's also rich in historic districts, fine restaurants, interesting shops, and tree-lined streets. It began, however, as a working class neighborhood that attracted European immigrants in the 1800s, particularly to the area around North Avenue. Farther north, the neighborhood along Fullerton Parkway, was decidedly upscale, as the restored brownstones here indicate. During the nation's early experiments with urban renewal, the area weathered considerable chaos as feisty residents, many of them artists, successfully fought the wholesale destruction of the beautiful 19th-century buildings in Lincoln Park. They argued, and proved, that renewal could result from preservation as well as from demolition.

This lakefront neighborhood has Lincoln Park, Chicago's largest park, as its eastern border. The 1,212-acre linear park is larger than New York's Central Park. It was designed, in part, by the landscape architect Jens Jensen. The Swedish-born Jensen saw poetry in the midwestern prairie of his adopted homeland and incorporated it into his park designs.

The Lincoln Park area stretches from North Avenue up to Diversey Parkway and west to Racine. This walking tour begins at the heart of the Lincoln Park community, at the intersection of Halsted Street, Fullerton, and Lincoln Avenue. At this crossroad are Children's Memorial Hospital and DePaul University. To reach this area from the Loop, catch a Howard Street Line train heading north. Get off at Fullerton and walk 1 long block east along this parkway, past lovely brownstones and churches, to Halsted and Lincoln. Buses go to Lincoln Park as well; the best choice is the No. 11 Lincoln Avenue bus, which stops in the Loop on Chicago Avenue between State and La Salle. This tour is best made without a car; it ends several blocks from where it begins and parking is at a premium.

Begin by heading north up Lincoln Avenue. The street, which runs through the neighborhood on a diagonal, starts the day sleepily (some shops don't open until nearly noon), and really comes to life at night. Farther up the block is a microcosm of urban living. The people who stroll up and down this thoroughfare are as diverse as the city: politicians, television stars, socialites, lots of quite ordinary folk of all ages, as well as hippies and a bag lady or two. Enjoy it, move with the crowd (the sidewalks are narrow), and you'll feel right at home.

On the left just north of the intersection where the tour begins is the *Three Penny Cinema,* a theater with grimy charm and good popcorn. Across the street is the *Biograph,* the legendary movie house where G-men tracked down their number one enemy, bank robber John Dillinger. He and his treacherous female companion, known as the lady in red, attended a 1926 screening of *Manhattan Melodrama.* She had clued the lawmen that she and her sweet-

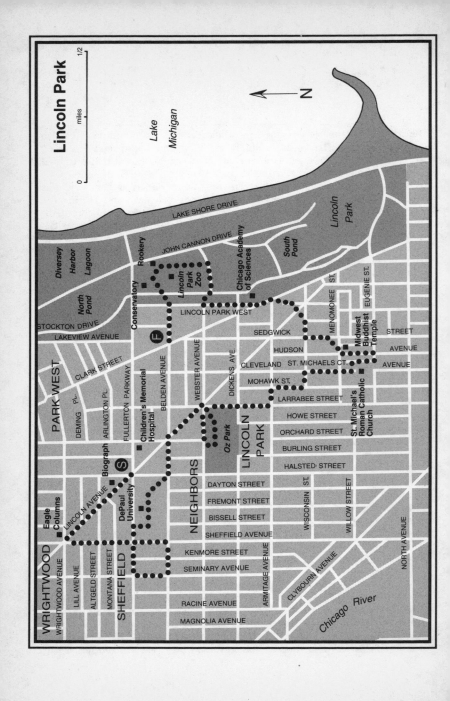

heart would be there, and as the two of them left the theater, Dillinger was riddled with bullets. Some crime buffs say that the man that was killed wasn't really Dillinger, and that the criminal quietly retired to Indiana.

For the music-minded, this block offers a choice of avant-garde clubs: *Lounge Ax* (2438 N. Lincoln; phone: 525-6620); *Irish at Lilly's* (2515 N. Lincoln; phone: 525-2422); and *Irish Eyes* (2519 N. Lincoln; phone: 348-9548). There also is vintage folk at *Earl's Pub* (2470 N. Lincoln; phone: 929-0660), run by Earl Pionke, the legendary "Earl of Old Town," a book in himself. This crusty barkeep with a soft heart has fed many struggling would-be singing stars and given them a place to sleep. Among those he indulged are the late Steve Goodman, who wrote "The City of New Orleans," and singer-songwriter Bonnie Koloc.

The shops here are as eclectic as the music. There is *Uncle Dan's Army & Navy Store* (2440 N. Lincoln; phone: 477-1918), offering everything for the urban camper. *Kongoni* (2480 N. Lincoln; phone: 929-9749) — the name means "antelope" in Swahili — is run by two staunch conservationists. Every item is authentically African, and has been selected with environmental preservation in mind. *Omiyage* (2482 N. Lincoln; phone: 477-1428), which sells baubles for children of all ages, is also a delight.

Bookworms will love this area where the bookshops stay open late — most at least until after the movie houses' last shows have begun. To sample the shops, start with *Booksellers Row* (2445 N. Lincoln; phone: 348-1170), loaded from ceiling to floor with used books on every imaginable topic. Its invitingly cluttered shelves and the slightly must aroma of old books and wooden bookcases, make it look and smell like the epitome of an old-fashioned neighborhood bookstore. There also is the *Children's Bookstore* (2465 N. Lincoln; phone: 248-2665), offering a wonderful selection of preschool and juvenile reading. Next door is *Dan Behnke Booksellers* (2463 N. Lincoln; phone: 404-0403), which specializes in used books. Across the street is the singular *Guild Books* (2456 N. Lincoln; phone: 525-3667), known for political tomes, hard-to-get material, literary journals, and art books, as well as folk records. *Guild* also has a lecture space and frequently welcomes authors to speak.

If you've worked up an appetite, consider *Periwinkle Café* (2511 N. Lincoln; phone: 883-9797), especially if the weather is nice enough for dining alfresco; even in inclement weather, this café is heaven for chocoholics. Behind the bright red storefront sporting the Union Jack is the *Red Lion Pub* (2446 N. Lincoln; phone: 348-2695), one of the few places in town that advertises authentic British cooking. Owner (and noted architect) John Cordwell confides that this place is haunted, but he thinks he knows who the ghost is, and he's welcome to stay. The *Montana Street Café* (2464 N. Lincoln; phone: 281-2407) offers such American fare as Wisconsin duck and slow-roasted Colorado leg of lamb with Michigan cider gravy.

Lincoln Park is an umbrella community; within it are a number of distinct, smaller neighborhoods — Sheffield, Wrightwood, Lincoln Central, and Old Town among them — and each has its own neighborhood association. Separately, these quasi-governmental groups determine the course of development within the neighborhoods; together, they fight City Hall on common issues, like parking congestion, nasty bars, and high taxes. (For example, along

Lincoln Avenue, you have just sampled an area known as Wrightwood. Every July, this neighborhood sponsors a *Taste of Lincoln Avenue* festival and uses the proceeds to help improve the area's schools, parks, and public areas.)

Continue up Lincoln to the six corners where it intersects with Wrightwood and Sheffield. To the right are the Eagle Columns, a trio of bronzes created by local sculptor Richard Hunt. (This is truly public art; residents here spent 5 years raising the money for this sculpture, and then treated themselves to a huge block party for its 1990 unveiling.)

From here, walk south down Sheffield. Hunt's studio is at the corner of Lill and Sheffield Streets. Next door is the *Lill Street Gallery* (1021 W. Lill; phone: 477-6185). The gallery operates a cooperative exhibition space and provides a workshop for potters who fashion sculptures, functional pots, and almost everything else you can make with clay.

Continue south, walking along Sheffield to DePaul, a neighborhood named for the university at its center. The first stop is the *DePaul Bookstore* (near the intersection with Fullerton; phone: 341-8423); student dorms are above this store, a converted factory building.

Once mainly a commuter school, DePaul University is attracting a growing number of students from elsewhere around the country. A major renovation and expansion of this campus currently is under way. For a sense of the campus, walk 2 blocks west on Fullerton to Seminary and turn left; then walk 1 block south. A classroom and office building is on the left and a student union is on the right; both were constructed within the last 20 years. At Belden, turn left, stopping at Kenmore, the next corner. Look south to the graystone townhouses, many of which have been converted to university buildings.

DePaul is part of the Sheffield neighborhood, and is known for its exquisite gardens, which are shown off in mid-July during the *Sheffield Garden Walk*. South of the university, along Seminary, Kenmore, and Sheffield, are the private homes — dating from the turn of the century — that give Lincoln Park its charm; many of them are on the annual garden walk. After exploring this community, head back to Fullerton on either Kenmore or Sheffield to continue the tour.

The next part of this walk goes down an alleyway that offers an opportunity to peek into some picturesque backyards; it is a concealed pathway that even people who have lived in the neighborhood for years haven't yet discovered. Walk east on Fullerton under the El tracks, and at the first driveway on the right, enter the iron gates; walk about 100 feet to a brick alley and turn left. Here look for architectural salvage pieces, now used as yard ornaments, and for artwork and sculpture among the shady gardens. At the intersection of another alley, look up and to the left to see an iron totem sculpture attached to the second story of a brick house at 901 W. Fullerton. This yard is full of sculptures and iron work. Continue east down the alley for 1 more block. A sculpture by Lincoln Park artist John Kearney — a giraffe made of car bumpers that have been welded together — is on the right.

At the end of the alley, turn right to explore the McCormick Row House Historic District. These 19th-century brick residences once comprised the McCormick Theological Seminary, a Presbyterian institution that erected one of the neighborhood's first buildings. To the left, with a sculpture in front, is *DePaul Concert Hall,* which originally was the seminary chapel. Exit the campus onto Belden and Halsted.

Cross Halsted and go straight east 1 block, where Belden intersects Lincoln. Across the street is a 100-year-old pub called *John Barleycorn* (658 W. Belden), after the limey lush of legend. There's beer and music; paintings line the walls, the hamburgers are huge, and the atmosphere is welcoming. (During Prohibition, the pub became a "Chinese laundry," where it was the patrons and not the shirts that got washed.)

From here, walk 1 long block down Lincoln and head toward the land of Oz; at Webster, turn right into Oz Park, the area where writer Frank Baum lived when he created his famous children's books ("We're off to see the wizard, the wonderful wizard of Oz"). Named in honor of his beloved creation, this park boasts a castle-like playground that delights youngsters of all ages. Designed by Robert Leather, it's similar to installations he's done around the country.

Walk east on Webster along the park's border, then turn right onto Larrabee, the eastern boundary of Oz Park, and head south, crossing Dickens. This area is known as Lincoln Central, and, like the other area neighborhoods, it is managed by its own quasi-governmental neighborhood association.

Walk 1 more block south to Armitage. Notice the relatively recent construction here, a shift from the 19th-century brick buildings that have peppered this walk. This area is one of the sections of Lincoln Park that was demolished for urban renewal in the 1960s, before residents made a concerted push for preservation over demolition.

Continue east on Armitage for 1 block to Wisconsin, and the Ash Playlot, an unassuming neighborhood spot where you can rest for a while. From here, turn right on Mohawk Street and go south 1 block to W. Wisconsin, then turn right to N. Cleveland and head south. This is Old Town; ahead is St. Michael's Roman Catholic Church (1633 N. Cleveland), built to serve the German immigrants who first populated this area. From the cul-de-sac in front of the church, look up to see its elegant spire. The church was built between 1866 and 1869, but part of it, destroyed by the Great Chicago Fire of 1871, was rebuilt later. Step inside to see the high vaulted ceilings, the brilliant stained glass windows, and the sword-wielding figure of St. Michael. Listen for the chimes. Local lore has it that if you can hear the bells of St. Michael's, you are in Old Town.

The famous *Old Town Art Fair* is held along Wisconsin and Menomonee Street during the second weekend in June, as it has been for more than 4 decades. Each of the area streets has its own special charm, take your pick and explore them at leisure.

Old Town was the first section of Lincoln Park to be revitalized after World War II. The original residents previously had begun to abandon the area for the suburbs, leaving room for dedicated urbanites to move in, changing the neighborhood's character from aging working class to what's now referred to as gentrified. From St. Michael's, walk a short block east on Eugenie. At Hudson, turn left and, as you go around the corner, notice 1700 N. Hudson, the home of architect Walter Netsch and his wife, Dawn Clark Netsch, who for many years was a state senator and now is comptroller for the state of Illinois. Netsch's rooftop design studio is above the garage.

Continue north on Hudson for 1 block to another house of worship, the Midwest Buddhist Temple (435 W. Menomonee), a pagoda-type structure surrounded by oriental gardens. Go left down Willow a few steps and turn right into an alley that runs along the western edge of the Buddhist temple. Across the street is a pedestrian mall — actually a little park — with stone tables inset with boards for playing chess or checkers. Follow this path past two more of John Kearney's bumper sculptures, a pair of horses.

The path ends at Sedgwick. Turn left and go one-half block to Wisconsin, then turn right. At the corner of Sedgwick and Wisconsin is a community conversation area next to the Church of the Three Crosses. Catercorner from this spot is a new residential townhouse development, the award-winning Belgravia Terrace, where townhouses sell for about $1 million each. Formerly the site of a hospital, this is one of the last parcels of land reconstructed under urban development.

Walk to the corner of North Orleans and Wisconsin and angle through the commercial mall to Lincoln Avenue. Stop by *Ranalli's Pizza* (1925 N. Lincoln; phone: 642-4700) to try one of more than 100 imported beers. This is also the place for some of Chicago's best pizza (and one of the few places where the hungry can get something to eat in this neighborhood).

Continue northeast along the mall, to Lincoln Park West. Just ahead is the *Chicago Academy of Sciences* (see *Chicago at-a-Glance* in THE CITY); the *Chicago Historical Society* is 2 blocks down Clark Street to the right. Both are worth a visit, but first stroll through the park for which this community is named, beginning with the famous (and free) *Lincoln Park Zoo.*

Walk into the park at Armitage, in front of the *Chicago Academy of Sciences.* Walk a block north to the recently restored *Café Brauer,* an exquisite piece of Prairie School architecture designed in 1905 by Dwight Perkins, who also designed many of the city's public schools and fought for the establishment of the forest preserves, the large areas of greenery that surround the city. Café diners can order several light dishes and enjoy them outside by the small lake; paddle-wheel boats can be rented under the bridge to the south. The zoo begins here, just across the bridge east of *Café Brauer.*

Wander through the zoo; then follow signs to the newly restored Rookery, a rock garden designed in 1936 by curmudgeonly octogenarian Alfred Caldwell, a student of Jens Jensen and the dean of Chicago's landscape architects. A faithful restoration of this lovely place, where all manner of waterfowl are free to come and go, was completed in 1991. Lincoln Park Conservatory is 3 acres of greenhouses and gardens. The glass-walled conservatory building itself is a marvel, with a tropical jungle at its center and constantly changing displays in other rooms. Leaving the conservatory, walk west a short distance to Clark Street. From here, any bus goes back to the Loop; taxis also frequently pass here.

Walk 9: Clybourn Corridor

Clybourn Corridor, one of the hottest commercial areas in Chicago, was a thriving manufacturing district until it went upscale during the 1980s, when development in Lincoln Park inevitably pushed west. With the River North district as their primer, many real estate developers envisioned the conversion of Clybourn Avenue's factories and warehouses into trendy lofts and high-end retail shops.

It didn't quite happen that way. A number of people — a coalition of industrialists, social workers, and even some of the young urban professional types who had been moving into the area — realized that to drive out high-paying manufacturing jobs (some with wages of more than $20 an hour) and replace them with low-end restaurant and retail jobs was not exactly progress. Instead, they settled on a compromise called the Clybourn Planned Manufacturing District. The plan, set boundaries for industrial uses, buffer operations such as retail and restaurants, and residential areas. It was a new — and experimental — chapter in gentrification.

Because Clybourn still is in transition, it can be deceiving. Don't dismiss what appear to be abandoned warehouses and run-down houses. Look again. The backyards of those old wooden houses may sport new decks — some with Jacuzzis — and most likely the interiors of the houses are being renovated before work begins on the exteriors. This tour is most easily done using a car; there is ample parking in the area's numerous shopping malls. Clybourn also is accessible by public transportation; to get to the place where the tour begins, board either a Howard Street Line or Ravenswood Line train, purchasing a transfer on the train, and ride it to Fullerton Avenue. There, catch a westbound bus (ask the driver) and go about a dozen blocks to where Fullerton intersects Clybourn (if you cross the river, you'll have gone too far). Note that though parts of this area may look a bit seedy, it is quite safe to wander about freely, particularly during daylight hours.

The Clybourn Corridor runs diagonally southeast from Fullerton Avenue on the north down to North Avenue (once the city's northern boundary) near Halsted Street. Begin the tour south of Fullerton, at the intersection of Webster and Clybourn.

A few doors to the north of this intersection is *Vintage Posters International* (2211 N. Clybourn; phone: 975-7744), a gallery dedicated to original 19th-century European posters, such as one of France's Cote d'Azur train or one from a French cabaret. Across the street is *Wear in Good Health* (2202 N. Clybourn; phone: 929-0883), a designer clothing store featuring, as its sign declares, "clothes, plain and simple."

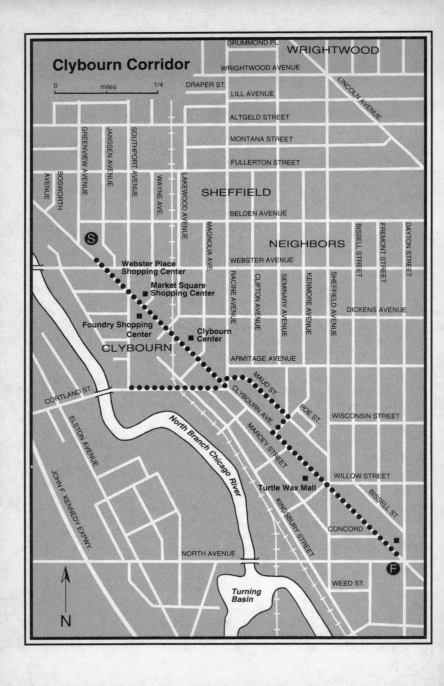

At the intersection of Clybourn and Webster there are three restaurants as diverse as the neighborhood: an excellent Thai café, *Rim Klong* (2203 N. Clybourn; phone: 883-0434); *Jake and Fanny's* deli and outdoor patio (across Webster; phone: 348-3300); and *Linda's* restaurant (2200 N. Clybourn), a long-time Clybourn fixture.

Anchoring the opposite corner is the *Webster Place Shopping Center,* site of the former Butternut Bread factory, which has a *Loews* 8-screen theater complex (phone: 327-3100) on the second level, and yet another Chicago institution, the *Great Ace* (phone: 348-0705), unlike any conceivable hardware store, on the first level.

Two other stores express the city's love affair with the Southwest: *Southwest Expressions* (*Webster Place*) next to the theaters; phone: 525-2626) and *Out of the West* (across the street at 2187 N. Clybourn; phone: 404-WEST) — both specialize in goods from that part of the country.

Continue south on Clybourn; the next section of the corridor is for antiques buffs — very affluent antiques buffs. If you're interested in a Chippendale chair in mint condition (and have a mint to spend on it) check out *Reflections Antiques* (2156 N. Clybourn; phone: 871-7078). A nearby store in the same general category is *Design Avenue* (2167 N. Clybourn; phone: 477-6669). *Interiors on Consignment* (2150 N. Clybourn; phone: 868-0797) offers high-quality goods.

The next stop on the left is the *Market Square Shopping Center,* one of the first pioneers of the resettled Clybourn Corridor. Its main store, *Treasure Island* (phone: 880-8880), is no ordinary grocery. Chicagoans, particularly those who actually live in the city, are as likely to bring out-of-towners here as they are to whisk them up the Sears Tower. This grocery features imported foods from all corners of the earth. Shoppers can easily lose track of time just browsing the aisles. There are a host of other stores in the shopping center, hidden behind the industrially inspired (or uninspired) façade. There is a designer sample store, a resale shop, and *Kiddleydivy* (phone: 929-2676), an upscale children's store.

Across the street is another shopping mall, offering more evidence of the community's affluence. The *Foundry Shopping Center* includes a *Pier 1 Imports* stuffed with interesting finds from the world over, *House of Teak* and a Scandinavian furniture store. *Habitat* offers wall coverings, and *Spaces* is for those who need to get organized. If it's time for indulgence, try some authentic French pastries from *Au Pain Chocolate* (phone: 871-6666); the shop's proprietor will be pleased to speak with you in French. Chicago's largest bookseller, *Kroch's and Brentano's,* has a major outlet here; in addition to selling books, this branch offers an extensive series of lectures and discussions conducted by leading authors from Chicago and elsewhere.

At this point along Clybourn, a single set of railroad tracks intersects Clybourn and Lakewood Streets, the tracks are so neatly paved you'll wonder if they're still in use. They are, and you can count yourself lucky if you witness the once-a-week delivery of sugar on its way to Peerless Confections some blocks north of here.

Farther up the block another shopping center, the *Clybourn Center,* between Magnolia and Racine Streets. This mall houses the *Wall Wizard* (2065

N. Clybourn; 868-1055), which offers ultra-sleek furnishings, and two children's stores, *Born Beautiful* (2045 N. Clybourn; phone: 549-6770) and *Head Over Heels,* which offer all the pampered child needs and then some. Farther down is *IF Designs* (2001 N. Clybourn; phone: 348-1040), selling contemporary furniture on the ground level of the Clybourn Commons Lofts, an office building.

At the intersection of Cortland and Racine, take a 2-block side trip to the right, venturing into what is still the industrial heart of the Clybourn Corridor. Two blocks west of this intersection is A. Finkl & Sons, a century-old foundry that still produces some of the nation's steel. It's safe to stand on the sidewalk and look in; it may be possible to see the workers pouring molten steel into forms. Charles Finkl, grandson of the firm's founder and now chairman of the board, helped lead the fight to form the Clybourn Planned Manufacturing District. Clybourn once was a typical Chicago neighborhood with worker housing surrounding its industrial plants. In the late 1940s, though, postwar prosperity enabled workers at plants such as Finkl to move to suburban areas, resulting in the neighborhood's decline until gentrifiers began moving in during the 1980s. For a look at a very modern section of this area, one where no traces of vintage Chicago can be seen, go back to Clybourn after looking at the Finkl plant, walk along Cortland Street, and at the intersection of Cortland and Racine, go left for a few steps on Racine to Maud Street. Turn onto Maud and follow it southeast. At Kenmore, another multi-street intersection, turn right to return to Clybourn.

This little side trip bypasses another strip shopping center, where *Mitchell's* restaurant (1953 N. Clybourn, between Armitage and Racine; phone: 883-1157), a favorite among locals, offers marvelous muffins for breakfast and the city's best BLT. *Stevie B's Rib Café* (1953 N. Clybourn; phone: 327-7750), also in the complex, is owned by restaurateur Steve Birger and actor Jim Belushi. Those in need of refreshment may want to backtrack.

Continue south on Clybourn; here are some of the older businesses on the street, such as *Artmark* (phone: 266-1111) and the nearby gift outlet at 1834 N. Clybourn, as well as the *Artists' Frame Service* (phone: FRAMING), the most comprehensive framing shop you'll ever see. The *Jayson Gallery* (1915 N. Clybourn) is next to *Lion Photo* (phone: 528-5585); whether you're building a darkroom or you just need a new lens cap, this is the place to go.

The final stop on this tour is *1800 Clybourn Center,* the former Turtle Wax factory (yes, that stuff with which you wax your car). Horwitz-Matthews, a Chicago development firm founded by two men who came out of the 1960s protest movements and also own a publishing company, artfully converted this complex of factory buildings into an urban shopping mall, one that turns shopping into theater. The shops inside are unique, from the *Real Nancy Drew* gallery to *Ancient Echoes* jewelry to the *Urban American Club* clothing store. There are amusing things to do here, too, like watch the fish in the aquarium on the lower level, fantasize you are Minnesota Fats at *Muddler's Pool Room* (phone: 944-7665), or play miniature golf at *Par Excellence* (phone: 278-4653), a course designed by local artists.

The acclaimed *Remains Theatre* (phone: 335-9800), another resident of the mall, offers off-Loop productions at affordable prices; one recent show was

David Mamet's *American Buffalo.* Follow the après-theater crowd to the *Goose Island Brewery* (phone: 915-0071), a discovery in itself. The shiny silver vats in which this micro-brewery and pub makes its own brands of beer are visible from the entrance. The brewmaster always offers at least five seasonal selections, such as Lincoln Park Lager, Old Clybourn Porter, or Honest Stout. Beer is served in pint glasses; if you'd like to conduct your own taste test, ask for the smaller, taster-size brews. The hearty menu features foods that go well with beer.

If you're still feeling hardy, continue walking the remaining 2 blocks of Clybourn, down to North Avenue. Most of this section has not been redeveloped, except there is the funky *Wayne's Ribs and Blues Bar* (1615 N. Clybourn). At the corner of North Avenue is the sparkling new *Crate & Barrel Outlet* (phone: 787-4775). Herein lies a tale of gentrification. This upscale home accessories and furnishings retailer, which today has stores from Texas to Boston, opened its first store on Wells Street in Old Town, a dozen blocks east, during the mid 1950s. The site was then considered a sort of outpost of civilization by the "lakefront liberals," with whom it was popular. Later, once the chain started opening other stores, the Wells Street store became an outlet for discontinued items. Three years ago, the outlet needed to expand, and rents on Wells Street had become too dear. So the shop moved west, helping to revitalize another neighborhood.

The area around North and Halsted is a microcosm of the changing Clybourn neighborhood, and of the changing city — an industrial stronghold that may bend and change with the times, may allow some new glitz to enter, but one that also refuses to give up all of its grit. If you are driving, return to North Michigan Avenue or the Loop by heading east on North Avenue, which intersects with LaSalle Street and Lake Shore Drive, the two quickest routes downtown. If you are on foot, the fastest way downtown is the train; there's a station at the intersection of North and Clybourn. Get on a train headed south to the Loop (there's only one choice, the other train goes north); the next stop is Clark and Division, then Chicago and State. The North and Clybourn train station is closed on weekends; a problem some residents and merchants are beginning to address. Your other choice, if you are on foot, is the North Avenue bus; again, buy a transfer so you can switch to a bus headed south at LaSalle Street.

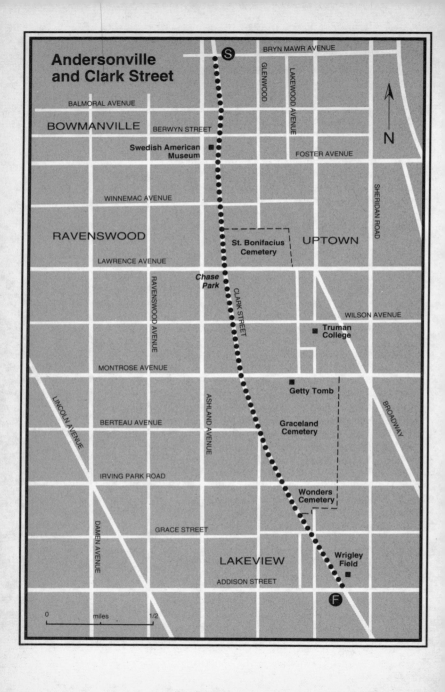

Andersonville and Clark Street

BRYN MAWR AVENUE

GLENWOOD

LAKEWOOD AVENUE

BALMORAL AVENUE

BOWMANVILLE BERWYN STREET

FOSTER AVENUE

Swedish American Museum

WINNEMAC AVENUE

SHERIDAN ROAD

RAVENSWOOD

St. Bonifacius Cemetery

UPTOWN

LAWRENCE AVENUE

Chase Park

CLARK STREET

RAVENSWOOD AVENUE

WILSON AVENUE

Truman College

MONTROSE AVENUE

Getty Tomb

LINCOLN AVENUE

BERTEAU AVENUE

ASHLAND AVENUE

Graceland Cemetery

BROADWAY

IRVING PARK ROAD

Wonders Cemetery

DAMEN AVENUE

GRACE STREET

LAKEVIEW

Wrigley Field

ADDISON STREET

N

0   miles   1/2

Walk 10: Andersonville and Clark Street

Clark Street runs parallel to Lake Shore Drive from the city's northern boundary to 23rd Street, near McCormick Place on the South Side. Historically, Clark has been a magnet for recent immigrants. Earlier this century, for instance, it provided a new home and renewed hope for generations of Italians, Swedes, and other Europeans. Since the early 1970s, however, a new generation of immigrants has established a beachhead here that is evident in the ethnic crazy-quilt of its restaurants. The area also has an extraordinary outdoor museum, Graceland Cemetery, and the nation's most gracious ballpark, *Wrigley Field,* home of the Chicago *Cubs.*

The segment of Clark Street between 5600 and 5200 North is main street for Andersonville, Chicago's vigorous Swedish enclave and one of the most concentrated Swedish neighborhoods in America. Major Swedish festivals held in Andersonville include a colorful mid-June street fair, featuring costumed folk dancing and choral singing, and *St. Lucia Day* (mid-December), with *Christmas* carolling and the traditional crowning of the Queen of Light.

This tour begins at Bryn Mawr Avenue in Andersonville (5600 North) and ends at Addison (3600 North), where every loyal North Sider's favorite team plays ball. This tour can be done by car or on the Clark Street bus, which runs the entire length of the street. To get to the starting point by car, head west from Lake Shore Drive on Bryn Mawr (5600 North). To get there on public transit, take the Howard Street train to Bryn Mawr and walk over (a 10-minute walk) to Clark Street. From Bryn Mawr, head south through the wonderful assortment of boutiques, specialty bookstores, offbeat second-hand shops, and eateries and groceries that encompass just about every kind of ethnic cooking imaginable.

The first stop is *Hollywood Antiques* (5657 N. Clark). The owners of this 3-room shop have a thing for Fiesta dinnerware, but the store's eclectic range of collectibles make it, as one local described it, "a great junk shop." A block farther down is the 50-seat *Kotobuki* (5547 N. Clark) Japanese restaurant, open for lunch Mondays through Fridays and dinner daily. Its specialties are sushi, sashimi, tempura, and beef teriyaki.

Don't like raw fish? Try *Machu Picchu* (5427 N. Clark), one of the few Peruvian eateries in the Midwest. Choose from among eight appetizers, including lobster soufflé and potato stuffed with a mixture of onions, beef, tomatoes, raisins, olives, boiled egg, and herbs. A like number of entrées include a popular pork dish served with a lively peanut sauce, duck in amaretto sauce, and filet of chicken accompanied by a potato prepared with a two-cheese sauce. The restaurant does not serve liquor, but patrons are invited to bring their own wine.

For a quick burger or to check on the home team, stop in at *Ashur's Sports Lounge,* where sports fans enjoy a big-screen satellite television set. *Timbuktu* (5416 N. Clark), across the street from *Ashur's,* offers a vast selection of clothing based on traditional African designs and styles. The owner, who may be behind a sewing machine, is always ready to answer any questions about the designs and their history. Pick up unusual African jewelry, bags, baskets, and lovely T-shirts.

Just ahead is the *Calo* theater (5404 N. Clark) and the *Tipanian* restaurant and cocktail lounge. The restaurant, with an easily recognizable red-and-white façade — prepares Szechuan and Mandarin Chinese, as well as Philippine, dishes; they also have live entertainment in the evening.

If pastries are a weakness, walk another block to a huge hand-painted medieval-style mural with princesses and knights. It covers the front of the *Swedish Bakery* (5348 N. Clark), a haven for tempting bread (including limpa and potato), pastries, cookies, muffins, and 20 different kinds of coffee cake — all at reasonable neighborhood-bakery prices. The genteel decor of the interior — pretty white wallpaper, a wooden bench, and a revolving cake stand — is reminiscent of a village tea shop. The sales staff wears traditional Swedish costumes (satisfying a Saturday morning craving can involve a wait of 20 minutes or more; get here early!).

Across the street is *Calo,* specializing in Italian food (and locally renowned for its pizza). *Calo* offers live entertainment, featuring popular music, with dancing on Wednesdays, Fridays, and Saturdays to help diners work off the delicious pasta and wine. Its celebrated baby-back ribs are the menu special on Thursday nights. This restaurant has its own parking lot — an important plus in an area where metered spaces are at a premium.

A few doors down is *Okee Chee's Wild Horse Gallery,* a gallery boutique dedicated to Native American culture, offering art, books, weavings, and handmade toys. From here, walk to the hand-me-down haven of *Camden Passage Antiques* (5309 N. Clark). This shop has vintage clothes, jewelry, and lots of odds and ends. It competes with the nameless second-hand shop on the other side of the street, which offers an array of inexpensively priced clothes, furniture, and bric-a-brac.

Food is the highlight of the next block, starting with the *Baskin-Robbins* ice cream shop (at the corner of N. Clark and Berwyn). Beyond that is *Andie's* restaurant (5293 N. Clark), with tantalizing Greek and Lebanese food, and *Reza's* Persian restaurant (5255 N. Clark). This last is an unusually good-looking neighborhood restaurant, with smart hardwood floors, vases filled with fresh pink carnations, and pretty Iranian prints adorning its brick walls. Try the yogurt-based appetizers, beef kabobs, and char-broiled combinations of shrimp, beef, chicken, scallops, and vegetables.

Down the street is *Valkommen,* a Scandinavian eatery that serves hearty breakfasts and lunches featuring sausages, ham, roast beef, and corned beef, along with seafood and salads. Satisfy a craving for herring, as Sweden's Queen Sylvia did during a 1988 royal tour, at *Wikstrom's* (5247 N. Clark) Scandinavian-style deli. *Wikstrom's and Erikson's,* another deli across the

street (5250 N. Clark), offers a veritable smorgasbord of Scandinavian goodies, including Swedish potato sausage, Danish brie, and Norwegian jahrlsberg
cheese, along with lutefish, packages of potato dumplings, sacks of yellow
peas, and an assortment of Scandinavian chocolate and candy.

The colorful display at *Woman Wild* (5237 N. Clark) only hints at the
delights within. Offering what it calls "treasures by women," this shop sells
gallery-quality textiles, pottery, and jewelry. These imaginative and often
brightly colored items are all original designs; they make great and unusual
gifts. Next door is the city's best feminist bookstore, *Women and Children
First.* In addition to books, the shop offers diverse merchandise, including
small gift items, unusual T-shirts (with readers and feline fanciers in mind),
note cards (both whimsical and profound), and a selection of jewelry. Pick
up a mystery novel by Chicago writer Sara Paretsky, whose tough female
protagonist, private eye V.I. Warshawski, roams the Windy City solving
murders.

Resale goods are the highlight of the next block. *Right Place* (5219 N.
Clark) has a variety of circa-1950 items — gaily colored clothing and plastic
goods. Across the street at *Books of Berwyn,* a small bright storefront has been
turned into a card and bookshop with a particularly good selection of children's books.

Heavenly Swedish waffles, piled high with whipped strawberries, thin pancakes smothered with tart lingonberries, and a side order of mild potato
sausage, served with a hot buttery cinnamon roll. Sound good? Head for *Ann
Sather* (5207 N. Clark). This Chicago landmark offers combination breakfast
plates that let diners sample both pancakes and waffles. Three-egg omelettes
are popular breakfast fare, and homemade bread (pumpkin, carrot, and the
like) is a special treat. Although famous for its breakfasts, this also is a good
and inexpensive spot for hearty lunches and dinners, such as meatballs, roast
duck, loin of pork, pan-fried chicken liver, and a Swedish sampler platter.
This most definitely is a family place. A series of murals along the wall
chronicle a Swedish fairy tale, and the restaurant presents readings of children's classics on Wednesday mornings.

The next stop is Graceland Cemetery, a dozen long blocks south and, thus,
worth a bus fare or returning to the car to drive. Graceland (enter where
Clark meets Irving Park Road; 4000 North) embraced the Victorian-age
belief that cemeteries should be places where the dead could lay eternally in
sweet repose and the living could enjoy a tranquil carriage ride through lush,
groomed landscape. Graceland is the final home of George Pullman, Potter
Palmer, Philip Armour, Cyrus McCormick, Marshall Field, and many other
luminaries (at least the Protestant ones) who built this city. Not only are
many of the city's architects buried here (Miës van der Rohe, Louis Sullivan,
and Daniel H. Burnham among them), they also designed some of the tombs.
(Architectural historians cite Sullivan's Getty Tomb as the beginning of
modern architecture in America. To build it, he looked not to models from
the past, but to his own vision of what American architecture could be.) The
Chicago Architecture Foundation (phone: 326-1393) gives tours of Graceland
on Sunday afternoons in the spring and fall. The foundation also sells a
self-guided tour.

Move on to Addison and *Wrigley Field,* where the Chicago *Cubs,* those guys who "just love to break your heart," play ball. The gloomy statistics: the *Cubs* haven't been in a *World Series* since 1945; the last time they won was 1908. This neighborhood is called Wrigleyville, and its residents fought the Chicago Tribune Company (a formidable foe in this town) for a decade over the issue of night games. The Trib eventually won and the lights went on in 1990, but on the neighborhood's terms. A warning: If it's game time, don't park here (assuming there's an available spot). One of the promises the neighborhood extracted from the city in return for approving night games is that residents get stickers for their cars; those without them get towed on game nights.

There are several places to eat a hot dog around here even if the team isn't playing. For atmosphere, try the *Cubby Bear Lounge* (1059 W. Addison) or *Bleacher Bums* (Waveland and Sheffield) at the other corner of the field. Those interested in more ethnic fare might want to try *Moulibet* (3521 N. Clark), a long block south. This is an Ethiopian establishment specializing in lamb, chicken, and vegetable dishes. Tej, a sweet honey wine, makes a good accompaniment to this very spicy food.

The Howard Street train stops at Addison (if there's a game, many people take advantage of its convenience). Hop on for an elevated ride through Lincoln Park on the way back to the Loop.

Walk 11: Argyle Street and Little Saigon

Argyle Street, named for a Scottish duke, used to call itself the new Chinatown. Today, neighborhood street markers more accurately identify it as Argyle International. The area, a few brief blocks between Broadway and Sheridan at 5000 North, has become an eclectic mix of nationalities. It's an outpost of the Far East in the Midwest, where Asian cultures, particularly Vietnamese, dominate. Chinese grocery stores, Korean hair salons, Thai bakeries, and Asian import stores line Argyle. Many shops have signs printed both in English and in the native tongue of the owner.

Getting here is easy: Hop on a Howard Street subway train in the Loop and head north. If it's rush hour, get on an "A" train; it's the only one that stops at Argyle Street. The station, decked out in green and red, is hard to miss. The train comes out of its subway tunnel at 2000 North and provides views of Lincoln Park, Lake View, and Graceland Cemetery along the way. Get off the train and head east toward Sheridan. The concentration of Vietnamese businesses on the stretch of Argyle Street bisected by the El have earned the area its familiar nickname: Little Saigon.

At Sheridan, turn right and walk 2 blocks south to the *Pasteur* restaurant (4759 N. Sheridan). Though it seems a typical storefront ethnic eatery, this shop, named after a street in Saigon, also has a certain stylishness about it. It is run by the Nguyen family, who have decorated the walls with photographs of their homeland. The restaurant's menu features 11 appetizers and 7 soup choices. Frequently named by critics as one of Chicago's best Vietnamese restaurants, *Pasteur* is a good spot for grazing.

Head back toward Argyle and cross the street. The *Superior* gift shop (1004 W. Argyle) has everything its window promises and then some: from vases to party decorations. The *Pho Xe Lua* Vietnamese restaurant (1021 W. Argyle), a little farther down the street, offers delicious and inexpensive lunches in a no-frills setting. The fixed-price lunch is $5. For something with more atmosphere, cross Argyle again to another Vietnamese restaurant, *Nhu Hoa Café*, which also offers Laotian dishes. Distinguished by its hot-pink awning and the neon palm trees in the window, it's known for crunchy egg rolls and fiery curry dishes.

The tumult of activity along Argyle Street is reminiscent of a Far East city. People preoccupied with shopping zigzag though the bazaar of exotic shops; delivery trucks loaded with pungently scented foods line up along the curb; and the air rings with the sing-song music of the Vietnamese language. Among the most authentic groceries in Little Saigon is *Hoa Yang*, at the corner of Kenmore Avenue. A vat of iced-down fresh fish sits right inside the

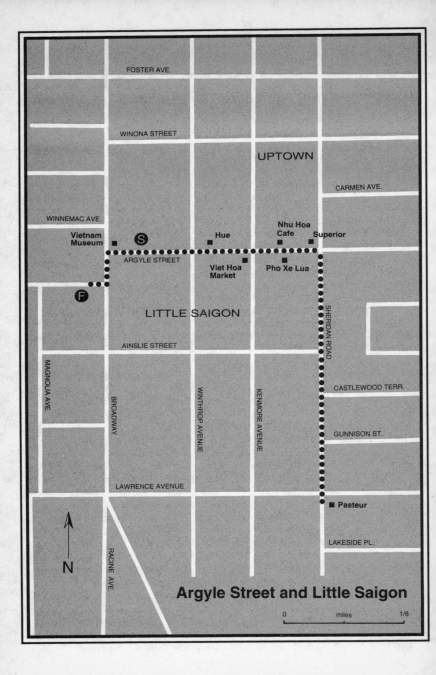

FOSTER AVE.

WINONA STREET

UPTOWN

CARMEN AVE.

WINNEMAC AVE.

Vietnam Museum

S

Hue

Nhu Hoa Cafe

Superior

ARGYLE STREET

Viet Hoa Market

Pho Xe Lua

F

LITTLE SAIGON

AINSLIE STREET

SHERIDAN ROAD

MAGNOLIA AVE.

BROADWAY

WINTHROP AVENUE

KENMORE AVENUE

CASTLEWOOD TERR.

GUNNISON ST.

LAWRENCE AVENUE

Pasteur

N

RACINE AVE.

LAKESIDE PL.

Argyle Street and Little Saigon

0   miles   1/8

doorway. The shelves inside are stocked with noodles of bewildering variety (have you ever seen noodles made of tapioca?), as well as canned quail eggs, bottled vegetables, 50-pound bags of rice, and a seemingly endless assortment of tea, which almost fills an entire aisle of the store. Across Kenmore, the *Viet Hoa Market* (1051 W. Argyle) is pure Vietnamese, crammed with fresh and frozen fish, exotic spices, oriental vegetables, spiced tea, and flavored rice, as well as an array of hand-painted tea pots, Vietnamese cooking utensils, and inexpensive ceramic bowls.

Another Vietnamese stop is the *Hue* restaurant (1138 W. Argyle), which is known for its variety of seafood dishes. *Hue* also has an extensive menu that features such delicacies as asparagus and crab soup and spicy chicken with lemon grass and peppers. It has no liquor license, but diners are permitted to bring their own beer or wine.

On the other side of Broadway at Argyle is the *French Baker,* a reminder of Vietnam's years as a French colony. (Some say that the mix of French and Chinese influences is what makes the food so good.) The bakery offers enticing French loaves and croissants, as well as a light Vietnamese lunch at small café-style tables.

Argyle turns into a residential area west of Broadway. Vietnamese families live in the decrepit-looking brownstones and narrow wooden houses of this neighborhood. In just a decade and a half, these refugees have carved out a distinct and self-sufficient community here. Near Argyle on the east side of Broadway is the tiny storefront *Vietnam Museum* (5002 Broadway, see *Museums* in THE CITY), a reminder of the controversial war that chased these people from their homes. The tiny storefront museum, filled with uniforms and equipment, maps, photos, and other memorabilia, is open only on Friday, Saturday, and Sunday afternoons. It is located just down the street from *Kim's Cleaners* and *Chiquini's* Mexican restaurant, a block that clearly celebrates Chicago's ethnic melange.

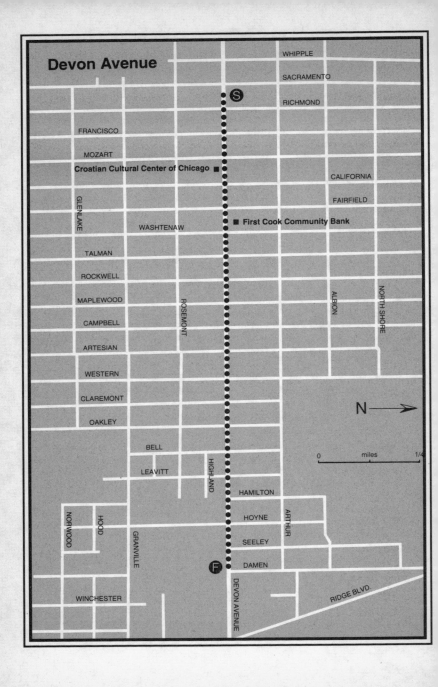

Devon Avenue

WHIPPLE

SACRAMENTO

Ⓢ

RICHMOND

FRANCISCO

MOZART

Croatian Cultural Center of Chicago ■

CALIFORNIA

FAIRFIELD

GLENLAKE

WASHTENAW

■ First Cook Community Bank

TALMAN

ROCKWELL

MAPLEWOOD

ALBION

NORTH SHORE

CAMPBELL

ROSEMONT

ARTESIAN

WESTERN

CLAREMONT

OAKLEY

BELL

N →

LEAVITT

HIGHLAND

0   miles   1/4

HAMILTON

NORWOOD

HOOD

HOYNE

ARTHUR

GRANVILLE

SEELEY

DAMEN

Ⓕ

WINCHESTER

DEVON AVENUE

RIDGE BLVD.

Walk 12: Devon Avenue

Elderly Jewish men shopping at a kosher butcher; Indian women with caste marks on their foreheads looking at colorful fabric; Russians, Greeks, Palestinians, and even a few Italians. You'll find them all along Devon Avenue, where every few blocks Chicago's diverse ethnic communities come together like bands in a rainbow. Once strictly a Jewish enclave, many of the original residents — now senior citizens — remain, surrounded by flourishing Eastern European bakeries, Middle Eastern groceries, Indian markets, and even a Croatian community center.

This walk starts at 3000 W. Devon, at the intersection of Richmond Avenue, and heads east. To get here, either drive or take a train and bus. By car, take the Kennedy Expressway northwest to the Diversey (2800 North) exit and head north on Western Avenue. Devon is about a 15-minute drive from the exit; this section of Western is where Chicago's car dealerships are concentrated. To get here by train, take the Howard Street Line to Howard, walk downstairs to the bus terminal and get a No. 155 Devon Avenue bus.

At the Richmond intersection, where the *New Kumoon* (2927 W. Devon), a Mandarin restaurant with carry-out stands, the rich ethnic mix of this area begins. Across the street, *Cosmos Food and Liquors* heralds its ethnic diversity with a sign proclaiming: "Greek and Syrian groceries, Kosher foods and wines." Inside are olives, packages of figs, dandelion greens (for making *horta*), wheels of Greek cheese, and crumbly feta.

Rosenblum's Judaica (2905 W. Devon), a book and gift store, features Hebrew cards, religious gifts, and a selection of special children's books with such titles as *How Uncle Murray Saved Seder*. In the window are silver menorahs, a magnetic spelling board with Hebrew characters, and ceramics of stern elders and studious rabbis.

Across the street is the popular *Hashalom,* a storefront restaurant with baskets and tapestries decorating its plain white walls and blue vinyl covering its tables. Its deliciously authentic Middle Eastern food combines Moroccan and Israeli preparations. Popular dishes include couscous, bourekas, and falafel. Another popular suggestion is shakshouka, a classic Israeli dish made with fresh tomatoes, onions, peppers, tomato sauce, two eggs sunny-side up, and pita bread. Top off the meal with rich Israeli coffee.

The side streets here are quiet, tree-lined avenues of 2-, 3-, and 4-story row houses and brownstones, but Devon itself is a bustling corridor of noise and activity, teeming with Asian immigrants, pungent with spicy smells — and carelessly strewn with litter. Import shops, jewelers, even a factory outlet — *Gregory and Son Nuts,* offering chocolate and nuts — can be found here.

Heading east to the intersection of Devon and Mozart (otherwise known as North Croatia Drive) heralds another heady ethnic mix. Dominating the south side of Devon is the huge Croatian Cultural Center of Chicago, a long, flat, unattractive cement building that is windowless and decorated with horizontal red, white, and blue stripes across its façade. Peek inside its cool, dark interior at walls adorned with portraits of Croatian kings and paintings of coastal scenes; perhaps its heavy chairs and tables are decorated for an upcoming wedding.

On the north side of Devon is a fruit market with crates of seasonal melons and mangos stacked on the sidewalk. The *Kosher Karry Deli* (2828 W. Devon), provides knishes, kugel, and other fare for bar mitzvahs, as well as bakery and deli goods for neighborhood patrons. Half a block east is *Levinson's Bakery,* where the aroma of freshly baked pastries inevitably lure passersby inside along with the Jewish grandmothers who congregate here. Bagel varieties include plain, egg, onion, poppy seed, pumpernickel, and sesame. For those who can't resist the temptation of calorie-laden pastry, there is some consolation: No preservatives are used in these baked goods. Notices for dances for Jewish singles are posted on the front window; passing by outside you're as likely to see a woman in a sari as an orthodox rabbi.

On the north side of Devon, the *Three Sisters Delicatessen* (2854 W. Devon) offers Russian groceries, including a variety of smoked fish — shad, herring, mackerel, sable, and sturgeon. At the corner of N. California, tempting cookies, cakes, and pastries sit in the window of yet another bakery — *Gitel's* kosher bakery (2745 W. Devon). Inside, shop for a wedding cake, study color snapshots of creations inscribed with "mazel tov," and pick up a copy of the *Jewish Sentinel* ("the voice of Chicago Jewry since 1911"). Two doors down at the *Phase II* portrait gallery, paintings of Golda Meir, Albert Einstein, and other celebrated figures are available. The *Russian-American Bookstore* (2746 W. Devon), is an interesting stop, complete with books, samovars, portraits of Lenin and Gorbachev (or whoever may have replaced him), and red banners.

Striking another note of incongruity is the First Cook Community Bank (2720 W. Devon), with its brick colonial architecture featuring dormers and white shutters. Outside is the *Spirit of the Fighting Yank,* a statue of a grenade-wielding American GI.

The *Gandhi India* restaurant (2601 W. Devon), is typical of the restaurants in the neighborhood's colorful Indian enclave. Although it may lack atmosphere, there's ample compensation in the good, inexpensive food. A daily, all-you-can-eat buffet is a bargain at $5.95. The punjabi bread is delightful, and the tandoori chicken and vegetarian dishes are tasty. Even if you don't opt for a full meal, take a short break and sample the combination appetizer plate and a glass of Taj Mahal beer.

"Little Bombay" begins in earnest along the stretch of Devon immediately east of Washtenaw. In fact, many of the Indian and Pakistani restaurants in this section of Devon advertise singers and musicians "direct from Bombay." *Al Mansour* (2600 W. Devon), plastered with posters promoting Indian movies, offers audiocassettes of contemporary and popular Indian singers. *Jai Hind Foods and Video* (2658 W. Devon) is typical of the food markets that vie for business along the next few blocks. Shoppers in saris peruse jars of chutney, tandoor paste, and sacks of rice to the omnipresent chant of Indian pop music and the pervasive aroma of pungent spices. An entire wall is stacked high with a variety of beans, curry and other powders, and seeds such as mustard and cumin. A dining area in the rear has a half dozen tables, and a offers a buffet of South Indian specialties and sticky desserts.

Tucked amid Devon's teeming Asian community, *Ebner's Meat Market* (2649 W. Devon) is another throwback to the neighborhood's Jewish origins. Window signs offer homemade chopped liver and kishka and proclaim that its operations are "under rabbinical supervision."

At the intersection of Talman, *Shada* (2629 W. Devon) displays its filmy saris in a kaleidoscope of color on mannequins with delicate Indian features, their hands gracefully folded. Selections of saris also are found at *Indira Fashions* (2625 W. Devon) and *Sari Sapne* (2623 W. Devon). Across the street, *Kadmar Plaza* (2646 W. Devon), an Indian grocery, opens onto yet another reasonably priced sari store (four saris for $100), which has floor-to-ceiling shelves crammed with bolts of cloth in a rainbow of colors and the inevitable Indian music playing in the background.

Along this section of the street, shady benches off the main sidewalk offer a place to rest. In good weather, neighborhood folk buy take-out food at nearby restaurants and lunch on the benches. If the weather isn't cooperating, try the *Viceroy of India* (2520 W. Devon), an airy, elegant restaurant with a daily all-you-can-eat lunch buffet. Its specialties include tandoori cooking, yogurt marinades, and mulligatawny soup.

If inexpensive Italian food is more your style, try *Villa Palermo* (open only for dinner) on the corner of West Devon and North Campbell. A block up, the neighborhood's delightful ethnic mix offers yet another food option: gyros sandwiches, spinach pie, saganaki, and baklava at the *Pantheon Greek* restaurant (2447 W. Devon). Across the street is the *Bombay Bazaar* and the Rosel School of Cosmetology.

Devon Street continues to change and its cultural diversity blossoms as stores close and new ones replace them, building on the ethnic smorgasbord. On the southwest corner of Devon and Artesian, *K-Econo* is the sort of discount emporium where transistor radios can be found among samurai swords, soccer balls from Pakistan, even a wall clock laminated with a picture of John Wayne. On this same block, where it's common to see women strolling under the shade of sun umbrellas, *Woolworth's* is a curious anachronism. Contemporary styles at the *GAP* clothing store, too, seem out of place amid the saris. Farther east, a Korean grocery (2114 W. Devon) carries sweet cakes, rice crackers, jars of boxthorn tea, packages of dried anchovies and seaweed, and dishes and pots.

Although Hispanic influence is still light here, there are a couple of Mexican restaurants tucked in among the Kosher delis and Indian restaurants. There also is a Caribbean dance hall, the *Olympic Reggae Club* (2340 W. Devon) in the area. The *Babylon Bakery* (2302 W. Devon) tempts passersby with delectable continental pastries. A mainstay in this area is the Sulieman brother's *Farm City Meats* store, where Fayez Sulieman declares that the Palestinian market sells "lamb, beef, goat, and chicken — but *no pork.*" Alongside the meat cases are pita bread, sacks of rice, and, acknowledging Devon's melting-pot character, flour burritos. At the *Natraj* Indian restaurant (2240 W. Devon), vegetarian meals are the specialty. Try masala dosa, a South Indian dish of crêpes filled with potatoes and onions. The *Natraj* has all-you-can-eat dinner buffets daily and a special Sunday lunch buffet featuring food from Southern India. It is easy to have a huge meal here for under $10 per person. Continue up the last 2 blocks of the street to 2000 W. Devon and the end of this tour, where Indian and Middle Eastern commercial outlets are gradually overshadowed by chain outlets like *7-Eleven* and *Burger King*.

Return to the city via the same route you came.

Walk 13: Halsted — The World on One Street

Locals claim it's possible to live an entire life without ever leaving Halsted Street, and they're probably right. A tour of this street can take a day, a week, a month, or more. This miniature universe stretches for 20 miles through metropolitan Chicago, from 4000 North to 12000 South. The busy thoroughfare is lined with hundreds of ethnic restaurants, as well as nightclubs, theaters, several ethnic neighborhoods, a university, a peddlers' market, and the Union Stock Yards, source of much of Chicago's early wealth.

Named for two Philadelphia brothers who financed the real estate acquisitions of Chicago's first mayor, William B. Ogden, Halsted shoots straight south through Lake View, Lincoln Park, West Loop, Greektown, Hull House, Maxwell Street, and from there into several ethnic enclaves, ending near historic Pullman. To get the full flavor of Chicago's variety, this is the tour to take. You can do it by bus, getting on and off to explore selected sites, or hoof it, arriving and departing by train. The No. 8 bus runs the full length of Halsted, starting at 3700 North. The Howard Street train stops at Addison, 3 blocks from where the tour begins, and at North and Clybourn. (The station at North and Clybourn is currently closed on weekends, which means you have to take a North Avenue bus east if you want to end the tour there.) A car is an impediment on the northern end of Halsted; it's not a problem from North Avenue south.

An excursion down this lengthy boulevard is easily broken into two parts if there isn't time to do it all at once. The first leg starts at the northern end of Halsted and runs south to the off-Loop theater district near North Avenue. A separate tour can be made of the downtown section of Halsted, starting at Madison Street, cutting through Greektown, and passing the University of Chicago to Maxwell Street.

Just south of the bus terminal at 3700 N. Halsted, where this tour begins, are two aromatic spots catering to sybarites: the *Chicago Plant and Flower Warehouse* and *Coffee Tree and Tea Leaves.* Across the street is one of those unexpected architectural treasures that abound in Chicago, the Chicago Park District storage building (3640 N. Halsted). The extraordinary terra cotta work on the façade seems unwarranted for such a commonplace, utilitarian structure.

Like so many major American cities, Chicago has seen the growth of an open, activist gay community since the early 1970s. Over the past 2 decades, that community established a center along North Halsted. Today, in the 3600 block, the *Brown Elephant Resale Shop* (3641 N. Halsted) sells its warehouse

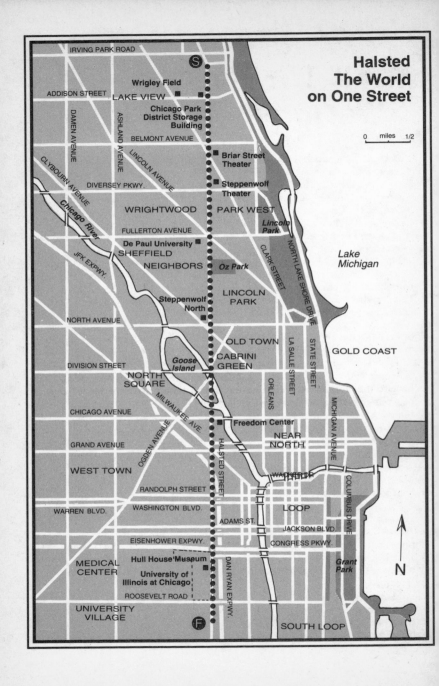

Halsted
The World
on One Street

0 miles 1/2

IRVING PARK ROAD

Wrigley Field

ADDISON STREET LAKE VIEW

Chicago Park
District Storage
Building

DAMEN AVENUE

ASHLAND AVENUE

LINCOLN AVENUE

CLYBOURN AVENUE

BELMONT AVENUE

Briar Street Theater

DIVERSEY PKWY.

Steppenwolf Theater

Chicago River

WRIGHTWOOD

PARK WEST

Lincoln Park

JFK EXPWY.

FULLERTON AVENUE

De Paul University

SHEFFIELD

Oz Park

NEIGHBORS

Lake Michigan

CLARK STREET

NORTH LAKE SHORE DRIVE

LINCOLN PARK

Steppenwolf North

NORTH AVENUE

OLD TOWN

LA SALLE STREET

STATE STREET

GOLD COAST

Goose Island

CABRINI GREEN

DIVISION STREET

NORTH SQUARE

ORLEANS

MILWAUKEE AVE.

CHICAGO AVENUE

Freedom Center

NEAR NORTH

OGDEN AVENUE

GRAND AVENUE

MICHIGAN AVENUE

WEST TOWN

HALSTED STREET

COLUMBUS DRIVE

RANDOLPH STREET

WACKER

WARREN BLVD.

WASHINGTON BLVD.

LOOP

ADAMS ST.

EISENHOWER EXPWY.

JACKSON BLVD.

CONGRESS PKWY.

Grant Park

MEDICAL CENTER

Hull House Museum

University of Illinois at Chicago

DAN RYAN EXPWY.

ROOSEVELT ROAD

N

UNIVERSITY VILLAGE

SOUTH LOOP

full of previously owned items to benefit an AIDS clinic. *Vortex* (3631 N. Halsted) is one of several gay bars in the area.

At the corner of Addison and Halsted is the Town Hall (23rd District) Police Station. The building was originally the Town Hall for a community named Lake View. In the 19th century, this was a resort area, far from the city's heat (the lake was a lot closer to Halsted Street than it is now). But by 1890, Chicago had expanded to the borders of Lake View and the community was annexed, as were many others over years of relentless growth. Across the street is an architectural remnant of another time, a 1950s diner called *Checker's.*

The next few blocks are loaded with restaurants, among them are: *Bangkok* (3542 N. Halsted), authentic Thai decor and food; *Ooh La La!* (3335 N. Halsted), a tempting mix of French and Italian dishes; *Yoshi's* (3257 N. Halsted), pricey Japanese with a French accent; *A Taste of Morocco* (3255 N. Halsted), just what it says; *Mickey Hornick's Chicago Diner* (3411 N. Halsted), a vegetarian delight; and *Nookies Tree* (3334 N. Halsted), for quick but quality dining. At Cornelia Street, just around the corner, is *Cornelia's* (748 W. Cornelia); its classic Italian dishes are frequently served with a side portion of classical music.

Fine antiques stores also are abundant on the 3400 block of North Halsted. Though you may not be in the market for a chifforobe, intriguing smaller items also can be found at the *Brokerage* (3448 N. Halsted); *Formerly Yours* (3443 N. Halsted); or the *3434 Shop* (3434 N. Halsted). *Jeffery Stephen's Ltd.* (3324 N. Halsted), an interior designer, can help create the right setting for any purchase.

If old furniture isn't your cup of tea, stop at *99th Floor* (3406 N. Halsted), where the clothing is, well, unusual. For a time-warp experience, step into *Caffè Pergolesi,* a bright yellow coffeehouse (3404 N. Halsted), and step back into the 1960s. In addition to the inevitable coffee, it offers solid fare like lox and bagels and hearty vegetable stews. The restaurant with the bright red British telephone booth outside is *Roscoe's* (3356 N. Halsted). *Town Hall Pub* is another great 1960s folk place. And art lovers will enjoy browsing in the *Art Mecca Gallery* (3352 N. Halsted), *Gallimaufrey Gallery* (3345 N. Halsted), or *Silver Moon* (3337 N. Halsted).

Fans of mystery writer Sara Paretsky, who has become a role model to a growing group of Chicago authors that set whodunits in their hometown, may recognize the corner of Belmont and Halsted as the place where private investigator V.I. Warshawski lived when her apartment was torched and she just missed going up along with it. Another antiques store across Halsted (and just around the corner to the right) is *Victorian House Antiques* (806 W. Belmont). This lovingly restored, if not too elegant, "painted lady" is as renowned for its hauntings as for its household goods.

The area of Halsted between Belmont and Fullerton is best visited at night, when the streets come alive with people looking for some of the best entertainment in town. Chicago has long been known as a place where actors can make their mark, and today that often means working in this neighborhood. At 3133 North is the *Briar Street Theater,* which began life as a stable, then became a sound stage and, finally, a theater. It hosts revivals, experimental productions by established playwrights, plus dance and jazz troupes. Nestled between Halsted and Clark at Wellington is the *Wellington.* Once called the *Ivanhoe* (hence the crenelated façade), this theater languished during the 1980s and was only rejuvenated in the spring of 1990. At 2851 North is *Steppenwolf North,* the former home of the Tony Award–winning *Steppenwolf Theatre Company* (now in a new building near North Avenue). This company launched the careers of such renowned actors as John Malkovich, Glenne Headley, and Gary Sinese, all of whom are still involved with the group. Although this nonprofit theater is no longer affiliated with the company, it remains dedicated to offering some of the best productions on the North Side.

Before the show or after, refuel at any one of the many fine (and exotic) restaurants along here. They can't all be listed, but among the more unusual or pleasurable is *Helmund's* (3201 N. Halsted), which offers Afghan food in a somewhat upscale environment. *Canoe Club* (2843 N. Halsted) boasts "Wisconsin" fare; no, that's not just cheese and cranberries, it's lots of fish and hearty breakfasts, too. The 2600 block is jammed with an international menu of restaurants, including the Peruvian *La Llama,* Italian *Arrivederci,* the acclaimed *Terczak's, Uncle Tannous's* Lebanese food, *Szechwan Kitchen, Stevie B's Rib Café,* and *Itto Sushi.* Stuffed? Get a little exercise (very little) at the billiard parlor *Corner Pocket* (2610 N. Halsted), or drop in for a palm reading at *Astrologer's Medium* (2615 N. Halsted), which frequently hosts weekend psychic fairs. If the wail of Chicago blues is in the cards, two of the city's best clubs are in the 2500 block: *Kingston Mines* and *B.L.U.E.S.* (see *Nightlife* in THE CITY).

During the day, you may want to hop a cab or bus from Belmont to Fullerton, where Halsted is more hospitable to daytime activities. Between Armitage (2000 North) and North, the street is loaded with the kind of shops that appeal to the neighborhood's residents: young urban professional families who can afford upwards of $800,000 to purchase the utterly charming old houses lining the area's side streets. This is the place to buy something for the kids at home, the grandparents who are staying with them, or even the boss who gave you a few extra days off. The stores are too numerous to mention; if what's in the window is appealing, walk in and have a look around.

In the 1800 block, there's a delightful array of domestic architecture: squat wooden Chicago cottages, new townhouses, brick cottages, a few brownstones, plus some refurbished 4-story walk-ups. Though the first floors of many have been converted to storefronts, some remain private dwellings.

Two restaurants in this area deserve special mention. One is *Café Ba-Ba-Reeba!* (2024 N. Halsted, see *Chicago's Best Restaurants* in DIVERSIONS), a tapas bar where an entire evening can speed by amid the hot and cold appetizers (tapas) popular among Spaniards after their afternoon "siesta." It's another eating event from Richie Melman, mastermind of the outrageously popular '50s-style diner *Ed Debevick's* (see *Eating Out* in THE CITY) in River North. This neighborhood's other outstanding restaurant is *Blue Mesa* (1729 N. Halsted), featuring authentic Southwestern cooking and tortillas that transport the soul to the land of canyons and cactus.

The gala opening of the new *Steppenwolf* theater (1650 N. Halsted; see *Theater* in THE CITY) last year (with *Another Time,* starring Albert Finney) got as much press attention in New York as it did in Chicago. That isn't all that surprising, since the company had previously sent acclaimed productions of *Balm in Gilead* and *Grapes of Wrath* to Broadway, the latter to win several Tony a wards. The new building has a 500-seat main stage, as well as a smaller stage for experimental works. Across the street from the *Steppenwolf* is the two-theater *Royal-George* complex, which also has a cabaret and wine bar to round out an evening's entertainment.

At Halsted and North Avenue are two new projects; one, the renovated Yondorf Hall, harks back to the neighborhood's early days. Once a community center with a second-story theater and numerous meeting rooms, it dates from when this was a heavily German manufacturing district. Most recently, it housed a discount liquor store in a neighborhood most people preferred to ignore. It was a dilapidated eyesore until the area began to change and a Canadian banking group bought and restored the building to its current state. On the west side of Halsted is a new shopping center anchored by the *Crate & Barrel Outlet Store*. Now a national institution, the chain got its start on Wells Street, a dozen blocks east of here.

There's lots going on at this rather chaotic intersection. To the east, along North Avenue, are several new or refurbished townhouse developments; to the southeast are a housing project for senior citizens and, in cheerfully colored glazed brick, a *YMCA* that serves both the upscale Lincoln Park area to the north and the poverty-stricken residents of Cabrini-Green to the south. South on Halsted, where it meets Clybourn, is the *Golden Ox,* established 70 years ago when this was a working class area. It still serves hearty bratwurst, strong beer, and other German fare.

The bus goes past renovated lofts housing offices and galleries to the right and, south of Division (1200 North), Cabrini-Green, the housing project frequently cited as the worst of a bad idea. Just south of here the street crosses the tip of Goose Island, at the intersection where the North Branch of the Chicago River splits into two channels. The huge Material Service complex is to the right (gravel and building materials); beyond that are old manufacturing and warehouse buildings now advertising expensive lofts. On the left at Chicago Avenue (800 North) is the massive "Freedom Center" where the *Chicago Tribune* is printed. At Randolph Street, look west to see Chicago central market, where fresh produce is brought in each morning and distributed to stores and restaurants. To the east, between Halsted and Desplaines, was the locus of one of Chicago's most notorious public brawls, the Haymarket Riot.

The fracas began when John Bonfield, an overzealous police inspector, sought to break up a meeting of socialists and anarchists in the Haymarket Square. The assembly had been called to protest the slaying of six men several days earlier at the McCormick works. When the police intercepted the Haymarket crowd as it left the square near the corner of Desplaines, someone in the crowd tossed a bomb, killing seven policemen and wounding many others. A brief gun battle followed, and large numbers of civilians and police were injured. Seven men, all associated with the anarchist newspaper *Arbeiter Zeitung,* were executed for the crime, though the real culprit in the bombing may have escaped.

Stay on the bus until the neighborhood changes again — this time to lively Greek restaurants and nightspots. If you want to walk around Greektown, get off the bus at Monroe or Adams, 100 or 200 South. This neighborhood is chock-full of great places to eat, and any choice you make is sure to be a good one (don't be shy about walking in, looking at a menu, and walking out; proprietors are used to browsers here). Some suggestions: *Greek Islands* (200 S. Halsted), decorated with blue-check tablecloths and popular with University of Illinois faculty; *Rodity's* (222 S. Halsted), somewhat rougher, considerably noisier, and popular with locals; and the *Courtyards of Plaka* (340 S. Halsted), definitely the most upscale, with an extensive wine list.

Also along this part of Halsted are other Greek institutions like the *Athenian Candle Company* (300 S. Halsted), which sells soaps, creams, and incense. The *Athens Grocery,* in the same block, offers plump Greek olives floating in vats of oil, crumbly feta cheese, and halvah, a sweet treat made of ground sesame seed. For a magnificent selection of airy Greek pastries, try the *Pan Hellenic Bakery* next door; in addition to baklava and various cakes dripping with honey, there are round and flat breads and marvelous cheese and spinach pies, a meal by themselves.

For after-dark amusements (this neighborhood is bustling until 11 PM or so), try the *Parthenon* (314 S. Halsted), where cries of "opaa" (hooray) accompany flaming platters of saganaki — a popular cheese appetizer that was actually invented in Chicago. There's belly dancing at *Neon Greek Village* and a few other locations along here. There's plenty of parking nearby, and restaurants and nightclubs will validate tickets from any of the lots on the east side of Halsted.

Just south of Greektown is the Eisenhower Expressway, a main artery for traffic heading in and out of the Loop. To end the walk here and head back downtown, hop on the train that runs down the middle of the highway.

If you continue walking, pause at the top of the overpass to take in the view of the University of Illinois at Chicago to the southeast. Since the campus was constructed nearly 30 years ago, its "brutalist" architecture has been frequently criticized as too harsh for what should be a nurturing environment. The dorms just south of the expressway were an attempt to soften the visual effect.

When the university was built, the area was still composed of several large brick turn-of-the-century buildings collectively known as Hull House. One of Chicago's more successful attempts at social engineering, Hull House was the nation's first settlement house, an institution that provided English courses, crafts workshops, health care services, and job training for generations of immigrants. Founded by early feminists Jane Addams and Ellen Gates Starr, Hull House served the Greek neighborhoods to its north, the Italian community to its west, and the Jewish market area to its south, as well as several other ethnic enclaves. The settlement was named for Charles J. Hull, the previous owner of the "country home" Addams acquired in 1889 to begin her experiment in urban welfare. That original 1854 building still stands at 800 S. Halsted, in jarring contrast to the buildings surrounding it. Maintained by the university as a museum, it contains many exhibits about the work of Hull House. Open from 10 AM to 4 PM weekdays, noon to 5 PM Saturdays.

The next street south is Taylor. Two blocks east and 1 block south is DeKoven Street and the site where Patrick O'Leary's barn stood until October 8, 1871. According to city folklore, a clumsy cow kicked over a kerosene lantern that night and ignited the blaze that torched the entire city. The Great Chicago Fire killed at least 300 of the city's residents and left one third of the rest homeless. On the positive side, as a result of the fire, Chicago had an opportunity to redesign itself and change the face of American architecture in the process.

This walk concludes at Maxwell Street, 1200 South, but 6 blocks from here is Pilsen. Once a Bohemian neighborhood, Pilsen is now largely Mexican, and has a thriving artists' community. Eighteen blocks beyond that is Bridgeport (home to two Chicago mayors named Daley), 10 blocks farther on are the old stockyards (now a struggling industrial park; no meat has been butchered there since the late 1960s) and the old *Chicago Amphitheater,* site of several presidential nominating conventions. Historic Pullman, where the railway cars of the same name were built, is at 12000 South (see *Walk 16: Pullman Historic District*). If you've come by car, take Roosevelt Road east to LaSalle, State, or Michigan, to return to the Loop. One side trip worth considering is a cruise through Chicago's largest Italian community, which is chockablock with restaurants, as well as street vendors selling Italian ices. To get there, walk 3 blocks west on Taylor Street (1000 South).

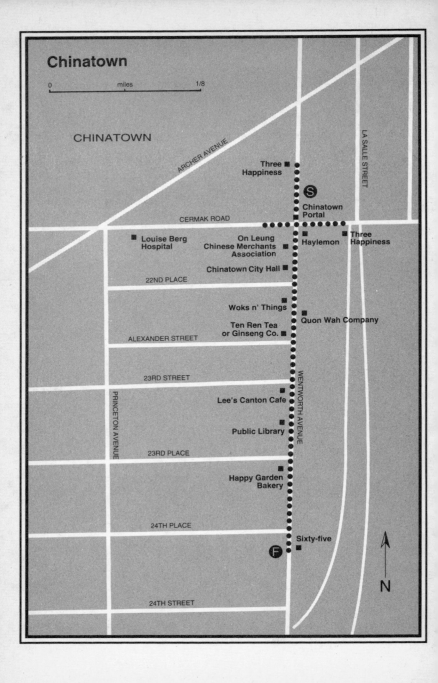

Walk 14: Chinatown

Chinatown insiders always seem to know something the rest of us don't, like how to shop for seaweed, who sells the best squid, or how to order dim sum. Fortunately, Chicago's Chinatown, like the city itself, is fascinating and comprehensible, perhaps even more accessible than its counterparts on either of the coasts. From the Loop, pick up the train on the elevated Wabash tracks, and after passing over old railyards, get off at Cermak, which is also marked Chinatown. If you are driving, Chinatown is just northeast of the junction of the Dan Ryan Expressway and Adelaide Stevenson Expressway. Then head south along State Street to Cermak (2200 South) and turn right; there's a large lot at Cermak and Wentworth. (Be sure to leave your car here; parking anywhere else in Chinatown verges on the impossible. Area residents have a simple way of reserving spots: They line the gutters in front of their houses with crates and 5-gallon cans; though illegal, it's an honored signal in the neighborhood.)

Enter Chinatown through the portal that arches across Wentworth Avenue at Cermak Road. Though relatively new (it was erected in 1975), this imposing structure is akin to porticoes in China dating back at least to the 10th century. Like similar entries in other cities, this is more than a gateway to a city within a city, it is a spiritual gateway, connecting the immigrant Chinese population with its historical roots. Notice particularly the way the transverse beam linking the heavy posts turns up like a tongue of fire at each end, gracefully tempering the massiveness of the supporting beams. This countering of forces is typical of classical Chinese architecture.

The tourist area of Chicago's Chinatown is shaped like a T. A segment of Wentworth Avenue forms the north-south axis, and a brief stretch of Cermak Road crosses the T. The houses on side streets radiating west from Wentworth are the homes and schools of Chinatown's residents (which still includes some of the Italian families that were once concentrated here).

As dim sum — tasty dumplings and other bite-size items of incredible variety — has grown in popularity, the number of restaurants offering these delectable tidbits has skyrocketed from one or two to well over a dozen. The first, and possibly still the best, is *Three Happiness,* which has two locations: a storefront at 2130 Wentworth and a more spacious layout occupying the second floor of a ramshackle building on the corner at 209 W. Cermak.

Inside, harried and generally indifferent waiters and waitresses push carts laden with goodies in and out of cramped spaces, stopping here and there to disburse duck feet steeped in star anise, steamed rice noodles, lion's head meatballs, and upwards of 50 other succulent dainties. Despite the shortcomings of its service (the staff can be slow and disinclined to negotiate the narrow aisles to the farthest tables), waits of an hour or more are common on weekends. Nonetheless, for variety, quality, and price — two people can eat quite well here for under $15 dollars — *Three Happiness* can't be beat.

There are several other restaurants on Cermak that merit more than passing interest. *Wing Wah,* west of Wentworth beside the firehouse, has only recently emerged from obscurity, but the cognoscenti have long known that this is the place for such dishes as snails in black bean sauce and whole pike steamed with golden noodles. The problem has been that most of the day's specials listed on the walls were in Chinese and too few waiters could translate. These days, what isn't printed in English will be explained by one of the establishment's bilingual waiters. *Haylemon,* on the southeast corner of the Cermak-Wentworth intersection, offers both dim sum and a regular menu. In an effort to spread the abundant luncheon crowds more evenly, the management now offers patrons a 10% discount *after* 4 PM. There are those who rate *Hong Min's* dim sum even more highly than that of *Three Happiness.* Pork buns and fresh noodles with seafood have been singled out for particular praise.

For a quick snack, pop into *Friendship Café* and sample its dim sum or a moon cake flavored with sweet bean paste. *China Arts & Gifts* can yield an occasional bronze or porcelain antique lurking behind the Hong Kong cinnabar-and-lacquer bric-a-brac. Proprietor James Che does a small trade in treasures that hold no interest for the grandchildren of the immigrants who brought them to this country. *Bark Lee Tong* (229 W. Cermak), does a brisk business in herbs and traditional home remedies.

From here, walk back to Wentworth, turn right, and stroll down the center of Chinatown. At 2216 is the On Leung Chinese Merchants Association, scene of more than one gambling raid. Red-and-green pagoda towers rise at each end of the building. Between them, a glossy green tile roof stretches over two tiers of colonnaded balconies. Mustard-yellow and jade-green tile insets — notice the pair of foo dogs — dot the otherwise somber brick.

For cookware sufficient to whip up an emperor's banquet, visit *Woks n' Things* (2234 S. Wentworth). This kitchenware emporium stocks knives fine enough to skin a frog and cleavers hefty enough to dismember a whole pig. Bamboo steamers, ladles, woks, and all the attendant paraphernalia can be found here at prices that range from reasonable to ridiculously inexpensive. Several doors down, *Oriental Boutique* (2262 S. Wentworth) sells kimonos and Susie Wong dresses, and *Sun Sun Tong* mingles postcards and appealing plaster figurines with royal jelly and herbal remedies. *Doug Kee Co.* (2252 S. Wentworth) spreads canned and dried foods, trinkets, and oversize woks through three large rooms without the clutter ordinarily found in such establishments.

Across the street is *Quon Wah Co.* (2241 S. Wentworth), a no-frills grocery store. In this store's chaotic jumble of goods is everything from litchi nuts in syrup to octopus. This block of Wentworth also includes *Emperor's Choice, Chiu Quon Bakery,* and *Mandar Inn.* This last restaurant, once a trend setter, now seems stodgy compared with others in Chinatown. *Emperor's Choice* excels at soups; 14 are listed on the menu, ranging from an aromatic meal-in-a-bowl called Eight Treasure Winter Melon to the refined and expensive ($22) shark's fin with crab.

Serious tea drinkers will find it difficult to resist a stop at *Ten Ren Tea* or *Ginseng Co. of Chicago* (2247 S. Wentworth). While the merely curious tend to buy fragrant hibiscus tea, well-heeled connoisseurs go for the aptly named king's tea, priced at nearly $120 a pound.

Lee's Canton Café (2300 S. Wentworth) operates an ice cream parlor where one can indulge in a dish of red bean ice cream and wash it down with a sweetly satisfying cold drink made from lotus nuts. The Chinese Christian Union Church on the corner of 23rd Place, an otherwise straitlaced affair of tan brick, flaunts a handsome green pagoda roof at its northern end and red-lacquer doors and window frames.

Chang Ying Ginseng Hong (2314 S. Wentworth) is made for souvenir hunters: among its collectibles are imported toy cars, fat plaster Buddhas, Chinese movie posters, decorated chopsticks, and soapstone carvings.

The Chinatown branch of the Public Library (2314 S. Wentworth) has three display cases devoted to ceramics and Chinese costumes. *New Hong Bakery & Café* (2339 S. Wentworth) offers western and Chinese pastries, a red bean freeze, and cold soybean juice — an acquired taste, it's a milky fluid that tastes something like starchy rice tea. The less adventurous would do well to visit the *Baskin-Robbins* two doors north.

The *Chinese Press Co.* (2400 S. Wentworth) prints Chinese wedding invitations; and to celebrate the occasion, *Happy Garden Bakery* (2358 S. Wentworth) will make bean paste or lotus moon cake pastry, as well as flaky coconut puffs. *Mei Wah* (2401 S. Wentworth), across the street, displays glistening carp and red snapper on shaved ice; in a nearby alcove are bitter melon, lotus root, dried mushrooms in huge 5-pound bags, plus shelves of tea and condiments.

Two of the best places for Hong Kong-style food are also two of the street's newest restaurants: *Sixty-five* (2409 S. Wentworth) offers sweetly pungent smoked crab, barbecued filet mignon, and aromatic West Lake duck; next door, the larger and somewhat more garish *Evergreen* serves sautéed dried squid, chicken steamed with black mushrooms and savory Chinese sausage, and huge clams steamed with black beans.

While window shopping, keep an eye open for spontaneous events along the street. The brass band you pass may be playing for a funeral at the Bowman Funeral Home (2236 S. Wentworth). During the *Chinese New Year* (4 weeks or so after January 1) some energetic young men slip into a gaudy fabric dragon to wriggle the length of Wentworth, scaring bad luck away. Watchers can help the evil spirits on their way by tossing sputtering firecrackers about with abandon. Shopkeepers along the route pass small money gifts wrapped in lucky red through the creature's mouth. It's all great for photos, but it only happens once a year.

Return to the Loop via the same route you took to get here.

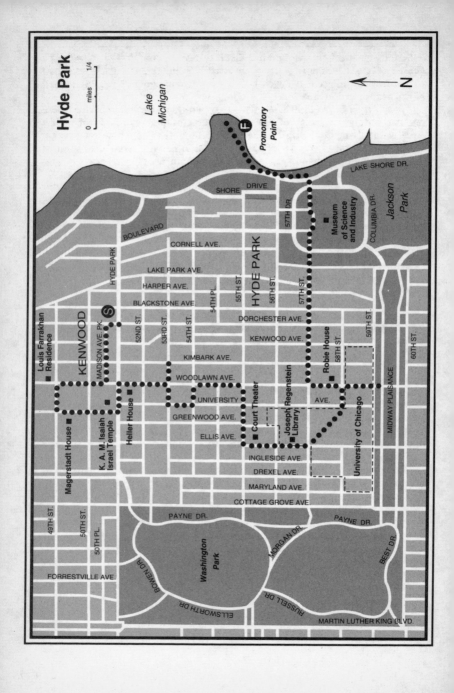

Walk 15: Hyde Park

The University of Chicago, and its tradition of intellectual and architectural excellence, dominates Hyde Park. At last count, 54 Nobel laureates had been associated with the university, which, though barely a century old, has distinguished itself as a bastion of economics and the social sciences. The university has fostered much of the urban renewal in Hyde Park and some of the city's great architects have designed for the campus. The university neighborhood is a fascinating community in its own right: It's the most successfully integrated area in the city, and its residents, whether associated with the university or not, maintain parks, lakefront, and flora, as well as schools and bookstores.

Hyde Park today is an architectural compromise between tradition and the forces of redevelopment. Whole blocks of shops, bars, and apartments have been torn down to keep the district from deteriorating. Nonetheless, many fine old homes and businesses have been lovingly maintained. A walk through Hyde Park and Kenwood is a safe and delightful trip through a college town in the middle of a large city. Neighborhood residents, like U of C students, tend to be intellectual, ideological, and idiosyncratic.

Hyde Park stretches from the lakefront west to Washington Park, and from 60th Street north to Hyde Park Boulevard at 53rd Street. The most convenient way to get to Hyde Park is to drive; street parking is limited but available. It is also accessible by public transportation: Take the downtown No. 6 Jeffery Express bus from State Street or take the METRA train south from stations underneath Grant Park. Whether traveling by bus or train, get off at Hyde Park Boulevard (the conductor might call it 51st Street) and walk 3 blocks west to Dorchester. This walk is about 2 miles long and takes about 2 hours, making a few stops along the way.

Walk half a block north on Dorchester and go through the iron gate on the west side of the street. This is Madison Avenue Park, a private, cooperative, ethnically mixed area that stretches 2 blocks. Walk west and watch children run and play down the grassy strip in the center. The houses and apartments on either side help separate this small community from the city just outside it.

When you've ambled the length of Madison Park you'll be on Woodlawn Avenue. Walk north to 49th Street. This is Kenwood, a neighborhood of landscaped boulevards lined with spacious estates and wooded gardens. Most of these architectural gems were built between 1890 and 1910. On the northeast corner of 49th Street and Woodlawn is the secured compound of Louis Farrakhan, the controversial leader of the Nation of Islam. (His private security force guards the house and the area around it.)

Go west on 49th Street to Greenwood Avenue, then turn south. The Magerstadt House (4930 S. Greenwood) is a massive brick residence designed by a contemporary of Frank Lloyd Wright. Its wide overhang and horizontal thrust recall Wright's Prairie style. A 1968 remodeling restored the house to its original 1906 appearance.

Continue south on Greenwood to Hyde Park Boulevard. The massive Byzantine structure on the northeast corner is K.A.M. Isaiah Israel Temple. K.A.M. stands for Kehilath Anshe Maarav (Congregation of the Men of the West). Founded in 1847, it is the oldest Jewish congregation in the Midwest. The synagogue was designed by Alfred Alschuler in 1924.

Stroll east on Hyde Park Boulevard 1 block to Woodlawn, then turn south. At 5132 South is Frank Lloyd Wright's Heller House. Though it was built in 1897, the projecting eaves and spacious feel hint at the typical design of Wright's later residences. The Prairie style, as it came to be called, used a bold horizontal sweep to evoke the Midwest's dramatic openness and natural beauty.

East of Woodlawn on 53rd Street is an eclectic shopping district full of small boutiques and interesting ethnic restaurants. This is where the neighborhood comes to shop and stroll. After taking a breather, retrace your steps on 53rd and go 1 block beyond Woodlawn to University Avenue, then turn south. The houses along this block are renowned for their gardens. At 54th Street, turn back east toward Woodlawn, noting the colorfully decorated graystone houses of local artists.

At Woodlawn, proceed south to 55th Street. East of the intersection are contemporary row houses designed by I.M. Pei. Once a popular bohemian neighborhood of artists and intellectuals, this was one urban renewal project that some area residents felt unnecessary. Nonetheless, such projects have helped keep Hyde Park stable, integrated, and safe, while other areas of the South Side deteriorated.

The *Woodlawn Tap,* on the corner of Woodlawn and 55th Street, is a neighborhood institution, as is owner Jimmy Wilson, who has tended bar near the University of Chicago campus for 50 years. His tavern opened in 1948 and has periodically expanded into adjoining rooms. *Jimmy's,* as it is familiarly known, is a favorite hangout for philosophers, poets, and construction workers, who, in Chicago, are as good as philosophers. Jimmy keeps an encyclopedia behind the bar, as well as Greek and Latin dictionaries and the complete works of Shakespeare to settle arguments. Stop in for a cheeseburger and a beer; in the afternoon, Jimmy might be sitting at the end of the bar smoking a cigar and helping himself to the stock.

Just west of *Jimmy's* is a fire station. In the 1950s, in a ramshackle building that stood here, a group of comics calling themselves the *Compass Players* started an improvisational troupe. These mixed nuts, among them Mike Nichols and Elaine May, went on to establish *Second City,* now located on Wells Street, north of the Loop.

Continue walking west on 55th Street for 3 blocks to Ellis Avenue. Dozens of bars and nightspots featuring jazz and blues used to line this street, but when they started to go to seed in the 1950s, the university bought them up and tore them down. When you reach Ellis Avenue, go south. On the left is the modern *Court* theater, a professional company that presents first class performances. Two blocks east of the theater is the university's *David and*

Alfred Smart Gallery, showcase for an impressive collection of visual and decorative art. The gallery has a bit of everything, from the classical to the contemporary.

The next block south on Ellis, dominated by the Joseph Regenstein Library, once held a large athletic field. The University of Chicago is perhaps the only school in the world that could graduate professional football's first coach (Amos Alonzo Stagg) and have the temerity to tear down the football stadium named in his honor to build a library. Even more daring than that, in 1942 the university allowed Enrico Fermi and a group of scientists nicknamed the "suicide squad" to use the field house to conduct a risky experiment in nuclear fission. The result was the world's first self-sustaining nuclear reaction. For good or ill, the atomic age was born on this spot in December 1942. The event is commemorated by Henry Moore's looming sculpture *Nuclear Energy.* Locally known as "the Reg," the 5-story library attracts scholars from around the world and also is the campus's busiest social center.

Continue south on Ellis to 57th Street, where the university's mix of architectural styles becomes most apparent. Hitchcock and Snell Halls, the Gothic stone buildings on the left, are undergraduate dormitories. To the right is the modern Kersten Physics Teaching Center. Behind Kersten is the John Crerar Library, the Midwest's largest medical library. Also on the right is the brutalist-style Hinds Geophysical Sciences building and its taller cousin, the Cummings Life Sciences Center. The red brick building at the corner is the *University Bookstore,* which has, in addition to its extensive stock of books, a small and very busy deli.

On the other side of Ellis is the limestone Administration Building. When it was erected in 1947, it was the first campus building to break with the university's customary Gothic architecture. In 1969, when a popular instructor was denied tenure, radical students staged a sit-in here. Unlike such protests at other universities around the country, officials didn't call on the police to put an end to it and simply allowed the demonstrators to stay in the building for 2 weeks.

Walk east through the Administration Building and wander through the university's main quadrangle. Students study, relax, and occasionally march on the grass in the summer, but the quad is beautiful year-round, surrounded by towering trees and imposing Gothic buildings that create an academic oasis. Notice particularly the snaggletoothed gargoyles, U of C's unofficial mascots, that stare down from every rooftop.

Walk east across the quad and exit between the tennis courts at the corner of University and 58th Street. Across the street to the right is the Oriental Institute, a branch of the university that is one of the world's foremost sponsors of archaeological digs in the Near East. The institute's museum (see *Chicago at-a-Glance* in THE CITY) showcases the history and art of the ancient Middle and Near East. Among its treasures are Sumerian and Assyrian statues, Persian jewelry, and Egyptian mummies (no admission charge.)

Across 58th from the Oriental Institute is the Chicago Theological Seminary. In the basement of the building is the *Seminary Cooperative Bookstore,* internationally acclaimed and simply the best academic bookstore to be found anywhere. Professors in town for colleagues' funerals have been known to skip visiting the deceased's family in favor of browsing through the store's cozy aisles — and the family usually understands.

Stay on 58th Street and head east to Woodlawn Avenue. On the right is the Rockefeller Chapel, an imposing limestone pile with stained glass windows in grand Gothic-cathedral style. Named for John D. Rockefeller, who donated the millions necessary to found the university in 1892, it is and will always be the tallest building on campus according to the terms of Rockefeller's bequest.

To the left across the street is Robie House (5757 S. Woodlawn), the most famous and influential of Frank Lloyd Wright's houses. Built in 1909, its sweeping eaves and horizontal lines, make it one of the best examples of the Prairie style. Equally as important was the interior of the residence for which Wright designed everything, including the furniture and carpeting. It has all been lovingly maintained by the University's Alumni Association, which uses the house as its offices. Free tours are given Mondays through Saturdays at noon.

Walking south from here on Woodlawn, you'll come to 59th Street and the Midway. Today this is just an undistinguished strip of urban greenery, but in 1893 it was the glittering midway of the *World's Columbian Exposition,* a celebration of the 400th anniversary of Columbus's landing in the New World (the opening was postponed from October 1892 because of construction delays). In the city that had already built the world's first skyscraper, the architects of the fair erected acres of neo-classical-style buildings along here. Louis Sullivan is said to have complained that the exposition would set American architecture back 50 years. Judging from what remains of the great fair, the visionary architect had the last laugh.

Return north on Woodlawn to 57th Street and turn right. This quiet, tree-lined stretch of 57th is a hodgepodge of apartments, restaurants, and bookstores. If the kids are along, there's also a large park and playground on the north side of the street. *57th Street Books* (1301 E. 57th) is a branch of the *Seminary Co-op* that features a large children's area, as well as a wide selection of periodicals from around the world. Farther east is *O'Gara & Wilson Ltd.* (1311 E. 57th); the oldest bookstore in the city, it's a homey shop with towering shelves of used volumes and a fluffy cat that prowls the aisles.

East of here there are three restaurants in a row: *Edwardo's* (1321 E. 57th) is part of a local chain that serves a delicious Chicago-style deep-dish pizza, as well as other Italian entrées. *Medici on 57th,* right next door, is a favorite college hangout serving pizza, hamburgers, and desserts in a dark, casual atmosphere — the kind of place where customers feel free to scratch their names into the tabletops and write graffiti on the bathroom walls. Even if you don't stop in, check out the stone carving of proprietor Hans Morsbach and the gargoyles eating pizza and drinking coffee on the exterior. *Ann Sather* (1329 E. 57th; see *Eating Out* in THE CITY) offers delicious, reasonably priced Swedish specialties (try the cinnamon roll).

Farther east is *Salonika* (1440 E. 57th), an economical Greek-Mexican-American restaurant that's a favorite with cash-strapped students, as well as local policemen and residents. Another block east is *Powell's Book Store* (1501 E. 57th), a 2-story paradise of used books that opens early and closes late.

Directly east of *Powell's* is the Metra Electric viaduct, where you can catch a train back downtown. The next street east is Stony Island, a stop for the No. 6 Jeffery bus back to the Loop. If you still have the energy for it, don't pass up this opportunity to visit the *Museum of Science and Industry* (see *Memorable Museums* in DIVERSIONS), just 2 blocks southeast of *Powell's*. The museum, in what was the *Columbian Exposition*'s Palace of Fine Arts, is Chicago's most popular tourist attraction. It features more educational exhibits than are possible to see in an entire day of exploring. Here you can tour a coal mine and a World War II German submarine, watch trains ply the 3,000-square-foot model of the *Santa Fe Railroad,* or see a thrilling Omnimax movie in the Henry Crown Space Center. If you chose to save the museum for another day, you might want to walk just a little bit farther east, across Lake Shore Drive to Lake Michigan. Stroll along the beach to Promontory Point, where you can sit and contemplate the view of the downtown skyline.

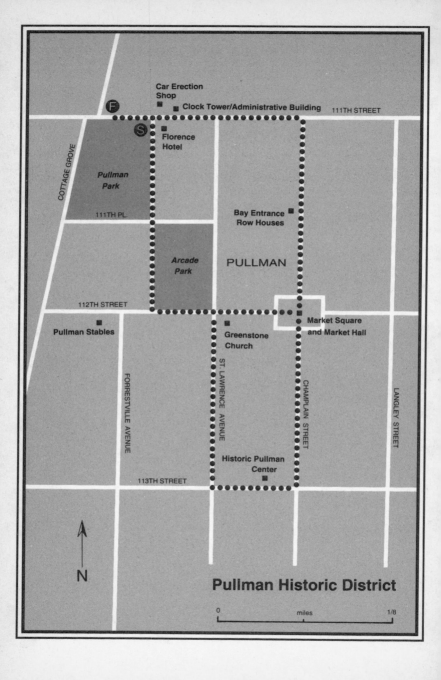

Car Erection Shop

Clock Tower/Administrative Building

111TH STREET

F

S

Florence Hotel

COTTAGE GROVE

Pullman Park

111TH PL.

Bay Entrance Row Houses

Arcade Park

PULLMAN

112TH STREET

Pullman Stables

Market Square and Market Hall

Greenstone Church

FORRESTVILLE AVENUE

ST. LAWRENCE AVENUE

CHAMPLAIN STREET

LANGLEY STREET

Historic Pullman Center

113TH STREET

N

Pullman Historic District

0   miles   1/8

Walk 16: Pullman Historic District

The town of Pullman was another of Chicago's experiments in social engineering. The nation's first planned industrial community, Pullman was built in the early 1880s by George M. Pullman, industrialist and founder of the Pullman Palace Car Company. The company manufactured railroad sleeping cars, a necessary luxury for those who could afford it in the days when a cross-country trip by rail could take 4 or 5 days. The premise of the town of Pullman was the enlightened theory that workers who lived in pleasant and hygienic surroundings would be more productive. Pullman added his own twist to the theory: since it was an investment, the town also had to turn a profit.

Built near the shores of Lake Calumet 14 miles south of the Loop, the workers' village was designed by noted architect Solon S. Beman and landscape architect Nathan F. Barrett. It was a nominally utopian plan, with a bank, a hotel, and a marketplace — plus a church, schools, and a library, a gas works, and (novel at the time) separate storm and sanitary sewers. With its clean, gas-lit streets and pastoral setting (in those days it was surrounded by farmland), it was far from the squalor of most Chicago neighborhoods. It was a pedestrian-scale community that was pleasing to the eye and nourishing for the spirit.

But it didn't last long. An economic depression in 1893 caused railroads to cut back drastically on new car orders. George Pullman responded by cutting back on his work force and lowering wages for the remaining workers. He did not, however, lower the rent or utility bills of Pullman residents. When a grievance committee went to him and appealed for such relief, the members were fired. In May 1894, the unionized employees went on strike, leading to one of the most contentious chapters in American labor history. Eventually, other railroad workers across the country staged sympathy strikes, refusing to move trains carrying Pullman cars. Since those same trains also hauled the US mail, President Grover Cleveland eventually called in federal troops to break the strike and the union. Strike leader Eugene V. Debs wound up in jail and became a cause célèbre, and in 1897 Pullman died one of the most hated men in America.

By an order of the Illinois Supreme Court, the company sold all its properties not relating to the railroad car business, including Pullman. This was accomplished by the early years of this century, when the company deeded Pullman to the city and the Chicago Park District. The neighborhood went into a long decline, and by the mid-1950s it was on the verge of becoming a slum.

In the past 20 years, however, Pullman has experienced a renaissance. Designated a state, city, and national landmark because of its town-planning and historical significance, Pullman is being restored with public and private initiatives, mainly through the efforts of the Pullman Civic Organization and the Historic Pullman Foundation. To get to the village, take the Dan Ryan Expressway (I-94) south to the 111th Street, Pullman exit; head west to the second stoplight. Pullman also is accessible by METRA train; pick one up at the underground station near Randolph and North Michigan and get off at 111th Street (it's a 30-minute ride).

This walk begins at the *Florence* hotel, named for Pullman's favorite daughter. In 1975, the Historic Pullman Foundation saved the building from destruction and restored much of it, including Pullman's own suite on the second floor. The Queen Anne–style building, with gables, turrets, and a 200-foot verandah, had the district's only bar in George Pullman's day — and its use was restricted to hotel guests. Today the *Florence* hotel restaurant and bar is open for lunch Mondays through Fridays, for breakfast and lunch on Saturdays, and for its modest but famous brunch on Sundays (phone: 785-8181; call for reservations, as well as for information about the variety of tours provided by the foundation; maps and other materials about Pullman are available in the hotel lobby).

Across 111th Street from the *Florence* hotel are Pullman's most prominent remaining structures, the Clock Tower/Administrative Building and the Car Erection Shop (1881-1907). The original hand-wound clock and bell still keep time, chiming on the hour. Pullman's palace cars were finished in the Car Erection Shop before being shipped off to robber barons, captains of industry, and others who could afford them. In 1991, the State of Illinois purchased these buildings and the *Florence* hotel, intending to develop them into the *Pullman State Historic Site,* a museum about the railroads and transportation.

From the factory building, walk south through Pullman Park and Arcade Park, once an elaborate flower garden, to 112th Street. There, directly southwest of Arcade Park at 112th and Forrestville, are the Pullman Stables, which also housed the village fire department. Two carved horse heads adorn the entrance. For sanitary reasons, all the town's horses were boarded at these stables. Residents could rent a horse and buggy here for picnics or errands in the city.

Walk 1 block east along 112th Street to St. Lawrence Avenue and the beautifully restored Greenstone Church, now owned by the United Methodists. Built of green serpentine stone from Pennsylvania, the Gothic-revival building was designed to enhance the town's architecture rather than to serve any particular congregation. Pullman leased it to whatever denomination could afford to pay the rent. The city's founder initially ignored the requests of Catholics and Lutherans for their own houses of worship, but he relented in 1888 and leased a plot of land to Swedish workers so they could build a Lutheran church. A year later, Holy Rosary Roman Catholic was built on vacant land west of the town.

Walk east along 112th Street to the intersection of South Champlain and Market Hall, originally the town's only shopping area. Its first floor consisted of 16 stalls where fresh produce was sold; on the upper floor were a dance hall, gymnasium, and meeting rooms. Greatly in need of restoration, Market Hall had its top floor removed half a century ago; the rest was damaged by fire in 1974. Market Square is surrounded by four arched, colonnaded apartment buildings, which George Pullman had built for some of his guests attending the 1893 *World's Columbian Exposition.*

From Market Hall, walk south to 113th Street along Champlain Street, noticing how the housing designs vary. Turn right onto 113th Street to the Historic Pullman Center at 614 East; originally a boarding house, it now holds a multi-media presentation about Pullman.

From here, wander north again along St. Lawrence through Market Hall to Champlain Street. Among the most attractive of Beman's residential designs in the town are the Bay Entrance Row Houses, found in the 1140 section of Champlain. Head north again to 111th Street where Pullman's executives lived. The houses here are on a much grander scale than the workers' housing in other parts of the village.

The end of the Pullman tour is just a block from the *Florence* hotel and the train station, where you can catch a train back to the Loop.

Index